# UNDERSTANDING SOCIAL IMPACTS

Volume 110, Sage Library of Social Research

# ⑤ SAGE LIBRARY OF SOCIAL RESEARCH

# UNDERSTANDING SOCIAL IMPACTS

## ASSESSING THE EFFECTS OF PUBLIC PROJECTS

# KURT FINSTERBUSCH

Volume 110
**SAGE LIBRARY OF
SOCIAL RESEARCH**

 **SAGE PUBLICATIONS**   Beverly Hills   London

*For information address:*

SAGE Publications, Inc.
275 South Beverly Drive
Beverly Hills, California 90212

SAGE Publications Ltd
28 Banner Street
London EC1Y 8QE, England

Printed in the United States of America

**Library of Congress Cataloging in Publication Data**

Finsterbusch, Kurt, 1935-
    Understanding social impacts.

    (Sage library of social research ; v. 110)
    Bibliography: p.
    1. United States—Public works—Social aspects.
I. Title.
HD3887.F52        302.4'8        80-17586
ISBN 0-8039-1015-0
ISBN 0-8039-1016-9 (pbk.)

FIRST PRINTING

# CONTENTS

*To Meredith*

*For her impact on my life*

# PREFACE

The social impact assessment field from the beginning has needed a summary of knowledge about major social impact areas. Social scientists who do social impact assessments do not have the time to look thoroughly at the literature on social impact areas; they need a summary of this literature. For years I have tried to persuade several government agencies to contract for such a compilation, but their research funds had to be used for more immediately applicable studies. I tried to persuade various colleagues to take up the task. They all agreed that a summary was necessary but were too preoccupied at the time. So was I, but I was developing an inner obligation to tackle the project. When I discussed my plans with Sara McCune, President of Sage Publications, she immediately recognized the need for the work and agreed to publish it. I am indebted to her for the encouragement and prodding which enabled me to produce this compendium.

I wish to thank my department and the University of Maryland for sabbatical leave for the spring semester of 1979 to work on this book. I am also grateful to the entire office staff of the department for speedily and accurately translating my hieroglyphics into typescript.

Credit also should be given to Jerry Delli-Priscoli and the Institute for Water Resources of the U.S. Army Corps of Engineers, because this book has benefited from work which I and my research associates, Gail Gorham and H. C. Greisman, did for them on a reference handbook on social effects measurement techniques. In this connection the chapter on noise and leisure/recreation and the discussion on population movements in Chapter 2 draw upon the work which Gail Gorham did for the Institute for Water Resources, and the discussion of the development of community in America benefits from the work of H. C. Greisman.

I would like to thank Lynn Llewellyn for reading and commenting on the manuscript. Finally, I dedicate this book to Meredith for her companionship and encouragement.

## Acknowledgements

I gratefully acknowledge the permission granted by the following publishers and authors to reproduce or extract material from their works: The Joint Center for Urban Studies of MIT and Harvard University for extracts in Chapter 3 from Richard P. Coleman, "Attitudes Toward Neighborhoods: How Americans Choose to Live" (Working Paper No. 49); University of Pennsylvania Press for extracts in Chapter 8 from Clifford R. Bragdon, *Noise Pollution: The Unquiet Crisis*; David Myhra for extracts in Chapter 6 from his paper, "Projection and Mitigation: Examples of Successful Applications at Nuclear Power Plant and Western Coal Mining Sites"; American Institute of Physics and James D. Miller for extracts in Chapter 8 from James D. Miller, "Effects of Noise on People," (*Journal of the Acoustical Society of America,*) Volume 53); Mirra Komarovsky for extracts in Chapter 10 from her book, *The Unemployed Man and His Family*; Yale University Press for Table 10.12 from E. Wright Bakke, *Citizens Without Work*; the Regional Science Association for Table 7.2 from Gerald Hodge, "The Prediction of Trade Center Viability in the Great Plains" (*Regional Science Association: Papers,* Volume 15); The Johns Hopkins University Press (1) for Table 10.6 from Bennett Harrison, *Education, Training and the Urban Ghetto,* (2) for Figure 9.1 from Marion Clawson and Jack L. Knetsch, *Economics of Outdoor Recreation,* and (3) for calculations from *Economics of Outdoor Recreation* used in Chapter 9; John Wiley & Sons for Figure 2.1 from Earl W. Morris and Mary Winter, *Housing, Family and Society*; Harper & Row for Table 9.5 from Neil H. Cheek, Jr. and William R. Burch, Jr., *The Social Organization of Leisure in Human Society*; Lexington Books for Table 9.2 from John D. Owen, *Working Hours: An Economic Analysis*; the Rural Sociological Society for Table 7.1 from Glenn V. Fuguitt, "The Places Left Behind: Population Trends and Policy for Rural America" (*Rural Sociology*, Volume 36), and for Table 3.1 from William J. Haga and Clinton L. Folse, "Trade Patterns and Community Identity" (*Rural Sociology*, Volume 36); the American Enterprise Institute and the Roper Organization for Table 9.6 from "Television: The Daily Fix; Stare Time Up to 3 Hours a Day" (*Public Opinion*, Volume 2); the Motion Picture Association of America, Inc. for portions of Table 9.4 from "The Public Appraises Movies," *A Survey for Motion Picture Association of America, Inc.*; to William R. Freudenburg for extracts from his paper with L. M. Bacigalupi, A. Clay, C. Landoll, and K. N. Deeds, "Subjective Responses to an Energy Boomtown Situation: A Preliminary Report on Research in Progress in Four Western Colorado Towns"; and to Robert J. Havighurst for extracts from his book with H. Gerthon Morgan, *The Social History of War-Boom Community*.

*—Kurt Finsterbusch*

*Chapter 1*

# INTRODUCTION

Social impact assessment (SIA) is a growing field of applied social science. Unlike other fields, however, it has lacked a summary of existing knowledge in the field. This book attempts to provide such a summary. It pulls together the available knowledge in each major social impact area and is designed to be primarily a resource for social impact assessors. It can also serve as a guide for students.

The organizing concept of this volume is the social impact area, and the impact areas which most concern us are those which include the impacts of large public construction projects. Such projects produce an infinite array of social impacts. When these are reduced to the most important and the most frequent and are grouped under general headings, they reduce to 13 impact areas:

(1) Population Changes*
(2) Employment Changes*
(3) Displacement and Relocation*
(4) Neighborhood Disruption*
(5) Noise Impacts*
(6) Aesthetic Impacts
(7) Accessibility Changes
(8) Leisure/Recreation Impacts*

  (9)   Health and Safety
 (10)   Citizens' Reactions
 (11)   Stressful Community Growth*
 (12)   Community Decline*
 (13)   Land Use Changes

The following chapters examine eight of these impact areas (designated by asterisks). Each summarizes the available and relevant knowledge base for social impact assessors, discussing the impacts of projects, and explicating the more general phenomena involved in each impact area.

The impact areas and the remaining chapters are related as follows. Common social impacts of large construction projects are population changes (Chapter 2), alterations in people's habitats or neighborhoods (Chapter 3), and the displacement and relocation of inhabitants and activities from the project area (Chapter 4). Occasionally whole communities are relocated (Chapter 5). In addition, when large construction projects occur in rural areas they often create boom towns (Chapter 6), which generally become bust towns after construction is completed (Chapter 7). Another common impact, usually classified as social, is noise (Chapter 8)—a negative feature of the construction stage of projects in populated areas and of the operation stage of certain facilities such as highways and airports. The last two impact areas reviewed in this book are leisure and employment, which cover the bulk of everyone's waking hours. Projects provide or displace leisure/recreation facilities and services (Chapter 9). Projects also can provide enough employment to substantially reduce the local unemployment rate. This is a major benefit of large construction projects. In this book, however, we focus on unemployment rather than employment. Social impact assessors need an understanding of the social and psychological problems of the unemployed. Construction projects tend not to have unemployment impacts, but many government actions do and many of these require EISs. Many government actions, including environmental regulations, cause employment in some industries and unemployment in others. Generally, the net employment increases but the positive net picture hides from view the misfortunes of many. Since the new jobs do not go to those laid off by the government action, unemployment remains an adverse social impact of such policies (Chapter 10).

The emphasis in this book is on the demographic and social impacts of the above eight impact areas. Many of these also have economic aspects, which, while not ignored in this work, are not discussed at length. It is for the social impact assessor to study the remaining social impacts.

Five additional impact areas which are logical candidates for inclusion in this review are not treated in separate chapters. Three are at least minimally covered in this book—land use, accessibility, and citizens' reactions. Most aspects of land use impacts are usually included in economic analyses and need not concern us here, but some of the social aspects of land use impacts are included in our chapter on the residential habitat. This chapter also touches upon accessibility, which is discussed further in the population movement and relocation chapters. Finally, most of the chapters touch upon citizens' reactions.

We do not include a chapter on aesthetics or health and safety impacts. Too little relevant material exists to warrant a chapter on aesthetics, and health and safety impacts are not normally addressed by the social impact assessor. For example, traffic engineers estimate accident potentials of various highway designs, and other technical experts estimate pollution levels and the health hazards which they present.

Now for a caveat and a suggestion. As all social scientists know, social life is wonderfully complex and full of rich nuances and subtleties. However, the emphasis in this work, as in any summary, is on the general patterns, and thus, the unique variations are averaged out of view. Averages, unfortunately, do not stir the emotions, and social impact assessments should promote some concern on the part of readers or they are inadequately representing the reality they report. Accordingly, we quote some analysts who write eloquently about conflicts which they observed or heard from the people affected. The suggestion is that the social impact assessor should be in touch with affected parties. Interviews and field work are essential to sensitive and effective SIAs. Secondary sources may be adequate for describing objective conditions but do not promote sympathetic understanding of the consequences of the project. Seeing and hearing are absolutely necessary for SIAs, and neither this work nor any other should be substituted for firsthand observations.

## What is Social Impact Assessment?

Social impact assessments are evaluations of policy alternatives in terms of their estimated consequences. In the process some new alternatives and some modifications of the proposed alternatives may suggest themselves, but basically SIA occurs after the policy alternatives have been determined. The complete policy process involves four stages: (1) formulation of policy alternatives, (2) selection of an alternative for implementation, (3) implementation, and (4) evaluation and modification. SIA is a decision tool for the second stage in which the alternative for implementation is selected.

Currently the major use for SIA is in the evaluation of alternative designs for public construction projects. For example, the social impacts of alternative alignments for a proposed highway would be compared against each other and against the consequences of not building the highway at all. Other types of public construction projects for which SIA is applicable and currently required by law include, dams, power plants, airports, urban renewal, tunnels, rail transit, and pipelines.

As an area of applied social science, SIA was born with the National Environment Policy Act (NEPA) in 1969. This act requires an environmental impact statement (EIS), which evaluates impacts on the environment for all actions, funded or conducted by the federal government, which significantly affect the environment. The social environment is included in the act's concept of the environment; therefore, SIA is included in EIS. As required by NEPA, SIA is a component of a multidisciplinary evaluation of the consequences of alternative courses of action.

The original purpose of NEPA was to protect the environment as much as possible from irreparable damage from public construction projects and from environmental policies. The inclusion of SIAs in EISs expands their purpose to include the protection of social units—that is, individuals, households, organizations, neighborhoods, and communities—from adverse consequences of public actions.

Normally, public actions have widespread benefits, as in the case of highways or power plants. However, they also have negative side effects which may outweigh the benefits. The EIS's purpose is to guarantee that the full range of benefits and dysbenefits (costs and negative consequences) are given consideration in the decision to carry out a proposed public action. How much consideration various benefits and dysbenefits receive is influenced by the EIS but is not determined by it. In the final analysis the policy decision is a judgment by an individual or a group and is not a scientific conclusion. It may be based on relatively systematic and objective information, including a SIA, but the assignment of weights to various benefits and dysbenefits to determine a best choice inevitably involves subjective judgments and political considerations. Different groups champion different alternatives, and often the.decision maker is caught in the middle.

At a minimum, the SIA identifies the full range of significant social impacts. At a maximum, the SIA would also report on the attitudes and probable reactions of all interested parties to the policy alternatives and would recommend modifications of the alternatives which would minimize dysbenefits and maximize benefits.

## Applications of SIA

The main applications of SIA are for environmental impact statements, technology assessments, AID project evaluations, and many other government project evaluations. Social impacts are considered in all policy decisions to a degree, but often they are not considered in a formal and systematic manner, which is the defining characteristic of SIA. It is convenient to date the beginning of SIA with NEPA in 1969 and to identify the bulk of SIAs as part of EISs. Hard and fast lines, however, cannot be drawn between SIAs and less systematic considerations of social factors. In fact, we would criticize many SIAs for EIS for investigating so few social impacts as not to qualify as SIAs. In other words, the borders of the field of SIA are not clearly marked.

## ENVIRONMENTAL IMPACT STATEMENTS

NEPA requires EISs for all federal actions affecting the environment. In practice, two types of actions are subjected to EIS review: individual projects and agency programs. Individual projects such as highways, dams, and power plants account for the majority of EISs and are the prototype public actions for the discussions of impacts in this book. Some of the early EISs were minimal documents of eight to ten pages of text with almost no coverage of social impacts. Some evaluated only the chosen alternative and provided little evidence for their assertions, which made them practically useless as decision documents. Today, the caliber of EISs is much higher and the documents are much longer. Recently, the Council on Environmental Quality promulgated new regulations governing the EIS process. These regulations are designed to reduce paperwork and the length of time of EISs while increasing their effectiveness, and were a reaction to excessively long documents which went into the more trivial impacts. For example, the EIS for the proposed Kaipa-rowits Power Plant and Transmission System in Utah ran over 2500 pages, which suggests that the EIS process was getting out of hand. The days of flimsy EISs are past.

To convey some idea about the nature of EISs we will briefly describe three cases, two of projects and one of a program. They are not representative but illustrative. The first is the EIS for the rebuilding and improvement of the lower West Side Highway in New York City for the Federal Highway Administration, and the second is the EIS for the Dickey-Lincoln School Lakes Dam by the Army Corps of Engineers. The third is the EIS for the Fish and Wildlife Service's Mammalian Predator Damage Management Program.

### West Side Highway EIS

The draft EIS for the West Side Highway which was accepted by the Federal Highway Administration in 1974 is an impressive document of 335 large, glossy, multicolored pages with countless pictures, diagrams, maps, tables, and graphics. It clearly represents a massive effort and is based on many technical reports which are footnoted but not included. Its coverage of impacts is inclusive, exhaustive, and relatively balanced. Nevertheless, its traffic projections and the estimates of economic costs and benefits that derive therefrom have been criticized. For example, the critics say the induced traffic estimates—that is, additional trips which the facility would stimulate—are too low.

The debate over the West Side Highway EIS raises the following question: Are EISs science or politics? They are political documents because they are part of the policy-making process, and policies have different effects on various groups. They are more than politics, however; they also can, and usually do, include scientific investigations—systematic and objective research. How these investigations are reported is subjectively determined. What is reported, what is left unreported, and how the facts are reported (or slanted) may be dominated by politics or by a professional ethic against bias and dishonesty. But even honest people will disagree on what an unbiased report is, so they can never be fully scientific. In any case the West Side Highway EIS seems to come as close to unbiased reporting as can be expected in a political document.

The avoidance of bias is reflected in the report's conclusion, which is quoted in full:

CONCLUSION
This summary of the probable beneficial and adverse effects of each alternative, and the more complete descriptions contained in other sections of this Statement, point up the complexity of the problems and issues which confront all participants in the decision-making process for the West Side Highway Project.

The five alternatives which have been presented here for consideration offer a wide range of possible actions and, therefore, a similarly wide range of potential impacts on the West Side and Manhattan. No single alternative can be shown to be beneficial in every category of social, economic and environmental effects. Nor can any one alternative be shown to respond positively and fully to the Goals and Policy Statements adopted by the Steering Committee at the outset of this planning process.

Consequently, this Environmental Impact Statement emphasizes the fact that making choices in order to provide optimum future conditions within the West Side Study Corridor will necessarily and properly reflect the balancing of various competing values [p. 311].

In other words, the study failed to reach a conslusion. No one alternative was recommended as clearly superior to the others.

The five alternatives which the West Side Highway EIS considered ranged from the "Maintenance Alternative" to the "Outboard Alternative." The former is limited to repairing the existing highway which had to be closed because an elevated portion had collapsed and the remainder had badly deteriorated. The Outboard Alternative removes the existing West Side Highway and waterfront facilities (landfills to the pierhead line), builds a six-lane interstate highway plus a new transitway submerged in the landfill, and converts the waterfront to parks and housing developments. The Maintenance Alternative was estimated to cost $86 million to construct and the Outboard Alternative $1,415 million. The latter, however, was estimated to save users approximately $86 million a year by 1995 over the former. The other three alternatives are Reconstruction (more extensive remodeling than the Maintenance Alternative), Arterial (which would replace West Side Highway with a new at-grade highway in the same location) and Inboard (submerge the new highway near the present bulkhead line). A transitway also figured in the Arterial and Inboard plans.

The major concerns of the EIS were the servicing of transportation needs in the lower West Side and the long-term and short-term impacts on population, housing, and land use characteristics of the nearby communities. The Inboard and Outboard Alternatives would increase the highway capacity and add a transit system (either rail or express buses) and encourage more development of the area than would the other alternatives. The study's summary of the social impacts of the Maintenance and Outboard Alternatives are as follows:

## SUMMARY COMPARISON

The Maintenance and Reconstruction alternatives would stimulate no highway related redevelopment, and would initiate few positive effects on adjacent communities. By reinforcing existing land uses on the West Side and precluding positive land-use changes far into the future, these alternatives would likely produce counter-productive effects for both adjacent communities and the City alike.

The Outboard alternative would have the effect of spreading future changes over a longer period of time, beyond the ten year construction period, and focusing redevelopment energies on newly created off-shore land rather than adjacent upland areas. Both public and private commitments to such an extensive redevelopment proposal would be large, but the longer lead time provided would allow for the formulation of community oriented control mechanisms and an orderly development program. The potential for new housing in off-shore areas could be used to moderate demand in adjacent communities and relieve pressures for residential expansion into those industrial areas that the City is attempting to stabilize. Extensive open space is another resource which could be developed for the benefit of local communities. Although long-term in nature, the Outboard alternative would create conditions that stimulate extensive, deliberate changes as distinct from the less controlled and largely deteriorating changes of the Maintenance and

Reconstruction alternatives, the speculative conditions of the Arterial alternative, and the limited changes of the Inboard alternative [p. 172].

In addition to the transportation, economic, and indirect development impacts, the EIS carefully examines visual effects; displacement and relocation; construction impacts; noise, air, and water pollution; energy consumption; and parks and waterfront access.

### Dickey-Lincoln Hydroelectric EIS

The second EIS to be described is the Dickey-Lincoln School Lakes hydroelectric, flood control, and recreation project involving two earth-filled dams which would create 88,650 acres of lakes. The project would supply peak load electric power, and it was compared with 24 alternative peak load power sources. The most economical alternative was found to be the oil-fired gas turbine. The Dickey-Lincoln Project would effect an annual savings in power costs compared with gas turbine of $23.5 million a year when fully developed. Annual economic benefits from recreational use, redevelopment, and the prevention of flood damages are small relative to the hydroelectric output.

The SIA component of the EIS includes a socioeconomic profile of the project area and an assessment of socioeconomic impacts. The socioeconomic profile describes the area in terms of the demographic factors ethnicity, religion, education, occupation, local government, municipal services, housing, economic activities, recreation, aesthetics, and noise. The assessments of socioeconomic impacts cover mainly demographic changes; demand on municipal services; relocation of 161 households; employment opportunities; recreational opportunities; noise; and impacts on agriculture, forestry, and industry.

Most of the anticipated social problems result from an influx of about 2700 workers and dependents during the peak construction period into an area containing about 16,000 inhabitants. The report identifies problems but avoids estimating their severity. For example, the following is the report's entire discussion of two aspects of municipal services:

*Solid Waste.* Of the four communities most likely to receive the greatest development, three have inadequate solid waste disposal systems.

*Medical Services.* The increase in numbers of residents would extend the shortage of health services. This shortage would be further intensified by accidents suffered by workers [p. 4-17].

The report is especially cautious in predicting the social problems which may arise as newcomers adjust to new social conditions and old-timers adjust to the changes the newcomers precipitate. All these matters are condensed into one paragraph.

At peak construction, there would be about 1,200 workers, mostly men without families, living in a far more rural setting than most are used to. This has the potential of creating social problems for local residents and construction workers. It would also create the need for a variety of services and an increase in local business generally [p. 4-16].

The major failing of the EIS is that it does not clearly indicate if the local people will benefit from the project. The reader is advised that they will have greater economic and employment opportunities on the one hand, and that social problems and municipal service shortages will occur on the other hand, but not how these and the other impacts add up for the local residents. The reader is not told what the local residents want out of life and whether the project will advance or diminish their goals.

### Mammalian Predator Control EIS

The third EIS to be reviewed assesses the U.S. Fish and Wildlife Service's Mammalian Predator Damage Management Program (1978). The EIS examines the current program in 13 western states and compares it with eight alternative programs. It supports the current program without actually stating its support.

The current program is reactive and not proactive. The Fish and Wildlife Service answers requests only for technical assistance from federal, state, and local agencies and private individuals. All requests are investigated, and, if warranted, the predators (primarily coyotes) are destroyed (73,000 in 1977). The program results

in significant reduction in numbers of predators in localized areas with resultant lesser losses of livestock (primarily young sheep, goats, and cattle). Other impacts include the occasional loss of nontarget animals and possible disruption of natural predator-prey relationships in those areas where predator populations are reduced.

There are also impacts on humans who are opposed to the killing of animals, or who are opposed to disrupted natural predator-prey relationships [pp. iii-iv].

The major benefits of the program are the savings in livestock which the study estimates netted $48 million for livestock producers in 1977 and $102 million in consumer savings because of increased supplies and lower prices. Since the program only cost $3,485,000 of federal funds and $5,368,000 of state and local funds, the EIS claims that it is economically beneficial. Critics claim, however, that the savings for livestock producers and consumers are greatly inflated. Very little hard data underlie the estimates, and skeptics question whether the program is cost-effective.

The main objection to the program is the ethical opposition to killing coyotes and a larger concern of some environmentalists that cattle and sheep producers interfere too much in the natural environment by over-stocking the ranges and killing off all animals that prey on livestock. The larger sentiment is not even explained by the EIS, and the humane objection to killing coyotes is not presented with any understanding. Instead, the study points out "that there are negligible impacts on general public attitudes as a result of the Service's predator damage control program" (p. 98).

The public comments on the program were thoroughly analyzed by Llewellyn et al. (1979) using a systematic content analysis methodology, and the results were compared with national surveys of attitudes toward predator control. Both in the public comments and the national surveys, public opinion strongly supports the conservation and environmental viewpoint. The public accepts the need for a predator management program, but favors nonlethal control techniques and a policy based on taking only "offending animals." The livestock producers, on the other hand, expressed in their comments the desire for an expansion of the program and the use of all control techniques, including the reintroduction of the poison, 1080, which often eliminates nontarget animals. In sum, the EIS greatly underestimated the attitudes of the public against lethal methods, especially slow-acting poisons, steel leghold traps, the slaughtering of cubs, and aerial gunning. The public is not so adverse to fast-acting poisons and shooting from the ground but favors guard dogs, repellent chemicals, and birth control techniques for controlling predators.

Probably the most important social impact of this program is its offense to humane sentiments. The role of the social impact assessor was primarily one of assessing public attitudes. This is a pattern which applies to many other programs affecting the environment. Many program EISs, however, involve a greater variety of social impacts than the Predator Control Program and involve complex SIAs. Some of the program EISs for 1975 are listed below:

San Mateo community development—Department of Housing and Urban Development
Natural Gas Emergency Standby Act of 1975—Federal Energy Administration
Timber management program—Bureau of Land Management
Manufacture of floating nuclear power plants—Nuclear Regulatory Commission
Proposed coal leasing program—Bureau of Land Management

## OTHER APPLICATIONS OF SIA

The applications of SIA are nearly infinite. When the PTA studies the effects of an elementary school closing, it is conducting a SIA. Professionally conducted SIAs, however, are usually performed by a government agency, a private contract research firm, or occasionally by university researchers or nonprofit organizations. They generally evaluate government policies, programs, or projects and generally do so for EISs. Since EISs are required only when the natural environment is significantly affected, many education, health, welfare, social control, and community service programs do not require an EIS. Nevertheless, their social impacts are evaluated before they are put into practice. Increasingly, the language and methodology of SIA are becoming affixed to the programs in many agencies, including HEW, LEAA, and Labor. AID reacts differently: It regularly requires SIAs for its many worldwide projects but labels these "social soundness analyses."

Professionally conducted SIAs are not limited to the federal government; state and local governments and private foundations conduct or sponsor SIAs as well. For example, the Charles F. Kettering Foundation recently funded a Rand study, "Urban Impacts of Federal Policies," and the Sacramento County Community Development and Environmental Protection Agency now requires SIAs for development projects.

The most challenging application of SIA is in technology assessments (TA). A TA is a policy study that assesses all significant impacts of the use of a new technology in order that government actions might prevent some of the negative consequences. The following partial list of TAs sponsored by NSF indicate their range.

Earthquake prediction
Life-extending technologies
Remote sensing of the environment
Cashless-checkless society
Integrated hog farming
Orographic snowpack augmentation in the Colorado River Basin
Alternative work schedules

Some of these technologies would significantly alter lifestyles, such as alternative work schedules, life-extending technologies, and the checkless-cashless society. Others such as integrated hog farming would affect only a few people—in this case, mainly hog farmers. The complexity and challenge of the SIA would vary accordingly.

## SIA Methods

How is SIA conducted? What data-gathering methods are used in SIAs? There are four major sources for SIA information: the literature, experts, project data, and direct experience. The literature includes basic research on social impact areas, case studies of similar projects or events, and theories and/or empirical findings which can be applied to the SIA situation. This book should make this task easier. By reviewing this book and the rest of the literature the assessor can be saved the arduous task of reinventing the wheel.

Since reviewing the literature is arduous in itself, assessors might be tempted to rely on experts for the guidance which the literature would provide. While we recommend using experts, we caution the assessor against relying completely on them. Certainly, experts can be useful in quickly filling in knowledge gaps when assessors have to report on types of impacts which are beyond their expertise. However, experts are prisms that color the literature they report, and their comments on the project situation include biased judgments. Both the literature and firsthand experience should be used to cross-check the contributions of experts.

Project data include quantitative and qualitative descriptive information on the project or other government action and on its setting or situation; this information is obtained from documents and published information. Direct experience provides additional project data and information on affected parties; it includes field observations, interviews with informants and affected parties, and questionnaire surveys of respondents who report about themselves and their families. These are traditional methods used in the social sciences.

The social impact assessment is strengthened by the judicious synthesis of the four types of data. The literature provides many ideas about what to expect in the study situation, but by itself it is an unreliable guide, since every situation has unique aspects. Experts also provide initial hypotheses about social impacts and can identify what information needs to be obtained. Guided by experts and the literature, the data-gathering process can be focused on verifying or revising the estimates of impacts derived from the literature search and the polling of experts. A cardinal rule is that assumptions, expectations, and conclusions should be checked. For example, the literature on the hardships of relocating families suggests that the poor are likely to experience more hardships than the middle class. The poor supposedly are more neighborhood-dependent and have fewer resources for making the adjustment to new habitats. In an SIA for a proposed highway, however, I found the poor families in the study area to be the least attached to their neighborhood: They viewed it as dangerous and a bad influence on their children, and they had few objections to moving, especially since the highway department was mandated to pay them what was necessary to put them into "decent, safe and sound housing."

## A Conceptual Framework for SIAs

Research is guided by conceptual frameworks, theories, and methods in the production of data. The choice of methods and theories to be employed is dependent upon the specific requirements of the study situation and cannot be prescribed in a work such as this. A conceptual framework for most SIAs, however, has been developed by the author and will be summarized here (see Finsterbusch, 1975, 1977, for more extensive discussions).

### IMPACTS ON INDIVIDUALS

Most social impacts affect individuals (or families), organizations, and/or communities. Generally, impacts on individuals are best monitored within a quality-of-life framework which includes both descriptions of measurable changes in a person's objective conditions and subjective responses to these changes. We recommend organizing the quality-of-life framework around 10 aspects of human life. Individuals can be viewed as

  (1)  organisms with biological needs;
  (2)  personalities with psychological needs;
  (3)  friends and relatives with social needs;
  (4)  workers with employment or production needs;
  (5)  consumers with desires for goods and services;
  (6)  residents desiring attractive and compatible habitats;
  (7)  commuters and travelers with transportation needs;
  (8)  citizens with freedoms, rights, and political opportunities;
  (9)  cultural beings with intellectual, cultural, and spiritual needs; and
(10)  pleasure seekers who enjoy entertainments, recreation, and leisure.

The biological needs are basic and involve nutrition, sleep, exercise, and good health. Health and safety hazards are the main social impacts in this area; the ultimate impact is death. Physical stress is often associated with psychological impacts which run the gamut from love and self-actualization to loneliness and fear. As a general rule, superior physical and social conditions are associated with positive psychological states of mind. Because good measurements of psychological states are expensive, most quality-of-life calculations are limited to objective social conditions. Some interviewing of affected parties, however, is essential to make sure that the assessor's assumptions about external conditions and internal states are not a house of cards.

SIAs examine impacts on social relations and social activities. Government actions might bring relatives or friends together or separate them and increase or decrease participation in social groups or organizations. Since people can make new friends, decision makers may discount these social impacts unless the assessor succeeds in portraying how the impacted parties feel about them.

Direct impacts on workers, consumers, residents, and commuters are widely reported. The indirect impacts are generally ignored, however, with the result that important consequences of policies are overlooked. For example, unemployment leads to lower self-esteem and declining authority in the family when it lasts several months (see Chapter 10). Another example is the various changes in activity patterns which result from changes in gas prices.

Direct impacts on people as citizens and consumers of culture, religion, and leisure are less frequently addressed but are important to the quality of life. These aspects of life may not seem essential, but they are sources of fulfillment and self-actualization for many people. It is necessary, therefore, to empirically investigate their importance.

## IMPACTS ON ORGANIZATIONS

Impacts on organizations are easy to monitor. Organizations have ostensible goals which can be used to guide the SIA. Social impacts on organizations are changes which help or hinder the organization attain its goals. Two other guiding concerns of organizations are whether the policy threatens the survival or the autonomy of the organization. Organizational theory and research repeatedly demonstrate the concern of organizations for survival and autonomy in addition to their stated goals. SIA information on these three objectives of organizations is easy to obtain because representatives of the organizations are almost always happy to supply such information when asked. When projects negatively affect a business it is usually quick to say so. Since politics is the game, however, assessors must be suspicious and find ways to check if public statements agree with real interests.

## IMPACTS ON COMMUNITIES

Impacts on communities are both easy and hard to monitor. Communities are fairly open social units to study and regularly publish considerable information about themselves. Many impacts are readily apparent and open to public investigation. On the other hand, community impact analyses lack focus. Communities do not have goals like organizations but are arenas in which many individuals, groups, and organizations seek to achieve their goals, often in competition with one another. One way to study community impacts is to treat the community government as another organization and to break community impacts down into impacts on individuals, groups, and organizations. This approach lacks an integrating focus. An alternative approach, which we recommend, is to view the community as a single social system which produces quality-of-life conditions for its members. This view is partly fictitious because many of the organizations which provide employment, consumer goods and services, health care, cultural opportunities, religious services, and recreation are not subunits of an integrated system or parts of an organized whole. They are not controlled or guided by a community decision-making unit as are the subunits of a formal organization. Nevertheless, the communities are the loci for the delivery of most quality-of-life components to individuals and families. They can be considered effective or ineffective to the extent that they are good places to live—that is, they provide for a high quality of life. Furthermore, although the community government does not literally direct and control the many organizations in the community, nevertheless it is responsible for overall community planning and some regulating of the multifarious activities within its borders in order to advance the general welfare as defined by the pluralistic political process. Hence, it may be considered a minimal system with a low degree of "systemness" (see Buckley, 1967).

When communities are viewed as social systems, social impacts on communities can be examined in terms of inputs, structures, activities, and outputs. The outputs are quality-of-life conditions for individuals and families—housing; health care; education; employment; transportation; consumer goods and services; and social, political, cultural, religious, intellectual, and recreational opportunities. Human, intellectual, financial, material, and natural resources are fed into the structures which produce these outputs by their activities. For example, teachers and administrators using books and classrooms teach students in the process of providing education for children. It is important, however, not to overlook the role played by the individual in providing for his own quality of life. Education is the joint product of the teaching of teachers and the learning of students. The organizations and groups in the community provide the conditions and the opportunities for the individual to obtain, partly by his own efforts, the quality-of-life factors.

According to the framework which views the community as a social system, projects and policies impact on communities by reducing or expanding inputs, altering structures, or increasing or decreasing activities. This framework is quite simple to use and is a common-sense method for organizing impact observations. The knowledge required for conducting community impact assessments, therefore, is an understanding of all of the factors which enter into the production of quality-of-life conditions at the community level. It should be noted that within this framework the assessment of impacts on communities is congruent with the assessment of impacts on both individuals and organizations.

## Regulations Pertaining to SIAs

In discussing how to conduct a social impact assessment, mention should be made of the official regulations governing impact assessments for legally required EISs. Section 102(2)(c) of the 1969 National Environmental Policy Act (NEPA) states:

> All agencies of the Federal Government shall . . . (c) include in every recommendation or report on proposals for legislation and other major Federal actions significantly affecting the quality of the human environment, a detailed statement by the responsible official on—
>
> (i) the environmental impact of the proposed action,
> (ii) any adverse environmental effects which cannot be avoided should the proposal be implemented,
> (iii) alternatives to the proposed action,
> (iv) the relationship between local short-term uses of man's environment and the maintenance and enhancement of long-term productivity, and
> (v) any irreversible and irretrievable commitments of resources which would be involved in the proposed action should it be implemented.

More recently, the Council on Environmental Quality (CEQ) in the *Federal Register* (November 19, 1978) issued new regulations for NEPA which seek to improve the efficiency and effectiveness of the EIS process. Three major provisions are to make EISs more efficient: (1) Limits are set on the number of pages and the length of time of EISs; (2) only competitive alternatives are to be assessed; and (3) only important issues are to be addressed. These provisions are a response, in part, to the criticism that EISs were heavily padded with nonessential details and were wasteful of time, paper, and money (see, for example, Friesema and Culhane, 1976; Bardach and Pugliaresi, 1977). The new regulations, therefore, would eliminate the study of nonessential issues. But who decides which issues are critical and which are nonessential? The new regulations specify that the authorized agency determines which issues are "deserving of study in the EIS . . . in consultation with affected parties" (p. 55982). The regulations suggest that the input of affected parties be obtained in a "scoping" meeting in the early stages of the EIS process. With affected parties helping to define the critical issues for investigation, the EIS should be more relevant and provide better feedback to decision makers. It hardly needs saying that the SIA should be particularly responsive to the concerns of the impacted parties.

The effectiveness of the EIS process is to be increased by three major provisions: (1) early guidance from affected parties as described above, (2) stronger linkage of the EIS to the actual decision-making process, and (3) naming the persons responsible for each part of the EIS. To ensure a stronger linkage between the EIS and the agency decision, the agency is "to produce a concise public record, indicating how the EIS was used in arriving at the decision" (p. 55980). To encourage higher professional standards in the production of "accurate documents as the basis for sound decisions" CEQ requires that "[a] list of people who help prepare documents, and their professional qualifications, shall be included in the EIS" (p. 55980). Many of these provisions are excellent in concept and they address real problems. How much they affect practice is yet to be seen, but any pressure for greater relevancy should sharpen the SIAs and EISs.

### Criticisms of SIAs

It must be admitted that SIA work to date has a generally poor reputation. Some SIAs are fraudulent justifications for political decisions made without regard for negative social impacts. Most are honest efforts, however, and if deficient, lack in design or level of effort. The latter has occurred when highways are designed with only a few person weeks allotted for assessing social impacts. In other cases the level of effort is more adequate, but the SIA consists of mechanically addressing a checklist of social impacts, and generally the list is very short.

A more critical evaluation of the quality of the SIAs which are performed for EISs is presented by Friesema and Culhane (1976), who judged them to be too narrow in coverage and of very low quality. "The primary deficiency of social impact assessment in EIS's is that the statements usually consider only one social consequence—the economic impact of the project" (1976: 343). The economic consequences are carefully detailed because they provide the primary justification for the project. Other social consequences are "rarely considered." Even when they are considered, they are inadequately addressed. Little information is presented, and almost no analysis is provided.

It is common for EIS's not to assert the directionality of the effects. much less the magnitude. Possible social impacts, if noted at all, are merely listed. Nor are the implications of change in some social variable likely to be discussed [1976: 343].

Finally, Friesema and Culhane review numerous methodological deficiencies of SIAs for EISs.

We point out that one reason for the inadequacy of most SIAs is the small knowledge base from which they start. Little useful knowledge has been produced on social impact areas, and the available knowledge has not been summarized for the convenience of social impact assessors. This book addresses the second problem, but the first will not vanish soon. The basic research which has been devoted to most major social impact areas is only modestly useful and ignores many of the most relevant topics. The exceptions are research on boom towns, noise, and leisure/recreation. The current studies of boom towns are useful for SIAs and can serve as guides to future boom-town impacts. The work on the psychological effects of noise is also directly relevant to SIAs. Much still remains to be done in this area, but a reasonable knowledge base has been developed. Finally, considerable research has investigated leisure patterns. Most of it is atheoretical and highly descriptive, but we know how people use their leisure time, so that leisure patterns can be taken into account in SIAs.

Much work has been done on population movements and how residents relate to home and neighborhood. Most of this work, however, is too general to accurately guide SIAs. We know where, how often, and why people move, but not much about the population movements associated with specific types of government actions. We know what factors contribute to satisfaction with neighborhood and housing, but not how much dissatisfaction results from specific types of neighborhood changes induced by government actions. The available literature in these impact areas, therefore, is useful as a general guide but fails to answer the specific questions which impact assessors must handle.

The remaining impact areas are seldom studied. Bust towns, household relocation, community relocation, and the social aspects of unemployment have been the subject of few studies. Basic research in these areas is badly needed. For example, a few case studies of bust towns exist but not enough to know how towns which will lose industry can best adapt. Or consider the subject of decommissioning facilities such as power plants, army bases, railroad lines, or mines. Some studies describe the economic impact of these changes in the community, but none go deeply into the hardships for the people dependent on these facilities for their livelihood. Many of these workers are long-term employees and residents. What work will they get? Where will they go? How will the families adjust?

The paucity of research on social impact areas is most surprising for relocation and unemployment. These have been frequent impacts of government actions for years. Many construction projects relocate residents and many government actions decrease employment. The number of people displaced and the number of employees laid off are almost always presented in EISs and earlier assessment reports. In addition, the economic aspects of these impacts have been widely studied. The social aspects, however, have not; they are generally ignored in SIAs as well as in basic research. It is hoped that the SIA community can influence the basic research community to look deeply at these areas of social impact.

## Accomplishments of SIAs

SIAs affect public policy decisions. We do not know how much influence SIAs have on decision-making and how often, but from the stories of specific decisions we know that they have influenced a number of decisions. A study of the impacts of the extension of Kennedy Airport into Jamaica Bay advised against the extension and called for policies for reducing the noise impacts on the surrounding residential area (Jamaica Bay Environmental Study Group, 1971). This report, in conjunction with public protest, influenced the New York Port Authority's decision. Pikarsky (1967) reports how the SIA outweighed the economic/engineering assessment in the selection of the alignment for the Chicago-Crosstown Expressway. CEQ (1976) reports on numerous changes in policy decisions brought about by the EIS process, and in some of these cases the SIA played a prominent role. For example, the Interior Department prohibited jet aircraft from intruding on Grand Teton National Park; the Corps of Engineers has canceled or stopped 12 projects and deauthorized many more; the Transportation Department has canceled or modified scores of major highway and airport projects; the Defense Department modified a number of demilitarization projects; and the General Services Administration altered the siting of the Kennedy Library and Museum from near Harvard Square to Columbia Point.

Since it is in CEQ's interest to find benefits from the EIS process, its optimistic report of EIS effects probably is biased. However, more neutral observers also argue that the EIS process has positive benefits. Friesema and Culhane (1976) give EIS a backhanded compliment in this regard. After severely criticizing EISs for low quality, they observe that bad decisions seldom are due to bad information and that the EIS process has changed the politics of decision-making. It opens the decision-making process to environmentalists and negatively affected parties and provides a basis for court actions against projects. Their assessment of the effects of the EISs in which they have participated is that "agency decisions have been altered to some degree in approximately half" of them.

Our own evaluation of the effectiveness of EISs generally and SIAs specifically is sanguine. They have affected the political game. Assessors who work on social impacts become advocates within their agency for greater consideration of social impacts in the agency's decisions. At the same time, the SIA provides opportunities for active publics to input into the decision-making process. We do not deny that SIAs at times have been completely ignored, and that the blood, sweat, and tears of social impact assessors have sometimes been in vain. Nevertheless, progress is evident, and as SIAs become more competent and social impact assessors graduate to higher ranks in the agencies, SIAs will become more influential.

*Chapter 2*

# POPULATION MOVEMENT

Social impact assessment almost always begins with a demographic analysis of the characteristics of the impacted population and estimates of population changes that the project or policy will cause. The analysis of these population changes is essential to project planning. It is also basic to the remainder of the social impact assessment, because the magnitude of other social impacts often depends on the magnitude of the population changes.

The present chapter presents a summary of demographic studies of macro and micro population movements. Three major topics will be reviewed. First, the macro picture of population dynamics in the United States will be described. What are the regional and national population trends? What are the lessons of fertility and cohort analyses? Second, the methodology for estimating population changes generated by specific projects is presented. Third, the patterns of residential mobility are analyzed. This is the micro picture of population dynamics which describes who moves and why.

## National Demographics: Macro Population Dynamics

One of the distinguishing features of the better SIAs is evidence of an awareness of the larger social and demographic context for the project or policy. The assessor is seldom required to describe the larger context; never-theless, knowledge of it should inform his work. One of the rare times when a description of the larger demographic context was required was the EIS for Locks and Dam #26 on the Mississippi River. The original EIS was contested in court and judged to be deficient because it failed to consider regional effects of improving the shipping capacity of the northern Mississippi region. The EIS had to be redrafted. Even for projects with more localized effects, knowledge of future demographic trends are important for predictions of impacts which occur 10 or 20 years in the future. In this section we briefly summarize the current population picture in the United States and how it is changing. These details provide only the minimal general demographic knowl-edge expected of assessors.

The U.S. population is around 223 million people as it enters the 1980s, according to the census count (227 million including estimated undercount and 232 million including estimated illegal aliens), and it is still growing. The important fact to note, however, is that both its long- and short-term rate of growth have slowed considerably. The U.S. population increased 4.4 times from 1800 to 1850 and 3.3 times from 1850 to 1900. It doubled again by 1950, and increased only 47 percent from 1950 to 1980.

## BIRTH AND FERTILITY RATES

Birth rates have cycled from Depression lows to highs in the fifties to current lows. Births jumped from 2.9 million in 1945 to 3.8 million in 1947. In the next decade, births rose slowly and peaked at 4.3 million in 1957. They declined to a low point of 3.1 million in 1973 and remain low today. Meanwhile, the post-World War II birth rate peaked at 25.2 per 1000 population in 1957, steadily declined to 14.9 in 1973, and has remained around that level up to the present. Related to these trends, the average size of families decreased from 3.70 in 1965 to 3.31 in 1979.

The fertility rate of American women has declined steadily from 3.6 in 1956 to below the replacement rate. The fertility rate is the number of children per woman aged 15-44, calculated in terms of expected completed family size. The replacement rate is a fertility rate of 2.1, and in 1975 the fertility rate was only 1.8. Since high past growth rates result in a much larger number of people in the high reproduction ages than in the high death rate ages, births will exceed deaths for four or five decades even with fertility rates below 2.1. Nevertheless, the annual increase in the U.S. population (births minus deaths plus net immigration) has declined from an average of 2.8 million between 1955 and 1965 to less than an average of 1.9 million. The Census Bureau projects a slight increase in the annual population increment to 2.2 million per year in the 1980s, but then a decline to about 1.5 to 2.0 million in the subsequent years.

## AGE COHORTS

It is important to note the changing age composition of the population. After World War II there was a baby boom followed by a baby bust in the late 1960s. The boom cohort, called the giant generation, places severe strains on social institutions as it passes through the life cycle. The giant generation hit the elementary and junior high schools in the 1950s and the junior high and senior high schools in the 1960s. The additional number of children was large enough to make the society noticeably more child-oriented. In the late 1960s it arrived on college campuses and contributed to campus unrest and the free and easy lifestyles of the period. In the 1970s the giant generation reached young adulthood and significantly affected job and housing markets. Meanwhile, smaller cohorts entered the elementary schools, forcing school closings. According to Morrison (1978), between 1970 and 1977 the 5-13 age group declined 12 percent, the 25-35 age group increased 32 percent, and the over-65 age group increased 18 percent. The increase in the elderly has been reflected in "grey power" and new concerns for that group's needs.

This story of the past guides our understanding of the future. Unusually large or small cohorts affect the institutions and culture of the society. Table 2.1 shows the absolute changes in the population within six age groupings from 1960 to 1990. The 1980s will be a period of decline for the college-age population, slow growth for the 25-35-year-olds, and very rapid growth for the 35-45-year-olds. These changes will impact on housing markets, schools, the economy, and all facets of life. If the 25-35-year age group is largely composed of apartment dwellers and the 35-45-year age group contains largely house dwellers, as Alonso (1978) argues, then the return to the cities of the 1970s may reverse to create a new wave of suburbanization in the 1980s. The new suburbs, however, will have fewer children and will reflect other lifestyle changes.

## HOUSEHOLD COMPOSITION

Changing lifestyles in the 1980s will reflect the new options available because of the low fertility rates and the high proportion of women in the labor force. They will also reflect changing marriage patterns: later age of marriage, high divorce rates, more unmarried couples living together, more female and male single-parent families, and so on. The husband/wife/children household with husband working, wife not working, and children under 18 at home may be thought of as the typical household, but it represented only 13 percent of all households in 1977 and will be even less typical in the future if current rates continue (see Table 2.2). Because age of marriage has increased from 1960 to 1977, the percentage of males 14 and over that were never married increased from 25.0 percent to 30.2 percent, and for women 19.0 to

TABLE 2.1   Five-Year Changes in U. S. Population by Age Class, for
            Population 18 Years and Older, 1960-1990 (numbers in
            thousands)

| | Age Class | | | | | |
| Period | 18–24 | 25–34 | 35–44 | 45–54 | 55–64 | 65+ |
|---|---|---|---|---|---|---|
| 1960-1965 | 4035 | −542 | 215 | 1529 | 1340 | 1503 |
| 1965-1970 | 4762 | 2925 | −1296 | 1263 | 1696 | 1925 |
| 1970-1975 | 2917 | 5625 | −326 | 459 | 1113 | 2333 |
| 1975-1980 | 1859 | 5254 | 2906 | −1070 | 1424 | 2521 |
| 1980-1985 | −1610 | 3187 | 5655 | −241 | 539 | 2378 |
| 1985-1990 | −2704 | 1227 | 5216 | 2854 | −961 | 2519 |

SOURCE:   Bureau of the Census (1970, 1977, 1978).

23.4 percent. The practice of unmarried couples living together is increasing;
this type of household increased 2.3 times from 327,000 in 1970 to 754,000
in 1977. Female-headed families increased 37 percent in the same period, and
male-headed families increased 21 percent. The number of divorced persons
per 1000 married persons with spouse present rose from 47 in 1970 to 84 in
1977 (Bureau of the Census, 1987a).

The above discussion of current and future demographic changes in the
United States presents national trends. These will be reflected in local trends
and should be taken into account in impact assessments. The prediction of
local trends also requires an understanding of residential migration trends
which are favoring some regions and types of localities over others.

## REGIONAL TRENDS

Three major changes are taking place in residential migration in the United
States. First is the movement West—and more recently South—of jobs and
people. Second is the spreading and thinning out of populations in the largest
cities. Third is the slowing of growth of most of the largest metropolitan
centers (absolute decline in one-sixth of them) and the reemergence of
growth in the nonmetropolitan places. About half of this nonmetropolitan
growth is related to metropolitan areas. It entails the spread of population
beyond the current Standard Metropolitan Statistical Areas (SMSA). An
SMSA typically consists of a county with a city of 50,000 or more inhabitants plus the surrounding counties that are metropolitan in nature and
integrated with the central city by commuting boundaries. There are 259
SMSAs in the United States, and the nonmetropolitan areas surrounding them
are growing faster than are the SMSAs.

TABLE 2.2  Distribution of Adult Americans by Types
of Households (percentages)

| | |
|---|---|
| Living in single-breadwinner nuclear families | 13 |
| Living in dual-breadwinner nuclear families | 16 |
| Living in no wage-earner nuclear families | 1 |
| Living in child-free or post-child-rearing marriages | 23 |
| Living in extended families | 6 |
| Living in experimental families or cohabiting | 4 |
| Heading single parent families | 16 |
| Other single, separated, divorced, or widowed | 21 |
| | 100 |

SOURCE:  Bureau of Labor Statistics (1977).

The other half of the growth of nonmetropolitan areas is in rural areas.
Many once stable, small towns and cities are experiencing growth which they
are often poorly equipped to deal with. Almost two-thirds of the nation's
nonmetropolitan counties have gained migrants in the 1970s, compared with
one-quarter in the 1960s and one-tenth in the 1950s. The pattern of nonmetropolitan growth is more balanced now than earlier, since many previously lagging areas have revived and some previously growing areas have
stabilized (Morrison, 1978).

The regional population shifts have been pronounced in the past two
decades. The westward movement throughout America's history has been
accentuated in this period, and a strong southward movement has developed.
Table 2.3 presents the regional population and population changes for nearly
three decades. These population changes are intimately tied to shifts in
economic activity and employment which are also increasing rapidly in the
South and West.

## Construction Projects and
## Population Growth

Many of the impacts of a construction project on local communities result
from the additional population which the project brings into the area. If
migrants are few relative to the population of the area, the impacts are
minimal. Obviously, the following factors affect the extent of the impacts:

(1) number of workers required,
(2) number of workers who will commute from current homes and
number of workers who will migrate to the area,

TABLE 2.3  Regional Population Change 1960 to 1978 (numbers in thousands)

| Region | Population Totals | | | Amount of Increase | | | Percentage Change | | |
|---|---|---|---|---|---|---|---|---|---|
| | 1960 | 1970 | 1978 | 1960–1978 | 1960–1970 | 1970–1978 | 1960–1978 | 1960–1970 | 1970–1978 |
| Northeast | 44,678 | 49,061 | 49,081 | 4403 | 4383 | 20 | 9.9 | 9.8 | – |
| North Central | 51,619 | 56,590 | 58,251 | 6632 | 4971 | 1661 | 12.8 | 9.6 | 2.9 |
| South | 51,973 | 62,813 | 70,626 | 18,653 | 10,840 | 7813 | 35.9 | 20.9 | 12.4 |
| West | 28,053 | 34,838 | 40,100 | 12,047 | 6785 | 5262 | 42.9 | 24.2 | 15.1 |

NOTE:  Population data for 1960 is for April 1 as presented in Bureau of the Census (1976). Population data for 1970 is for April 1 and data for 1978 is for July 1, both from Bureau of the Census (1978b).

(3)  where the migrants settle,
(4)  the household composition of incoming workers, and
(5)  the size of the community.

The number of workers required should be available from the contractor. However, for comparative purposes we present in Table 2.4 the labor force requirements for construction and operation of various energy facilities as calculated by White et al. (1978). The size of the community should also be known. In this section the bases for estimating the other three parameters will be discussed. The way migrants will distribute themselves in the nearby area depends on many factors, and predictions should be stated cautiously. Two generalizations, however, can guide these predictions. First, migrants generally prefer the largest community in the region of the project. Even though smaller communities may be geographically closer to the project site, the largest community will attract the largest number of migrants (Denver Research Institute, 1975). Second, construction workers will settle where unused housing already exists, or they will settle in trailers. Thus, housing markets, zoning, and trailer court developments will affect settlement patterns.

## ESTIMATING MIGRATING WORKERS

The proportion of the project labor force which is supplied locally varies considerably. At one extreme among the 14 projects studied by Mountain West Research (1975) is the Weyodak Project near Gillitte, Wyoming, where only three of the 92 construction workers were supplied by the local area. At the other extreme, the San Juan 1 Project near Fruitland, New Mexico, had a 79 percent local construction work force.

Many factors affect the ratio of local to migrant workers. (For purposes of this discussion all workers who live in the same town before and after they started work are considered local even though they might drive several hours to work). The main factor is the size of the required project labor force relative to the area's available labor supply which consists of the unemployed and movable workers of the required skills. The general pattern is for the available local labor to supply mainly unskilled labor, bricklayers, carpenters, millwrights, and cement finishers. This is the finding of Table 2.5, which summarizes the localism of the combined labor force for 14 projects surveyed by MWR.

## ESTIMATING MIGRATING POPULATION

MWR uses its study of 14 energy-related construction projects to ascertain the family status of nonlocal workers (see Table 2.6). The assessor needs to carefully estimate the family status of nonlocal workers in order to estimate

TABLE 2.4   Construction and Operational Personnel Requirements for Energy Facilities

| Facility (and size)[a] | Duration Years | Construction | | Operation | | Construction/ Operation Employment Ratio[d] |
|---|---|---|---|---|---|---|
| | | Peak Employment | Peak Population[b] | Employment | Population[c] | |
| Coal | | | | | | |
| Surface Mine (12.7 MMtpy) | 5 | 210 | 630 | 550 | 2,200 | .4 |
| Underground Mine (12.7 MMtpy) | 6 | 820 | 2,460 | 2,530 | 10,120 | .3 |
| Gasification (250 MMcfd) | 5 | 4,680 | 14,040 | 590 | 2,360 | 8.1 |
| Liquefaction (100,000 bbl/day) | 7 | 5,220 | 15,660 | 3,060[f] | 12,240 | 1.7 |
| Power Plant (3000 MWe) | 8 | 2,540 | 7,620 | 440 | 1,760 | 5.8 |
| Oil Shale | | | | | | |
| Surface Mine (140,000 tpd) | 4 | 710 | 2,130 | 660 | 2,640 | 1.1 |
| Underground Mine (140,000 tpd) | 4 | 710 | 2,130 | 1,180 | 4,720 | .6 |
| Retort and Processing (100,000 bbl/day) | 6 | 2,680 | 8,040 | 650 | 2,600 | 4.1 |

TABLE 2.4  Construction and Operational Personnel Requirements for Energy Facilities (Cont)

| | | Manpower Requirements (person years) | | | | | |
| | | Construction | | Operation | | | Construction / Operation Employment Ratio[d] |
| Facility (and size)[a] | Duration Years | Peak Employment | Peak Population[b] | Employment | Population[c] | |
|---|---|---|---|---|---|---|
| Crude Oil | | | | | | |
| Production[e] (100,000 bbl/day) | 7 | 3,920 | 11,760 | 3,050 | 12,200 | 1.4 |
| Natural Gas | | | | | | |
| Production[e] (250 MMcfd) | 5 | 1,700 | 5,100 | 790 | 3,160 | 2.2 |
| Uranium | | | | | | |
| Open Pit Mine (1200 tpd) | 5 | 80 | 240 | 180 | 720 | .4 |
| Underground Mine (1200 tpd) | 5 | 440 | 1,320 | 840 | 3,360 | .5 |
| Milling (1200 tpd) | 3 | 90 | 270 | 110 | 440 | .8 |

MMTpy  = million metric tons per year
MMcfd  = million standard cubic feet per day
bbl/day = barrel(s) per day
MWe  = megawatt-electric
tpd  = tons per day

a. The facility size listed is that assumed in the impact analyses in White et al. (1977). Data are from Carasso et al. (1975: 6.30-6.31) and involve uncertainties of −10 to +20 percent; data for developing technologies (coal liquefaction, gasification, and oil shale processing) involve uncertainties of −30 to +75 percent.
b. Using a population/employment multiplier of 3.0.
c. Using a population/employment multiplier of 4.0.
d. The larger the ratio, the greater the employment decline when construction ends.
e. Includes exploration (including dry holes), development, and production. See Carasso et al. (1975: 6.7-6.15).
f. See Carasso et al. (1975). This figure is among those with the greatest uncertainty. In addition, economies of scale are not incorporated into coal liquefaction facilities over the 21,000 bbl/day plant assumed by Bechtel.
SOURCE: White et al. (1978: 286).

TABLE 2.5  Occupational Distribution of Construction Workers—All Projects

| Occupation | Total Work Force | Number of Local Workers | Local Workers as Percentage of Total |
|---|---|---|---|
| Supervisory | 222 | 73 | 32.9 |
| Professional technical | 181 | 32 | 17.7 |
| Craftsmen | 1609 | 625 | 38.9 |
| Ironworker | 246 | 85 | 34.6 |
| Cement finisher | 37 | 19 | 51.4 |
| Millwright | 52 | 27 | 51.9 |
| Boilermaker | 63 | 27 | 42.9 |
| Pipefitter | 359 | 102 | 28.4 |
| Electrician | 347 | 94 | 27.1 |
| Painter | 42 | 17 | 40.5 |
| Carpenter | 356 | 219 | 61.5 |
| Plumber | 6 | 2 | 33.3 |
| Mechanic | 46 | 16 | 34.8 |
| Sheet metalworker | 18 | 6 | 33.3 |
| Bricklayer | 7 | 4 | 57.1 |
| Welder | 30 | 8 | 26.7 |
| Laborer | 427 | 243 | 56.9 |
| Operatives | 394 | 159 | 40.4 |
| Clerical and other | 308 | 118 | 38.3 |
| TOTAL | 3141 | 1251 | 39.8 |

SOURCE: Mountain West Research (1975).

the increased demand on housing, schools, and other services. In addition, single and married workers have different lifestyles that need to be taken into account when discussing changes in community life. MWR computed the average family size of married nonlocal workers to be 3.784 compared with 3.970 for married local workers. Finally, in Table 2.7 MWR works out the total direct population influx per 100 nonlocal construction workers, which averages out to 228. This figure should be used as a best guess for total population influx when the nonlocal labor force has been estimated and no other information is available. Unfortunately, individual projects vary from 145 to 288, so the marital and family status of expected migrants should be obtained, if possible, to develop more accurate estimates of the direct population growth.

TABLE 2.6    Marital Status and Number of Children Under 18 of Local and
             Nonlocal Construction Workers—All Projects

|  | Percentage of Local Workers | Percentage of Nonlocal Workers |
|---|---|---|
| Single | 23.3 | 18.5 |
| Divorced or widowed | 5.9 | 6.1 |
| Married, no children | 16.7 | 21.5 |
| Married, one child | 13.6 | 15.0 |
| Married, two children | 17.3 | 16.7 |
| Married, three children | 10.7 | 10.0 |
| Married, four children | 6.9 | 7.4 |
| Married, more than four children | 5.5 | 4.6 |
| TOTAL | 100.0 | 100.0 |

SOURCE: Mountain West Research (1975).

MWR attempted to develop a model to predict the number of local workers which community$_i$ supplies to project$_j$ ($LW_{ij}$). The variables in the model were:

$C_i$ = size of community

$P_j$ = number of employees on project j

$D_{ij}$ = distance between i and j

OC = total population of other communities within 100 miles of the project

OP = total employment on other projects within 100 miles of the project

Below is their multiple regression equation containing the above variables which explained 53 percent of the variance in $LW_{ij}$ for 68 combinations of projects and communities.

$$LW_{ij} = 12.723 + .0024C_i + .055P_j - 006D_{ij} - .1720P - .00030C$$

## ESTIMATING THE EMPLOYMENT MULTIPLIER

Employment multipliers estimate the amount of indirect or induced employment which results from the consumer expenditures of the project labor force and their families. The most common techniques for estimating induced employment use economic base models. The local economy is

TABLE 2.7  Average Population Influx per 100 Nonlocal Construction Workers

| Project Number and Name | Worker Single, Widowed, or Divorced | Worker Married, but Family Absent | Family Present | | | Total Population Influx per 100 Nonlocal Construction Workers |
|---|---|---|---|---|---|---|
| | | | Worker | Spouse | Children | |
| Coronado 1, 2, 3 | 8.7 | 30.4 | 60.9 | 60.9 | 69.6 | 230.5 |
| Craig 1, 2–Yampa Power Plant | 27.2 | 30.8 | 42.0 | 42.0 | 57.4 | 199.4 |
| Hayden 2 | 22.8 | 31.1 | 46.2 | 46.2 | 64.4 | 210.7 |
| Colstrip 1, 2 | 34.0 | 24.7 | 41.2 | 41.2 | 94.8 | 235.9 |
| Center–Milton R. Young | 25.0 | 36.1 | 38.9 | 38.9 | 69.4 | 208.3 |
| Leland Olds | 17.1 | 37.1 | 45.7 | 45.7 | 78.1 | 223.7 |
| San Juan 1 | 21.7 | 21.7 | 56.5 | 56.5 | 73.9 | 230.3 |
| Emery | 13.3 | 46.7 | 40.0 | 40.0 | 73.3 | 213.3 |
| Huntington 2 | 10.6 | 34.8 | 54.7 | 54.7 | 93.8 | 248.6 |
| Jim Bridger 2, 3 | 21.3 | 14.0 | 64.7 | 64.7 | 123.0 | 287.7 |
| Texaco Lake Expansion | 34.2 | 24.6 | 41.2 | 41.2 | 56.1 | 197.3 |
| Sun Oil–Cordero Mine | 65.3 | 17.3 | 17.3 | 17.3 | 28.0 | 145.2 |
| Texas Gulf Sulphur | 32.9 | 25.7 | 41.3 | 41.3 | 67.7 | 208.9 |
| Wyodak | 21.6 | 18.2 | 60.2 | 60.2 | 67.0 | 227.2 |
| TOTAL ALL PROJECTS | 24.6 | 26.5 | 48.9 | 48.9 | 78.9 | 227.8 |

SOURCE: Mountain West Research (1975).

divided into basic and nonbasic (service) sectors. The former export from the community their goods and services, and the latter provide goods and services to the community. The economic base method for calculating the employment multiplier is to calculate the ratio of basic to nonbasic employment in a community prior to the proposed project and to multiply the new project labor force by this ratio.

This technique for computing the employment multiplier has had unsatisfactory results when empirically tested (Moody and Puffer, 1970; Lewis, 1976; Garrison, 1972; Muller, 1976; Richardson, 1973; Meidinger, 1977). It assumes that induced employment/project employment ratios replicate the nonbasic/basic sectors ratios of the past. However, Meidinger (1977) shows how volatile this ratio is from year to year. Furthermore, the nonbasic/basic ratios aggregate many individual economic activities into a single average which may differ considerably from the effects of a new project.

Lewis (1976: 68) recommends "using some combination of regional input-output models and case studies of different kinds of actions in a variety of regions." He warns that results in one region may not apply to other regions but are better guides than export-base-type multipliers. He draws attention to the industry-specific employment multipliers of Lofting and McGauhy (1968) based on an input-output study of the California economy. The multipliers range from .10 for trade to 1.09 for construction and are much lower than those which result from export-base methods.

The approach which Muller et al. (1978) recommend in the place of the economic base method is a time-series analysis relating the change in personal income from a new project to the change in indirect employment. Both methods estimate indirect employment, but the economic base method uses the number of project jobs, and Muller et al. use the addition to local income generated by project employees. The main advantage of the personal income approach is its ability to take into account long-distance commuting. Project jobs do not increase indirect employment when workers leave the area to spend their income.

In small rural communities both the economic base method and Muller's technique could greatly overestimate induced jobs because labor in the service sector may be underutilized. According to Garrison's study of new plants in five rural counties,

[t]he multiplier effect on employment was rather small. Only 98 new jobs in trade, finance, services and other local consumption of nonbasic activities were attributed to the new plants, which had a combined local employment of 1,177. The analysis suggests that considerably larger infusions of new industry would be necessary to eliminate the under-utilization of labor and capital in the nonbasic sector of small rural communities and to produce a significant effect on employment and investment in these enterprises [Garrison, 1972: 337].

Muller et al. applied their method to estimating indirect employment for the Trident Submarine Base on the Puget Sound in Washington. They first computed the relationship between personal income from direct employees (X) and indirect employment (Y) based on annual data from 1965 to 1974. This relationship is expressed in the formula $Y = 204 + 28.7X$ (millions of dollars), which explained 88 percent of the variance in indirect employment. Next, they estimated total personal income affecting indirect employment to be \$98.6 million. Using the formula, they predict the Trident Base will generate 3033 "indirect" additional jobs (see Muller et al., 1978 for details).

## Residential Mobility:
## Micro Population Dynamics

One of the major impacts of projects and policies is residential mobility. Projects directly cause residential mobility by displacing homes. Projects also create and/or eliminate jobs and thereby indirectly cause some workers to move to obtain new jobs. Furthermore, projects may induce some residents to move by aesthetically affecting residential environments and by changing residents' accessibility to jobs, friends, schools, churches, goods, services, and other destinations. In this section we review the literature on residential mobility patterns in order to provide basic background information for assessors. This information should inform studies of relocation, employment, and residential impacts and should guide predictions about the population movements associated with new projects and policies.

We discuss four aspects of residential mobility patterns which are particularly relevant for understanding the social impacts of projects and policies. First, we describe and interpret the high frequency of moving in the United States. Some of the statistics on residential mobility may seem alarming, but they are less alarming when examined more closely. Most moves are desired and take place within the same community. Furthermore, mobility rates differ markedly for various groups and fortunately tend to be lowest in groups which are the most adversely affected by moving. Second, we examine why the national mobility rate is so high and then why individuals move. Many moves are associated with changes in the circumstances of the moves, such as marriage, divorce, graduation, or change of job. The majority of local moves, however, are to make housing adjustments, and most of these are considered improvements. Third, we consider the effects of moving on individuals. Moving is stressful, involves adjustments, and severs social ties. Most people adjust successfully and are happy about having moved; but some do not. Finally, we focus on involuntary moving, which is of particular importance to assessors. We review the fragmentary research which has compared voluntary with involuntary moving.

FREQUENCY OF RESIDENTIAL MOBILITY

Between 1970 and 1975, 45.6 percent of the people in the United States aged five years and over changed their residence (Bureau of the Census, 1975). According to Long and Boertlein (1976), the average person is expected to move 12.9 times. This is a nation of movers. Nevertheless, the United States is not very different in its mobility patterns from certain other western nations. In 1970 the percentage of people moving in five years was 47.0 in the United States, 51.4 in Australia, and 46.6 in Canada (Long and Boertlein, 1976). In contrast, England and Japan had five-year mobility rates of 37.2 and 35.9, respectively. The mobility rate in the United States, therefore, is among the highest in the world, but it is not unique. Almost half of the population moves within five years, and almost one-fifth moves each year. These statistics seem shocking and justify books like Packard's *A Nation of Strangers* (1972) and Gordon's *Lonely in America* (1975). Before deploring the situation, however, we need to examine mobility statistics in greater detail in order to be clearer about their meaning.

Table 2.8 presents the residential mobility rates for five-year age groups. The most mobile group is aged 20 to 24 years. They leave their parents' homes and go to colleges, start families, join the army, get jobs, and so on. People are still highly mobile in their late twenties, but they are beginning to settle down. Average mobility rates are recorded for people in their thirties and below average rates for the remaining adult age cohorts. Among children,

TABLE 2.8   Percentage of Population Residentially
Mobile, by Age: Around 1970

| Age at End of Migration Interval | 1-Year Interval | 5-Year Interval |
|---|---|---|
| 1 to 4 years | 28.8 | – |
| 5 to 9 | 19.7 | 55.6 |
| 10 to 14 | 15.0 | 43.8 |
| 15 to 19 | 18.1 | 44.5 |
| 20 to 24 | 44.4 | 75.4 |
| 25 to 29 | 34.7 | 78.4 |
| 30 to 34 | 23.4 | 63.6 |
| 35 to 39 | 17.8 | 50.4 |
| 40 to 44 | 13.6 | 40.3 |
| 45 to 49 | 11.5 | 34.1 |
| 50 to 54 | 9.9 | 30.5 |
| 55 to 59 | 9.3 | 28.3 |
| 60 to 64 | 8.6 | 27.3 |
| 65 and over | 8.4 | 28.1 |

SOURCE: Long and Boertlein (1976: 9).

the first four years are the most mobile, which suggests that a new child may be one important reason for moving to new quarters, presumably larger ones. We might add that similar mobility curves for age cohorts characterize other countries.

Most residential moves are voluntary, which suggests that mobility rates should be highest for groups that experience the greatest net gains from moving. Table 2.9 fits this pattern. Moving occurs most frequently among age cohorts which are the most capable of adapting to the disruption of moving and which are likely to benefit most from moving. Migrants tend to be younger, better educated, and wealthier than nonmigrants. They tend to be people who are least likely to experience employment difficulties in their place of origin or destination (Garn, 1978: 24).

Although the high mobility rates in the United States are seen by some as a cause for alarm, they are gradually decreasing. According to the Bureau of the Census (1977), the "average annual rate of moving in 1958-61 was 20.1 percent, compared with 19.1 percent in 1968-70. The rate declined to 17.7 percent for the 12 months between March 1975 and March 1976" (p. 1). For 15-year-olds and older, the five-year rate dropped from 49.5 to 46.3 from 1960 to 1970 (Long and Boertlein, 1976). If high mobility is bad for the quality of life, as some suppose, things are improving slightly.

Another factor which should be taken into account is the distance moved. Most moves involve short distances and allow the maintenance of many social relationships. Around 1970, 61.6 percent of the movers moved within the local area, and another 16.9 percent moved within the state. Only 18.0 percent moved between states, and 3.5 percent moved from abroad (Long and Boertlein, 1976).

Who are the movers and who are the stayers? Surprisingly, rural and urban persons have similar five-year mobility rates. For persons five years and over,

TABLE 2.9   Percentage of Male Population 18 Years and Over Who Stayed in the Same House from 1970 to 1975 by Income Groups (excluding the movers from abroad and nonreporters)

| 1974 Income Group | 18 Years and Over | 19 to 24 Years | 25 to 34 Years | 35 to 44 Years | 45 to 64 Years | 65 Years and Over |
|---|---|---|---|---|---|---|
| Less than $3000 | 63.3 | 64.6 | 33.3 | 49.0 | 62.7 | 77.0 |
| $3000 to $4999 | 57.8 | 43.9 | 23.5 | 44.1 | 69.6 | 78.7 |
| $5000 to $6999 | 52.0 | 35.5 | 20.8 | 51.3 | 69.3 | 82.0 |
| $7000 to $9999 | 47.9 | 24.5 | 23.1 | 49.2 | 72.3 | 77.0 |
| $10,000 to $14,999 | 53.5 | 20.7 | 25.0 | 56.7 | 78.4 | 79.2 |
| $15,000 or more | 58.0 | 16.4 | 23.3 | 55.3 | 76.5 | 80.0 |

SOURCE:  U.S. Bureau of the Census (1975: 41).

55.2 percent of persons in SMSAs resided in the same house from 1970 to 1975 (exclusive of nonreporters and movers from abroad) compared with 56.1 percent of persons outside SMSAs. The movers residing in SMSAs in 1975 were more likely to have moved within the same county than were movers residing outside the SMSAs (61.1 percent compared with 53.5 percent); however, both groups of movers were equally likely to move within the state—79.9 percent compared with 77.7 percent (U.S. Bureau of the Census, 1975: 61).

The poor and the rich tend to move the least, as shown in the first column of Table 2.9. However, income is associated with both age and mobility, so the mobility of income groups should be compared within age groupings in order to get an accurate picture. In the 65 and over category, all income groups have the same high level of residential stability over a five-year period. The upper income groups move the least in the 35-44- and 45-64-year cohorts, and they move the most in the 18-24-year cohort, probably because they can afford to move out of their parents' homes earlier than young people with less income. In a survey of about 5000 families, Goodman (1974) reported that stability increases as the ratio of family income to family income needs increases. Defined this way, the poor are the most mobile and the rich the least mobile.

Mobility rates differ markedly for married and unmarried persons. Single male primary individuals had five-year interval mobility rates of 61.7 percent between 1970 and 1975 compared with 45.0 for married male heads of households. These differences are not accounted for by age differences for the two groups. For example, in the 45-64 cohort, married male heads of households had five-year interval mobility rates of only 23.9 percent compared with 46.3 for single male primary individuals.

The mobility picture differs greatly for males and females and slightly for blacks and whites. The five-year interval residential mobility rate for single male primary individuals was 61.7 percent between 1970 and 1975 and 38.2 percent for single female primary individuals. Finally, the overall differences between black and white five-year interval mobility rates are modest: 48.9 percent for blacks and 43.8 percent for whites.

## WHY DO PEOPLE MOVE?

### Explanation of National Mobility Rates

We begin with the broad picture and ask why the United States has very high levels of residential mobility. First, high rates of mobility are an outcome of high levels of industrialization. In agricultural countries most people are literally tied to the land unless severe overpopulation forces the surplus to migrate to the cities. In this country less than five percent of the labor force is in farming. Some farm workers are migratory, but the farmers and farm managers are stable: Only 22.9 percent of them changed residence from 1970 to 1975. Very few nonfarm workers are tied to the land; some are tied to their localities—such as doctors or insurance salesmen, who build up a clientele in an area—but many workers move to follow opportunities.

Another feature which contributes to America's high levels of mobility is its migration history (Long and Boertlein, 1976). This is literally a nation of immigrants, so the idea of mobility is more basic than the idea of stability. To some extent, mobility begets mobility. Long and Boertlein observe: "[P]ersons who were living outside their state of birth in 1965 were over three times as likely to move between states in the 1965-70 interval as persons living in their state of birth in 1965" (1976: 22, 23).

### Explanation of Individual Mobility

The reasons for moving may be classified roughly as either circumstantial (that is, involving a change in circumstances) or environmental (involving the desirability of the home or neighborhood). Major circumstantial reasons include (1) the formation of new households (usually because of marriage), (2) the dissolution of households by divorce or separation, (3) employment and education demands, or (4) forced relocation. People go away to college, join the army, transfer to a new job, marry and divorce, and change their residences in the process. Major environmental reasons can be (1) insufficient space because of growth in the family, (2) the desire to move to a better neighborhood, (3) the desire to own a home, and (4) too much space because of a decline in family size.

In most cases residential mobility is either desired by the movers or is required to attain other desires such as marriage or a job. It is a positive experience with some unavoidable negative consequences. In this section on the reasons why people move, positive effects of moving are prominent. In the subsequent section, the negative effects of moving are prominent.

The simple explanation for voluntary moving is that people move to improve their well-being. Migration behavior studies show that a substantial portion of migrants move in order to improve their economic situation, and succeed in doing so. Most interstate and long-distance moves are motivated by employment considerations, whereas most moves within metropolitan areas are motivated by housing considerations, and few are work-related (Goodman, 1974; Zimmer, 1973). Zimmer looked at central-city and suburban residents in three sizes of metropolitan areas and found that only 3.3 to 5.6

percent gave work-related reasons for their last residential move within the metropolitan area.

## Explanation of Interstate Mobility

For an understanding of the reasons households move between states see Tables 2.10 and 2.11. Most households move for employment reasons. Family-related reasons are the next most frequent. It is interesting to note that climate is the fifth most important reason on the list for interstate migration. Among the old (age 55 and over) 22.2 percent moved to be closer to relatives, 19.8 percent moved because of retirement, and 12.1 percent moved to a better climate. In absolute numbers, however, more young adults (107,000 ages 20-34) moved to other states because of climate than did old persons (89,000 over 55).

## Explanation of Local Mobility: Goodman

A major study of local moves is reported by Goodman (1974), based on a national panel of about 5000 families. "Approximately 20% of the local moves between 1969 and 1971 were by individuals or family subgroups leaving their original household to form or join another" (Goodman, 1974: 80). These moves Goodman calls splitoffs, and he excludes them from his analysis in order to study less "automatic" moves. Splitoffs are accounted for by children leaving parents, by divorce and separation, or by remarriage.

Goodman (1974) studied local non-splitoff movers in terms of plans to move and actual moves between 1969 and 1971. The reasons given for moving by families planning to move fall into four categories, as follows:

| | |
|---|---|
| Housing consumption reasons (more or less space, less rent, better neighborhood, want to own home, better house) | 64% |
| Productive reasons (to take another job, to get nearer work) | 15% |
| Response to outside events, involuntary reasons (dwelling unit coming down, being evicted, armed services) | 10% |
| Ambiguous or mixed reasons (to save money, all my neighbors moved away) | 10% |

Most local moves, therefore, are due to housing adjustments. This finding is borne out in other studies.

TABLE 2.10  Reasons for Moving Given by Household Heads Who Moved Between States in the 12 Months Preceding the 1964, 1975, and 1976 Annual Housing Surveys, by Age and Sex

| Reasons for Moving | Both Sexes | | | Male | | | Female | | |
|---|---|---|---|---|---|---|---|---|---|
| | 20–34 years | 35–54 years | 55 and over | 20–34 years | 35–54 years | 55 and over | 20–34 years | 35–54 years | 55 and over |
| All Heads (000's) | 3371 | 1557 | 733 | 2797 | 1339 | 502 | 574 | 218 | 231 |
| Percent moving because of: | | | | | | | | | |
| Job transfer | 25.4 | 30.9 | 6.0 | 28.9 | 34.0 | 8.2 | 8.2 | 11.9 | 1.3 |
| New job or looking for work | 28.3 | 23.2 | 4.9 | 29.5 | 25.0 | 6.4 | 22.6 | 11.9 | 1.7 |
| Other employment reason | 2.0 | 3.1 | 2.6 | 2.1 | 3.4 | 3.2 | 1.4 | 1.4 | 0.9 |
| Enter or leave Armed Forces | 6.3 | 2.6 | – | 7.4 | 2.9 | – | 1.0 | 0.5 | – |
| Attend school | 7.5 | 1.2 | 0.4 | 7.1 | 1.0 | 0.6 | 9.6 | 2.3 | – |
| Wanted change of climate | 3.2 | 5.8 | 12.1 | 2.9 | 6.0 | 14.1 | 4.5 | 4.6 | 7.8 |
| Retirement | 0.0 | 3.3 | 19.8 | 0.0 | 3.2 | 25.7 | – | 3.7 | 6.9 |
| To be closer to relatives | 5.2 | 5.3 | 22.2 | 3.9 | 5.2 | 12.7 | 11.1 | 9.6 | 42.9 |
| Other family reason | 8.2 | 9.4 | 11.2 | 6.1 | 6.6 | 8.0 | 24.0 | 29.4 | 19.0 |
| All other reasons | 11.2 | 11.6 | 17.3 | 10.3 | 10.5 | 17.3 | 16.0 | 17.4 | 16.9 |
| Not reported | 1.7 | 2.6 | 3.3 | 1.8 | 2.0 | 3.6 | 1.2 | 6.0 | 2.6 |

– means no sample cases fell in the category.
0.0 means that the computed percentage was less than 0.05.
SOURCE:  Long and Hansen (1979: 9).

TABLE 2.11    Detailed Reasons for Moving Given by Household Heads
Moving Between States in the 12 Months Preceding the 1974,
1975, and 1976 Annual Housing Surveys, According to
Number of Households and Total Persons

| *Detailed Reason for Move* | *Percent Distribution* *Households* |
|---|---|
| **EMPLOYMENT** | |
| Job transfer | 23.8 |
| Entered or left U.S. Armed Forces | 4.8 |
| Retirement | 3.4 |
| New job or looking for work | 23.6 |
| Commuting reasons | 1.0 |
| To attend school | 5.4 |
| Other | 2.4 |
| **FAMILY** | |
| Needed larger house or apartment | 0.8 |
| Widowed | 0.7 |
| Separated | 1.2 |
| Divorced | 1.0 |
| Moved to be closer to relatives | 7.5 |
| Newly married | 1.6 |
| Family increased | 0.1 |
| Family decreased | 0.1 |
| Wanted to establish own household | 1.6 |
| Other | 2.7 |
| **OTHER** | |
| Neighborhood overcrowded | 0.4 |
| Change in racial or ethnic composition of neighborhood | 0.2 |
| Wanted better neighborhood | 1.1 |
| Wanted to own residence | 0.9 |
| Lower rent or less expensive house | 0.8 |
| Wanted a better house | 0.3 |
| Displaced by urban renewal, highway construction, or other public activity | 0.1 |
| Displaced by private action | 0.3 |
| Schools | 1.0 |
| Wanted to rent residence | 0.2 |
| Wanted residence with more conveniences | 0.2 |
| Natural disaster | 0.1 |
| Wanted change of climate | 5.1 |
| Other | 5.5 |
| Not reported | 2.1 |
| Interstate migrants (thousands) | 5,843 |

SOURCE:  Long and Hansen (1979: 6).

Goodman used a multiple classification analysis to study the association of ten characteristics of households with moving and obtained the following results:

| Household Characteristic | Strength of Association (ETA) with Moving |
|---|---|
| Housing tenure (own/rent) | .38 |
| Mobility history (year of most recent past move) | .34 |
| Age of head of household | .33 |
| Life cycle stage | .28 |
| Index of crowding | .24 |
| Poor family (yes/no) | .07 |
| Race | .07 |
| Commuting hours | .06 |
| Commuting cost | .06 |
| Housing expenditures (actual/expected) | .04 |

Goodman's study confirms the repeated finding that owners move less than renters. It is easier for renters to move (owners have heavy transaction costs of selling) and owners tend to develop a psychological stake in their houses and neighborhoods. Goodman's second finding is that movers move again. The more recently one has moved in the past the more likely one is to move in the present. The third finding is that mobility declines with age, as already noted in the previous section. Mobility is also related to life cycle—that is, age and whether single or married and with or without children. Children and marriage decrease mobility, except for new families with young children. The latter move to adjust to their changing needs (see also Chevan, 1971). Another finding is that crowded households tend to move. On the other hand, surplus space generally does not precipitate a move to more economical quarters. Finally, five other factors had small correlations with moving but were statistically significant with a large sample of 5000 families.

When these ten variables are combined in a multiple correlation analysis with moving, the multiple r = .47 and $r^2$ = .22. Age of household head and renting are the two most prominent factors in the multiple correlation. It is worth noting that poverty and race have no independent effects; their correlation with moving is due to the tendency of these groups to rent and be crowded.

The fact that many local moves are for the purpose of upgrading housing is reflected in the differentials in housing expenditures before and after moving. Among owners, housing expenditures of nonmovers increased 12 percent and of movers 52 percent between 1969 and 1971. Among renters, housing expenditures of nonmovers increased 12 percent and of movers 47 percent. Furthermore, the average crowding for movers was less after moving.

### Explanation of Local and Nonlocal Mobility: Roistacher

Roistacher (1974) used the same national survey as Goodman but analyzed the moving patterns of a different population. Instead of looking at local non-splitoff movers, she examined the moving behavior of households with the same head for all five years from 1968 to 1972. This group constituted 70.5 percent of the households but only 57.6 percent of the movers. The moving rate of all households was 46.0 for the five-year period and 35.1 for the families with no change of head.

An important part of her analysis is the relationship between reasons for moves and distance of moves. Using same-county moves as local moves and all other moves as long-distance moves, she found that most housing-consumption-related moves are local (82.5 percent) as expected but that over half (54.1 percent) of the job-related moves are also local. Of involuntary moves, 65.9 percent are local, and 72.7 percent of ambiguous moves are local.

Roistacher examined the household characteristics which account for moving. As in Goodman's study, age of household head and owner/renter status had the highest direct association (zero order, eta) and highest Beta weights with moving. The direct association indicates the degree of association with nothing else controlled, and the Beta gives a rough idea of the relative importance of the various independent variables in explaining the dependent variable. Other variables which contribute to explaining moving are change in income, family size, and change in family size. Each of these factors supports the idea that moving is related to housing adjustments.

Roistacher analyzed how involuntary movers differed from voluntary movers. Involuntary movers had substantially lower average incomes than other movers and concomitantly higher percentages on welfare, percentage black, and percentage female-headed households. The latter three variables, however, have no association with involuntary moving when income is controlled; they contribute almost nothing to the multivariate correlation explaining whether moving was involuntary or not. The variable which is most highly associated with involuntary moving and has the highest Beta weight is family income. Secondary factors which explain involuntary moving are owner/renter status, age of head, and change in family size. However, it should be noted that the multiple correlation explains only five percent of the variance in voluntary/involuntary moving, largely "because involuntary moving is a low probability event: only 18% of the movers move involuntarily" (Roistacher, 1974: 60).

### Explanation of Voluntary and Involuntary Mobility: Rossi

Rossi (1955) studied 924 families drawn from four census tracts in Philadelphia. The dependent variables in his analysis were moving expectation, moving desires, and actual mobility within eight months of the interview. Since 96 percent of those who planned to stay did stay, and since 80 percent of those who definitely planned to move in 10 months moved, Rossi accepts "a family's reported intentions about moving . . . as a good indicator of how that family will actually behave" (p. 107).

In reporting Rossi's findings we use his own excellent summary.

About one out of every four residential shifts must be classified as either involuntary or as the logical consequences of other decisions made by the household. Involuntary moves include evictions and destructions of dwellings. Moves which must be looked upon as forced by other decisions include moves made as a consequence of marriage, divorce, or separation, job changes involving long distance shifts, or severe losses in income.

Among voluntary moves—where the household had a clear choice between staying and moving—the most important factor impelling households to move was dissatisfaction with the amount of space in their old dwellings. Other factors, in order of their importance, were complaints about their former neighborhoods, and about the costs of rent and maintenance in their old homes. No other category of complaints received any significant amount of mention as important factors in moving decisions.

The important things the respondents had in mind in choosing their present homes from all those available them were, in rank order: space in the dwelling, particular dwelling design features, dwelling location, and, finally, cost. However, costs appeared as the major consideration in the actual choice, followed by space, location, and neighborhood in that order. Apparently, the most important attribute of a dwelling is its dimensions, but then if two or more dwellings of roughly equal size are considered, the cheaper one is finally chosen. Costs are the "clinching" factor in the choice point of housing selection [Rossi, 1955: 9].

### Explanation of Voluntary and Involuntary Mobility: Butler

The final study to be reviewed here is a national survey of residential preferences and moving behavior of 1476 metropolitan households, reported in Butler et al. (1969) and Butler and Kaiser (1971). In comparing mover and nonmover households, significant associations were found for moving with age of household head and renting as in the previously discussed studies and with large household size, full families with young children, more recent mover, nonwhite, living far from work place, living in central city, living in worse housing, and living in worse neighborhood. Many of these correlations easily translate into reasons for moving. For example, the association of moving with full families with young children suggests that such families seek larger space. These translations, however, should be tested. For example, it is not necessarily the case that the moves of those living far from the work place are for the purpose of getting closer to work. "There was no evidence that households improved their accessibility as a result of the move" (Butler and Kaiser, 1971: 485).

### Other Explanations of Mobility

There are many other studies of moving and moving decisions (Barrett, 1973; Chevan, 1971; Simmons, 1974; Speare et al., 1974; Michelson, 1977; Quigley and Weinberg, 1977; Goldstein, 1973; Abu-Lughod and Foley, 1960; Newman, 1974; Fredland, 1974); most of Butler's findings are confirmed in these studies. The main regularities in moving behavior are now well established. Moving is intimately associated with the life cycle, with single young adults and young married couples without children being the most mobile and the elderly being the most stable. Children provide both an incentive to move and an incentive to stay. They create the need for more space so that families with young children are fairly mobile. As the children grow older, however, parents are reluctant to uproot them from their friends and schools.

The major reason why moving is associated with life cycle is that certain events which generally require moving are most probable at certain ages. Young adults leave their parents, go away to college, pursue career opportunities, experiment with lifestyles, experience a jump in standard of living with their first steady jobs, get married, and start families. As a result, young adults are likely to move several times. Middle and old age are associated with fewer disruptive events; moving because of job changes, marital status changes, and housing choices occur, but less frequently than for young adults.

The characteristics of individuals which are associated with moving are renting as opposed to owning, young age, unmarried, and no children if married. The poor also are more prone to move than is the middle class, which is largely a function of the association of youth and renting with lower income. Blacks move more frequently, but not when renting and crowding is taken into account.

Morris and Winter (1978) summarize the literature on moving in Figure 2.1. The most important immediate cause is a disposition to change residence. If the household has sufficient income, it can act on this disposition and move. The other variables we have reviewed are in the model as direct causes of the disposition to move or indirect causes through neighborhood satisfaction and/or housing satisfaction.

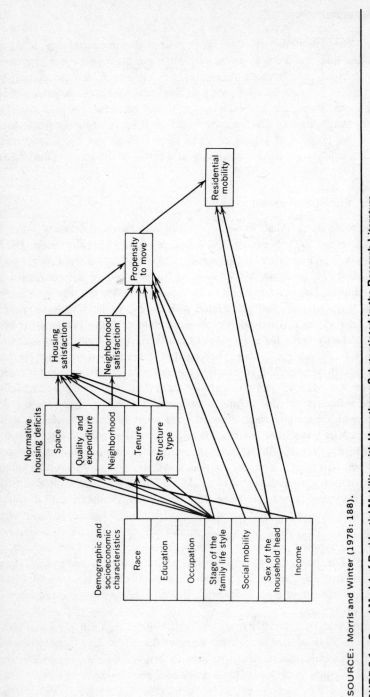

SOURCE: Morris and Winter (1978: 188).

FIGURE 2.1 Causal Model of Residential Mobility with Hypotheses Substantiated in the Research Literature

## THE EFFECTS OF MOVING

Moving is stressful, but when it is voluntary the advantages probably outweigh the disadvantages. The amount of stress of moving has been scaled relative to other stressful events by Holmes and Rahe (1967) and it receives the same score as marriage. This comparison should serve as a reminder that stressful events may be more positive than negative. In this section some of the negative effects of moving are reviewed.

### Moving and Social Ties

An obvious effect of moving is the weakening of social ties, and the extent of the effect is dependent on distance. This effect is minimal for local moves for adults, but even local moves outside the neighborhood can be disruptive for adults with neighborhood-based social networks (see Fried, 1963). One reason why adult social ties are not weakened more by moving is because people often move to areas where their close friends or relatives are living (Blumberg and Bell, 1959; Tilly and Brown, 1967). In addition, Litwak (1960) shows that distance need not weaken family ties, and Jacobson (1971) argues that the social relations of the geographically mobile are more stable than commonly reported. On the other hand, Young and Willmott (1957) found that in the London area moving from the city to a suburb had a marked negative effect on kinship interaction.

The effects of moving for children's social ties is less ambiguous than for adults. All moves outside the neighborhood sever most of the friendship ties of children. In this regard it is fortunate that mobility for children is highest in the preschool years when the child relates primarily to family members and experiences little social loss with moving. Teenagers, for whom neighborhood and school friends are very important, have about an even chance of not moving until they finish high school (see above).

Another group whose social networks can be disrupted even by short moves is the elderly, for whom travel is inconvenient. They have the further disadvantage of not making new friends easily.

The effects of moving on the amount and intensity of social ties is mixed. Moving involves the weakening of social ties, as discussed above, but it also involves the development of new friendships. McAllister et al. (1973) found in a two-wave national survey of metropolitan women that movers were like nonmovers in the percentage that increased, decreased, or retained their interaction frequency with neighbors and friends between interviews. For strictly neighborhood interaction, however, a much higher percentage of movers had increased their levels of interaction than had nonmovers. The authors conclude that in the short run, at least, residential mobility heightens local interaction. A curvilinear relationship is postulated to exist between local interaction and duration of residence such that there is a heightened search for social contacts on arrival which trails off after an introductory period only then giving way to a gradually deepened social life [McAllister et al., 1973: 203].

Most studies, however, fail to distinguish between stages of adjustment to the new environment, and, therefore, report increasing numbers and intensity of social ties with increasing length of residence (Philliber, 1976; Janowitz and Kasarda, 1974).

Another situation in which moving might increase visiting with neighbors is the move to the suburbs. Gans (1963) studied the move from city to suburbs and found that movers increased their visiting. In the suburb he studied there was considerable new housing, and interaction was required to get things going and to deal with the unusually large number of problems. He also found that 23 of the 55 moving couples moved to the suburb in order to do more visiting, and 83 percent of those succeeded. Selective migration, therefore, contributed to the positive effects of moving on the frequency of social interaction in Gans' study.

In another report on the McAllister survey, Butler et al. (1973) found that movers decreased their formal organizational participation. Zimmer (1955) reports similar findings from a single-wave survey; he found that both membership and leadership in formal organizations are correlated with length of time in the community.

### Adjusting to the Move

Another impact of moving is unhappiness or depression. Satisfaction with the move is dependent upon the degree of desire for the move in the first place and the degree of adjustment after the move. Forced relocation is particularly upsetting. Most people do not want to move and object strenuously if there is a chance that their objections may prevent their moving. Fortunately, most people do adjust even to forced relocation. The adjustment period varies. Fried (1963) describes the forced relocation of people who were heavily dependent on intense neighborhood social networks. Six months to two years after moving at least 46 percent of the women and 38 percent of the men "give evidence of a fairly severe grief reaction or worse" (p. 152). Studies of moving in more normal samples find that most movers adjust quickly (Butler et al., 1973; Landis and Stoetzer, 1966; Jones, 1973). For example, Butler et al. (1973) found that moving has little effect upon the extent of unhappiness and alienation of both the men and women in their sample.

Moving requires different types of adjustments and places different types of demands on all members of the family. In long-distance moves, most men are quickly integrated into a social network at their new work place, but nonworking wives may or may not be invited into the social networks of their new neighborhood. Furthermore, in local moves, women's networks are more likely to be disturbed than are men's networks because they are more likely to be neighborhood-based. Perhaps the differentials in the disruption of social ties of men and women account for the differences in happiness and satisfaction with the move expressed by men and women (Butler et al., 1973). Not only is adjustment more difficult for wives, but the demands on women are generally greater than the demands on husbands. Jones (1973) reports that 78 percent of women in her sample agreed that "the wife is the key person in establishing the home and making the move successful" (p. 212). This greater responsibility of women for the moving process may explain the greater incidence of symptoms of mental disorder for women as reported by Butler et al. (1973).

Smith and Christopherson (1966) studied family adjustment to nonlocal moving and noted that adjustment difficulty increases with age. This means that parents have more difficulty adjusting than children and that the elderly generally have considerable difficulty. They also observed that adjustment becomes easier with each move, and the improvement in adjustment tends to be the greatest with the third move. Finally, they found that people moving from a smaller to a larger community adjusted better than did people moving from a larger to a smaller community.

### Moving and Mental Illness

Moving probably contributes to mental illness, although the effects are small in most cases. There is a fair amount of research which finds migration to be related to mental illness (see especially Malzberg and Lee, 1956; Malzberg, 1967), but some studies find no relationship (see Lazarus et al., 1963, and Sanua, 1969, for reviews of this literature). Sanua (1969: 336-7) concludes his review with this comment on the ambiguous nature of the findings: "A general conclusion which we can draw from this review is that some migrations are related to greater risks in mental health and some migrations are related to favorable mental health." Positive effects are more likely when the move is voluntary (Leighton et al., 1963) and when migration is between similar types of communities (Srole et al., 1962). Gans (1963) finds that the moves to the suburbs which he studied had more positive than negative effects on mental health. "Most interview respondents report improvements in health and disposition" (p. 191). Also in the study by Butler et al. (1973) described above, women movers evidenced more symptoms of mental disorders than did women nonmovers, but the opposite was true for men. Since long-distance moves are primarily job-related, they are more likely to be voluntary for men than for women.

### Effects of Moving On Children

We conclude our review of the effects of moving with a discussion of its effects on children. The evidence is mixed: Many students of childhood development hold that stability is important to the development of an emotionally stable and well-adjusted child (for example, Bettelheim, 1971; Mead, 1966). A number of studies seem to support this theory by finding that moving is related to mental disturbance and behavior problems in children (Tietze et al., 1942; Stubblefield, 1955; Gordon and Gordon, 1958; Kantor, 1965). However, moving families may be less well adjusted on the average before moving than nonmoving families. The effects of moving, therefore, are not easy to discern.

Tietze et al. (1942) found length of residence in the same house to be negatively related to each type of mental disturbance they studied in children in Baltimore. Gordon and Gordon (1958) used the files of psychiatric clinics in four counties and found emotional disturbances greater where mobility rates were greater. Using case studies, Stubblefield (1955) traced emotional disturbances in a number of children to moving. He suggested the following situations as contributing to the disturbances: (1) children receive less attention during the moving and settling-in process; (2) children may be rejected or ignored by their new peers; (3) children experience separation grief from old friends; and (4) children may not be adequately prepared for the move because they are told at the last minute.

Kantor's before-and-after study (1965) of over 400 families moving a short distance complicates the interpretation of the above findings. She found moving children to have more behavior problems both before and after moving than did nonmoving children, and the moving children did not significantly change their rates of problem behavior. In other words, the problems are there before the move, so the extent to which moving caused disturbances is unclear.

The association of problems with moving for children is further complicated by a study by Barrett and Noble (1973), who found that a population of 318 long-distance moving children showed less aggression, inhibition, and learning disabilities (as reported by parents) than did children in a nationwide test and the same levels as tested middle- and upper-class children. These findings suggest that moving has no negative effects. However, children who had moved in the previous six months were reported as more aggressive, more inhibited, and as having more learning disabilities than children who had moved more than six months previously. Only the learning disabilities differences, however, were highly significant.

Barrett and Noble also asked parents to judge whether the move had a good or bad effect on their children. For 81 percent of the children, the effect was judged to be "good" or "none," for 6 percent "mixed," and for only 13 percent "bad." The authors conclude that, "within the limits of this study, it is our view that the long distance move should be laid to rest as a special variable in children's disorders" (1973: 188).

The effects of moving on the academic performance of children are also unclear. Several studies find no relationship (Evans, 1966; Bollenbacher, 1962; Northwood, 1967; Fitch and Hoffer, 1964; Greene and Doughtry, 1961). For example, Greene and Doughtry (1961) found little relationship between their index of mobility and many measures of children's academic performance. The few significant correlations that emerged showed that more mobile students tended to have better grades than the less mobile. Since it is not known whether they were more capable students prior to the move, firm conclusions cannot be drawn from this study.

Northwood (1967) studied changes in school performance for both moving and nonmoving children. He examined school records for several years before and after relocation for urban renewal or highway projects, and concluded:

> The forced relocation of school and home of children in the Topeka Urban Renewal and Highway Projects did not result in significant damages to them in school progress and behavior as measured by such indicators as grade-point average, absence rates, grade failures, withdrawals, dropouts, and other test scores [1967: 266].

However, it should be noted that Northwood's findings were based on a sample of 83 selected children, and school records were available for only 50 of these children.

Levine et al. (1966) found that the number of previous schools attended was negatively related to grades for elementary students in an inner-city school. Kantor (1965) cited evidence that moving is associated with poorer school performance among lower-class children but not for upper-class children, who often do better after moving. Finally, Long (1975) found that frequent interstate migration is associated with an increased likelihood of being enrolled below the modal grade for age among children whose parents are not college graduates. For children of college graduates frequent interstate migration is associated with a reduction of grade skipping. Interstate migration is most likely to be undertaken by well-educated persons whose children tend to do well in school, and for this reason children who have made frequent interstate moves are less likely to be behind in school than less mobile children [1975: 369].

Adverse effects of moving on children would occur mainly in four areas: (1) loss of friends and difficulties in making new friends, (2) worsened family relations, (3) school performance and adjustment to school, and (4) mental disorders or behavioral problems. The previous discussion pointed to two effects of mobility: First, school performance is not adversely affected as a general rule, but seems to be adversely affected for lower-class children. Second, moving may have some effect on mental disorders in the first few months, but its effects dissipate fairly quickly. In the area of family relations, the effect of moving is seldom studied except in clinical case studies, which discover some serious problems, but these problems might be rare in the population of moving children. In the friendship area the effect of moving on children's friends was studied by Barrett and Noble (1973). When asked "Did your child find it easy to make friends?" mothers of moving children reported that 80 percent of the children found it easy to make friends. Barrett and Noble also studied the effect of moving on adjustment in school. When asked "Did your child find it difficult to change schools," parents of 74 percent of the children said "no." The general finding, therefore, seems to be that most children adjust well to moving, but some experience negative consequences.

## INVOLUNTARY MOVING

Involuntary moving occurs when households desire to stay but must move because of circumstances beyond the family's control. There is no sharp line, however, between voluntary and involuntary moving. Eviction by landlords and displacement by urban renewal, highways, or dams are classified as involuntary moves, but some of the households would have moved voluntarily. About one out of every five people in the United States moves every year—most of them voluntarily. On the other hand, moves which are classified as voluntary are not voluntary for all members of the household. Children often do not want to move, but their wishes do not prevent the move. Wives might prefer that the family stay and may reluctantly consent to the moves which are required when their husbands change jobs. Even when a company moves to another area and the employees must move or quit, they are not forced to move; they are free to stay and find other jobs. Nevertheless, such moves are classified as involuntary.

### (1) Frequency of Involuntary Moves

It is difficult to estimate the amount of involuntary moving. In 1972 the federal government compensated over 50,000 claimants with relocation payments. Federally sponsored projects, therefore, relocated from 100,000 to 200,000 people (depending on the average size of the household). March (1970: 3) estimated that in the 1960s "approximately 100,000 families [were] forced to move each year because of urban renewal and highway construction." The highway and urban renewal booms are past, and a new philosophy and/or new politics against rampant displacement is taking hold in federal and local governments; thus, displacement by federally sponsored programs has declined. At certain times and places, however, displacement has been great. Stone (1976: 3) reported that in Atlanta "[d]uring the time that redevelopment activity was at its height, the city pursued a policy under which one-seventh of its population was displaced by government action." When one adds to the above sketchy estimates the innumerable evictions, housing destroyed by fires and floods, and health- or employment-related involuntary moves, the number is substantial. Based on a national sample of 5060 families, Roistacher (1974) observed: "Each year one in seven families who move does so involuntarily" (p. 41).

### (2) Voluntary and Involuntary Moving Compared

The hardship of involuntary moving is normally greater than the hardship of voluntary moving, but little research has measured the differences. The major relevant study is by Butler et al. (1973), who studied a national sample of 1561 households which were interviewed in both 1966 and 1969. The authors compared four sets of people by cross-cutting desire to stay or move with moving or staying: voluntary stayers, involuntary stayers, involuntary movers, and voluntary movers. These four groups were compared on their organizational activity, visiting patterns, and physical and psychological problems.

The voluntary stayers were the most likely to belong to and participate in organizations and to visit families in the neighborhood. Surprisingly, they were similar to the other groups in their levels of alienation, unhappiness, and mental disorders. In comparison to voluntary stayers, therefore, the movers are slightly less active socially, but do not seem to suffer much from moving. Likewise, the differences between voluntary and involuntary moving are quite small.

No differences were found between voluntary and involuntary moving heads of households in belonging to or participating in organizations. For wives and single males, however, the involuntary movers belong to and participated in organizations less than the voluntary movers. Voluntary and involuntary movers had similar patterns of visiting families *in* the neighborhood. Among males, the voluntary movers more frequently visited families *out* of the neighborhood than did involuntary movers, and voluntary movers are slightly less likely to feel closer to in-neighborhood people than out-of-neighborhood people. These findings are unexpected, since involuntary movers were assumed to have stronger social ties to their old neighborhood and could be expected to visit friends in their old neighborhood more than could voluntary movers. The meaning of these findings must remain in doubt, however, since Butler et al. did not report whether involuntary and voluntary movers differed with respect to length of stay, distance of move, and other factors. In summary, both voluntary and involuntary movers have fairly similar informal and formal social ties.

The two groups differ, however, in terms of physical and psychological problems. Among males, involuntary movers are much more alienated, in much poorer health, and have slightly more mental disorders than voluntary movers. Oddly enough, however, fewer of them are unhappy. Again, the lack of reported information on the characteristics of these two groups before moving prevents an accurate interpretation of these findings.

Among females, involuntary movers were similar to voluntary movers in terms of happiness and physical health. They had slightly more mental disorders and less alienation. The consequences of involuntary moving for women, therefore, are not significantly different than the consequences of voluntary moving.

Another important study which compared voluntary and involuntary movers is that of Key (1967). He compared voluntary movers and nonmovers to respondents displaced by highways and urban renewal. The differences between voluntary and involuntary movers are minimal and easily might be due to the different composition of the two groups. Key first considered the effects of moving on housing and then on family life. His major finding on the effects of moving on housing is that both voluntary and involuntary movers tend to upgrade their housing and to like their new housing.

Key's major finding on the effects of moving on family life is that it is generally negligible and occasionally positive. Moving and type of move had negligible effects on the relationship of the respondent to the extended family and on actual marital status. On an index of interaction with the immediate family, the involuntary movers increased their intrafamily interaction but voluntary movers and nonmovers decreased it. Key cannot explain this finding. For those who experienced changes in their married life, the movers were more likely to increase their satisfaction and cohesiveness than were the nonmovers. From this Key concludes that "at the level of the family, mobility apparently has some positive consequences" (1967: 122).

Key also studied the effects of moving on the relationship of residents to their neighborhoods. Moving and type of moving had both positive and negative impacts on this relationship. Moving significantly reduced neighboring and use of neighborhood facilities but also resulted in increased liking for the neighborhood and the feeling that movers were a part of the neighborhood. Among movers, involuntary movers improved their neighborhood situation more often than did voluntary movers. Involuntary movers were more likely to feel a part of the neighborhood and to move to where they had relatives in the area. However, only those displaced by urban renewal were less pleased with their new neighbors than with their old neighbors.

The studies by Key and Butler et al. challenge common assumptions about the negative effects of moving and especially of involuntary moving. Their analyses were not extensive enough, however, to explain many of their findings or to demonstrate that their findings would stand if the groups were truly comparable—that is, made equal on relevant dimensions such as income, life cycle, owner/renter, and length of residency at time of first interview. Therefore, these studies indicate the need for further research.

## Summary and Conclusion

At the macro level of population dynamics much is known about current trends. Population growth is slowing down because of very low fertility rates. The 1980s will see a giant generation in the 35 to 45 age category and a midget generation aged 15 to 25. These exceptional generations create many problems for most of the institutions in America. Other population movements include residential migration which tends to be westward and southward. Most of the metropolitan centers are experiencing a slowing down or halting of growth, while nonmetropolitan communities are growing. Finally, in the metropolitan areas of the largest cities the population is spreading out. These are a few of the basic demographic facts about the United States of which assessors and policy planners should be aware.

Assessors often are required to estimate population movements associated with specific projects or policies. The intensity of many other social impacts are contingent upon these population changes, requiring fairly accurate estimates. In this chapter a methodology for making these estimates is presented which describes how to estimate the percentage of workers who will migrate to the area of the project, the number of dependents they will bring with them, and the additional employment in the local economy which local expenditures of the new industry and its labor force will induce.

This chapter also briefly reviewed the literature on residential mobility covering the frequency of residential mobility, why people move, the effects of moving, and the unique aspects of involuntary moving. This literature provides insight into the positive and negative consequences of moving on individuals and families which is so important for assessors. It can guide assessors in estimating the adverse consequence of induced residential mobility and in designing measures for investigating these consequences.

The United States has one of the highest residential mobility rates in the world, though not the highest. The rate differs greatly for various age groups and is highest for people in their twenties and lowest for people over 50. In fact, the annual residential mobility rate for the former is four times that of the latter. Higher-than-average rates also are obtained for the better educated and richer, but when age is controlled the very poor tend to be more mobile than the rich, and both more mobile than middle-income groups. In addition, single people and males move more than married persons and females.

In general, the highest mobility rates apply to the groups which have the most to gain and the least to lose from moving. Most moves are voluntary and are made to improve the movers' opportunities or housing. Most interstate moves are employment-related; most local moves are housing-related. Less than 10 percent of all moves are involuntary moves due to evictions, displacement, armed services, and other factors. The major difference between the voluntary and involuntary movers is that the latter had substantially lower average incomes.

The effects of moving vary considerably in their intensity for various groups. Moving is stressful for everyone; adjustment is easy and rapid for some, while a few never adjust. In general, the elderly are the most adversely affected, and men seem to adjust more quickly than women. It should be noted that not all of the commonly expected negative impacts of moving in fact occur. For example, movers interact as frequently with neighbors or friends as do nonmovers. Also, moving is not clearly related to mental illness. Some migrations are related to favorable mental health and others are related to mental illness. Nor does moving clearly cause behavioral and emotional problems in children or lower school performance. The emotional problems of children which are detected in some studies seem to dissipate quickly. Most children seem to adjust well to moving; a minority evidences serious problems.

One other set of comparisons which failed to produce expected findings is between voluntary and involuntary movers. The differences between the two groups are small and more or less balance out. For example, among males, involuntary movers were more alienated and in poorer health, but fewer of them were unhappy. Other studies look at additional dimensions, but, in sum, the involuntary movers are not noticeably more adversely affected by moving than are voluntary movers.

*Chapter 3*

# RESIDENTIAL HABITAT:
# HOME AND NEIGHBORHOOD

"For a man's house is his castle."

This well-known quote by Sir Edward Coke implies that a house not only provides space for living but also protects against the outside world. In the three and a half centuries since that statement, changes in the outside world have made castles and fortresses obsolete and man more vulnerable to changes in his environment. Many government projects and policies affect people's residential habitat in a variety of ways. Under the law of eminent domain, a person's property can be taken from him for public purposes, and the household is paid off and sent packing. Highways and airports can increase background noise to levels that interfere with conversations and sleep. Other physical impacts include air pollution, barriers across paths of travel, altered views, changes in pedestrian safety, and the removal of neighbors and services.

It is important to remember that homes and neighborhoods provide not only shelter and services but also social and psychological functions for their residents. The latter are more difficult to understand, to assess, and to compensate. The government can compensate an owner for the physical and economic features of home and neighborhood, but not the social and psychological features. For the latter personal adjustments are necessary. However, if impact assessors understand the social and psychological functions of neighborhoods, then projects might be planned so as to minimize their negative impacts. Both home and neighborhood are the settings for many memories and the objects for emotional attachments. With time they give a sense of rootedness, belonging, and security. Residential displacement or neighborhood disturbance by government actions cause severe psychological loss for some (long-term residents and the elderly) and slight inconveniences for others. The following discussion should help impact assessors to anticipate and understand the differential effects and to plan projects so as to minimize psychological losses.

We begin this chapter with a sketch of the changes which a large-scale construction project (exemplified by a highway) might cause in a neighborhood. Because of the history of the regulations governing environmental impact statements, these impacts tend to be catalogued under the concept of community cohesion. We have observed much confusion in the SIA literature over the meaning of community cohesion and how it should be studied. The second section of this chapter, therefore, defines this concept and provides a methodology for its investigation.

It will be argued that community cohesion should be analyzed at the neighborhood level in urban/suburban areas and at the level of village, town, or small city in rural areas. It follows that social impact assessors need to understand how residents relate to their neighborhoods or rural communities in order to anticipate and interpret how projects impact on the social environments of residents. The bulk of this chapter focuses on the resident-neighborhood relationship in urban/suburban areas (rural communities are discussed in Chapters 5 through 7). The weakening of neighborhood solidarity and the psychological importance of neighborhoods for residents in the past century is reviewed. The concept of "neighborhood" is defined and compared with the public's notions of their neighborhood. The functions of neighborhoods are discussed, and the degree to which various groups are attached to their neighborhoods are analyzed. Attachment is traced in terms of measures of satisfaction, social ties, and desire to stay or move.

This chapter explains not only how residents relate to their neighborhoods but also to their homes. The functions and meanings of homes for their occupants are identified, and the bases for attachment to homes are reviewed. Finally, we compare the relative importance of characteristics of neighborhoods and houses in the choice of housing and in the motivation to move.

Three chapters discuss how residents relate to their environment and how public actions affect them through their residential habitat. In this chapter we describe how residents relate to home and neighborhood and how neighborhoods function in order to understand how neighborhood changes resulting from public actions affect individuals. Chapter 4 examines the problems of displacement and relocation, and Chapter 8 analyzes how noise affects people.

### Social Impacts of Public Projects
### on Neighborhoods and Residents:
### The Case of Highways

How do construction projects impact on neighborhoods and their residents? A brief description of the various social impacts by project stages is presented below. It represents a summary of the literature and the author's research (Finsterbusch, 1976a; Federal Highway Administration, 1974, 1976; Llewellyn et al., 1975; Hamilton et al., 1980; Burkhardt and Shaffer, 1972; Vlachos, 1976; Lane et al., 1975).

#### PLANNING STAGE

Once neighborhood residents, neighborhood leaders, developers, or businesses learn that a highway is being considered, social and economic impacts on the neighborhood begin. Since development is closely associated with highways, land speculation is likely to begin immediately. Some homeowners, on the other hand, who have reasons to believe that the highway will remove or worsen the attractiveness of their homes will try to sell and relocate. When knowledge of the possibility of the highway spreads, people may hesitate to buy houses in the likely highway corridors. Residents and landlords will not be willing to put in improvements; nor will banks finance them (see Miller, 1971).

This stage is the time for residents to react to the planned highway. Citizen groups may be formed and civic associations may become active. After all, a highway project creates costs for some and benefits for others, so it is appropriate for residents, businesses, and other interested parties to try to influence the decision in their best interests. This activism brings people into close contact with their neighbors in a common purpose which can be gratifying to them, but it also takes time away from their other leisure activities and relationships. Sometimes these groups are even willing to sustain legal fees and to challenge highway decisions in the courts. In sum, the interests at stake are so important to the affected parties that some organizations will use resources and some individuals will devote considerable time to protect or advance them. These reactions should decrease considerably when highway departments develop equitable solutions to the difficult problems of the unequal distribution of costs and benefits of projects. Compensation, for example, is one method commonly used for increasing the equity of projects.

Highways affect people's tangible self-interests and their deep feelings as well. Impacted parties experience a range of strong feelings—usually negative—including despair, frustration, and grief. The changes associated with highway locations in one's neighborhood generally are anticipated negatively (Burkhardt and Chinlund, 1971; Buffington et al., 1974; Colony, 1971). Residents fear displacement, resent the unattractiveness of the highway, regret the stimulation to development which highways bring, and disapprove of the general disruption of things. Displacement may ultimately improve the overall situation of the relocatees because of relatively generous additive payments, but most people are concerned about the inconveniences of moving, the disruption of social relationships, and the time required to learn how to best exploit a new area's resources. It takes time to establish good relations with persons providing services, such as doctors, dentists, and mechanics. For some people, especially long-term elderly residents, relocation is very painful. Most people impacted by highways, however, are not displaced. The negative impacts on the nonmovers are less serious than the impact of displacement, but only displacement is compensated. In sum, until corridor residents are somehow compensated they have reasons to dislike the prospect of a highway being located in their neighborhood, and some people may be anxious during the waiting period. The sooner the highway location is decided, therefore, the better off will be the corridor residents psychologically.

Another impact of the planning stage is the change in people's expectations of the future. The despair, frustration, and grief mentioned earlier is only a small part of this impact. In addition, government planners, businesses, developers, realtors, banks, real estate sellers and buyers, and others factor into their plans the probable existence of the highway and act accordingly. Because of people's anticipatory actions and investments, the longer the highway location decision takes, the greater the social and economic costs of not building the highway (unless the no-build option was a strong possibility from the beginning). It should be pointed out, however, that most of the parties involved have sought speculative gains against the risk that the highway would not be built, and highway departments have no obligations to speculators.

Another impact of the planning stage that warrants consideration is the impact of the highway location decision process on the rapport the government has with the citizens. The attitudes and beliefs of citizens toward government and of government personnel toward citizens are likely to undergo change as interested parties interact with the government and with each other over the location issue. Trust either will be built up or torn down with consequences for future citizen-government interactions.

## LAND ACQUISITION STAGE

Once the route is chosen and receives the necessary levels of approval, land is acquired and structures and residents are displaced from the highway corridor. The principal social impact of this stage is the experience of displacement which is traumatic for some, especially the elderly and long-term residents. Displacement involves the investment of time in the search for and move to the replacement housing. The general rule is for households to upgrade their housing and for a fair number of renters to buy homes. With the present level of additive payments, and some additional personal funds, relocatees are usually better off in terms of their housing and their economic worth. The main economic disadvantage of relocation seems to be the difficulty of finding mortgage money and the higher mortgage interest rates. However, relocatees generally suffer psychologically and socially due to the disruption of close and meaningful social ties and the severance from familiar surroundings and services. Of course, these consequences are minimized if they relocate in the same neighborhood.

Highways also relocate businesses and services including shops, service stations, laundries, banks, restaurants, bars, barber and beauty shops, repairmen, schools, churches, doctors, dentists, hospitals, and more. Some of these may be marginal organizations and/or depend for survival on their long-term established customers and members from the area. They will not survive relocation, so many of them liquidate (at a loss) rather than relocate. Others will relocate but generally suffer short-term economic or membership losses. They probably will receive adequate compensation for their property and moving costs, but not for the many subtle costs of relocation such as those required to develop new customers, ease cash flow problems, adjust to the new layouts, smooth disrupted schedules, and counteract high turnover because some workers will not commute the extra distance.

Displacement of residents, businesses, and services affects the residents, businesses, and services which remain in the neighborhood; however, usually these impacts are not large. The remaining residents will suffer some disrupted friendships and may lose nearby businesses and services they used. Businesses and services lose some customers or constituents, but most of these social, business, and service relationships can be continued after relocation, although generally at greater inconvenience and travel costs. The same discussion applies if people's places of employment are relocated.

If the highway causes substantial displacement, the housing market tightens in the area and prices increase. In exceptional cases overcrowding and its attendant psychological problems may result. If the acquired structures are not demolished quickly, they are likely to be vandalized. Meanwhile, the property is likely to become overgrown and unkempt. Thus, the highway corridor becomes unsightly to the neighborhood and depresses real estate values. In the long run, highways increase real estate values because of the increased accessibility which they provide. It should not be assumed, however, that long-run gains are adequate compensation for short-run losses. In fact, some of the residents who are negatively impacted will have moved before the positive impacts are experienced.

Other impacts of the acquisition stage include possible pressures for rezoning; more rapid development of the area; possible loss of park lands, woods, countryside, and historical sites; and possible changes in the character of the neighborhood and community. Many of these impacts continue into the construction and postconstruction stages. The neighborhood is also affected by the displacement of places of employment, shops, schools, churches, hospitals, and so on. Finally, the community loses the taxes from the acquired properties, although the positive effects of highways on land values are likely to increase net taxes in the long run.

## CONSTRUCTION STAGE

The construction stage impacts neighborhoods and individuals negatively. Exceptions are the construction jobs and business created, most of which go to people outside the corridor disrupted by the highway. The corridor neighborhoods are inconvenienced by detours, disrupted traffic, congestion, lost business, dust, noise, truck traffic, safety hazards, and hindered emergency services. The highway begins to interfere with neighborhood travel patterns. Sometimes vibrations damage nearby structures (the damage may be compensated). Certainly the entertainment value of work-watching is not adequate compensation for these inconveniences.

## POSTCONSTRUCTION STAGE

The positive impacts occur when the highway is opened to traffic. The highway decreases the travel time, gas consumption, accidents (probably), and inconvenience of users. It increases accessibility for residents, businesses, emergency services, and facilities in the area. For residents it increases access to jobs, schools, stores, recreation, hospitals, churches, and nonneighborhood friends and relatives. These effects are substantial and are reflected in generally increased land values (Gamble et al., 1973; Adkins, 1957; Buffington, 1964) and therefore higher taxes.

However, many negative effects often derive from the highway traffic. Nearby residents may be subjected to increased noise, air pollution, and a less desirable view. To counter these effects they may install insulation and soundproofing, air conditioning, fencing, shrubs, and landscaping. They will also have to expend more time and money on house-cleaning, painting, and maintenance.

The neighborhood is affected in many ways, many of which are negative from the point of view of the long-time residents but positive from the point of view of the agencies, businesses, and services in the area. The highway encourages zoning changes which tend to increase population density and reduce the rustic or suburban character of the neighborhood. Outsiders travel into the area and crowd roads, shops, parks, services, and parking, and compete for local jobs and facilities. Over time, further commercial development will adjust supply/demand ratios for services, but the increased density of activity changes the character of the area. The highway may even make the neighborhood more accessible to crime and vandalism. The integration and cohesion of the community is likely to decline as different classes of people move into the new multidwelling housing in rezoned areas. Neighborhoods divided by elevated or at-grade highways generally develop new functional boundaries. Pedestrians and bikers have reduced accessibility unless facilities are built to help them cross the highway.

The general reorganization of traffic patterns helps some businesses, schools, churches, and services and adversely affects others. The highway gives some businesses and services greater visibility and accessibility, but businesses and services on the previously traveled routes decline. Mass transport may be assisted by the new highway, but it is more likely that the highway encourages private rather than public transportation. On the whole, however, the net benefits of highways are positive, and that is why states build them and citizens pay for them. The majority of citizens want highways as long as they go through somebody else's back yard.

## Definitions of Community Cohesion

### DEFINITION OF COMMUNITY

Assessors are required to report on project impacts on community cohesion according to EIS regulations. This task is made more difficult by the failure of this directive to define community cohesion. Both "community" and "cohesion" are terms with a variety of meanings and applications. For the term community Hillery (1955) found 94 definitions in the literature up to 1953, and Sutton and Munson (1976) found 125 from 1954 to 1973. In analyzing the 125 definitions, the latter study "discovered that community is said to be one or sometimes several of eighteen different predicate nominative ideas" (1976: 20), which range from territory and social system to sense of belonging and having things in common.

Both studies attempt to derive a modal definition of community from the works that they review. The resulting two modal definitions can be used for SIAs. Hillery states: "Most students, however, are in basic agreement that community consists of persons in social interaction within a geographic area and having one or more additional common ties" (1955: 111). We recommend this as a minimal definition of community. Sutton and Munson propose a more elaborate modal definition of community which we recommend as the standard definition.

Community is a social, demographic and territorial entity which has
characteristic patterns of multiple services/facilities, solidarity, collective action, and modes of social interrelationship [1976: 12].

The major difference between the two definitions is that Sutton and Munson
include the provision of multiple services/facilities in their definition. Therefore, they would not define a strictly residential area as a community, but
Hillery would. The convergence in these definitions far outweighs the diver-
gence. Both definitions consider a territorial unit a community only if it
involves some undefined amount of social interaction among its members,
some undefined degree of solidarity, and some undefined amount of member
identification.

Our own review of the literature on community suggests that Hillery and
Sutton and Munson have systematically and adroitly extracted modal definitions. It also suggests that territorial units above the size of the town or small
city in rural areas (larger cities are urban places) and the macro neighborhood
in urban areas have the characteristics of community in so slight a degree as
to make them inappropriate units for measuring project impacts on community cohesion. We recommend, therefore, that community cohesion be examined at the level of neighborhood or town in rural areas and at the level of
micro or macro neighborhood in urban/suburban areas.

We have provided a working definition of community, but impact assessors
also need an intuitive grasp of the social phenomena to which the term
points. They can gain this type of insight from Erikson's *Everything in Its
Path: Destruction of Community in the Buffalo Creek Flood* (1976). Erikson
came to a new understanding of the meaning of community when he
interviewed the survivors of this disastrous flood in West Virginia which killed
over 125 people and destroyed the homes of over 4000 others. His artful
report on this tragedy is one of the most enlightening descriptions of
community in print. The following excerpts provide some indication of the
meaning of community for the people of Buffalo Creek.

The people of Buffalo Creek . . . were wrenched out of their communities [and] torn away from the very human surround in which they
had been so deeply enmeshed [p. 186].

Communality on Buffalo Creek can best be described as a state of mind
shared among a particular gathering of people. . . . It is a quiet set of
understandings that become absorbed into the atmosphere and are thus
a part of the natural order. . . . And the key to that network of
understanding is a constant readiness to look after one's neighbors—or,
rather, to know without being asked what needs to be done [pp. 189,
190].

The difficulty is that people invest so much of themselves in that kind of social arrangement that they become absorbed by it, almost captive to it, and the larger collectivity around you becomes an extension of your own personality, an extension of your own flesh. This pattern not only means that you are diminished as a person when that surrounding tissue is stripped away, but that you are no longer able to reclaim as your own the emotional resources invested in it. To "be neighborly" is not a quality you can carry with you into a new situation like negotiable emotional currency; the old community was your niche in the classical ecological sense, and your ability to relate to that niche meaningfully is not a skill easily transferred to another setting. This situation is true whether you move into another community, . . . or whether a new set of neighbors moves in around your old home [p. 191].

## DEFINITION OF COHESION

The concept of cohesion has not been subjected to as rigorous an analysis as the concept of community, and there is less variation in its usage. Nevertheless, it is an awkward concept when applied to communities. It evolved as a characteristic of fairly small groups, and refers to the binding of the group together. It does not translate readily to large social units in which most people have little or no interaction with each other.

The Theodorsons (1969: 57) provide a useful definition of social cohesion:

Cohesion, social. The integration of group behavior as a result of social bonds, attractions, or "forces" that hold members of a group in interaction over a period of time. When there is a high level of social cohesion the group is attractive to its members. Members have strong positive feelings toward the group, want to remain in the group, and like each other.

Schachter (1968), in the *International Encyclopedia of the Social Sciences* states; "The social forces that draw and keep men together may be called cohesion, or cohesiveness" (p. 542). What are these forces? Schachter mentions "the prestige of the group; the attractiveness of group activities; the attractiveness of the members of the group" (p. 543). The group is attractive to the extent that it satisfies needs—needs for prestige, fellowship, security, material benefits, and so on. The manner of group interaction is also a factor: The more cooperative, consensual, and free the interactions are, the greater the group attractiveness.

Many of the factors causing group cohesion also cause community cohesion. Community cohesion is advanced by high prestige, attractive activities, attractive members, cooperative and voluntary relationships, and abundant provisions for individuals' needs. Community cohesion is decreased by worsening conditions, declining activities or declining participation in activities, and less interaction or less friendly relationships. The latter condition is likely when heterogeneity and turnover increase.

In summary, community cohesion refers to the amount and quality of social relations and interactions in rural communities or urban/suburban neighborhoods and to the attraction to or identification with these units. Projects can negatively affect community cohesion by reducing the attractiveness of the environment and interfering with the provision for the material, social, and psychological needs of individuals. Interference with social relationships, interactions, and activities are especially injurious to community cohesion.

## Measurement of Community Cohesion

### LOCATING COMMUNITY BOUNDARIES

Community cohesion is as difficult to measure as it is to define. The first problem is to establish the borders for the communities being studied. In rural areas concentrated population settlements are isolated from each other so that the community center is generally readily identified. The borders are more difficult to determine. The traditional method for determining rural community boundaries was to determine the trading area for the businesses in the town or the catchment areas for noncommercial services such as schools and churches (see Galpin, 1915; Kolb and Day, 1950). The border of the community was then the composite of these borders, and early empirical investigations indicated that general trade areas provided the best boundaries "for describing the idea of a community" (Kolb and Day, 1950: 52). Later research, however, suggests that retail trade areas in rural regions are much larger than residents' community of identification.

Since the reliability of using trade areas for defining community boundaries is in doubt, some would prefer to be expedient and to use political boundaries. These do not always coincide with people's loyalties and interaction patterns, but they are definite, well established, and the units for much published or available data. Seiler and Summers (1974) recommend using township boundaries on the basis of a survey of 1171 residents of 10 townships in four counties in rural Illinois. They conclude: "Township boundaries regularly coincide with community boundaries" (1974: 259). They acknowledge, however, that community boundaries might be smaller than township boundaries, but their methodology could only demonstrate that community of identity seldom crossed township boundaries.

We recommend yet another method. Open-country residents should be asked to identify their community of identity. According to Haga and Folse (1971), modern transportation has substantially lengthened the distances that people travel for retail goods in rural areas, but their "affectual relations" (represented by church membership in the study) and "community of identity" remain fairly close at hand (see Table 3.1). Their study is based on a sample of 252 heads of households who were open-country residents surrounding 36 rural villages in four counties in central Illinois. The authors point out:

> Only the affectual relations involved in church membership approached the close clustering of perceived identity. We found that the mean distance between an open country respondent and his community of identity was 3.785 miles. The mean distances for church membership, grocery shopping, and furniture purchases, respectively, however were 4.175 miles, 5.725 miles, and 8.750 miles [Haga and Folse, 1971: 45].

On the basis of this study we judge retail trade areas in rural regions to be too large for significant cohesion in terms of social interactions and relationships (affectional ties). The best way to establish community boundaries is to question residents about the community of which they feel a part. A less costly procedure is simply to use distance. According to Haga and Folse, "rural residents tend to identify with the physically closest perceivable community. Only 2.6 percent of the open-country respondents deviated from this pattern" (1971: 49). This method, however, needs further testing in other rural areas.

TABLE 3.1  Percentage Distribution of Respondents in Each Zone of Distance Between Place of Residence and Community of Identity, Church, and Trade in Groceries and Furniture

| | Percentage of Respondents Who Lived: | | |
|---|---|---|---|
| Relationship to Community | Less than 5 Miles from Indicated Place | 5 to 10 Miles from Indicated Place | More than 10 Miles from Indicated Place |
| Community of identity | 85 | 8 | 7 |
| Church membership | 72 | 11 | 17 |
| Groceries | 61 | 22 | 17 |
| Furniture | 35 | 25 | 40 |

SOURCE: Haga and Folse (1971: 45).

In urban/suburban areas "community" is most appropriately identified with neighborhoods, and the best method for determining neighborhood boundaries is to ask individuals to draw them on city street maps. Individual maps are then redrawn on a common map, and boundaries that are commonly accepted become clearly visible. This method also identifies where boundaries are unclear, which is important to know. (For a fuller discussion of this method, see Haney and Knowles, 1978). A more expedient method for drawing neighborhood boundaries is to use the boundaries marked out by planning commissions or neighborhood associations. These may differ widely from the neighborhood maps of residents, and should be at least spot-tested by minisurveys before being used (seeing Finsterbusch, 1976b, on the use of minisurveys). Another simple method is to use the catchment areas for elementary schools or some other important neighborhood facility. School integration policies and school closings, however, have caused elementary school and neighborhood boundaries to diverge considerably in recent years. A more promising method for distinguishing neighborhoods is to examine statistical indicators block by block and draw neighborhood boundaries where changes occur in the indicators (see Hill, 1967). The work of social area analysts indicates that it is important to differentiate residential areas in terms of three dimensions: economic, family, and ethnic characteristics (Shevsky and Bell, 1955; Bell, 1959; Tyron, 1955).

## MEASURING COHESION

Identifying communities (that is, either rural communities or urban/suburban neighborhoods) and their boundaries is only part of the problem of measuring changes in community cohesion. The second problem is selecting measures of cohesion. In small group research cohesion is measured by social interaction patterns or by sociometric choice—that is, the ratio of best friends in the group to best friends outside the group. One measure of community or neighborhood cohesion, therefore, could be the proportion of "best friends" for a sample of residents that reside in the community or neighborhood. The number of relatives living in the neighborhood is another indicator. Traditionally, however, neighborhood cohesion is indicated by a neighborhood interaction scale which uses a set of questions to score residents on their degree of intimacy with their neighbors (see Bernard, 1937; Bott, 1957; Wallin, 1953; Caplow et al., 1964). For example, Caplow et al. (1964: 69) created a neighborhood interaction scale out of six questions which classify respondents as not recognizing their neighbors, recognizing them, talking to them outside, mutual aid or common activities with them, and entertaining in each others' homes.

In addition to residents liking other members of the community or neighborhood, community cohesion involves identification and satisfaction with the community and the amount of social activities and interactions within the community. Identification and satisfaction have been measured by the desire to stay or the intentions to move and by questions about how satisfied the respondent is with the community or neighborhood and with various aspects of it (see Fessler, 1952; Marans and Rogers, 1975; also, works cited later in the section on neighborhood satisfaction). Social activities are generally measured by participation in neighborhood or community associations and neighborhood-based voluntary organizations. Social interactions are generally measured by how often people visit with their neighbors.

Smith (1975) provided the most complete review of measures of neighborhood cohesion. His personal recommendation was to use a multidimensional approach based on four levels of neighborhood cohesion: "(1) use of physical facilities, (2) personal identification, (3) social interaction, and (4) value consensus" (p. 146). We support his idea that neighborhood cohesion is multidimensional, but, unlike him, think that personal identification and social interaction are more central to the concept of cohesion than are the use of neighborhood physical facilities and value consensus. The latter two characteristics contribute to personal identification and social interaction, but if the former characteristics emerge on other grounds, the neighborhood is still very cohesive. On the other hand, without identification and interaction the neighborhood cannot be defined as cohesive.

Another multidimensional approach which merits attention has been developed by Burkhardt et al. (1971), who recommended the use of six dimensions: (1) neighboring (interaction), (2) use of local facilities, (3) participation in local organizations, (4) identification, (5) commitment (desire to stay), and (6) evaluation (satisfaction).

All of the above measures require interviews with a sample of residents and, therefore, are relatively costly measures. Census variables have been used as inexpensive surrogate measures for community cohesion in urban areas, but not without certain difficulties. Census tract boundaries seldom coincide exactly with neighborhood boundaries, and block data lack most of the variables which can be used as surrogate measures for cohesion. The main surrogate indicator for community cohesion for census tracts is length of residency as measured by the percentage of residents five years in the home. Long-term residents have had the chance to build up neighborhood social relations and identification with the neighborhood. In stable neighborhoods, the people one encounters on the streets or at bus stops, gas stations, stores, banks, the PTA, and so on are familiar and may even be friends. Length of residency also is an indirect measure of satisfaction with the neighborhood, since dissatisfied residents move at the first opportunity.

One of the shortcomings of length of residency as an indicator of satisfaction with the neighborhood is the possibility that residents stay because they are trapped (Droettboom et al., 1971). They may be dissatisfied with the neighborhood but stay because they have nowhere else to go. This situation can be discovered by taking into account the vacancy rate. A high vacancy rate indicates that people want to leave the neighborhood more than people want to move in. Abandoned houses also indicate that a neighborhood is undesirable even if turnover is low. Abandoned housing cannot be obtained from census publications or other convenient sources but can be observed while driving through the area.

Two other sets of census variables are related to community cohesion: indicators of homogeneity and family neighborhoods. As a general rule homogeneity contributes to cohesion. Planners and policy makers may have compelling reasons for wanting to mix groups in residential areas, but in so doing they make cohesion more difficult, although not impossible. Income, ethnic, and racial homogenity are especially important for community cohesion. This is not to say that ethnic and racial groups cannot live together harmoniously; they definitely can when they are at the same income level. We point out, however, that most of the exceptionally cohesive neighborhoods are ethnically and racially homogeneous.

Family neighborhoods are generally more cohesive than neighborhoods of largely single people. Consider first the measure of cohesion which is based on the percentage of best friends living in the neighborhood. Most family members score higher on this measure than do single people. Elementary school children have all of their friends in their neighborhood. Adolescent children have friendship networks that extend short distances beyond the neighborhood but are generally centered in the neighborhood. Nonworking wives tend to develop close friendships in the neighborhood. Finally, parents often make neighborhood friends and acquaintances through their children. Another reason why family neighborhoods tend to be more cohesive than nonfamily neighborhoods is that many neighborhood activities are centered on children, and children provide motives for parents to be concerned about and involved in their neighborhoods. Finally, once children begin to depend emotionally on their friends, families are loathe to move, and stable neighborhoods tend to be cohesive.

## The Transformation of Neighborhoods
## in the Twentieth Century

### URBANIZATION AND NEIGHBORHOODS

The nature and function of neighborhoods have been transformed in the past century, and impact assessors should be aware of these changes. The process of urbanization and the mobility provided by the automobile have weakened the psychological and social importance of neighborhoods for their residents. At the start of this century most Americans lived in open country or rural neighborhoods. Today most Americans live in urban or suburban neighborhoods. The urbanization of the United States in percentage terms has been substantial since 1840, with the exception of the 1930s. The percentage of urban dwellers was 10.8 percent in 1840, passed 50 percent between 1910 and 1920, and reached 73.2 percent in 1970.

The impact of urbanization on neighborhood life was perceptively described by Wirth in 1938 (and more recently by Milgram, 1970). City life is overstimulating compared with rural life. Surrounded by more people than they can enjoy and more stimuli than they can absorb, urbanites isolate themselves emotionally from their environment and from other people. They become impersonal and superficial in many of their relationships and relatively indifferent to much of what happens around them. Accordingly, they remain relatively uninvolved with neighbors and neighborhood events. As a result, the neighborhood normative social order is fragile and not compelling. Later scholars have established that this view of urban life is an exaggeration. Urban residents have rich social networks (Fischer et al., 1977; Hunter, 1978), and normative orders of considerable strength exist even in slums (Gans, 1962a; Whyte, 1955; Suttles, 1968). Many city and suburban neighborhoods are homogeneous and, therefore, exhibit a fair amount of sociability (Gans, 1961, 1962b). However, the social networks of the urban/ suburban middle and upper classes generally are not based in the neighborhood (Gulick et al., 1962; Wellman and Leighton, 1979; Wellman, 1979); and wherever neighborhood normative orders are strong they depend heavily upon class, racial, and/or ethnic norms. Furthermore, as Tamney (1975: 98) points out, urban relationships

> are not part of some larger social structure of obligations and privileges. Granted urban life does not mean isolation or atomization. But it does mean a profound change in the nature of social relations. In the city the relationships we have are not unified or tied together; they are not part of a common structure. Rather they are experienced as discrete events. Social life lacks unity.

In the popular literature this pattern is generally criticized. However, Gulick et al. (1962: 341) regard it as functional in freeing people from the oppression of closed circles, and Wellman and Leighton (1979) point out that these "branching" networks allow "additional resources to be reached" (1979: 384).

An important difference between urban and rural neighborhoods and between neighborhood life today versus a century ago is the degree of need for mutual aid. Today in most urban neighborhoods residents are not interdependent and have little need for each other. The urbanite depends upon public services and insurance policies and employs service workers and professionals for needs that neighbors would serve in earlier times and in rural places. However, there are exceptions, and in neighborhoods where borrowing, assistance, and exchange of services are still practical, neighborhood identification remains strong.

The type of neighborhood that is often found in today's urban areas is a "community of limited liability" (Janowitz, 1967). Most residents demand more from their community than they are willing to invest, and when the community fails to serve their needs they move out or reduce their involvement. Of course, if withdrawal is widespread and fairly complete the neighborhood is socially disorganized and usually a dangerous and desperate place to live.

## THE EROSION OF NEIGHBORHOOD ATTACHMENT

Several processes have eroded the psychological importance of neighborhoods in urban/suburban areas. First, ethnic and cultural homogeneity was much stronger in many urban neighborhoods a half-century ago than now. According to Stein (1964), "The cities of the twenties were extremely heterogeneous entities composed of more or less culturally distinct, spacially segregated sub-communities" (1964: 279). Americanization undermined the ethnic distinctiveness of many urban neighborhoods. Other ethnic enclaves dispersed to the suburbs as their members advanced economically. Other ethnic neighborhoods dissolved as housing deteriorated and lower-income groups with different backgrounds moved in, hastening the exodus of the remaining ethnics. The ethnic groups which resettled in the suburbs tended to congregate in a few communities but without the same degree of concentration which they had in the central city.

The second process which has weakened the psychological importance of urban neighborhoods is the separation of living quarters and workplaces. Traditional working-class urban neighborhoods were in walking distance of work, so work associates lived within walking distance of each other. The exodus of industry from the city and the development of mass transit and the automobile separated work and home and dispersed work associates. Additional work/home separation resulted from the transformation of the retail trades from neighborhood family stores to supermarkets and shopping malls. This process also shifted shopping from a neighborhood activity to a section or community-wide activity.

The third process which weakens neighborhood ties is urban redevelopment. Slums were leveled for urban renewal or highways in accord with faulty notions of community improvement. Planners thought that deteriorated housing signalled oppressive and debilitating environments which engendered hopelessness and sapped the will of slum dwellers to make good in society by legal means. Rebuilding these areas was judged to be a social service. Not until the 1960s did the thinking of urban planners change. The writings of Gans, Fried, and Jacobs demonstrates the vitality of the neighborhood life of many of these supposedly blighted areas, while some of the massive renewal projects generated almost no socially constructive neighborhoods and soon became towers of terror. Clearly, the costs far exceeded the benefits for many of these projects.

Subsequent renewal programs or private sector redevelopments were smaller in scale and increasingly emphasized renovation of structures as opposed to new buildings. They were less harmful to neighborhoods but were designed to improve their structures and upgrade their population. With the new population, however, came new social patterns and the decline of the old neighborhood way of life.

Other factors which have weakened neighborhood life are changes in transportation and communication and the high rates of residential mobility. Before the horse-drawn streetcar was introduced around 1870, almost all movement was by foot. In the 1880s and 1890s the electric streetcar was introduced, followed by rapid transit electric trains around the turn of the century (Kasarda, 1978). Each development allowed residential communities to be located farther and farther from work. The reorganization of residential patterns was underway. The electric street railway came into widespread use for intracity transportation after 1910, peaked in 1920, and declined rapidly thereafter in favor of automobiles and buses. The adoption of the automobile increased rapidly from 1900 to 1930 from a few owners to almost one per household. Motor vehicle registration increased from 8000 to 26,352,000. Both motorized and electric transportation greatly reduced residents' dependence on their neighborhoods for work, social relationships, goods, services, and recreation. Transportation changes have contributed to the drastic decline in the use of neighborhood-based services and institutions (except for schools) since World War II (Janowitz and Street, 1978). The telephone, which spread rapidly after 1900, reduced the need for face-to-face contact and weakened neighborhoods further. Yet another blow to neighborhood vitality is the pattern of residential mobility which for three decades has been around 19 percent per year.

In summary, the nature and functions of neighborhoods have been transformed in this century. Neighborhoods have become less distinctive and internally less homogeneous. Residents satisfy more of their material and social needs outside the neighborhood. In spite of these changes, some neighborhoods have unusual vitality and dense social networks. Furthermore, a significant minority of residents are deeply attached to their neighborhoods. Public projects, therefore, should be designed to disrupt neighborhoods and displace residents as little as possible.

## Defining Neighborhoods

As in the case of community, there is no consensus about the definition of neighborhood. Most scholars would agree with Keller (1968), who says that neighborhood "refers to distinctive areas into which larger special units may be subdivided" (1968: 87). The disagreement among scholars is over the kind of distinctive areas to which it refers. Ley (1974) applies it to a block-long street, and Suttles (1968) applies it to an area having 30,000 residents. The Theodorsons (1969: 273) provide two definitions for it as follows:

Neighborhood.

1) A small territorial unit, usually a subdivision of a larger community, in which there is some sense of local unity or identity. Because the neighborhood is small, contacts are face to face, and many relationships tend to be primary, that is, close and enduring. However, according to this definition, a neighborhood also includes families that have little if any interaction with each other. The neighborhood usually provides essential services for the local residents.

2) An informal primary group found within a limited area. In this sense, a neighborhood includes only those families within a limited area who are friendly with each other.

Mann (1968) defines neighborhood in a manner which suggests a much larger area than does Theodorsons' definition:

Neighborhood: This concept may be defined both physically and socially. Physically it refers to a part of town or city made distinct by boundaries such as main roads, railways, rivers, canals and open spaces and having a certain similarity of housing type within the area. Often a shopping centre with local institutions such as churches, public houses and branch libraries may be the focal points of the neighborhood. Socially a neighborhood may be characterized by social similarities of the residents, often especially by similarity of social class or ethnic type.

We suggest using the term neighborhood as indicated in the following hierarchy of spacial units for urban areas:

(1) House or apartment as the basic residential unit;
(2) block (set of houses) or low-rise apartment house;
(3) block group (set of blocks), low-rise apartment complex, or high-rise apartment house;
(4) micro neighborhood (set of block groups) or high-rise apartment complex;

(5)  macro neighborhood (set of micro neighborhoods);
(6)  section of the city (set of macro neighborhoods);
(7)  city or urban area.

These spacial units generally are not clearly demarcated. They are heuristic concepts which provide only rough guidance for the study of urban areas. This hierarchy can be abbreviated in some urban areas by combining block group and micro neighborhood and/or combining macro neighborhood with section of the city. Within this hierarchy of spacial units, micro neighborhoods might range from 150 to 5000 residents and macro neighborhoods from 1000 to 40,000 residents depending upon densities, type of housing, social patterns, and spatial arrangements. Only in areas of high-rise apartment complexes would the upper ranges of micro or macro neighborhoods be found. Since no consensus exists on the use of these terms, the ranges are partly arbitrary. We have used Herman (1964) to define the upper limits of macro neighborhoods: She divided West Philadelphia into 26 neighborhoods ranging from 10,000 to 40,000 residents.

Four elements characterize neighborhoods, according to Keller (1968): geographic boundaries, ethnic or cultural identity, psychological unity, and concentrated use of facilities. Few areas possess these characteristics in significant measure, so few neighborhoods in the ideal sense exist. Nevertheless, most urban residential areas have these characteristics to some degree which justifies the continued use of the term "neighborhood" in analyzing residents' geographic attachments.

Quite apart from the way social scientists define neighborhoods is the way residents understand the term. Coleman (1978) asked people in Kansas City, Boston, Houston, Dayton, and Rochester how they defined their neighborhood; they learned that people had "three or four gradations in geographic definition of 'neighborhood,' each with a different social and symbolic meaning" (1978: 3). These definitions differed for residents of single-family homes and apartment dwellers as follows:

To single-family home occupants, "neighborhood" in the smallest sense refers to "the houses around my house—really the whole block—the range of distance where I would let my children play;" or, phrased another way, "It's a circle with a radius equal to one black with my home the center." This is "the immediate neighborhood." At the next level up, the neighborhood boundary line tends to be drawn where the market value of housing noticeably changes or there suddenly becomes apparent a different mix in value of housing. This line marks off those neighbors with whom one feels socioeconomic brotherhood from those with whom one doesn't; it can be drawn one block away or one mile. When neighborhoods are not so homogeneous in housing quality that boundary lines by market value cannot be drawn readily, then people turn for their geographical definition to neighborhood names, school district boundary lines, the region embraced by a civic association, or the dividing force of major traffic arteries. These become important in any event—forming often a third-level definition of "neighborhood," if not second-level. The broadest levels of neighborhood definition in the geographical (or physical) sense refer to whole suburbs or townships—or beyond that, the whole "southwest section of Greater Houston" or "the southeast area of Rochester."

For apartment dwellers, "neighborhood" can mean something as small as their own building (or complex)—or perhaps, at the second level up, it may include a whole series of adjacent apartment buildings or two-family houses. Apartment residents do not readily consider single-family homes that surround or abut their apartment building as part of their neighborhood; they tend to feel no bond with the residents in these single-family homes; they think of themselves as differentiated in life style and circumstances by the variation in structural choice. The largest definitions of neighborhood given by apartment dwellers tell what "part of town" they looked in when shopping for their present quarters. This may be a street name—as "the Westheimer area" in Houston or "Park Avenue area" in Rochester—or the name of a whole suburb or township. Typically, it is the label they looked under in the rental want-ads.

Both single-family residents and apartment dwellers resist the idea of including within their neighborhood any area they would not want to live in, no matter how close. They will say: "My neighborhood doesn't extend as far north as 'X' Street—you find a different class of people there." One Rochester man was more poignant in his expression of this attitude: "I used to think of 'Z' Street as part of my neighborhood, but not now, since welfare people have begun moving in there" [Coleman, 1978: 3-5].

In this chapter urban and suburban neighborhoods are treated together. This is appropriate because, according to Gans, "when one looks at similar populations in city and suburb, their ways of life are remarkably alike" (1967: 288). Most of the city-suburban differences in variables such as community involvement and frequency of contact with neighbors are due to socioeconomic differences rather than to factors which are inherent in urban or suburban conditions (Fischer, 1975). Furthermore, it is likely that self-selection explains any residual differences (National Research Council, 1974: 54-56). Berger's study (1960) is particularly well suited for demonstrating that urban/suburban conditions have little effect on neighborhood life. When his subjects were moved en masse to suburbia by their company, he did not find significant changes in neighborhood patterns.

Although urban and suburban neighborhoods are similar enough to be treated together, they are not entirely alike. Fischer and Jackson (1976) identify some small but statistically significant effects of suburbanism on neighboring, and Milgram (1970) describes how the urban conditions of large numbers, density, and heterogeneity are experienced "as overloads at the level of roles, norms, cognitive functions, and facilities. These overloads lead to adaptive mechanisms which create the distinctive tone and behaviors of city life" (1970: 1468).

## The Functions of Neighborhoods

Neighborhoods provide a number of functions for their residents and affect their lives in a number of ways. Assessors need to understand these functions in order to properly interpret how projects impact on neighborhood functioning and thereby impact on individuals. The main functions of neighborhoods are social contact, assistance, security and social control, status or identification, and the socialization of children. Other functions are organizational ties; local services; accessibility to jobs, goods, services, and activities; recreational facilities; political participation; and providing an acceptable physical environment. Neighborhoods differ considerably in their level of functioning on the various functions, and the level of functioning on various functions has been found to be strongly correlated by Warren (1977). The functions of neighborhoods will be reviewed briefly in this section after noting two major neighborhood styles which affect the way neighborhoods function.

### INTIMATE AND ALOOF NEIGHBORHOODS

Keller (1968) noted that there are two basic neighborhood styles which define the neighbor role very differently. In some neighborhoods neighbors are supposed to be friendly and helpful and in others neighbors are supposed to mind their own business and not ask favors. In the former, intimacy is valued; in the latter, seclusion is valued. Keller hypothesizes that the major factor which accounts for these differences is the degree to which people are in need of aid and social support from each other. This pattern of neighborhood dependency and friendliness is common in rural villages and uncommon in cities. It is found, however, in certain types of city neighborhoods: "Ethnic minorities, immigrant colonies, working class enclaves and even middle class suburbs in a somewhat different sense show a marked inclination and need for neighboring" (1968: 48). One would think that it would also be found in very poor city neighborhoods because the need for aid is great. Keller observes, however, that suspicion and fear prevent the development of collective norms of cooperative neighboring in many of these impoverished areas.

## NEIGHBORHOODS AS THE CONTEXT
## FOR SOCIAL RELATIONS

Considerable research has sought to determine the extent of social networks and social contacts in cities. Dating back to Wirth's classic article, "Urbanism as a Way to Life" (1938), the urban condition has been seen as conducive to superficial, nonobligating, and transitory social relations and not conducive to intimate associations. Much of the research on urban social relations in the 1960s and 1970s has considerably modified this view by showing that urbanites have active social networks. For example, Key (1965) compared social contacts of people in communities at five levels of the rural/urban scale: rural, village, small urban, Terre Haute, and Indianapolis. The respondents in Indianapolis had above-average contacts with immediate family, extended family, informal groups, work groups, and formal groups. They had below-average contacts only with neighbors, and this type of contact showed a consistent increase as the size of the community decreased. Thus, the low neighboring found in cities should not be interpreted to indicate that urbanites have few intimate social relationships. His work dovetails with the summary of empirical research on metropolitan America by a special committee of scholars under the auspices of the National Research Council, which concluded:

> At present, the best evidence suggests that metropolitan experience involves an increase in the number and variety of impersonal (secondary) relationships and that frequency and quality of personal and intimate (primary) relationships has remained virtually unchanged [1974: 51].

From studies such as Key's one would conclude that individuals in cities have reasonably strong social networks but that only a minority of urban residents are rooted in their neighborhoods. Wellman strongly states this view in his provocative article, "Who Needs Neighborhoods?" (1972). The finding of one survey which he reviews is: "Only 13 percent of the respondents' intimates lived in the same neighborhood; the great majority, 63 percent, lived in other parts of Metropolitan Toronto and 24 percent lived outside of Metropolitan Toronto" (p. 96). He argues that most residents' important ties are interest-based and are not neighborhood-based. Modern urban life, it seems, has weakened the classical relationship between propinquity and friendship (Festinger et al., 1950; Caplow and Forman, 1950) but, we argue, it has not nullified it. As Gans (1961) pointed out, proximity is more likely to lead to friendship among similar than dissimilar people. Thus, interests and propinquity interact in the formation of friendships.

As a general rule, social ties in urban neighborhoods tend not to be intimate and psychologically crucial, but important exceptions have been documented. For example, Gans' *Urban Villagers* (1962a) describes intimate neighborhood-based social networks in the West End of Boston (see also Fried, 1963, 1967). The exceptions to the general rule seem to occur most often in long-established, occupational, cultural, and ethnic enclaves. In these cases the neighborhood not only provides intimate social relations, but also is important to the maintenance of a distinctive way of life. These neighborhood enclaves, therefore, provide very important psychological and social supports for their residents.

As noted above, most neighborhoods are the contexts for mainly superficial social relations. Because they are superficial, they have relatively slight effects on mental health (Langner and Michael, 1963: 287-289). They are sources of aid, provide some sense of security, counter alienation and isolation, and, when necessary, provide some of the emotional support that everyone needs.

Why are most relationships with neighbors not intimate? The answer seems to be that most people satisfy their deeper social needs in the family and outside the neighborhood. Keller (1968) relates the decline in intimacy in neighborhoods to the increased intimacy of modern families and to the transportation and communication advances which make it possible to maintain intimacy conveniently with people beyond the neighborhood.

There are many exceptions to the general rule that family and nonneighbors provide sufficient primary social ties. Children, the elderly, the handicapped, and others without ready means of transportation are dependent upon neighbors for close social relations. When relative immobility is combined with living alone, the need for intimate neighbors is very great. Unfortunately, the accepted pattern in most neighborhoods is for superficial relations with neighbors, and many of the people who need close ties to neighbors become socially starved. Often the elderly become lonely hermits even though they desire intimacy and are surrounded by thousands of people. After a while they withdraw into their shells to minimize the pain of their loneliness.

## THE NEIGHBORHOOD AS A SOURCE OF
## SECURITY AND SOCIAL ORDER

The neighborhood provides security in three major ways: by keeping out dangerous people; by controlling the behavior of people in the public areas of the neighborhood; and by making friends, foes, and neutrals identifiable. Both the wealthy suburban neighborhood, which is protected by distance from poor neighborhoods, and the carefully guarded luxury apartment houses provide security largely by keeping out dangerous people. Furthermore, the lifestyle of these residential places make most potentially dangerous people conspicuous because of their dress and manners and thereby discourages their visits to the neighborhood. Finally, these neighborhoods are heavily policed.

More ordinary neighborhoods provide security, to the extent that they do, by controlling the behavior of people while they are in the neighborhood. It is not possible to keep undesirable persons out of these neighborhoods, but they can be hindered from destructive acts. The classic exposition of this process is Jacobs' *The Death and Life of Great American Cities* (1961). She describes how the sidewalk shopkeepers and tenement residents in her neighborhood watch the streets, and, whenever anything out of place begins to occur on the street, people appear in doorways and windows. Anyone intending criminal or inappropriate actions are made aware that they are being watched and that the neighborhood will do something to stop them if they put their plans into action. She lived in a neighborhood which was safe because the people in the neighborhood were concerned about what went on around them. They minded more than their own business and effectively controlled undesirable behavior. Long-term residents provide this service, as do streetside shopkeepers. It is also important to have bustling street life from early morning to late at night, since lonely streets can be especially dangerous.

The third way that neighborhoods provide security is by allowing individuals or groups to protect themselves. In relatively dangerous and insecure neighborhoods the residents over time can distinguish friends and enemies and can recognize dangerous situations. They must view most strangers with distrust and devise countless strategies for navigating public space without mishap. In the worst neighborhoods the home and the friendship group are like frontier outposts in hostile territory (Ley, 1974). Beyond the front door constant vigilence is exercised. These neighborhoods are dangerous, but because they are familiar their shoals are navigable.

The home as frontier outpost in ungoverned wild territory does not describe all slum neighborhoods. Suttles (1968) described how a segmented social order was maintained in one slum neighborhood. This social order was based on ethnic and neighborhood solidarities and age- and sex-graded groupings. Social realtions are restricted to the safest ones, which include family, one's ethnic group, and people for whom someone in the group can vouch. A fair degree of social order is maintained by the groups which have authority over various spaces, and, though intergroup tensions exist, the groups keep it under control.

The above discussion describes how neighborhoods provide security, but security is only one component of the social control which neighborhoods should provide. Wilson (1968) argues with considerable force that the failure of cities is basically their failure to stop improper behavior in public areas—that is, the general lack of social control, including the control of "crime, violence, rebellious youth, racial tension, public immorality, delinquency" (1968: 28). This failure should not be blamed on the police because the police by themselves can exercise little social control. Most social control is exercised by parents, peers, and neighborhood citizens. The urban crisis, according to Wilson, results from the failure of urban residents to exercise social control in their environments. He asserts that "it is the breakdown of neighborhood controls (neighborhood self-government, if you will) that accounts for the principal concerns of urban citizens" (p. 28).

### THE NEIGHBORHOOD AS A SOURCE OF AID

One of the major differences between rural and urban neighborhoods is the amount of aid neighbors solicit from and offer to each other. Furthermore, within both urban and rural neighborhoods the extent of aiding has declined over the years as government and insurance programs reduce the dependency of families on neighbors for both their regular needs and for recovery from crises. Nevertheless, neighbors still provide aid ranging from the cup of sugar to caring for children while the parent is on an errand. Assistance from neighbors is still an important component in the meaning and significance of the neighborhood for its residents, especially for lower-income families without kin in the area (Herberle, 1960; Litwak and Szelenyi, 1969). In fact, Keller (1968) uses the norms about what aid can be asked of neighbors as a major dimension for comparing neighborhoods, as discussed earlier.

### THE NEIGHBORHOOD AS A SOURCE OF STATUS AND IDENTIFICATION

To some extent, people are judged by where they live. Neighborhoods with bad reputations give their residents a bad name to live down. Conversely, neighborhoods with good reputations give their residents an identity of which to be proud. Neighborhood status may be based on the society-wide norms of wealth or on subgroup norms for specific lifestyles. As everyone knows, expensive neighborhoods confer status and the presumption of respectability. The status of wealthy neighborhoods is further enhanced by age and tradition. Ross (1962) described how the Beacon Hill area in Boston is well known as an upper-class neighborhood and source of status identification for its residents.

Certain other neighborhoods are judged favorably by certain subcultures because of their special style and/or special inhabitants. For example, a Greenwich Village address suggests cultural and intellectual interests and a liberated view of life, and the neighborhood appearance seems to conform to these images. However, not everyone thinks Greenwich Village is a respectable address. Certainly some parents in the rural areas of the Midwest wish their daughters lived in a less avant garde neighborhood. Another important dimension on which people's preferences differ is the activity level of the neighborhood. Some people identify with quiet relaxed neighborhoods and others with lively neighborhoods.

The basis for positively valuing neighborhoods varies from class to class, according to Coleman (1978). His upper-status groups (professionals and managers) expressed a concern about respectable neighbors, good architecture, suburban seclusion, good schools, and the right part of town. A minority preferred quality city neighborhoods. His middle-class groups (white collar and elite blue collar) also wanted good schools, quiet neighborhoods, suburban lifestyle, but were not choosy about the part of town or architectural features. His working-class groups used fewer criteria: They wanted to avoid deteriorated and/or messy neighborhoods and had definite ideas about the kind of people (for example, welfare families) they did not want in their neighborhoods. His lower-class sample had little hope for satisfying their neighborhood preferences, so they were relieved if the neighborhood was not overly dangerous and their housing was in decent shape (Coleman, 1978: 9-18).

It is important to notice the exceptions to the general rules. For example, in each of Coleman's groups whites preferred white to mixed neighborhoods, but some whites and blacks wanted to live in racially integrated neighborhoods. The desire for racial mixture was also found by Hunter (1975) in his replication 25 years later of Foley's (1952) neighborhood study. Hunter found that its sense of community had increased because it was racially mixed. New residents were attracted to that neighborhood in part because it was a successfully integrated neighborhood.

## THE NEIGHBORHOOD AS CONTEXT FOR THE SOCIALIZATION OF CHILDREN

Socialization of children is an important function of neighborhoods and a priority concern of parents with children in the home. The neighborhood usually contains an elementary school and is the basis for assignment to junior and senior high schools. The neighborhood is the source of most children's peer groups, which greatly influence their social development. It is also the source of adult role models and an important context for the observation of social norms in action. The neighborhood school, role models, and peer groups, along with the family and the media, are the major agents of socialization.

Some neighborhoods subject children to influences which their parents think are constructive, while others socialize children into delinquent pathways. Maccoby et al. (1958) found that high-delinquency areas were much more socially disorganized than low-delinquency areas with similar socioeconomic status of residents. They argue that "the lack of social integration appears to have certain direct effects in a lowered level of social control of delinquent and pre-delinquent activities" (1958: 51). Shaw and McKay's (1931) early studies of the areal distribution of juvenile delinquency lead them to make the following observations:

> Children who grow up in these deteriorated and disorganized neighborhoods of the city are not subject to the same constructive and restraining influences that surround those in the more homogeneous residential communities farther removed from the industrial and commercial centers. . . . Very often the child's access to the traditions and standards of our conventional culture are restricted to his formal contacts with the police, the courts, the school, and the various social agencies. On the other hand his most vital and intimate social contacts are often limited to the spontaneous and undirected neighborhood play groups and gangs whose activities and standards of conduct may vary widely from those of his parents and the larger social order. These intimate and personal relationships, rather than the more formal and external contacts with the school, social agencies, and the authorities, become the chief sources from which he acquires his social values and conceptions of right and wrong.

> Delinquency persists in these areas not only because of the absence of constructive neighborhood influences and the inefficiency of present methods of prevention and treatment, but because various forms of lawlessness have become more or less *traditional* aspects of the social life and are handed down year after year through the medium of social contacts. Delinquent and criminal patterns of behavior are prevalent in these areas and are readily accessible to a large proportion of the children [quoted in Burgess and Bogue, 1964: 595-596].

The importance of neighborhood effects on the socialization of children is well understood by parents who take it into account in choosing a place to live. One reason for the flight to the suburbs is the desire of parents to improve the neighborhood influences on their children. I observed similar parental concerns in a study of a poor neighborhood that lay in the path of a proposed highway. I found that the mothers had little attachment to the neighborhood because they abhorred what it was doing to their children.

## OTHER NEIGHBORHOOD FUNCTIONS

Neighborhoods also provide organizations and associations which meet specific needs of residents and provide social contact in the process. Examples of neighborhood organizations include the Boy Scouts, Little League, country clubs, Y.M.C.A., swimming pool associations, music groups, senior citizen associations, garden clubs, churches and synagogues, neighborhood associations, Alcoholics Anonymous, and the American Legion. Many of the social relationships involved in these organizations are warm and intimate even though they may be temporary and do not involve the private lives of the participants (see Wireman, 1978).

Most of the local residential services are provided by the municipal government, but the quality of the services varies somewhat from neighborhood to neighborhood. The neighborhood also provides the environment for the home which may be noisy or peaceful, beautiful or ugly, clean or polluted, light or dark, filled with or empty of greenery, littered or unlittered, and contain well-maintained or deteriorating buildings, yards, and streets. The neighborhood provides other resources such as parks, playgrounds, libraries, and rivers. In a sense it also provides accessibility to some jobs, goods, services, and activities but not to others.

Neighborhoods also perform an important political function which is overlooked by most community sociologists. Janowitz and Street (1978) have clearly articulated this neglected function of neighborhoods.

> The local residential organization is the catchment area for fashioning accountability and developing links to political institutions. This is especially the case in a society in which responsibility is widely diffused and readily avoided. Within the social space of family residence, persons have the opportunity and, in varying degrees, the necessity of aggregating their competing self-interests. . . .

> Because the political system emphasizes territorial representation, and because the expansion of the governmental functions includes many welfare state functions that are geographically based, local residential political participation and local residential political decision making have grown in importance since the end of World War II. The local family-residential social organization remains the catchment area in which the metropolitan-wide and societal-wide constituencies are mobilized. However, at the same time, it is the arena—actual and potential—for balancing competing interests and conflicting aspirations [1978: 94, 97].

## Understanding Attachment
## To the Neighborhood

A neighborhood serves various needs of its residents as described in the previous section. As a result, individuals are emotionally attached to their neighborhoods to varying degrees. In this section we summarize the findings on the attachment of individuals to their neighborhoods in terms of three interrelated dimensions: satisfaction with the neighborhood, neighborhood social ties, and the desire to stay or move. A major component of the assessment of project impacts on neighborhoods and their residents is the examination of changes in these three dimensions. Some argue that the use of local facilities is another indicator of attachment to the neighborhood (Stone, 1954; Burkhardt et al., 1971). Neighborhood attachment is modestly related to local facility use (Stone, 1954), but not as strongly as to local social ties. Therefore, we do not treat local facility use as a major dimension of attachment to neighborhood in this section.

## SATISFACTION WITH THE NEIGHBORHOOD

Most people are satisfied with their neighborhoods. In a large national sample Andrews and Withey (1976) asked residents, "How do you feel about this particular neighborhood as a place to live?" Only nine percent said they were dissatisfied and the other respondents answered as follows: delighted, 18 percent; pleased, 39 percent; mostly satisfied, 24 percent; and mixed, 10 percent. Lee and Guest (1979) report that 82.3 percent of the combined Annual Housing Survey samples for 1974, 1975, and 1976 rated their neighborhoods as excellent or good, 15.1 percent rated them as fair, and only 2.6 percent rated them as poor.

What explains the different degrees of satisfaction with and attachment to one's neighborhood? Several studies find that satisfaction with the neighborhood is significantly related to amount and intensity of social contacts, length of residency, and certain variables, such as home ownership, which indicate investment in the neighborhood. For example, Janowitz and Kasarda (1974) analyzed a survey of 1648 residents by the Royal Commission on Local Government in England, and conclude:

> Whether or not a person experienced a sense of community, had a strong interest in the affairs of the community, or would be sorry to leave the community was found to be strongly influenced by his local friendship and kinship bonds and formal and informal associational ties. Participation in these local social networks, in turn, was found to be influenced primarily by length of residence in the community [1974: 230].

Their findings hold up in other studies. For example, using similar variables, Hutchison (1977) obtained the same results from a survey of 200 residents of South Chicago. The evidence on the importance of length of residency for satisfaction with the neighborhood is particularly strong (Ermuth, 1974; Kasarda and Janowitz, 1974; Hunter, 1974; Philliber, 1976; Marans and Rodgers, 1975; Nathanson, 1964).

In addition to social ties, length of residency, and home ownership, many other variables have been found to be correlated with satisfaction with the neighborhood. Perceptions of neighborhood conditions and upkeep play an important role (Butler et al., 1969; Campbell et al., 1976; Foote et al., 1960;

Fischer et al., 1977; Lansing et al., 1970; Galster and Hesser, 1979; Lee and Guest, 1979; Marans and Rodgers, 1975), as do positive perceptions of neighbors (Campbell et al., 1976; Fried and Gleicher, 1961; Galster and Hesser, 1979; Lansing et al., 1970; Marans and Rodgers, 1975). Convenience, traffic, noise, and fear of crime are other features of the neighborhood related to neighborhood satisfaction (Butler et al., 1969; Campbell et al., 1976; Hartnagel, 1979; Kasl and Harburg, 1972; Lee and Guest, 1979; Marans and Rodgers, 1975). We also note that neighborhood satisfaction is higher in the suburbs than in the central city and is higher for whites than blacks (Lee and Guest, 1979).

Since many of the variables which cause satisfaction with neighborhood are themselves correlated, multivariate analysis is required to determine which variables have independent effects on neighborhood satisfaction. Philliber (1976) surveyed a sample of 800 residents of Gary, Indiana. Seven questions on attitudes toward one's neighborhood and one's neighbors were combined into an index of subjective integration into the neighborhood. A path analysis showed the importance of length of residence, home ownership, and family structure (low = unmarried, medium = married without children, and high = married with children) for contact with neighbors and for subjective integration into the neighborhood. These three characteristics of households always emerge as important in neighborhood and mobility studies.

Philliber's study focused on personal characteristics to explain degrees of neighborhood satisfaction. Characteristics of the neighborhood and the assessments of these characteristics by residents are even more important. Campbell et al. (1976), in a national sample of 2161 residents, found that assessments of five neighborhood attributes by residents explained 32.4 percent of the variance in their satisfaction with their macro neighborhoods, while the personal characteristics of life cycle stage, race, length of residence, family income, education, and occupation only explained 7.6 percent of the variance in neighborhood satisfaction and explained only an additional variance of 2.3 percent when added to the assessments of neighborhood attributes. The relative importance of the five neighborhood characteristics as assessed by the respondents is reflected in their beta coefficients as follows: evaluation of neighbors, .37; conditions and upkeep of housing, .25; safe to walk at night, .11; convenience, .10; and importance of locking doors, .07.

This ranking suggests that the people of the neighborhood are the main contributing factor to satisfaction with the neighborhood, and that the quality and maintenance of housing in the neighborhood is the second most important factor. It does not explain how these two variables affect each other.

The importance of neighbors in neighborhood satisfaction is also emphasized by Gans (1962a) in his intensive field study of the Italian community in the West End of Boston. The residents had many social ties and deep roots in the area and were therefore attached to the area. They were greatly disturbed by their displacement for a highway and urban renewal. Apart from their intimate friends and relatives in the area, however, most did not care much about the West End. Gans found that

> there was relatively little interest in the West End as a physical or social unit. West Enders were concerned with some of the people who lived in the area, but not with the entire population. Their interest in the physical features of the area was limited generally to the street on which they lived, and the stores which they frequented. . . . Only after it was too late did people begin to realize that they did have some feelings about the entire area [1962a: 105].

Fried and Gleicher (1961) conducted a survey of West Enders as part of the same study and reported: "For the great majority of the people, the local area was a focus for strongly positive sentiments and was perceived probably in its multiple meanings, as home" (1961: 308). Strong positive feelings about the West End were strongly related to positive attitudes toward neighbors, moderately related to the number of kin in the area, and strongly related to the percentage of the five closest persons residing in the West End. While explaining the strong attachment of West Enders to their neighborhood, Fried and Gleicher observed how "the residents of slums are 'at home' in the street" (p. 311) and treat the public places around their homes as part of their personal territory. Working-class residents have less of a subjective boundary between home and environment than does the middle class.

The above discussion has focused on neighborhood satisfaction in terms of micro or macro neighborhood areas as defined earlier. It should be noted, however, that in some of the studies reviewed "neighborhood" was not defined for the respondents, and some of them may have had smaller areas in mind when they gave their opinions about their neighborhoods. Now we will consider attitudes toward the block or small area around the house and report the findings of Lansing et al. (1970). They studied satisfaction with "the five or six other buildings nearest to you around here" (p. 245). Their index of satisfaction was based on four attitude questions evaluating this small area: (1) attractive/unattractive, (2) pleasant/unpleasant, (3) good place/poor place, and (4) like what I see. The most significant predictors of satisfaction with the area as indicated by standardized multiple regression coefficients in descending order were evaluations of the area as (1) poorly kept up/well kept up, (2) unfriendly/friendly, (3) noisy/quiet, (4) similar/dissimilar neighbors, and (5) adequate space near home. When zero-order correlations were used the same variable had the highest correlations, except that the fifth-highest correlation is with "rating of places near home for children to play" (1970: 131). The greater importance of neighborhood appearance over desirable neighbors to block satisfaction may be due to its conceptual overlap with Lansing et al.'s measure of block satisfaction, or it may indicate that appearance is supremely important at the block level. Other variables related to block satisfaction in the Landing et al. (1970) study were investment quality of the home, frequency of casual interaction with neighbors, and privacy in yard from neighbors. Additional variables related to satisfaction with the area around the house in a study reported by Marans and Rodgers (1975) were uncrowded, safety of neighborhood streets, low traffic level in the neighborhood, many trees in the neighborhood, and clean air.

Satisfaction with neighborhood has been treated as a discrete dependent variable in the above discussion, but it overlaps with satisfaction with both community and home. These three variables cluster together in the smallest-space analysis of Campbell et al. (1976) which looked at 17 domains of satisfaction variables. They conclude "that people do not clearly differentiate between their housing, their neighborhoods, and their communities" (1976: 256).

Because neighborhood satisfaction is related to community satisfaction (see also Marans and Rodgers, 1975), it is instructive to note people's preferences about communities. Fischer (1975) uses Gallup Opinion polls to show that overall satisfaction with life decreases with size of community. The message seems to be that rural life is better than urban life and suburban life is somewhere in between. Campbell et al. look specifically at community satisfaction and neighborhood satisfaction, finding that both decrease markedly with increasing size of community (see also Lee and Guest, 1979; Marans and Rodgers, 1975). A greater percentage of urbanites than suburbanites do not like their neighborhoods, and rural residents are the most satisfied with their neighborhoods. Fischer reviews other studies and concludes:

> Perhaps the most accurate summary statement is that there is a general American value preference for the rural or small-town ideal, even if it can only be realized in the suburban tract home. At the same time, the reality of economic life means that metropolitan residence is chosen. The implication, which may be serious, is that many if not most urban residents benefit materially from their place of residence, but feel that this is not where the "good life" is led [1975: 205].

The studies reviewed earlier indicate that most people—but especially families—prefer uncrowded, unpolluted, quiet, and safe residential areas with many trees, little traffic, good schools and services, privacy, and spaces for children to play and for family activities. At the same time, they want the economic and entertainment opportunities of the city. Suburban or peripheral urban areas which are readily accessible to the city center seem to most satisfactorily combine these values.

## NEIGHBORHOOD SOCIAL TIES

The most thorough discussion of social networks and social relations is by Fischer et al. (1977). Social relations are examined in terms of intimacy, frequency, duration, and source; social networks are examined in terms of density, homogeneity, dispersion, and dominant source of respondent's friendships. The important part of their study for our purpose is its findings on the factors which determine the intimacy and frequency of neighborhood social ties. The most prominent factor is length of residency (see also Gates et al., 1973; Smith et al., 1954), even when many other characteristics of people and neighborhoods were controlled. However, length of residency is also a result of local social networks in that the more involved residents are in neighborhood social relations, the more reluctant they are to leave.

Three other characteristics of families strongly affect the strength of local social ties according to Fischer et al. (1977) and other studies: children, working wives, and social class. Children generate neighborhood social contacts and neighborhood involvement (Greer, 1956; for an exception see Caplow et al., 1964). On the other hand, children tend to interfere with extralocal relations. Women's employment is another factor affecting neighborhood ties. "Wives who are not employed outside the home link themselves and their families to the neighborhood more closely than do working women" (Fischer et al., 1977: 147; see also Gans, 1961). Social class affects neighborhood social ties in complex ways. Middle- and upper-class adults are more likely to participate in local voluntary activities and casual neighboring (Fischer et al., 1977; Fischer and Jackson, 1976; Gates et al., 1973; Janowitz and Kasarda, 1974; Smith et al., 1954) but are less likely to have relatives or intimate friends in the neighborhood (Fischer et al., 1977; Janowitz and Kasarda, 1974).

Some characteristics of home and neighborhood are associated with strength of neighborhood ties, but when characteristics of the family and other factors including home ownership are taken into account, the characteristics of home and neighborhood generally do not have a direct effect on neighborhood ties (Fischer et al., 1977). Variables of this type are house value, median income of the neighborhood, and median house value of the neighborhood. Some other neighborhood characteristics, however, directly affect the amount of neighboring and the density of neighborhood networks according to Fischer et al. (1977). Neighboring and network density are greater in neighborhoods that (1) are racially, ethnically, or occupationally homogeneous; (2) are suburban; (3) have large amounts of organized local activity; and (4) have low crime rates.

Other studies generally support the findings of Fischer et al. and sometimes identify additional factors which are related to the quality or intimacy of neighborhood social ties. Janowitz and Kasarda (1974) found family life cycle to be significantly related negatively to neighborhood social ties (in terms of standardized partial regression coefficients with community size, length of residence, density, and socioeconomic status being controlled). When they tested for the effects of community size, they found that "location in communities of increased size and density does not weaken networks of kinship and friendship" (p. 230). Sutcliffe and Crabbe (1963) also found no significant differences in the incidence of neighborhood friendly contacts in the inner city, suburb, and rural areas when age, sex, education, religion, and occupation were controlled. The incidence of neighborhood "best friends," however, was somewhat higher in the suburbs than in either the inner city or rural areas.

## THE DESIRE TO STAY IN THE NEIGHBORHOOD

The desire to stay in one's neighborhood is strongly related to neighborhood satisfaction and neighborhood social ties, as one would expect (Bach and Smith, 1977; Galster and Hesser, 1979; Foote et al., 1960; Caplow et al., 1964; Fernandez and Dillman, 1979; Hutchison, 1977; Janowitz and Kasarda, 1974; Kasl and Harburg, 1972; Redpath, 1974; Speare et al. 1974). Length of residency and home ownership are two other variables associated with the desire to stay (and low mobility rates) in study after study (Speare, 1970, 1974; Kasarda and Janowitz, 1974; Pickvance, 1973; Fischer et al., 1977; Rossi, 1955; Morrison, 1967, 1970b; Meyers et al., 1967). Other factors which are related to the desire to stay in one's neighborhood are: the value of one's home (Fischer et al., 1977), the quality of the physical conditions of home and neighborhood (Kasl and Harburg, 1972; Newman, 1974), and the crime rate or the level of fear of crime (Droettboom et al., 1971; Kasl and Harburg, 1972).

People may like their neighborhood and still want to move in order to own a home or to have sufficient space. In a study of 1486 recent house movers, Barrett (1973) asked the open-ended question: "Why did you move from your previous residence?" (p. 95). Two reasons dominated the list of answers. Thirty-two percent wanted to own a home and 30 percent said their previous accommodation was too small. The third largest response (given by only 11 percent of the households) was dislike for the area of the previous home. Stegman's (1969) study of 841 moving families had similar results, but found space needs even more prominent on the list of reasons for moving, and home ownership and dissatisfaction with the neighborhood less prominent answers. It should be noted that among Stegman's 393 central-city movers, the second most frequent reason (second to space needs) was "forced to move."

Rossi (1955) studied 924 households' desire to stay or move and found 52 percent desiring to stay and 48 percent desiring to move. A second question asked whether they were "very anxious to move" (or stay); 25 percent were anxious to move and 23 percent were desiring to move but not anxiously. The major factors producing mobility desire were complaints about the social environment and about the physical characteristics of the neighborhood. Surprisingly, Rossi found that having most of one's friends or relatives nearby compared with distant did not reduce mobility desires.

About half of Rossi's sample were recent arrivals to their homes, and these 444 households were asked why they had recently moved. Of these, 273 were "voluntary movers," and Rossi had them identify which of their complaints were the most important in their decision to move. The three major sets of complaints were: space complaints, 45 percent; neighborhood complaints, 14 percent; and cost complaints, 12 percent. The breakdown of neighborhood complaints was as follows: social composition, 49 percent; physical structure, 23 percent; services, 13 percent; other aspects, 15 percent. As in the Campbell et al. (1976) study discussed above, Rossi found that attitudes toward the people of the neighborhood were paramount in residents' attachment to their neighborhoods. (For additional details in Rossi's study see Chapter 2).

## SUMMARY AND CONCLUSIONS

The work reported in this section describes several aspects of attachment to one's neighborhood and a range of factors which influence attachment. Aspects of attachment which were reviewed in this section were satisfaction with neighborhood, neighborhood social ties, and the desire to stay in the neighborhood. All of these are closely related to each other and to length of residency and home ownership. These findings suggest a strategy for impact assessors when attachment to neighborhood cannot be measured directly. They could use length of residency and home ownership, which can be obtained from census data, as surrogate measures for attachment to the neighborhood.

## Attachment to the Home

Some discussion of attachment to the home has already been presented in connection with the above discussion of attachment to the neighborhood. A few of these points warrant repetition. First, home ownership for most people is still the American dream and is an important contributing factor to neighborhood satisfaction, local social ties, and the desire to stay. Second, house value and median house value of the census tract are correlated with neighborhood satisfaction. Finally, two strong incentives for moving are the desire to own a house and the need for more adequate housing.

Attachment to home has not been examined as extensively as attachment to neighborhood. Nevertheless, the factors affecting attachment to home are fairly apparent, since they are mainly the physical and economic features of the home. Campbell et al. (1976) explains 34.5 percent of the variance in housing satisfaction by the occupants' assessments of four housing attributes. The Beta coefficients of these assessed attributes are one indicator of their relative importance: well-built structure, .31; size of rooms, .26; heating adequacy, .25; and costs, .11. The researchers also used objective housing attributes to predict housing satisfaction, but these only explained 12.1 percent of the variance in housing satisfaction. The relative importance of the five most important objective attributes as indicated by the Beta coefficients are as follows: rooms per person, .24; owned rather than rented, .11; value/rent, .10; type of structure, .08; and age of structure, .13. The importance of rooms and space per person for housing satisfaction has also been demonstrated by Steidl (1972) and Riemer (1945). The importance of ownership for housing satisfaction has been demonstrated by Back (1962), Dillman et al. (1979), and Morris and Winter (1978).

Campbell et al. also used a multiple regression analysis to explain the desire to move to another dwelling unit. Twenty-three independent variables (that is, explanatory factors) were included in the regression covering satisfaction with neighborhood and home; assessment of community, neighborhood and housing attributes; personal characteristics; and objective environmental characteristics. Only seven of the 23 variables had significant Beta weights in the stepwise multiple regression; together they accounted for 33.5 percent of the variance of the desire to move to another dwelling unit. Their relative importance as indicated by their Beta weights is as follows: satisfaction with housing, -.37; satisfaction with neighborhood, -.15; assessment of size of rooms, -.09; satisfaction with community, -.06; size of community, .05; and a special factor, .05. It appears, then, that people voluntarily move out of greater dissatisfaction with their housing than with their neighborhood. The importance of these two factors is reversed, however, in the choice of housing, as explained below.

## THE IMPORTANCE OF NEIGHBORHOOD
## RELATIVE TO HOUSE IN CHOICE OF HOUSING

Neighborhood considerations are important in the choice of where to move. The selection of new housing is based largely on neighborhood qualities once minimal space needs have been decided upon. As a matter of fact, neighborhood considerations seem to be more significant to the choice of new housing than characteristics of the house. Coleman (1978) asked about 500 people this question: "Next time you move, would you be willing to move to a less desirable neighborhood in order to obtain a more suitable dwelling?" (p. 6). The overwhelming response (89 percent) was "no." He asked another 400 respondents, "Suppose you found two places that cost the same and the difference was that one was in a neighborhood more to your liking and the other was more what you wanted in housing—which do you think you would finally choose?" (pp. 6, 7). Again, most (71 percent) gave neighborhood considerations precedence. Neighborhood considerations were very important to the other respondents, as Coleman notes: "Almost invariably people who take the minority position, and give greater weight to house, hedge their choice by saying: 'the house is more important so long as the neighborhood isn't too bad.' They say, in effect: a neighborhood, even to be considered, must meet a certain minimal standard" (p. 7).

The finding that neighborhood considerations are given more weight than characteristics of the home is supported by Stegman's survey of 841 recent movers (1969). He found it to hold more strongly for suburban movers than central-city movers. "Seventy-seven percent of the suburban movers chose a very good neighborhood with a less desirable house while only 51 percent of the central city movers chose likewise" (p. 26).

## The Functions and Meaning of Homes

The main function of housing is the provision of living space. By this obvious statement we want to underline the utilitarian attitude many people have about their houses. As noted earlier, the main reason why people move is the lack of sufficient space. People also move when the household size declines and they are no longer willing to pay and care for the surplus space. However, space is not the only criteria for housing satisfaction. People also want attractive and convenient living space and will invest in decor, appliances, and arrangement.

Housing serves more than utilitarian needs. People become psychologically attached to their homes, and this attachment is one reason why moving can be so stressful. People become emotionally attached to their homes through a process of identification. According to Rainwater (1966), "The house acquires sacred character from its complex intertwining with the self and from the symbolic character it has as a representation of the family" (p. 23). The primary purpose of housing is shelter, not just from the elements, but also from human threats and surveillance. Behind its walls one can relax and drop the public self which one presents to the outside world. Since one can be oneself in one's home and in few places outside one's home, the walls of the house serves as a type of boundary for the self. In this way the home is usually an extension of the person.

The psychological functions of the home for people vary with their class and circumstances. The major differences have been described by Rainwater

(1966): "The poverty and cultural milieu of the lower class make the prime concern that of the home as a place of security" (p. 24). He had in mind the urban slum neighborhood where people are very much afraid. In contrast, in less dangerous neighborhoods the home serves other functions for the lower class, most of which involve inviting people into the home. On the other hand, the middle class uses the home more for self-expression than for security:

> When, as in the middle class, the battle to make the home a safe place has long been won, the home then has more central to its definition other functions which have to do with self-expression and self-realization. There is an elaboration of both the material culture within the home and of interpersonal relationships in the form of more complex rituals of behavior and more variegated kinds of interaction. Studies of the relationship between social class status and both numbers of friends and acquaintances as well as kinds of entertaining in the home indicated that as social status increases the home becomes a locale for a wider range of interactions [Rainwater, 1966: 27].

Montgomery (1967) identifies seven human needs which housing serves: (1) protection from nature and man, (2) need for a sense of place or rootedness, (3) need for a wholesome self-concept, (4) need to relate to others, (5) need for social and psychological stimulation, (6) creative or transcendental needs, and (7) need to fulfill values. The following comments briefly touch upon the relationship of housing with these needs. The physical structure of the house protects from nature, man, and noise. One's home inevitably provides a sense of place which generally deepens over time. On the need for a wholesome self-concept as it relates to housing, Montgomery quotes a report by Hudson Guild Neighborhood House (1960):

> Housing is/has become a subject of highly charged emotional content: a matter of strong feeling. It is the symbol of status, of achievement, of social acceptance. It seems to control, in large measure, the way in which the individual, the family, perceives him/itself and is perceived by others [Montgomery, 1967: 6].

Accordingly, improvement in a person's housing tends to improve his or her self-concept. Likewise, "uglifying" or diminishing one's housing has the opposite effect (see Mintz, 1959). The need to relate to others is served by housing, in Goffman's language (1959), by providing a setting which contains the props that people employ in managing the impressions they make on others. The need for social and psychological stimulation is well served by most well-furnished and roomy homes, but poorly served by slum housing or high-rise housing which cuts children off from easily accessible public play space. Montgomery says housing should serve creative or transcendental needs, but does not say how. Finally, the need to fulfill values is related to housing in many ways, including the dimensions of beauty, privacy, individuality, family-centeredness, and mental health.

It is especially important that impact assessors and urban planners understand the impact of housing changes on the self-concept. The following comments by Back (1962) suggest why:

> People frequently see the home as an outer shell of the self. Where a person lives and how he lives determine the view which he has of his place in the community, his role, his status, and his style of life. Consequently, a major change in housing conditions implies a major adjustment of a person's self-concept. He may not be ready to accept this change, even if objectively it could be only for the better. The social reformer who sees in rehousing a major advance in general social conditions is sometimes baffled by the resistance of slum dwellers who see in the proposed change a threat to their self-image [1962: 3, 4].

Fried uses the term "spatial identity" to refer to the spatial component of the self-concept. It is related to other components of the sense of ego identity, but in different ways for various categories of people. The differences for the working and middle classes are particularly relevant for impact assessments.

> It appears to us also that these feelings of being at home and of belonging are, in the working class, integrally tied to a *specific* place. We would not expect similar effects or, at least, effects of similar proportion in a middle-class area. Generally speaking, an integrated sense of spatial identity in the middle class is not as contingent on the external stability of place or as dependent on the localization of social patterns, interpersonal relationships, and daily routines. In these data, in fact, there is a marked relationship between class status and depth of grief [for relocating]; the higher the status, by any of several indices, the smaller the proportions of severe grief. It is primarily in the working class, and largely because of the importance of external stability, that dislocation from a familiar residential area has so great an effect on fragmenting the sense of spatial identity [Fried, 1963: 157].

Another way of looking at the inclusion of housing in the self-concept is suggested by Cooper in her article, "The House as Symbol" (1972). She argues that people unconsciously seek a symbol of self when choosing a residence. The overwhelming majority of people (85 percent in one survey) describe their ideal house as a free-standing, single-family house with yard. This infers territorial rights and enhances the self-image. The high-rise apartment is almost universally rejected for family living. However, regardless of the type of housing one moves into, over time the occupants make it a part of themselves and find it easier to be completely themselves in that space more than any other. Why?

> Probably because the personal space bubble which we carry around with us and which is an almost tangible extension of our self, expands to embrace the house we have designated as ours. As we become accustomed to, and lay claim to, this little niche in the world, we project something of ourselves onto its physical fabric. The furniture we install, the way we arrange it, the pictures we hang, the plants we buy and tend to, all are expressions of our image of ourselves, all are messages about ourselves that we want to convey back to ourselves, and to the few intimates that we invite into this, our house [Cooper, 1972: 31].

## Summary

A major impact area for public projects is the residential habitat including both home and neighborhood. This chapter has discussed how projects impact on residential habitats, how community cohesion is defined and measured, how people relate to their residential habitat, and how neighborhoods and homes function for their residents.

Projects impact on neighborhoods even as they are conceived in the planning stage through the anticipatory activities of many interested parties. In the land acquisition stage residents and activities are displaced. The construction stage involves many inconveniences and unpleasant physical effects. After construction the way the facility is used determines the types and extent of impacts.

The next issue examined is the definition and measurement of community cohesion. For SIA purposes community can be defined as "a social, demographic and territorial entity which has characteristic patterns of multiple services/facilities, solidarity, collective action, and modes of social interrelationship" (Sutton and Munson, 1976: 12). Cohesion can be defined as "the integration of group behavior as a result of social bonds, attractions, or 'forces' that hold members of a group in interaction over a period of time" (Theordorson and Theordorson, 1969: 57). Community cohesion refers to the amount and quality of social relations and interactions and to the identification of members to the community. Understood in this manner, community cohesion should be examined at the level of neighborhoods in urban/suburban areas and of towns or villages in rural areas.

The measurement of community cohesion requires a method for identifying neighborhood or community boundaries. The survey is the ideal method, but often it cannot be afforded. In rural areas distance from population centers is normally an acceptable principle for drawing the boundaries between population centers of the community of identification. In urban areas neighborhood boundaries are harder to ascertain without surveys. Boundaries can be placed at break points in statistical indicators for city blocks, or official neighborhood boundaries can be used.

Surveys should be used in the measurement of the extent of community or neighborhood cohesion. Commonly accepted measures of cohesion are based on levels of interaction, extent of intimate relationships, and degree of identification. The main indirect measure for community cohesion in urban/ suburban neighborhoods is length of residency. Its worst errors can be discovered and corrected by examining vacancy rates.

Basic to an understanding of the functions of neighborhoods is knowledge of the transformation of neighborhoods in the past century due to urbanization and transportation improvements. The psychological importance of neighborhoods has declined considerably except for a few isolated ethnic and/or cultural enclaves. Americanization, the separation of living quarters from workplaces, and urban redevelopment have contributed to this decline.

Although neighborhoods have declined in importance, they still provide a number of functions for their residents. The main functions of neighborhoods are social contact, mutual aid, security and social control, status or identification, and the socialization of children. Other functions include organizational affiliations, political participation, accessibility, recreational facilities, and local services. It must be recognized that modern middle-class urbanites have social networks which are not neighborhood-based and tend to use nonlocal facilities and services. The elderly, handicapped, children, ethnics, lower class, and housewives, however, tend to be more neighborhood-dependent. The preservation and strengthening of neighborhoods, therefore, should be an objective in the planning of public projects.

Some residents are deeply attached to their neighborhoods, while others are aloof. The literature on neighborhood satisfaction, neighborhood social ties, and the desire to stay or move is reviewed. Studies show that most people are satisfied with their neighborhood. Variations in degrees of satisfaction are related most strongly to the amount and intensity of social ties, length of residency, and home ownership. Other variables associated with neighborhood satisfaction are perceptions of neighborhood conditions, perceptions of neighbors, convenience, safety, and low levels of crime, noise, and traffic. Multivariate analysis points to the people of the neighborhood as having the greatest effect on neighborhood satisfaction; the quality and maintenance of the housing as the second most important factor.

The most important factor in accounting for the intimacy and frequency of neighborhood social ties is length of residency, which in turn is also a result of close ties with neighbors. It is also noted that (1) the lower class tends to have neighborhood-based social networks, (2) children generate neighborhood social ties and involvement, and (3) neighborhood social ties are weaker when wives are employed.

Neighborhood satisfaction and social ties strengthen residents' desire to stay in the neighborhood, as do length of residency and home ownership. Other factors which contribute to the desire to stay are house value and condition, quality of neighborhood conditions, and low fear of crime.

The desire to move to different housing results mainly from the desire to own a house and the need for more housing space. Other important factors affecting attachment to the home are the perceptions of its various physical and economic features and satisfaction with the neighborhood. In choosing a house, however, the characteristics of the house are less important than the characteristics of the neighborhood.

Finally, the functions and meaning of homes are reviewed. The main function of housing is living space, but housing also serves important psychological needs. People become emotionally attached to and psychologically identify with their homes. The home becomes a symbol of the self, and occupants use their homes to express themselves. The home also provides a sense of place, a sense of security, and a place to be natural and completely oneself.

*Chapter 4*

# DISPLACEMENT AND RELOCATION

"The highway department caused my husband's death. He died one month after the move." This statement was made by one of the 494 relocatees interviewed in a study by Perfater and Allen (1976). Nine other elderly respondents also attributed the death of their spouse to relocation or worrying about relocation (1976: 49). Although death may result from relocation, most people adjust well and some people would have moved anyway (one fifth of the population moves each year). Because of the severity of the impacts of relocation on some residents, however, it should be viewed as a major social impact of construction projects.

Some of the effects of relocation are psychological stress; disruption of social ties and established social patterns; time, energy, and money devoted to finding new housing; changes in housing conditions, tenure and costs; changes in location causing changes in accessibility to job, service, and activities, and changes in the economic situation of relocatees. As a general rule, relocated households are sufficiently compensated by the government for their property. Residents tend to move to better housing, and many renters become owners. Commuting distances to jobs, services, and activities increase somewhat, but the changes which are the most strongly negative are the psychological costs of moving and the disruption of social patterns. In the following section we examine the groups of residents which are the most adversely affected.

## Impacts of Displacement and
## Relocation on Residents

### HOUSING CHANGES WITH RELOCATION

The general pattern is for displaced households to upgrade their housing. Two processes account for this pattern. First, low-income households which are in substandard housing are supposed to be relocated by the government in standard housing. Second, the households generally choose more expensive housing when they relocate even if this means greater costs to themselves.

The major legislation governing relocation by federally sponsored projects is the Uniform Relocation Assistance and Real Property Acquisition Policies Act of 1970. This act not only requires just compensation for the real property taken and actual moving expenses, but also provides limited payments toward higher costs of replacement housing. We call these additive payments, which are not to exceed $15,000 for owners and $4000 for renters. They compensate homeowners for (1) the difference between the acquisition price for the taken property and the actual costs of comparable replacement housing that is decent, safe, and sanitary; (2) less favorable financing including higher interest rates, and (3) settlement costs. Additive payments provide funds to renters to cover (1) necessary increases in rents to obtain comparable housing that is decent, safe, and sanitary, and (2) a down payment for the purchase of housing and reasonable acquisition expenses. If more than $2000 is required for the down payment, the tenant must pay half of the excess up to $4000 with his own funds. The act also provides (1) relocation assistance advisory services, (2) the requirement of at least 90 days' written notice to vacate; and (3) a guarantee of replacement housing so that if none is available, it must be provided or the federally funded project may not proceed.

The provision of additive payments helps assure that displaced residents gain rather than lose in terms of housing quality and housing economics as a general rule. As administered by the Federal Highway Administration, 29,000 people were relocated in 1973 to make way for federal aid highways, and the additive payments averaged about $3800 for homeowners and $1000 for renters (Federal Highway Administration, 1974). These additive payments make relocation financially worthwhile for some people, especially the poor.

One purpose of the additive payments was to ensure that displaced residents in substandard housing would have the opportunity to relocate in decent, safe, and sanitary housing. Even prior to the 1970 act urban renewal programs sought to relocate residents in standard housing. The result was a decline in substandard housing for displaced residents, but not its elimination (Hartman, 1964). In certain projects, however, outstanding results were achieved. Thursz (1966) reports on the relocation associated with the renewal of Southwest Washington, D.C. A sample of relocatees were interviewed before and five years after relocation. Only 22.2 percent were in "good" housing before relocation compared with 85.7 percent afterward. Before relocation 46.9 percent were in housing "needing major repair, dilapidated or unfit for use" and none afterward.

Another optimistic assessment of housing upgrading is presented in a study of 165 households relocated as a result of highway location since the Uniform Relocation Assistance Act in several areas in Texas (Buffington et al., 1974). The study concluded:

> Because of the relocation program, about 80 percent of the relocatees moved into equal or better housing and neighborhoods. . . . One hundred percent of those whose original dwellings did *not* meet the safe, decent, and sanitary requirements of the relocation program moved into replacement dwellings that met these requirements. Only six percent of the relocatees thought that they had downgraded the quality of their housing [Buffington et al., 1974: 34-37].

All things considered, it seems that residents in substandard housing have a good probability of improving their housing when displaced by federally sponsored projects (on this point see also Key, 1967; House, 1970).

Renters constitute another group that has a good possibility of improving their housing situation. Many renters take advantage of the $4000 maximum additive payment provided for them by applying it to the down payment on the purchase of a house. In a study of 250 relocated households in Cleveland, 40 percent of previous renters became homeowners with this federal aid (Colony, 1973), and 50 percent of previous renters became homeowners in the Texas study (Buffington et al., 1974).

Forced to move by a federally sponsored project, many people upgrade their housing using their own funds. The average value of housing for displaced residents increased even before the government's policy of additive payments was enacted. Now, with additive payments, about 75 percent of those who bought housing costing over $20,000 added personal funds to the relocation payments according to the Cleveland study. Residents displaced from inexpensive homes in the Clevand study, however, did not use personal funds in the purchase of new housing. It is important to notice this difference because it indicates that very different purchasing psychologies are operating for the most and least affluent relocatees.

In a study by Buffington (1974), the economic value of the upgrading was substantial. The economic upgrading was borne partially by the government and partially by the relocatees. On the average, for owners the replacement housing cost was $5272 more than they were paid for their old housing. Of this amount, the government paid approximately 35 percent in housing supplements and the remainder was borne by the relocatee. Renters who became owners were given, on the average, $1665 for down payments. Their average down payment was $1971.

In the process of upgrading, most relocatees incurred larger monthly costs. The median increase was $43 for original owners and $53 for original renters. The median increase in monthly house payments was $40, with the remaining increase representing costs for transportation and utility expenses. In some cases these increases in costs can cause economic hardships. In a study by House (1970), the proportion of families "experiencing difficulty meeting costs increased from 9% to 18%" (1970: 77).

Perfater and Allen (1976) examined the housing changes of the 494 relocatees in their study. Their findings further substantiate that the relocation program results in housing upgrading and tenants becoming owners. On the latter point they found: "Whereas 45% of the displacees were renting at the time they were first contacted by the Department, only 20% remained tenants after relocation" (1976: 27). Perfater and Allen also found that the costs of the upgraded replacement housing were borne by both government and relocatees. Thus, persons who rented after relocation paid an average of $10.45 per month more than was judged necessary to obtain comparable housing. "Owners tended on the average to pay approximately $3,140 more for their replacement housing technically comparable to the original home" (1976: 29). This upgrading is partly reflected in the slightly larger size of the average replacement home. It should be noted that the housing upgrading also resulted in increased property taxes.

Burkhardt et al. (1976) reported on subjective comparisons of original and replacement housing. "Sixty percent of the respondents were more pleased with their new homes than the old, while the reverse was true for 27 percent" (1976: 34).

Probably the best study for analyzing the quality changes in housing for relocatees is the Texas study, from which Table 4.1 is taken. Quality upgrading is indicated strongly in the size of the living unit; number of bedrooms, number of bathrooms; and the decent, safe, and sanitary designation. Buffington (1974), in another study, found even greater upgrading: Of 171 urban locatees in two major urban areas in Texas, 74 percent had upgraded their housing in terms of market value or monthly rents and 73 percent had upgraded in terms of an index based on 12 selected physical characteristics. The change in the quality of housing was perceived by these relocatees as upgrading by 68 percent. In the earlier study 70 percent judged their housing to improve, 21 percent found no change, 10 percent felt it had worsened (Buffington et al. 1974: 22).

TABLE 4.1 Quantity Changes in Housing Based on Selected Characteristics of Original and Replacement Dwellings, by Original Tenure of Respondent

| Quantity Changes in Housing | Original Owner | | | Original Tenant | | |
|---|---|---|---|---|---|---|
| | Up-graded | Down-graded | No Change | Up-graded | Down-graded | No Change |
| | Number | | | | | |
| Specific Characterisitcs[a] | | | | | | |
| Type of housing | 3 | 6 | 86 | 19 | 3 | 48 |
| Type of construction | 22 | 11 | 62 | 14 | 13 | 43 |
| Size of living unit | 48 | 24 | 23 | 49 | 14 | 7 |
| Number of rooms | 33 | 21 | 41 | 32 | 12 | 26 |
| Number of bedrooms | 24 | 13 | 58 | 36 | 6 | 28 |
| Number of bathrooms | 21 | 0 | 74 | 21 | 0 | 49 |
| DS&S designation[b] | 18 | 0 | 77 | 6 | 4 | 60 |
| Combined Characteristics[c] | 55 | 21 | 19 | 45 | 13 | 12 |

a. Those who moved into a more permanently constructed, larger dwellings upgraded their housing. Those who moved into a less permanently constructed, smaller dwellings downgraded. Those who moved into a dwelling of the same construction, size as original dwelling made no quantity changes in housing.
b. DS&S stands for "decent, safe, and sanitary." The frequency is determined by asking each respondent about the condition of the original and replacement dwelling and by calculating the habitable floor space requirements for the household. The habitable floor space was considered to be 80% of the exterior dimensions of mobile homes and 70% for all other dwellings. For a dwelling to be DS&S, the first occupant had to have at least 150 square feet of habitable floor space and at least 100 square feet (70 for mobile homes) for each additional occupant.
c. Respondents who upgraded more specific characteristics than they downgraded had accomplished overall quantity upgrading their housing. If the reverse was true, they had downgraded their housing on a quantity basis. If neither was true, they had made no change in their housing.
SOURCE: Buffington et al. (1974: 20).

Relocatees tend to improve the quality of their housing and also the status of their neighborhoods (1974: 52). These outcomes of forced relocation are identical to some of the reasons why people voluntarily move, as discussed in Chapter 2. Since about 20 percent of the population move every year, some displaced residents were eager to move to a better habitat before the acquisition of their property, so the project simply hastens their move and enables some upgrading through the additive payments.

While the general rule for households displaced by projects is to improve their housing, two negative factors should be noted. First, people who think they may be displaced allow their housing to deteriorate while awaiting acquisition. Often the waiting period is several years. If the wait is long enough to allow noticeable deterioration, the compensation will be based on a low assessment and will be disappointing to the relocatees. This pattern became a major source of dissatisfaction with a relocation program in Lynchberg, Virginia, according to personal communication with Michael A. Perfater of the Virginia Highway Research Council. In Lynchberg a highway was planned nearly a decade before being built, and housing seriously deteriorated in the highway corridor.

The second negative factor is that in a tight housing market the condemnation of sound housing must worsen the housing market in the short run. Because of the additive payments the relocatees are not adversely affected as a group, but other home seekers will be adversely affected because of inflation in the housing market (Sale and Steinberg, 1971).

## ECONOMIC IMPACTS OF RELOCATION

The major economic impacts for relocated residents are the higher cost of their new housing on the average and the additive payments discussed above. In both the Texas and Cleveland studies, replacement housing cost owners about $5000 more on the average than did previous housing. Renters also increased their housing costs either by renting more expensive housing or by buying houses which could rent for more than their previous housing. In the Texas study, renters increased their monthly payments by $21 on the average (Buffington et al., 1974: 76). It should be noted that the federal government will pay supplemental rent payments for only four years, after which time some households may be forced back into housing with lower rents.

The larger housing costs, monthly payments, and the additive payments are the major economic changes resulting from relocation; however, many additional small economic changes occur, and these generally increase costs. Since the houses are generally larger they cost more to heat, light, cool, clean, and maintain. The increase in labor for housework and maintenance are also increased economic costs. Furthermore, since commuting distances are somewhat greater, transportation and utility costs increased $8 per month on the average (Buffington, 1973). Except for transportation costs, the increase in expenses is associated with improved living conditions. The overall effect on quality of life of the increased housing expenses is unclear, however, because other consumption must be curtailed by an equal amount. However, the fact that the residents themselves decide to incur these extra costs suggests that they have positive overall effects—that is, higher marginal utilities than competing consumption desires.

Moving expenses can be neglected in assessing economic impacts, because generally they are adequately compensated by the government (Buffington et al., 1974; Colony, 1971). Of course, time costs of obtaining, moving into, and decorating new housing are not compensated and are important negative impacts of displacement.

Finally, displacement for highways probably increases relocatees' net worth on the average. Although too little data are available, and one can question whether the existing studies sufficiently accounted for what would have been the normal appreciation of previous housing, nevertheless, it seems that net worth generally increases modestly because of relocation. The average additive payment of $4800 for owners and $1100 for renters in 1973 by the Federal Highway Administration seems to be more than compensatory and, therefore, contributed to an increase in net worth. For example, the Texas study of the displacement of 170 households from low-value housing calculated that 93 percent of relocatees increased their net worth, and the average change in net worth was +$1485 (Buffington, 1973).

People's perceptions inevitably deviate somewhat from reality. Only 22 percent of the sample relocatees in the Texas low-valued housing study felt they were better off financially, while 38 percent felt they were worse off (Buffington, 1973). The perceptions of relocatees in the general Texas study were somewhat more positive: In judging their overall financial position, 29 percent claimed improvement, while 27 percent claimed worsening (Buffington et al., 1974: 32).

## TRANSPORTATION IMPACTS OF RELOCATION

One of the obvious criteria for selecting housing is the commuting time and distance to jobs and other destinations including social visits. When people are forced to move, they may have to commute longer distances. Partly to minimize this impact, most displaced residents try to relocate close to their original homes as long as they can reside in neighborhoods of equal or higher status (Buffington et al., 1974; Cooper, 1964). For example, in the Cleveland study, six out of 10 displaced households that were located for interview relocated within a mile of the proposed expressway (Colony, 1973: 57), and the median move in Key's (1967) urban renewal sample was 1.1 miles, excluding the 7.3 percent who moved out of town. Also, Burkhardt et al. (1976) found that only 14 percent of a sample of relocatees from six different communities moved more than 15 miles. In contrast, in Thursz' study (1966) of the renewal of Southwest Washington D.C., relocatees scattered widely (96 families interviewed were found in 37 different census tracts), and the majority of "those employed had to cope with greater distances and more difficult transportation problems" (1966: 50).

Many trips are to stores and services to which customers have no personal attachment, and they readily substitute stores and services available in their new neighborhood. Other services involve very special relationships based on loyalty, trust, warmth, and unique knowledge which take time to develop. These relationships are hard to replace; they have a low degree of substitutability. People normally are willing to incur greater commuting costs to maintain the same job, doctor, dentist, church, and social relations.

Using data from the general Texas study, we present in Table 4.2 the percentage of relocatees who say they commute greater or lesser distances for various types of trips since moving. There is a definite tendency for relocatees to commute longer distances, after relocating, to work, relatives, friends, church, and the doctor. We assume that, as a general rule, these trips were to the same locations as before relocation. In addition, the travel distance was greater for a number of the more substitutable destinations (shopping, banking, moviegoing). The explanation stated (but not demonstrated) in the text is that relocatees tended to move to the suburbs, and shopping trips tend to be farther in the suburbs.

The general Cleveland study found similar travel patterns (Buffington, 1973: 37, 56). About twice as many relocated heads of households commuted greater distances to work, and more relocatees traveled greater distances to church.

The general Cleveland study also provides data on the extent to which people change jobs and churches when relocated by a government project. As

TABLE 4.2   Percentage of a Sample of 165 Relocatees Using Specified Facilities Claiming to Travel Greater, Less, or About the Same Distance to the Facility after Relocation than Before

|  | Type of Facility | Distance to Facility Claimed to be: | | | Ratio of |
|---|---|---|---|---|---|
|  |  | Greater | Less | About the Same | Greater/Less |
| (A) | Involving Less Substitutable Relationships |  |  |  |  |
|  | (1) Place of employment | 44 | 23 | 33 | 1.9 |
|  | (2) Homes of relatives and friends | 33 | 17 | 50 | 1.9 |
|  | (3) Church building | 36 | 27 | 38 | 1.3 |
|  | (4) Doctor's office | 37 | 19 | 44 | 1.9 |
| (B) | Involving More Substitutable Relationships |  |  |  |  |
|  | (1) Shopping center (most used) | 44 | 24 | 32 | 1.8 |
|  | (2) Movie house | 29 | 16 | 55 | 1.8 |
|  | (3) Bank | 48 | 18 | 34 | 2.7 |
|  | (4) Schools | 30 | 44 | 27 | .7 |
|  | (5) Park (most used) | 26 | 28 | 45 | .9 |

SOURCE: Buffington et al. (1974: 72, 73).

many as 32 percent of relocatees changed jobs since relocation, but only five percent of those who changed jobs (less than two percent of relocatees) did so because their old jobs were too far from their new housing. As one would expect, relocation had a greater impact on the church attended. About the same percentage of church attendees changed congregations as heads of households changed jobs, but relocation was the cause of most of the changes in congregations. Six out of 10 relocatees who attend church attended the same church after relocation as before. In addition, most relocatees continued their memberships after relocation in other social activities. Only seven percent of relocatees reported dropping out of clubs, unions, or organizations when they moved (Buffington, 1973: 56).

## SOCIAL AND PSYCHOLOGICAL IMPACTS
## OF RELOCATION

Not many events are more distressful than being forced out of one's home. Against one's will one's entire life is changed by the move to new surroundings. All of the ordinary daily routines will be changed, even if only slightly, and many close and friendly relationships will be affected. In urban areas it generally turns out that life after the move is almost as enjoyable as before the move, but this cannot be known beforehand, and there is the possibility that irreversible harm will be done to important social relationships and favored behavior patterns. Some people suffer considerably from relocation, especially when it is forced. In other words, moving involves risks that are fertile grounds for fear. Consequently, news of displacement is "viewed as a crisis" by many relocatees (Burdge and Ludtke, 1973) and is viewed negatively by a majority (Thursz, 1966; Kemp, 1965; Johnson and Burdge, 1974; Fellman and Brandt, 1970; Colony, 1972). In an in-depth study of 10 displaced households in Vermont, "interviewees without exception spoke of this final realization that they had to move as severely traumatic" (Institute of Public Administration, 1973).

The reasons for moving are important to the way people anticipate the move. Voluntary and forced relocations have quite different psychological impacts. If the head of the household accepts a better job which necessitates moving, he is under psychological pressure to be optimistic about the consequences of the move. The rest of the family is also under some psychological pressure to "look on the bright side." According to the theory of cognitive dissonance, the above description should be the general rule; but many exceptions are to be expected. For example, some children might resent being forced to leave their friends, will blame the head of the household, and will want to make him or her feel guilty about causing them to suffer.

The important observation to be drawn from the above discussion is that in most cases of voluntary relocation at least one powerful member of the family has an "interest" in moving, and the family's anticipation of the move will be more positive because of this fact. Construction projects, however, cause forced relocations which have fewer psychological forces countering the natural fears of the results of moving. The period before moving, therefore, can have significant negative effects in terms of distress.

For some people the distress will be great and the postmove grief will be severe. Marc Fried (1963) tells of the widespread grief on the part of people relocated from the West End of Boston because of urban renewal in an article entitled "Grieving for a Lost Home." Among the 250 women interviewed two years later, 26 percent reported still feeling sad or depressed and another 20 percent reported a somewhat shorter period of sadness or depression (six months to two years). Men were somewhat less distressed; 38 percent of them reported one of these two responses. Perfater and Allen (1976) also found some cases of intense grief due to displacement, and suggested that the deaths of several elderly may have been due, in part, to displacement. Thursz (1966) found that 35 percent were "very sorry they had to move" even five years after moving.

The West End of Boston was not a typical community—it was a working-class neighborhood in which many residents had lived most of their lives. Relocation meant separation from familiar and valued settings and the close social ties experienced in these settings. In this and many other working-class areas the neighborhood is considered an extension of the home. This attitude is different from the typical middle-class attitude to physical location: The middle class has less local attachment, is less oriented to living their lives in the same familiar neighborhood, and is more oriented to moving to better jobs and better neighborhoods. The long-time residents of stable working-class neighborhoods do not have the psychological mobility of the middle class. The social and psychological loss from forced relocation often is also great in rural areas where farmers have a strong attachment to their homesteads (Burdge and Johnson, 1973; Burdge and Ludtke, 1973; Johnson and Burdge, 1974, Napier, 1973).

Several studies of relocation focus on changes in social patterns and interaction rates. Mogey et al. (1971) found that the elderly greatly reduced contact with relatives and friends and reduced satisfaction with neighbors and neighborhoods after relocation. Burkhardt et al. (1976) focused primarily on neighborhood interaction factors; a number of their findings point to some of the social costs of displacement. First, they found that neighboring declined with relocation. "The relocatees reported a substantial drop in neighborly assistance after the move" (p. 461), and "after relocation, the mean number of homes visited dropped from more than four to just over one" (pp. 46, 48). Second, "a substantial decrease in the use of neighborhood facilities occured after relocation" (p. 48). Third, participation in neighborhood organizations declined. "After relocation, the proportion of the sample participating in neighborhood-oriented clubs did not change significantly, but the number of clubs people belonged to decreased" (p. 49). Fourth, "there was a substantial drop in identification with the neighborhood as a place to live after relocation" (p. 50). At the same time, fewer respondents considered their neighborhood the best or better than most for persons like themselves when interviewed after relocation than when interviewed before relocation. It should be noted that this lower satisfaction with neighborhood in the new location does not emerge on the direct question, "How do you like this neighborhood in comparison with your previous neighborhood?" Fifty-one percent of the relocatees who changed neighborhoods said "better" and only 25 percent said "worse."

Burkhardt et al. also reported that "after relocation, the percent of persons with all or most of their friends in the neighborhood declined dramatically, from 23 percent to 8 percent, while the percent of persons with none of their friends in the neighborhood increased substantially, from 27 percent to 43 percent" (1976: 55).

Perfater and Allen (1976) analyzed some of the social effects of relocation for their 494 respondents and discovered some unusual findings. First, they examined the degree of satisfaction with the respondent's new home. "Fifty-eight percent of the respondents preferred their replacement dwellings and 23% preferred their original one" (p. 41). Relocatees who had lived in their original dwelling more than 20 years were just as likely to prefer their new dwelling as were relocatees who had lived in their original dwelling a shorter time. This finding is surprising because long-term residents adjust less well generally to relocation (Buffington et al., 1974; Perfater, 1972; Fried, 1963).

Another aspect of the social impact of relocation examined by Perfater and Allen addressed attitudes toward new and old neighborhoods and social contacts which the two neighborhoods provided:

> Thirty-six percent of the respondents preferred their previous neighborhood, 35% preferred their current one. . . . Those who preferred their old neighborhood cited neighbors and access to conveniences as the things they missed the most. These same individuals, when asked what was different about their new neighborhood, most frequently mentioned incompatibility with neighbors and environmental difference (i.e., noise, shade, dust, and dirt, woods, clean air, etc). From responses to these questions it appears that neighborhood satisfaction is closely related to neighbor satisfaction. When asked what effect moving had on friendships made in the old neighborhood, almost 50% of the respondents said that at least some friendships had been ended. When asked the extent to which new neighborhood friends had been made, 87% of the respondents reported that they had made at least some [1976: 43].

Thursz (1966) studied 98 relocatees five years after they were displaced from a slum by the renewal of Southwest Washington, D.C. Few relocated in the same area indicating that the disruption of social patterns was large for almost the entire sample.

> The majority of respondents indicate that they have maintained contact with old neighbors from Southwest, even though five years have passed (51.1 percent), and 42.3 percent indicate that some of their old neighbors have moved into the same building or close-by dwellings. In most cases, this represents only a single family. When asked specifically to indicate the pattern of contact between them and their former friends from Southwest, only 4.2 percent indicate that they maintain frequent and reciprocal contact with former neighbors [Thursz, 1966: 54].

The lack of close ties to old neighbors is surprising in view of the fact that almost two-thirds of the respondents had lived in Southwest for 10 or more years.

A majority in Thursz's sample improved their housing, and most rated other physical aspects of their new neighborhoods as superior to their old neighborhoods. In contrast, most rated the social aspects of their new neighborhoods as inferior. Only 18.6 percent agreed and 41.2 percent disagreed with the statement, "The people who live in this area are better neighbors." Only 26.8 percent agreed and 42.3 percent disagreed with "There is more neighborhood feeling here." Surprisingly, the old slum was considered safer than the new neighborhoods: Only 14.4 percent agreed and 54.6 percent disagreed with "It is safer for people to be out alone after dark in this neighborhood." Thursz also found very high levels of anomie and low levels of social integration among the relocatees. Five years after relocation, 26 percent "indicated that they had not made a single new friend in the neighborhood" (p. 54). Thursz developed the following thesis: "No matter how dirty, inadequate, and unsanitary the old Southwest was, it was also *home* for families that had been there for a long time. Under these circumstances, relocation tends to improve the physical conditions while worsening the social conditions. For many, the loss was deep and continues to be felt" (pp. 100-101).

In conclusion, the negative social and psychological effects of forced relocation are considerable and long-term for some relocatees but minor and short-term for others. It is not clear whether these negative social impacts are generally greater in the long run than any housing and economic benefits which may accrue to relocatees. About four years after relocation, more respondents were unhappy about moving than happy in Colony's study (1973), and five years after, about as many disliked as liked having to move in

Thursz's study (1966). On the other hand, 50 percent of respondents were mildly or very pleased with the entire relocation experience, and 42 percent were mildly or very upset in Buffington et al.'s study (1974). In addition, it is not known how well answers to survey questions measure the amount of the net negative or positive impacts of relocation.

## OTHER IMPACTS OF DISPLACEMENT AND RELOCATION

Public projects affect the sensitive relationships between the public and the state and federal governments. Governmental decisions about large construction projects are exceptional government actions in the extent to which they intrude into people's lives. They force people from their homes. They involve government coercion which is exercised through the right of eminent domain. Compensation is paid, but displacement is still coercion. The well-being of individuals is sacrificed for the good of the community. If the government seeks the good will of the people, it must be judicious in the use of this power. It must minimize and justify this use of force. Environmental impact statements, hearings, and citizen participation by letters, formal statements, meetings, and demonstrations are means for preventing grievous errors and for justifying the fairness of the final decision to the public. They are outgrowths of the increasing concern of the public over the impacts of government actions and the ways government decisions are made.

The impact of residential displacement for public projects on the government/public relationship depends largely on how the government proceeds. Adverse impacts are reduced when the government adequately informs the public, seriously considers a full set of possible alternatives (including the no-build alternative), allows sufficient time for relocation, is prompt and generous in relocation payments, and is represented by officials with helpful and concerned manners.

A significant impact of public projects are the public participation activities which they arouse. The fact that people are to be displaced often mobilizes community or neighborhood residents to public actions in opposition to the proposed placement of the facility. This impact has both positive and negative aspects. On the positive side, public participation strengthens democratic institutions, provides necessary information to government planners, instills in government personnel a greater sensitivity to the needs and desires of the public, trains people in the practice of public participation, and, when the government listens to the people, increases the loyalty of the public to the democratic form of government. On the negative side, public participation uses up many person-hours that people would prefer devoting to other activities, generally increases the costs of projects, causes greater delays, and sometimes prevents projects which would greatly benefit the larger community.

Last to be considered are the effects of displacement on the community. Each acquired property was a source of tax revenue which the county and/or city loses. The project itself might add to the tax base, as in urban renewal, or enhance the value of the surrounding area, as in the case of highways outside of central cities (Gamble et al., 1973; Federal Highway Administration, 1974). These positive impacts on taxes may outweigh the negative impacts of displacement on taxes. (Parenthetically, we observe that highways in central cities tend not to have a positive impact on property values; see Buffington, 1964, and Golden, 1968.) Another impact of displacement on the community is a tightening of the housing market and stimulation of the home building industry if the stock of suitable housing is noticeably reduced. Finally, the induced public participation may cause disruptions and antagonisms which reduce community pride and cause problems for the maintenance of public order.

## Displacement and Special Groups

The general rule is for displacees to adjust well to relocation, but there are many exceptions—especially the poor, elderly, long-time residents, women, children, and minority groups. In this section, the reasons why these groups suffer most from relocation are presented.

### THE POOR

Until recently, government agencies favored locating projects in poor rather than rich neighborhoods. The economics of acquisition and the political influence of the rich largely account for this bias. If displacement hardships were the critical consideration, however, the bias would be in the opposite direction. The poor are likely to be more dependent upon the social life and services of their immediate neighborhoods, and, therefore, suffer greater disruption of social ties upon moving (Cline, 1963). If only a few households are displaced, they probably can relocate nearby and continue life as before. Large-scale relocation from a poor neighborhood, however, can cause much distress and suffering, as in the case of the redevelopment of the West End of Boston discussed above.

In some poor neighborhoods strong social networks are found. An example is Brookline-Elm, described here by Fellman and Brandt (1970):

> 33% of our sample visit one or more relatives outside the immediate family almost every day, and 51% spend time with relatives at least once a week. Most striking is the physical proximity of these relatives; 60% of our sample have relatives in Cambridge, and 46%—almost half—have relatives within what they consider walking distance.

(Twenty-three percent of our sample have relatives outside the immediate family on the same block or in the same dwelling.)

Not untypical is the case of a woman whose widowed mother lives next door, whose married daughter lives two blocks away, and whose son lives near enough to stop each morning to see his mother on the way to work. In contrast to the mobile, isolated, nuclear family more common in the upper middle class, for working class people such as live in Brookline-Elm, the neighborhood itself provides the most important experiences of their daily lives.

In the same vein, it is significant that about sixty percent of our respondents report having friends within walking distance, with whom they get together at least once a week. Fifty percent of the residents do not have cars; even in the car-owning families the women are stuck at home during the day, as few families own more than one car. For people like these, relocation even two or three miles away is not a minor inconvenience but a major blow to their emotional stability and social life [1970: 287-288].

Obviously, Brookline-Elm is not only a poor neighborhood but also a stable one, so that length of residency accounts for much of the hardships of relocating. However, it is also a fact that the poor are more house-oriented and neighborhood-oriented, while the rich and upper middle class is more oriented to the larger community and the cosmopolitan society than is the lower class.

Havinghust and Feigenbaum's study (1959) in Kansas City described how the leisure style of the lower class centers on the home and on the immediate neighborhood. In addition, working-class families are more attached to their houses than are middle-class families, because they are more likely to have invested their own time in repairs and improvements.

Not always are the poor attached to their neighborhoods. Some poor neighborhoods are terrifying and drab places to live. In some of these dangerous neighborhoods, the residents are able to work out a surprising amount of social control and order, as in the Addams area of Chicago (Suttles, 1968). Nevertheless, some residents are eager for almost any way out of the neighborhood. Wolf and Lebeaux (1967) found very little emotional attachment of residents to the neighborhood in a Detroit slum, and the same finding is reported by Cagle and Deutscher (1970) in their study of urban renewal in Syracuse. In summary, the poor often are more negatively affected by displacement than wealthier groups with more resources and a more mobile lifestyle, but sometimes the poor are eager to move and view displacement as an opportunity. In the latter case they may be greatly benefited by relocation due to the additive payments which may be required to get them into decent housing.

## LONG-TERM AND ELDERLY RESIDENTS

It is obvious that long-time residents are more attached to their homes and neighborhoods than recent residents, and all studies confirm this assumption (see Chapter 2). It may be difficult for government officials and planners who are members of the more geographically mobile middle class to understand the depth of feeling that longterm residents have for their home and neighborhoods. For example, one woman said in public that even if she won a million dollars in the Irish Sweepstakes she would not move from her very modest home. The reason she gave was: "I sleep in the same bedroom where I was born" (Fellman and Brandt, 1970: 286).

Another group which has considerable difficulty adjusting to relocation, according to numerous studies, are the elderly (Buffington et al., 1974; Colony, 1973; Burkhardt et al. 1976; Niebanck, 1965; Niebanck and Yessian, 1968). They adjust less well to changes generally, but especially relocation. They do not make new friends easily and some elderly relocatees remain relatively isolated socially in their new neighborhood for the rest of their lives. Colony (1971: 64) found that 29 percent of relocatees age 61 and over had made no new friends in their new location several years after moving. Only five percent of relocatees age 20 to 30 had made no new friends.

Perfater and Allen (1976) paid special attention to the experience of the elderly in their study of relocatees. From their data we calculate that 53 percent of the respondents under 60 years of age said they had been upset by the impending move compared with 69 percent of those over 60 years old. They also found that the elderly made fewer friends in the new neighborhood than younger relocatees. Perhaps their most important finding, however, came from some unsolicited comments. "Ten of the elderly respondents attributed the death of a spouse to the overwork involved in trying to make the replacement housing equal to that which they had before" (1976: 48). Some comments by the elderly are revealing:

> My husband had suffered 2 or 3 heart attacks prior to contact by the highway department. I felt relocation killed him.
>
> I lost my husband by death due to his worrying where we were going and in moving our property.
>
> Relocation was too much for my husband.
>
> I hope when you have people move you don't expect old people to jump up and down. I've been down sick ever since I moved [pp. 58, 59].

Pastalan (1973) also found that forced relocation increased the death rates of the elderly.

The elderly build up intricate and fragile networks around themselves to meet their physical and social needs.

Forced by physical limitations and low incomes to rely heavily upon those living nearby, the elderly tend to spin a cocoon of social relationships revolving about local community organizations, which enmesh and protect their fragile existence. . . . Though this symbiosis is not universal, relocation processes tend to uproot and destroy whatever social and communal relationships may have developed among the elderly unless those among them can, if they so desire, move as a complete social unit [Schorr, 1975: 109].

A sensitive description of how the elderly—especially those with low incomes—experience relocation is presented by Niebanck (1965: 135-144). They lack an important opportunity for making new friends since they no longer work. They tend to live in older parts of urban areas which are also the types of areas that are candidates for urban renewal. However, these areas are also well suited to maintenance of meaningful long-standing friendships. "As age increases, these ties become stronger and the willingness to move is sharply reduced" (Niebanck, 1965: 135). Often these neighborhood friendships are enriched by a common ethnic background in an ethnic neighborhood.

The elderly are much more neighborhood-dependent than are younger adults. Niebanck reports on one study where "it was found that the great majority of [their] primary friendships were located within the neighborhood" (p. 136). They are also more dependent on convenient services which older neighborhoods provide.

The locational advantages of older areas are quite obvious, in view of . . . the needs for services, . . . many of which can be best provided in central locations. In appearance, many older areas seem to be entirely unsatisfactory for urban living, but in terms of locational characteristics they are superb. Each neighborhood usually has its own complement of stores, services, and clubs and institutional facilities, and it is situated in close proximity to hospitals, public facilities, and the unique advantages of downtown. The downtown business district has more than mere facilities to make it attractive. There is pleasure in seeing people, watching movement, experiencing the rhythm of the urban world, and feeling for the moment involved in more of life's dimensions than is really possible at any age [Niebanck, 1965: 136-137].

The elderly are also emotionally dependent upon the neighborhood for familiar reassuring surroundings. "Unfamiliar surroundings breed withdrawal and its concomitant loneliness and depression" (1965: 137).

Unfortunately, most of the attractive features of the old neighborhood for the elderly are weakened if the neighborhood is dangerous. The elderly must be secure enough to venture forth and use the neighborhood. At times, relocation of the elderly from dangerous areas is merciful.

## OTHER GROUPS

Finally, the special hardship of displacement for some other groups will be briefly outlined. Women, children, and minority groups suffer more from relocation than do men, adults, and white native Americans. Women and children are more dependent on people in the neighborhood for close friend-ships and repeated social interactions than are men and adults. Furthermore, the activities of women and children are much more limited to the house and the neighborhood. Hence, they have more to lose by moving. On the other hand, children make friends easily. Although they often lose all of their friends when they move, they recover from the loss the most quickly. Minority groups also tend to be more dependent on the neighborhood than white native Americans. The churches, clubs, bars, hang-outs, and recreation areas in which minorities feel at home are usually concentrated in one or a few neighborhoods. Unless the displaced minority households are able to relocate in the same neighborhood, they are likely to be removed from the services which are oriented toward that minority and the social networks in which they are completely accepted.

It is important to have a balanced view of relocation. One might underesti-mate its negative effects upon observing that most relocatees adjust well and many improve their housing and gain economically from additive payments. On the other hand, one might overestimate its negative effects upon observing some displacees who suffer great social and psychological loss. Furthermore, some construction projects destroy neighborhoods which provide people with extremely supportive, locally based social networks. Others destroy neighbor-hoods that few would miss, either because they were horrible environments or because the residents had geographically scattered intimate social relation-ships. Assessors should recognize the great variance in the effects of reloca-tion on residents and be able to predict the extent of suffering which relocation causes with a fair degree of accuracy. They can be guided by the general rule that the long-term residents and the elderly are affected the most negatively by relocation and that the poor, women, children, and minority persons may also suffer more than the average relocatee.

*Chapter 5*

# COMMUNITY RELOCATION

Sometimes a government project necessitates the relocation of an entire community. The generalizations in the previous chapter about forced relocation of residents may also apply when a community moves to a new site. However, community relocation has many unique aspects and needs to be studied in its own right. We have located very few studies of relocated communities, and will report in this chapter on two cases of reestablishing communities which were displaced by reservoirs. The first is a retroactive study of Hill, New Hampshire, which was relocated by the Corps of Engineers. The second is the account of the relocation of three communities around Arrow Lakes by the British Columbia Hydro and Power Authority as told by the employee of BC Hydro and Power who was responsible for resettlement planning.

**Hill, New Hampshire—
A Town That Moved Itself**

### THE RELOCATION STORY

The story of the relocation of Hill, New Hampshire, a town of almost 500 residents in 1940, is told by Adler and Jansen (1978). Severe flooding occurred in 1927, 1936, and 1938 along the Connecticut and Merrimack

Rivers which spurred New Hampshire to press the federal government for a comprehensive flood control plan. The Corps of Engineers studied the problem and proposed two reservoirs for flood protection along the Merrimack. One was the Franklin Falls Reservoir which was to flood Hill. As the plans for the reservoir moved ahead, the people of Hill discussed what they would do. Hill was a declining town with little remaining employment; thus, it made sense for the remaining businesses and residents to move to other communities. A different sentiment evolved, however, behind the leadership of the town's three selectmen and the support of "Hill's older, more established residents, who were distressed not only about the idea of giving up their homes, but also feared losing their friends and community" (1978: 21).

Fred Clark, Director of the New Hampshire Planning and Development Commission, presented a plan for building a new, carefully planned community to replace Hill and thereby keep the community together. An overwhelming majority of the townspeople in attendance accepted the idea. It would be much more economical than unplanned resettlement in a new site which would burden the town with high costs for providing services such as roads, sewers, water, and sidewalks. However, it would require cooperation and leadership. Both were forthcoming, and Hill successfully resettled. Not everyone moved to the new town, but most of the older, long-term residents did.

> In all, there were 88 residents whose land was purchased by the Corps of Engineers. Approximately 46 of these purchased lots in the new village. Some of those who did not relocate left on their own volition. They worked in nearby communities and moved for convenience, or felt Hill was a dying town and would never survive economically. Others, primarily the young, who had rented and had no capital to finance a house, or the old, who felt the strain of starting over again was more than they could handle, had no other option available than to leave and settle elsewhere [Adler and Jansen, 1978: 23].

The successful resettlement of Hill depended on a number of factors, some of which are not likely to occur in other community relocation situations. First, the new town would need an economic base. Fortunately, two small industries, the crutch and the needle factories, agreed to relocate with the town. Most of the remaining labor force commuted to nearby workplaces. The dam construction also provided work for about 15 men for a time. Second, an attractive site at a reasonable price had to be obtained for the new town. Fortunately, "the farsighted selectmen, on their own initiative, bought options on all three possible sites for the new village. . . . This was to prevent speculators from coming in and taking advantage of the situation by buying the future sites and selling lots for a large profit" (1978: 23). Third, leadership, consensus, and cooperation are required for such a project. The three selectmen had a good understanding of the situation and provided leadership in obtaining state aid and legislation, purchasing the site, and orchestrating the move. In addition, cooperation and consensus were excellent. Finally, a number of financial resources were required. Individuals partly financed their new homes from the Corps payments for their old homes, but many also needed mortgage money. Local banks in Franklin and Bristol were unwilling to write mortgages for Hill because the risks were high. However, the banks in Concord would give mortgages to Hill residents. The town also needed additional financing: It lost much of its tax base when the Corps took 30 percent of the assessed taxable property in Hill for the reservoir; but the state reimbursed the town for lost tax value. The state also arranged a $50,000 loan at one percent annual interest for Hill to purchase land and build streets and public buildings while awaiting the settlement for town property in the old village. The water system was financed with a $40,000 bond. These actions were made possible when the State legislature raised the debt limitations for Hill at the request of the selectmen.

## ASSESSMENT OF THE IMPACTS OF RELOCATION

What is the impact of community relocation as revealed in the story of Hill? It must be recognized that the experience of Hill is unique in many ways. It benefited from good planning, leadership, community participation, and community solidarity. These factors minimized costs and the negative impacts and made the moving experience a more positive one. Hill also benefited from state and federal help. It is hoped that some of the favorable circumstances of Hill can be duplicated in future community relocations with similar results.

Economically, the town did very well and individuals did reasonably well. The original settlement offer by the Corps to the town was rejected, and the final court settlement awarded by the courts nine years later was even less in constant dollars, so the town felt it was not properly compensated for its lost property. Nevertheless, Hill benefited economically from the move: The main benefit came from the state revenue subsidies to offset the loss of tax revenues. These payments were generous, based on generous assessments, and full compensation was extended 13 years past when about one-half of the lost tax base was returned to the tax books. Furthermore: "The state's payment of taxes for buildings in the old village, which were nearly all replaced in the new village by 1950, was like adding another $200,000 to the town's tax base" (1978: 53). Hill also benefited from $85,000 worth of construction of streets, sidewalks, and landscaping by a U.S. government WPA project. Finally, the total street area of the village had been reduced from two and one-half miles to one and one-quarter miles, which reduced the costs of maintenance and snow ploughing. On the negative side, some of the economic base of the town was lost. "The dowel factory moved away, and the stores, shops, restaurants, etc. were lost during this move. Only one general store remained" (1978: 47).

Since the 1940 compensation procedures of the Corps were far below the generous provisions of the Uniform Relocation Assistance Act of 1970, individuals were not offered generous settlements, nor were moving expenses paid. However, since Hill was a declining town, the residents could not have sold their property for much on the open market if the reservoir were not built. The relocation resulted in a halt in the decline in property values. The Corps was also generous in allowing owners to buy back their houses for salvage for a minimal fee. Many residents used old windows, doors, and other materials extensively in their new homes. Ten homes were repurchased and moved to the new town, although the savings over a new home were small. In addition, fire insurance rates were less for the relocatees because fire hydrants were better placed. Finally, the state revenue subsidies helped keep property taxes low for many years. Overall, individuals may have come out about even economically.

The noneconomic impacts were mixed and nearly impossible to judge as positive or negative on balance. The cooperation necessitated by the move strengthened friendships in the community and built community pride and identity. Some of the renters in the old town had the opportunity to become owners in the new community. The old village had been located in a scenic setting along the river. The new village was less scenic, but the town and each lot backed up to a green belt for beauty and privacy. In addition, the highway went near but not through the new town, eliminating traffic noise and danger.

The reestablishment of the village was of great benefit to some of the long-term residents who did not have to abandon old friendships. Relocation on an individual basis would have had more adverse effects. Nevertheless, even relocation as a community was traumatic for many who were forced out of the homes in which they had lived all their lives. Inevitably, some of the residents had to move away; the younger households, mostly renters, could not afford the price of a lot in the new village, and the older residents were not up to the effort required to rebuild.

Adler and Jansen conducted a survey of the current Hill population and compared the surviving relocated residents with the current nonrelocated residents. They summarize their findings as follows:

The major differences are that the relocated population is more involved with their community and is more content with services and the community generally.

The individuals who had experienced the relocation are proud of their town and still feel Hill is the best place to live. However, they miss many of the amenities which had characterized the rural existence they had known before the relocation. Some residents see the relocation as the cause of the changes the town has seen over the years; however, those changes are in fact characteristic of other rural communities in the region [1978: 83].

Certain implications of the Hill story warrant special mention. It demonstrates the potential advantages of reestablishing a community over one-by-one relocation. Friendships were maintained and deepened through cooperation in the reestablishment of the community. Community cohesion, identity, and pride were also enhanced. However, these benefits are not necessary consequences of community relocation and may not occur in other situations. In Hill the reestablishment benefited from good leadership and social solidarity from the beginning without which the reestablishment may have been frustrating and unpleasant.

## The Arrow Lakes New Communities

### THE RELOCATION STORY

Wilson (1973) tells the story of the relocation of about 500 of the 1100 residents of the Central Arrow Lakes area occasioned by the damming of Arrow Lakes in British Columbia. The other 600 left the region entirely. The moving began in 1966, three years before the reservoir filling, and focused on the three reestablished communities of Fauquier, Edgewood, and Burton and on the substantial migration to Nakusp. There was a limited amount of habitable land around the new shoreline and highway accessibility to only a small amount of this. BC Hydro and Power owned most of the shoreline land and provided most of the land for resettlement, but in limited areas. Thus, displaced households had limited relocation options, and most opportunities for relocation in the region involved dealing with BC Hydro and Power. Even a fair percentage of those who resettled in the town of Nakusp did so on land developed by BC Hydro and Power. The demographics of the main resettlement projects are shown in Table 5.1. Much of the resettlement story told by Wilson centers on the relationship between BC Hydro and Power and the displaced residents. Many misunderstandings and difficulties are reviewed. The major problem was in the level of compensation: Most displaced residents had properties with low market values but which provided good shelter and resources for supplementing their incomes. Most people had extensive gardens and raised much of their food. Some also marketed fruits or nuts. Compensation was based on market values far below the replacement value of

TABLE 5.1   Relocated Households in Three Reestablished
            Communities and in Nakusp

| Community | Estimate of 1965 Households | Relocated Households 1970 |
|---|---|---|
| Fauquier | 50 | 40 |
| Burton | 25 | 18 |
| Edgewood | 12 | 27 |
| Addition to Nakusp | | 50 |
| Total | | 135 |

SOURCE: Figures compiled from Wilson (1973).

these properties. Furthermore, the loss of the old property resulted in some changes in people's independent style of life.

The focus of our discussion, however, is on the lessons of the reestablished communities. Unfortunately, Wilson's account is journalistic, and an accurate account of these communities before and after relocation is missing. Hydro planned the new communities on the basis of surveys of people's relocation intentions. "These plans were then handed over to the reservoir engineer for engineering design, followed by development by contract" (1973: 78). Area residents were then allowed to purchase lots. Hydro equipped the communities

with services and facilities appropriate to their size and to modern standards. All have modern water systems, but Fauquier alone required storm drains and a piped sewer system (leading to a sewage lagoon) because of the impervious nature of its subsoil. . . . All have power and telephone services, those at Fauquier being underground. Each community had an elementary school, a community hall, at least one church, and a park. There are stores in all three and post offices in Fauquier and Edgewood; the latter also retaining its Red Cross outpost hospital [1973: 78].

## ASSESSING THE RESULTS

The new communities were designed and established by Hydro, which made all the decisions. The original residents apparently were minimally consulted. They petitioned Hydro (and some of these petitions are presented by Wilson), but Hydro always had the last word. Nevertheless, "a good majority were satisfied with their new circumstances" (1973: 137). Wilson summarizes the resettlement stories of the three communities as follows: "Burton developed relatively painlessly; Fauquier developed slowly amid considerable frustration to its residents; and Edgewood was enveloped in

protest and controversy from beginning to end" (p. 79). The major frustration in Fauquier was the early announcement by the minister of highways of
plans to build a bridge over the lake at Fauquier which were later dropped, to
everyone's disappointment. Other frustrations concerned the delays in the
building of stores and a community hall.

The main resentment in Edgewood was the feeling that Hydro sought to
encourage the expansion of Fauquier at the expense of Edgewood. One
episode which was the basis for this feeling was Hydro's unwillingness to
make additional lots available in Edgewood when unfilled applications
exceeded the available lots. Hydro did not expand the lots because it felt no
obligation to provide for people from outside the area who wanted to settle
in Edgewood. The residents of Edgewood felt differently on the issue, and
their feelings are expressed in a bitter letter to Hydro from the Women's
Institute of Edgewood: "The housing situation in Edgewood is most critical.
Numerous men who have obtained work here are being forced to leave
because no living accommodation is available for their families" (1973: 85,
86). Hydro did make one expansion of lots but soon was resisting new
pressures for another expansion. A second episode which indicated Hydro's
neglect of Edgewood was its efforts to get the BC Forest Service to relocate
its Edgewood Ranger Station to Fauquier even though Fauquier was not
central to the territory it governed.

The lesson in the different amount of relocation trouble for the three new
communities was described by Wilson in the following judgment:

> It may be that the major factor in all the troubles was simply the time
> required to get the essential things done. The longer it took to complete
> the compensation process, build roads, and establish the visible infra-
> structure of the new communities, the longer the period of indecision,
> turmoil, and trouble for the people concerned [1973: 79].

In accord with this view, the reestablishment of Burton was prompt and
relatively free of trouble.

The degree of relocation trouble, however, is not the only gauge of
relocation success. Edgewood had a stormy relocation experience, but the
community had a good record of cohesion and cooperation. Its new

> site was well known and had been chosen by the people themselves
> prior to the advent of Hydro; no mean advantage. The resettling group
> were all Edgewoodites, who seemed to have maintained their sense of
> community. . . .
>
> No drainage or sewerage works were required, thus it could be devel-
> oped and settled with a minimum of delay [1973: 88].

Edgewood also had leadership that was lacking in Fauquier, which explains in part the very different levels of community mobilization in these two communities. Fauquier also had "a much greater mixture of local origins among its residents" (p. 88) which worked against community mobilization.

Wilson conducted a survey which netted only 40 responses spread out over four communities. Despite the nonrandom and small sample, he derived from it the following picture of the four major resettlement areas:

> The responses suggest that there are considerable differences in morale between the new communities. Edgewood emerges as a fiercely proud, coherent, self-conscious community; it boasts of "unity in the face of oppression" and feels that it has emerged stronger than ever from its ordeal by water, and "no thanks to Hydro." ... Burton sounds depressed. Fauquier values its new services and its site, but still sounds somewhat unhappy. The settlers in Nakusp seem to have experienced the least upset and to appreciate the services and activities of the larger community, while feeling most the impact of higher taxes [1973: 141].

### Conclusion

Little can be generalized from the resettlement of only four communities, but two features of the relocation process emerge as critically important in these cases. First, the quality of the community leadership affects both the economic and social outcomes of relocation. Good leaders generate economic resources and effect savings by anticipatory actions. They also facilitate community cohesion and morale. The second important feature of the relocation process is its schedule. Long delays cause frustration, especially when the relocated community has to wait a long time for roads and an infrastructure.

*Chapter 6*

# BOOM TOWNS

The first three centuries of American history saw the formation of hundreds frontier boom towns. These towns are remembered with pride for their contribution to the white conquest of the continent and for the exciting lifestyles of their settlers. With the excitement however, went hardships and scarcity of goods and services. Young men looking for adventure and fortune were not put off by these difficulties, but boom towns were unpleasant places to live for most people. Today boom towns still arise when large construction projects or resource developments occur in sparsely populated areas. The existing small communities experience rapid population growth and the resulting problems or negative impacts. Many of these problems are the obvious consequences of the rapid population growth; others come as a surprise. Obviously, the new population increases the demand for housing and the full range of services provided at the community level faster than they can be supplied. It is less obvious that conflicts will occur between the preproject community residents and the newcomers, but most case studies report such problems. The experienced assessor might predict old-timer/newcomer conflicts, but the nature of the conflict and how it will be resolved is difficult to predict.

In this chapter we describe the social changes which commonly occur in boom towns. We begin with population changes and then trace the obvious supply/demand problems with their resulting fiscal problems. Finally, we describe the less certain institutional adaptations, social changes, and group conflicts which are likely to occur.

## Population Growth

The term "boom town" is applied to a rural community which experiences a substantial increase in economic activity causing rapid and disruptive population growth. The major types of new economic activity are (1) mining and resource development; (2) rural industrialization; (3) military installations; (4) power plants, dams, and other large construction projects; and (5) tourism, recreation, or retirement housing. Each type of economic activity produces different patterns of population growth, but all develop in the sequence of stages most typical of the boom town model: construction, operation, and shut-down. The construction stage produces the rapid and disruptive population increase, which peaks around the fifth or sixth year for large power plant construction. For dams and power plants, the operation stage requires fewer workers than does the construction stage. For military installations the operation stage may require more local civilian workers than the construction stage. Finally, many boom towns have a "bust" stage either after the construction of the facility or when it is shut down. In fact, some communities in the west have gone through several boom/bust cycles. Page, Arizona, went through two such cycles in 20 years (Little, 1977).

The rate of population increase is the major determinant of the extent of other impacts. Gilmore (1976) estimated that communities can readily absorb a five percent annual population increase but experience many problems when growth rates exceed 15 percent. We suggest, therefore, that an annual growth rate of 15 percent for three or more years would qualify a community as a major boom town. Some boom towns, however, have doubled their population in a single year.

## Supply/Demand Problems
## and Additional Tax Burdens

Rapid population growth places severe pressures on public services. It quickly exhausts the unused capacity of schools and other services, including water supply and sewerage. It overtaxes current systems, causing breakdowns, malfunctions, or deficient service. For example, Cortese and Jones (1977) reported that the water mains in Langdon (population 2200) broke over 100 times during the winter two years after construction began on an antiballistic missile site. As a result, a bigger water system was built. System expansion is the answer when funds are available. However, it is often difficult to estimate how much expansion is required. Overexpansion is a fairly common and costly planning mistake. For example, Sweet Home, Oregon, tripled the capacity of its water system in anticipation of a boom from nearby dam construction, but experienced rather modest growth, which left considerable unused capacity.

The disparity between supply and demand results not only in new construction, but also in an increased need for maintenance and operational personnel. The local government payroll expands in all categories because of the need for more employees, including teachers, policemen, firemen, inspectors, and administrators. With both payroll and contract costs escalating rapidly, indebtedness and interest payments follow suit. Unless the new industry or utility is paying substantial taxes to the community, property taxes must be raised. The natural sequence of events aggravates the problem. During the construction period, the demand for government services is high, but the tax payments by the industry or utility are normally low, since the facility is not yet producing. During the operation stage the situation is reversed: The need for tax revenue is diminished while tax payments are at peak levels. To solve these problems, it is often arranged that the industry prepays taxes to help the community in its financial crisis.

It should be pointed out that although population growth brings additional taxpayers, their taxes almost never compensate for the increase in public expenditures which they require. Newcomers generally rent or live in trailers and contribute little additional revenues for the community.

Supply/demand disparities also occur in the private sector to the detriment of the consumers. An acute housing shortage stimulates housing construction, but new houses accommodate only a small percentage of the new residents. Rented space and mobile homes provide much of the new housing. Property owners rent out almost any kind of spare room they have, including unused barns and sheds (Howard et al., 1975).

In the retail, commercial, and service areas business is good, but for some it is too good. Stores, restaurants, bars, barber shops, gas stations, and others experience increased business, and some cannot keep up with the increased demand. Fairly quickly, new retail and service businesses are established (which sometimes put some antiquated local establishments out of business), but demand generally keeps ahead of supply until the population levels off or declines. For consumers, the scarcity of goods and services and the attendant inflation in prices is a hardship. A particularly troublesome shortage is medical personnel, since these professions are underrepresented in rural areas normally and medical personnel are not attracted to boom towns (Cortese and Jones, 1977).

One long-run advantage of the population growth when supply/demand balances finally are achieved is the increase in consumer options as a wider range of entertainments and goods becomes available. Some of these changes may seem insignificant, but they add to the quality of life in various ways. For example, Cortese and Jones (1977) noted in Green River, Wyoming, the addition of a new pizza parlor and a new taxicab business; and in Center, North Dakota, a dentist started a new practice.

## Economic Problems

The major economic problem for community residents is inflation, a result of the supply/demand imbalance. The worst inflation occurs in the sky-rocketing costs of housing. Cortese and Jones (1977) reported: "In one community the school superintendent explained that an apartment tradi-tionally occupied by incoming teachers tripled in rent in less than two years" (1977: 80). Some of the preimpact residents profit from the inflation, including the price of labor, but many are losers. Those on fixed incomes such as the elderly are especially hurt. Also, some companies are forced out of business because they cannot compete with the construction jobs for unskilled labor (Howard et al., 1975).

Another problem for preimpact businessmen is adjusting to the new demands and/or competing with new businesses. Some fail because they are slow to adopt more competitive methods. Others quit because of new problems. Cortese and Jones (1977) reported that in one town "a local druggist was planning an early retirement because of the pressures of new business. . . . For a businessman used to the informal style of occasionally getting out of bed at 11 p.m. to fill a prescription for a neighbor, the pressure of doing it *every night* was too much" (1977: 81).

## Psychological and Social Problems

Boom town conditions are frustrating for both new and old residents (see Bates, 1978; Little, 1977; Cortese and Jones, 1977; Freudenburg et al., 1977; Freudenburg, 1978a, 1978b). The old residents experience the erosion of their way of life and increased problems on many fronts. They generally are favorable toward projects before they occur (Little and Lovejoy, 1979), but their attitude worsens when the project gets underway. Mountain West Research (1975) asked the long-time residents of five communities that were being affected by large construction projects

whether the effects of the construction were the same, better or worse than they had originally expected. . . . Only 14.5 percent said better, 32.8 said worse, and 52.4 percent said about what they had expected.

The reasons given most frequently for thinking the effects were better than expected were, "improved community facilities" (40 percent of those thinking the effects were better), and "financial benefits" (35 percent). The reasons given most frequently for thinking the effects were worse than expected were, "inadequate community facilities" (63 percent of those thinking the effects were worse), and "increased population" (22 percent) [1975: 60].

The new residents are frustrated by crowded housing (mainly trailers) and the lack of amenities—especially recreational opportunities. Not surprisingly, these conditions aggravate family relations and lead to marital tension, child abuse and neglect, and delinquency. Wives are bored and husbands are under stress at work. Reported cases of depression, alcoholism, and attempted suicide greatly increase, as do mental health cases. Children have adjustment problems in school, as indicated by low achievement, truancy, delinquency, drug abuse, and venereal disease. The above problems also affect the workplace in the form of high rates of absenteeism and turnover.

The number of crimes sometimes increases at a rate similar to the growth of population (Little, 1977), but usually increases much more rapidly than population (Hogg and Smith, 1970; Freudenburg et al., 1977). Even when the crime rate per thousand population remains fairly constant the perception of crime as a problem increases. The way crime is controlled and offenders handled also changes. Community social pressure becomes less effective in controlling behavior, including crime and delinquency, when the small homogeneous community undergoes rapid development (Freudenburg, 1978b). Likewise, law enforcement officials can no longer return petty offenders to family, friends, and religious leaders to keep them in line, but they increasingly "go by the book."

A social factor which affects many problem areas is the transiency of the newcomers. Not only are most of them newcomers, but most expect to leave in a few years (see Table 6.1 for appropriate survey results from five boom towns). As very few construction workers plan to stay in the community, they form little attachment to it. The vitality and spirit of neighborhoods and the community can be debilitated by the transiency of the residents.

## Intergroup Conflict

Although rural communities are not the homogeneous and harmonious places depicted in the common myths, they become increasingly heterogeneous and disharmonious with rapid development. The major axis of conflict is between the newcomers and the old-timers. Their conflict is multifaceted and includes styles of life, economic interests, political philoso-

TABLE 6.1   Plans for Staying in the Area—Residents of Currently Affected
            Communities

| | Percentage of Residents | | |
| Plans | Long Time Residents | Newcomer Construction Workers | Other Newcomers |
|---|---|---|---|
| Settle down here | 75.9 | 10.2 | 32.1 |
| Leave immediately | 1.1 | 5.2 | 3.0 |
| Stay as long as work is available | 10.2 | 51.0 | 12.1 |
| Uncertain | 4.2 | 7.0 | 13.8 |
| Leave at retirement | 4.0 | 21.5 | 22.0 |
| Stay until transferred | 2.8 | 2.7 | 13.4 |
| Other | 1.7 | 2.2 | 3.6 |
| TOTAL[a] | 100.0 | 100.0 | 100.0 |

a. Totals may not add to 100.0 percent because of rounding.
SOURCE: Mountain West Research (1975: III-18).

phies, and moral values. Some of the lifestyle differences derive from the
contrast between rural and urban patterns and has been perceptively analyzed
in the sociological tradition from Toennies (1957), Maine (1964), and Durkheim (1933) to Wirth (1938) and Redfield (1947). These discussions apply to
newcomer/old-timer value conflicts in boom towns, because the newcomers
tend to be more urban than the old-timers. Lifestyle differences also might be
based on ethnic, religious, and income differences in certain cases.

Boom towns invariably engender economic conflicts. The economic interests of the newcomers and old-timers diverge, and sometimes the boom
creates economic conflict among old-timers. The predominant economic
interests of old-timers are likely to be one or more of the following: farming,
ranching, lumbering, tourist industry, or business (mainly retail). Only the
last is likely to benefit from the boom development. Furthermore, the project
might compete with other interests for scarce resources—that is, land, labor,
water, and community support. For example, some projects compete with
farmers and ranchers for limited supplies of water, and some threaten agricultural interests by poisoning water supplies or degrading the productivity of
the land, as in strip mining. Environmental effects of the project also
adversely affect the tourist industry. On the other hand, commercial, retail,
and service businessmen generally are not affected by environmental impacts
of the project and tend to benefit from increased business. They are likely to
incur labor problems, but in general they gain economically from the boom.

Old-timers and newcomers often clash on political philosophy. Old-timers
may be politically conservative, believing in self-reliance and minimal govern-

ment. The newcomers probably are more liberal and expect government to act in the face of problems. When their numbers are sufficient, they elect new leaders and turn the town in new directions.

The newcomer/old-timer differences in social values overlap with other conflicts. The traditions and religious values of the old-timers are likely to be hostile to the less religious and more loose-living values of the newcomers. Some of the current energy boom towns in the west are occurring in predominantly Mormon areas, and Mormon teaching is against smoking and drinking. The construction worker's need for release is likely to find outlets which are not appreciated by the old-timers, Mormon or otherwise. Another group with values which are antithetical to the values of boom town newcomers are the American Indians (White et al., 1977: 313).

Conflict occurs along other axes as well. Some communities are unanimously pro-development, being more aware of the benefits than the negative effects. As the problems emerge this consensus breaks down, and conflict develops over how the community will respond to development. Many communities have pro and con development groups from the beginning with values and economic interests underlying the rift. Many rural communities do not have genuine party politics even though they might use the labels. The political process, therefore, tends to mask the basic rifts in the community and makes differences appear to be more a matter of opinions. The boom, however, blows the whistle on consensus politics and often aligns conflicts along party divisions.

## Institutional Adaptations

The boom demands responses from the local government that are unlike anything that it did before, such as planning, zoning, negotiating with the utility or project company, negotiating with government agencies, obtaining special state legislation, obtaining federal or state funds, devising new taxation schemes, and providing new services. Local business may be forced to adopt new practices to compete with new entrepreneurs who move in. Schools and law enforcement officials might have to deal with new drug problems. Even the work of social workers is altered (Bates, 1978). Cortese and Jones (1977) reported a dramatic change in the nature of the problems which social workers handle in the three boom towns they studied. These new demands on officials and businessmen exceed the abilities or oppose the values of a significant number of them. Officials resign, are voted out, or adapt. Businessmen sell out, go bankrupt, or adjust. In the process, institutions of the boom town are qualitatively changed.

## Selective Review of
## Some Boom Town Case Studies

The above discussion summarizes the general patterns commonly experienced in boom towns. A proper understanding of boom impacts, however, requires the details which case studies provide. In this section a number of case studies will be reviewed to elaborate on the general patterns and to discuss some special features of specific cases.

### I. THE ENERGY BOOM IN CRAIG, COLORADO

One of the most descriptive studies of boom towns is by Freudenberg et al. (1977) of the boom in Craig, Colorado. They reported on the transformation of the way of life in Craig due to coal development in the area. The population approximately doubled from 5000 to 10,000 in about four years. The city's budget increased from $800,000 in 1974 to over $5,000,000 in 1977. Freudenburg et al. described some of the multifarious changes which accompany booms:

Taxes have risen; rents and house prices have soared to the point where costs run roughly 2-3 times as high as costs for comparable units in the other towns; Craig's financial cost of living has leaped upward. . . . In the past few months, the town has gained one-way streets, a juvenile detention center, and a massage parlor of questionable legality; it has lost, through resignations, the city engineer, the water superintendent, the city clerk, the police chief, and even the mayor. Noise and construction, trailers and traffic, all are clearly in evidence: A city policeman reported that it had taken him as long as 28 minutes to get across the town's (formerly) two-lane main street at rush hour [1977: 7].

The authors succeed in the above passage in creating a picture of change and stress with a variety of surface indicators. They also reported crime statistics and survey results:

The town had never even bothered having a police department until November of 1975; they now have a very busy 22-person department with an annual budget of $300,000. The sheriff's department—which formerly handled complaints for the entire county including Craig—had a doubling of "offenses known" in just that one year, from 1974 to 1975.

Nor was the increase confined to minor crimes; another study (McKeown and Lantz, 1977), which compared analogous two-month periods in 1973 and 1976, found substantial increases even after controlling for type of complaint. During the same period that population was rising by about 100%, crimes against property were up 200%, and crimes against persons increased 900%. Meanwhile, family disturbances rose 250%, and child behavior problems rose an even 1000%; alcohol-related complaints rose 550%, and other drug-related reports went up 1400% [1977: 5-6].

A sample of residents of Craig were surveyed and compared with residents in three other towns without booms. Craig residents were more likely to fear for their safety (29 percent) than the residents of other towns (10 percent) and to find it necessary to lock their doors when leaving for a short time (72 percent versus 35 percent). They also were three times more often victims of crimes than were the residents of the other towns (23 percent versus seven percent).

The authors saw these changes as reflecting the destruction of the informal mechanisms of social control and functioning which operated effectively before the boom. On this point their analysis is particularly sensitive:

Not surprisingly, over the four or five generations that these towns have been inhabited, the residents have developed a fairly impressive set of informal mechanisms—or "natural systems," if you will—for performing social functions and generally taking care of each other. These mechanisms tend to be of the sort that sociologists can find nearly everywhere (to name a few noteworthy examples, they are ways of controlling deviance, socializing the young, giving people a sense of place, purpose, and personal worth, and taking care of the communities' weaker members and/or those in need or under stress). Yet all of these mechanisms tend to be quite admirably adapted to each community's own unique pattern of individuals and circumstances.

In what is probably the most characteristic single consequence of the large-scale impact process, these rather finely-tuned (and surprisingly delicately-balanced) arrangements are simply blown apart—scattered to the four winds by the sudden arrival of more new people than can be contained within them. The process requires no plotting, no nastiness—only numbers. The result is that a people who once took care of one another in a naturally-evolved and in fact almost automatic way—for they are often not even aware of doing so—are suddenly left with some very important machinery that's simply inoperative [1977: 4-5].

It is clear that the social system of Craig was in disarray. Surprisingly, however, the authors did not find individuals in Craig, except for the ranchers, more distressed or unhappy than individuals in the other towns. They concluded that individuals are fairly well able to cope with boom town conditions even when the preboom social arrangements are not able to cope.

## II. THE MINI-BOOM IN SWEET HOME

The description of institutional changes in boom conditions presented by Freudenburg et al. is supported by a study of a mini-boom in Sweet Home, Oregon. The construction of two dams nearby caused only a 21 percent increase in population in five years (a mini-boom), but some of the boom town problems occurred anyway and are reported in Hogg and Smith (1970) and Smith et al. (1971). Three aspects of boom development are carefully examined in the reports and will be presented here: law enforcement and crime rates, unemployment, and community value change.

Changes in law enforcement procedures in Sweet Home exemplify the interruption of informal mechanisms by boom changes as described by Freudenburg et al. Law enforcement in rural areas is likely to have a personal and informal character which is successful in preboom circumstances but which encounters difficulties when the number of newcomers becomes sizable. If political leadership changes during the boom period, the new leaders may be critical of "unprofessional" law enforcement practices and call for changes. This pattern occurred in Sweet Home. Hogg and Smith abstracted the following account from a student report by Ron Hart.

Sweet Home's Police Department has been a concern of both political actors and non-actors for many years. Some controversy stems from the chief of police's interactional and organizational style, which often seems unorthodox to both outsiders and formally legal-oriented Sweet Homers. This style is marked by a relativity and personalness which result in a department with limited set rules, procedures, or techniques. The police chief prefers using his knowledge of the social situation as a primary factor in enforcing the law, rather than the more formal definitions of legal versus illegal behavior as these are acted upon by power of arrest. Therefore, he has the reputation for preferring to drive intoxicated persons home rather than arrest them; rather than automatic referral to the courts, he has often referred breaches to the family of the offender; and he holds a very judicious attitude towards punishment of offenses that do not, in his mind, harm the social setting of the town. . . .

The feeling on the chief's part that people must be taken into account is evident in his style. To use the example of the introduction of radar, he first publicized the event in the local paper and then went to all of the service clubs and told them how it worked and why it was being introduced. Next, he set up neighborhood demonstrations where cars were stopped at random, the drivers told how fast they were going, and how the officer knew. He wanted it known that radar really worked. Finally, after three months of demonstrations and publicity, the first ticket for speeding was issued. . . . This style, according to the chief, is a very effective one for Sweet Home, but it is seen as "old fashioned" and conservative by some people in other formal political organizations [Hogg and Smith, 1970: 93-96].

This personal style of law enforcement required "a high degree of interpersonal interaction and contact. Obviously, the influx of construction workers would severely stress these informal means of law enforcement" (Hogg and Smith, 1970: 97).

According to official statistics as reported in Table 6.2, the crime rate increased sharply during the construction period, especially larceny. The large increase in drunks and drunken driving supports the stereotypical view that many construction workers drink as a major form of recreation. It is important to notice, however, that disorderly conduct arrests increased only as much as the population did. This statistic conflicts with the stereotype of construction camp rowdiness. Finally, it should be noted that after construction most categories of crime returned to near-preconstruction levels. The continued high traffic violations probably were due to the installation of radar.

The Hogg and Smith account of the Sweet Home mini-boom includes a detailed report abstracted from a student report by Mary Lemhouse analyzing the local employment office's caseload (1970: 58-69). The office was located in nearby Lebanon. A number of observations based on the report are presented here:

(1) Workers anticipate employment opportunities. Two years before construction on the dams would be available in quantity workers migrated to the area speculating on employment possibilities. Many drifted away without getting work, although many waited months before leaving.

(2) The employment office caseload fluctuated greatly as the weather affected construction activity.

(3) With the downturn of construction activity most laid-off construction workers leave the area. However, the lumber industry was able to absorb some of the excess labor.

A special feature of the report by Smith et al. (1971) of the Sweet Home mini-boom is its discussion of the shift in values in Sweet Home due to the inmigration of more urban/suburban residents. This inmigration began well before construction started on the dams, but the dams provided new water resources for recreational purposes that were attractive to urbanites and suburbanites. As a result, "When the dams became a probable reality for Sweet Home in the late 1950's, the residents interested in making the community more attractive voiced their desire to change Sweet Home's image" (p. 185) from a tough logging town to a neat, orderly, and picturesque town. Most residents did not participate in the governance of the

TABLE 6.2   Crime Statistic; for Sweet Home, Oregon

| Offense | Before Construction 1962 | Construction High 1963–1966 | Post Construction 1967 |
|---|---|---|---|
| | (Calendar year basis in percent of 1962 level) | | |
| Total offenses | 100 | 240 | 186 |
| Complaints received and answered | 100 | 156 | 139 |
| Traffic violations | 100 | 274 | 208 |
| Disorderly conduct | 100 | 122 | 187 |
| Grand & petty larceny | 100 | 575 | 100 |
| Drunks | 100 | 236 | 111 |
| Driving while under the influence | 100 | 210 | 117 |
| Assault & battery | 100 | 167 | 83 |
| Vagrancy | 100 | 187 | 56 |
| Population | 100 | 118 | 117 |

SOURCE: Hogg and Smith (1970: 98).

town which allowed the minority with developmental goals to gain control of the government. "Many of these new migrants took important positions in the community, positions which influenced the allocation of resources" (1971: 184). The newcomers wanted quality schools and improvements in municipal services; because of their growing influence, improvements were instituted and school and municipal expenditures increased.

### III. CALVERT CLIFFS NUCLEAR POWER PLANT

The next case study provides useful details on the labor and commodity markets. Howard et al. (1975) produced a brief report on the socioeconomic impacts of the Calvert Cliffs Plant in Calvert County, Maryland. Peak construction employment in 1970 was about 2500 workers, and operation employment was about 150. At peak employment the construction workers constituted a substantial portion of the locally employed labor force. In 1970 Calvert County had 20,682 residents and 7141 employed residents, of which only 53 percent worked in the county; many of the others commuted to jobs in the Washington or Baltimore SMSAs.

The plant was a boon for workers and a bane for employers. On the labor force impacts the authors observed the following:

The local labor force primarily participated in the power plant construction by filling unskilled and semi-skilled jobs. . . . The need for construction workers at the plant has caused local labor shortages particularly in tobacco stripper and other agricultural workers and in the lumber mills. Farm laborers realized as much as a threefold increase in their earnings by working at the plant where minimum construction wages started at $6.50. Many of these laborers have been reluctant to return to their former lower paying jobs having experienced union wages. As a result, farmers have experienced some difficulty in hiring workers and a number of lumber mills have reportedly gone out of business due to a lack of available local labor [Howard et al, 1975: 4].

The report also discussed how the plant inflated the housing market to the detriment of County residents.

High wages earned at the plant pushed rentals up to two and three times what they had formerly been. Farmers and other landlords enjoyed windfall income from renting even marginal living quarters. . . . Low moderate income housing and apartment projects have not been built. The result has been that the construction workers have been willing to pay higher rents for all available rental units in the County, thereby displacing former renters unable to spend more on housing. Instances are reported of County public employees, especially teachers, having been forced to seek housing outside the County [1975: 5].

Calvert County seems to have avoided the financial crunch which afflicts so many boom towns. The power company paid only modest taxes (corporate and real estate) during the construction period, but the county held the line on expenditures during the boom period.

No major increase in public services expenditures were brought about by the large influx of construction workers, although some sections of county government were presented with increased service requirements. . . .

School enrollment increased by approximately 1,300 students during the last seven years. School officials estimate approximately 250 of these students were a result of the construction force. School expenditures, as a percent of the total county budget, did not increase over the same period. The school budget has averaged 68% of the total county budget since 1967. (p. 12).

The report does not explain how the county managed without high power plant tax payments, but we suspect that the fiscal health of Calvert County may have resulted from the increased settlement of Calvert County by people working in Washington, D.C. and increased construction of recreation homes. Summer homes are economically profitable for the county in that they provide tax revenue, but their owners require few services (their children are educated elsewhere).

Calvert County rode out the boom period without fiscal problems and expects to profit handsomely from the power plant when it reaches the full operational level.

> The positive impact of tax revenues generated by the power plant in Calvert County will be great. It is anticipated that the county will receive between $12 and 14 million in annual tax revenues from the plant, when it is in full operation. This is twice the 1974 budget for the county and will appreciably affect the initiation of public improvements [1975: 9].

The county plans to use the additional revenues for "various major projects such as new or expanded health care facilities, new municipal and recreation facilities" (p. 10).

## IV. BRUNSWICK AND HATCH NUCLEAR PLANT BOOMS

Two other cases of communities with relatively positive experiences with boom conditions are reported by Peele et al. (1978) and Shields et al. (1979). They conducted a postlicensing study of two nuclear power plants: Brunswick 1 and 2 in Brunswick County, North Carolina and Hatch 1 and 2 in Appling County, Georgia. On the whole, the plants' impacts were relatively beneficial. Before construction, the two areas were underdeveloped economically and had too little opportunity for workers and businessmen. They benefited from the stimulation to their economies and the increases in their county tax revenues.

> In 1976 the Brunswick plant accounted for about 50% of that county's tax base, whereas the Hatch plant (only 75% complete) represented 60% of Appling County's tax base. The tax rate in both counties has been reduced, but at the same time government expenditures on new facilities (e.g., schools and office buildings) has increased. Undoubtedly, the increased tax base had been one factor underlying high acceptance of the nuclear plants [Peele et al., 1978: 116].

Even though the population of both areas increased by about 50 percent, community strains were modest. Housing was in short supply, but mobile homes filled much of the housing needs. The authors also reported that community services and schools were able to handle the increased demand. Most workers came without families. As a result, the rise in school enrollments was modest.

## V. ROCK SPRINGS, WYOMING, BOOM/BUST/BOOM

The next three case studies are reported here for their variations in community responses to boom prospects. The first ignored the advanced warnings of the boom, the second anticipated the boom, and in the third the company anticipated the boom. Myhra (1975, 1977) reported on boom conditions in three communities: Rock Springs, Wyoming; Skagit County, Washington; and Colstrip, Montana. His Rock Springs report is of special interest because Rock Springs had a history of booms and busts and yet failed to prepare for the 1970-1975 boom related to the construction of a power plant and oil drilling rigs.

> Their most recent bust period began in the 1950's and extended to 1970. Most of the miners and [their] families stayed in the area during the bust period. . . . When announcements were circulated that extensive mining activity was again being planned in 1970, very little attention was paid to it. The civic leaders in the community knew that housing would be required if development started, yet nothing was done in preparation. This is particularly important in Rock Springs because most of the land around the community is either owned by the Union Pacific Railroad or the Bureau of Land Management. Thus, one of the few ways of obtaining residential property there is for the city itself to buy several sections of land from either Union Pacific or the Bureau and then resell the land to private developers. No land was purchased by the city in anticipation of the coming energy growth, and not until 1975, after energy development in the Rock Springs area was at its peak, did the city move to purchase any land. However, by this time the city workers and their families at the numerous projects underway were forced in many cases to live out of camper trucks and, in some instances, tents [1975: 6].

Myhra explained the community inaction by a callous "attitude of 'what was good enough for us is certainly good enough for them' " (p. 6). (For a discussion of many other aspects of the Rock Springs boom see Section XI).

## VI. NUCLEAR POWER PLANT BOOM IN SKAGIT COUNTY, WASHINGTON

The major lesson of Myhra's (1975 and 1977) case study of Puget Sound Power and Light Company's proposed nuclear power plant construction in Skagit County, Washington, is the opposite of the Rock Springs case. The people of Skagit County had strong attitudes toward boom development and acted in their own behalf relative to the power company. They anticipated the project and thoroughly discussed its consequences. The majority favored the project for the economic opportunities and tax revenue it would provide, but also wanted to maintain the rural character of the area. They recognized that the county lacked adequate employment opportunities at the time and was slowly losing its more skilled population. Many natives, however, opposed the project altogether, because they feared it would cause undesirable boom conditions. In the end the majority of residents favored the plant but under carefully prescribed conditions. The major conditions were plant compliance with a zoning plan and prepayment of taxes to meet the new demands on schools and county services. The power company agreed and thus recognized its responsibility to mitigate the social impacts of plant construction.

## VII. COLSTRIP, MONTANA, A RECONSTRUCTED TOWN

According to Myhra (1975: 18), the Western Energy Company (WEC),

a wholly owned subsidiary of Montana Power Company, ... has expanded the small town of Colstrip from a population of 100 in 1970 to a population of over 3000 at present. This was achieved without the boom town atmosphere and adverse socioeconomic effects commonly associated with rapid population growth.

In order to recruit and retain workers, MPCO/WEC planned and built almost a new town out of the nearly abandoned Colstrip. Myhra elaborated on many of the details of the plan which combined attractiveness, flexibility in meeting a variety of housing needs, and low housing costs for its residents. Colstrip was planned and has operated as a company town, but, unlike the infamous company towns of yesteryear, Colstrip provides a much better residential environment for migrants than is available in other boom towns. In fact, Myhra was so impressed with the development of Colstrip that he advocated its emulation elsewhere. Some of its provisions as of 1975 were as follows:

A family renting a new house of 1200 square feet pays approximately $210 a month to MPCO/WEC. The rental fee includes all maintenance expenses, water and sewer, garbage collection, landscaping, range and refrigerator and insurance on the structure. The family is responsible for its own lawn care, use of electricity, furniture, side walk snow removal and personal property insurance.

Eventually, MPCO/WEC management plans to allow incorporation of Colstrip and the establishment of local self-government. Prior to this occurrence, MPCO/WEC wants to have Colstrip fully developed in terms of its planned housing and commercial and community facilities.

Thus, when the transfer takes place, within the next several years, Colstrip as an incorporated municipality will avail itself of all the usual sources of municipal revenue: property taxes, business and occupation taxes, admission taxes, licenses and permits, forfeitures and penalties, earnings from municipal utilities, shares of state-collected taxes and any payments in lieu of taxes [1975: 23-24].

## VIII.  ACCELERATED SUBURBANIZATION IN BUCKS COUNTY

Company towns are not the only type of planned communities which can greatly ameliorate the problems of boom developments. Planned residential developments can benefit boom towns. Breeze et al. (1965) described the impacts of the large Fairless Steel Works in Lower Bucks County, Pennsylvania. The planned community of Levittown which was being constructed in the area satisfied much of the new housing demand. Levittown had its own water and sewage system and planned and built schools, churches, parks, and other facilities along with the new houses. It had an advantage over the normal boom community because decisions on community development and services were efficiently made by the Levitt brothers. Most boom towns take too long to learn what decisions should be made and then have difficulty making them collectively. Unfortunately, planned communities like Levittown are not likely to occur in most boom situations because of the risks of busts. Levittown was planned for Bucks County because the area was developing as suburbs for Philadelphia on one side and Trenton on the other. Developers are attracted to areas with more predictable development potential than most boom towns.

## IX.  SENECA: BOOM TOWN IN WARTIME

According to Havighurst and Morgan (1951), Seneca, Illinois, had a population of 1235 in 1942. Two years later it had a population of 6600. A shipyward for LSTs was located on the Illinois River next to the town. Employment at the shipyard rose to 8000 in eight months, peaked at 10,600 in the summer of 1944, and went from 9000 to almost none in four months in 1945. In a very short time Seneca experienced a full boom and bust cycle.

A boom in wartime has two special problems: (1) they have an acute shortage of private capital and (2) the local and county governments are seldom willing to pay for the expansion of school, water, sewer, and other facilities for a temporary population. In Seneca the federal government had to fill the large gap. The extensive role of the federal government is illustrated in the way housing was provided.

All the existing housing facilities were filled to overflowing in an area thirty-five miles surrounding Seneca. All vacant dwellings were filled up in the neighboring cities. . . .

Trailers appeared in back yards and in vacant lots in Seneca. Single houses were remodeled into multiple dwellings, and spare rooms were rented in all the surrounding towns. But after all available living space was occupied, still more was needed.

The need for new housing could not be met by private business. The practical certainty that shipbuilding in Seneca would be stopped after the war, together with wartime prices and restrictions on building materials, made the investment of private capital in new housing a hazardous if not impossible matter, and the only alternative was public housing.

The Federal Public Housing Authority was called on to supply the need. The FPHA built, in total, 1,467 family units and a dormitory for 300 men. Made entirely of wood, these dwellings were expected to last ten to fifteen years. . . .

It was expensive housing, considering what the government received for its money; but speed, not cost, was the primary concern.

The first public housing in Seneca was a fleet of trailers of the Farm Security Administration. Although intended as temporary dwellings for construction workers, the trailers were kept in use, 225 of them, throughout the boom.

In addition to the public housing projects, several private trailer camps grew up on the outskirts of Seneca; and seventy-five private trailers were located in backyards and vacant lots. Non-government trailers reached a peak number of about 190 early in 1943.

Many private homes provided space for roomers and a few were converted into rooming houses. The number of people cared for in this way was not very large and probably never exceeded 350.

Havighurst and Morgan discussed the relations between old-timers and newcomers, which was kept to a minimum and involved an undertone of resentment. "Old-timers in Seneca tended to forget their own social differences and to feel as though they all belonged together when they faced the horde of strangers moving in upon them" (1951: 102). The two groups mixed in the churches, but none of the other organizations welcomed the newcomers. Even in most of the churches the newcomers did not feel really welcome. They formed social communities of their own so they did not feel deprived by the lack of interaction with old-timers. However, they did resent the scorn of the old-timers. One lady reported to the fieldworker:

> I took my little boy into the Sweet Shop to buy a paper and git him an ice-cream cone. The clerk, she said to him, 'Whaddye want? Well, you don't get no stool if all you want's an ice-cream cone; git right down!' Then she turned to another woman and said, 'That damned shipyard trash!' Right in front of my child, too. I went out of there without no ice-cream cone nor paper neither [Havighurst and Morgan 1951: 103].

When intermingling between old-timers and newcomers occurred it was confined largely to the upper class of the two groups. At this level friendships were formed quickly and parties were held. The mutual acceptance was symbolized by the marriage of an upper-class newcomer into an old-timer upper-class family.

Havighurst and Morgan (1951: 108) summarized old-timer/newcomer relations as follows:

> Relations between the old and new residents were kept to a minimum. This was largely because the newcomer was thought of, and thought of himself, as a man who comes today and goes tomorrow. It hardly seemed worth the effort to build up a social relationship with strange people for such a short time. The life of the newcomer to Seneca was characterized by:
>
> the feeling that he was there for a temporary stay;
>
> no sentimental attachments to the village or its institutions;
>
> unusual discomforts due to crowded housing conditions;
>
> freedom from the conventions of life in Seneca;
>
> minimal participation in local institutions;
>
> minimal social interaction with old-timers [p. 108].

## X. FAIRBANKS—A BOOM WITHOUT NEW FAMILIES

One of the few recent boom town studies which is reported in a commercial publication is the story of the oil pipeline boom in Fairbanks, Alaska, told by Dixon (1978). Fairbanks was the management center for the project, the location of a large pipeyard and construction camp, the project transportation and supply center, the project's service center, and the hiring and job termination point for all workers on the pipeline from Prudhoe Bay to Glennallen. In addition, many of the companies working on the project established their administrative centers at Fairbanks. As a result, demand was increased for banking, office supplies, repair equipment, warehousing, and office space, and the Fairbanks North Star Borough population increased 39 percent in two years from 45,571 in 1973 to 63,350 in 1975.

A unique aspect of the Fairbanks boom was the failure of a few normal boom effects to materialize. The Fairbanks North Star Borough School District expected 8844 students in the fall of 1974 without pipeline construction and 11,994 with pipeline construction. Only 20 of the expected additional 3150 students appeared, and the preparations for extra students—double shifts, expanded staff, and extra temporary classrooms—became unnecessary. The faulty projections allowed for the probability that many construction workers would come to Fairbanks without families, but they did not anticipate that almost all would come alone.

Another faulty expectation was that many more workers would come to Fairbanks seeking pipeline jobs than could be employed, so the surplus would either fill local jobs or be a burden on the welfare program. Unexpectedly, the local job market was plagued by a shortage of workers throughout the boom, and the welfare rolls declined substantially. The reason, in part, was Fairbanks' "campaign to discourage people seeking pipeline jobs from coming to Fairbanks unless they had adequate resources to sustain themselves" (1978: 119). An influx did occur, but welfare recipients (except unemployment insurance) declined.

> After pipeline construction began, the number of people and families receiving food stamps declined dramatically. From January 1973 to January 1976 there was a 90 percent drop in food stamp recipients in Fairbanks, from 3,007 persons to 310 persons. From 1972 to 1975, the number of public assistance cases in Fairbanks declined by 31 percent [p. 105].

While Fairbanks avoided the problems of high welfare needs, it suffered a severe local employment problem. More local people sought pipeline jobs than was expected, leaving many unfilled local jobs at the very time when additional local jobs were being created. The newcomers, however, did not fill local jobs: Most of them were determined to obtain pipeline jobs, and those that could not get pipeline jobs immediately left the area or relied on unemployment insurance to maintain themselves until they could get a pipeline job. The cost of living was too high for migrants to live on wages from local jobs, so they took such jobs only for a short time. This pattern contributed to very high turnover rates in local businesses and agencies. An extreme example involved the post office's 30 mail carrier jobs. It hired an average of 10 new carriers each month to keep these jobs filled. Overall, the Post Office had an annual turnover rate of 65 percent. The local labor supply remained a problem throughout the boom, but it was reduced somewhat by teenage labor. A survey of high school students found that one-half of them had jobs.

A thesis which Dixon developed in connection with unfulfilled expectations was the importance of preventive or anticipatory actions in altering the course of developments. The campaign to discourage unprepared job seekers was one of several examples cited. Another example of action which averted anticipated negative impacts was the city's conversion of several major traffic arteries into one-way streets to reduce automobile idling in the downtown area. This action was effective in reducing carbon monoxide levels below preconstruction levels in spite of increased traffic and preventing "one of the impacts most feared by people concerned about the Fairbanks environment" (1978: 119). Another anticipated impact of the boom was particulate air pollution, which would increase ice fog and reduce visibility and therefore hamper airport operations. The impact on airport operations was averted, however, when the airport installed a new instrument landing system. These and other examples were compiled by Dixon to illustrate that "a community is not merely a passive recipient of change; it has the power to affect the shape of change" (p. 119).

Although some of the anticipated negative impacts of the boom were avoided, many occurred as expected: inflation and scarcity of housing and other goods and services. Inflation was offset for some Fairbanks' residents by higher earnings on pipeline jobs and increased profits for businessmen, but the net economic situation of the average non-pipeline worker declined because inflation outgained wages. The higher earnings for pipeline workers generally was not due to much higher wages rates. For example, union laborers earned $9.60 an hour at both pipeline and non-pipeline jobs, and nonunion non-pipeline laborers earned from $4.00 and up. Pipeline workers, however, worked an extra 20 to 30 hours a week, and therefore commonly earned twice as much in a week. Union non-pipeline laborers generally earned around $1664 per week, and the pipeline laborers earned around $3536.

Inflation and scarcity are best illustrated by the housing market and the telephone service. In November 1973, posted vacancy surveys indicated a 7.2 percent vacancy rate in apartments. One year later the rate was 2.2 percent, and six months it was later 0.5 percent. The large complexes were fully occupied and had waiting lists. The housing scarcity was accompanied by increased rents which were sometimes exhorbitant. The State Commissioner of Commerce investigated the situation, declared a housing emergency, and imposed rent control. Thus, further inflation was moderated, but the action was not retroactive and did not apply to new housing.

The housing shortage was met in three ways: trailers, doubling up, and rooming houses. Dixon estimated that more newcomers were accommodated by doubling up than lived in trailers or campers. Residents opened their houses to visitors, guests, and tenants and "Fairbanks acted like a sponge" (p. 110). Dixon further estimated that about 25 rooming houses were started during the boom which were notorious for their crowded conditions.

> In some cases, a landlord would divide the basement of a house to accommodate as many people as beds would fit into the space. In some cases, there were not any beds. Most places charged $10 per night. In one of the more publicized dormitories, 45 people slept in a converted two-bedroom house [1978: 111].

The scarcity of goods and services is illustrated by the problems of the telephone company in servicing the expanded population. Three months after construction began the telephone company exhausted its capacity and could not service new customers until new equipment was installed, which was expected to take two years. A waiting list of 1564 people was quickly formed, and the existing service deteriorated from system overload. Telephone calls took several tries and, at times, several hours to complete. In one year the number of telephone trouble reports increased by 69 percent.

One would think that the businesses and agencies of Fairbanks would have been better prepared for the boom. Before accusing the businessmen of short-sightedness and poor business sense, however, one must consider their past experiences.

> In 1970 it appeared that the pipeline construction boom was imminent and many forward-thinking business persons in Fairbanks expanded their inventories and operations to accommodate the anticipated increased demands. Due to the delay in pipeline construction, their investments were not profitable and many sustained heavy losses. . . . These recent experiences, coupled with the long boom/bust history of Fairbanks, led many to believe that it was more realistic to view the pipeline period as a temporary boom and more responsible to react accordingly by limiting their investments. They applied the same principles to decision-making in the public realm and received reinforcement from consultants and state agency personnel. . . .
>
> To business and community leaders, it seemed more responsible to "only bet on a sure thing" [1978: 134-135].

Although this position of business and community leaders is too conservative, it recognizes the difficulty of predicting the future accurately enough to make profitable or effective investment decisions. As Corrigan (1976) observed in his review of western boom towns, "so many energy projects have been proposed, withdrawn, reviewed and revised that any community would be hard put to prepare for whatever might result" (1976: 1152). In this regard one should note that the cases reviewed in this chapter give further evidence that the general boom town patterns have many exceptions.

## XI. ROCK SPRINGS/GREEN RIVER, WYOMING

The case of the coal, oil, and trona mining boom in Sweetwater County, Wyoming, is described by Gilmore and Duff (1975). The towns most directly affected were Rock Springs (see also Myhra's account in Section V) and Green River. The county population increased over 100 percent from 1970 to 1974, which produced many negative boom effects. The authors described severe problems due to scarcities in housing, health, recreational, and educational services. Inflation, crime rates, and shortages of goods and services are other problems that they reviewed. They concluded emphatically, "The boom has seriously damaged the quality of life for county residents" (1975: 10). The quality of life was especially low for "fringe dwellers":

> A substantial share of the population increase since 1970 is housed in mobile home subdivisions or "colonies" sprawled in chaotic fashion throughout the unincorporated areas of the county. An estimated 1,000 mobile homes are presently located in these scattered, isolated fringe developments. These mobile home communities usually lack proper water, sewer, or sanitation facilities. The homes are poorly constructed and create a serious fire hazard.

> Such settlements offer little opportunity or encouragement for new-comers to participate in community life. Social cohesion suffers as alienation and emotional distress feed on each other. Alcoholism, petty crime, educational problems of children, and boredom of spouse are seen in higher proportions among fringe dwellers than among people living in established communities [1975: 12-13].

The ranking of problems by the percentage of county residents mentioning it as a problem in a survey was as follows:

   (1)   Inadequate housing (45%),
   (2)   poor traffic flows (27%);
   (3)   lack of entertainment and recreational facilities (23%);
   (4)   congestion and overcrowded conditions (20%);
   (5)   high prices and cost of living (20%);
   (6)   lack of paved streets and roads (19%);
   (7)   poor or overcrowded public school facilities (17%);
   (8)   inadequate medical facilities and shortage of medical personnel (15%);
   (9)   crime and drugs (13%);

(10)  inadequate shopping facilities and services (12%);

(11)  poor sewage disposal (11%).

A major thesis of Gilmore and Duff is that the adverse living conditions caused by the boom reduced "the profitability and productivity of industry" (p. 10). They cited shortfalls in production goals, high turnover rates (in some cases annual rates exceeded 100 percent), and cost overruns, concluding:

> All of these problems are primarily attributed to the difficulties of recruiting and retaining satisfactory employees. . . . [M]uch of this difficulty can be attributed to the quality of life problems besetting the community [1975: 15].

When interviewed, most residents were satisfied with their jobs but considered going elsewhere because of unsatisfactory living conditions.

## SUMMARY

The above cases of boom towns perform two functions. First, they indicate the kinds of problems to be anticipated in boom towns. Second, they demonstrate that few things are certain in boom towns. Large increases in school enrollments are expected in boom towns, but they failed to materialize in Fairbanks. Fiscal problems are expected, but they did not occur in Calvert Cliffs. Increasing crime rates are expected, but crime rates were fairly constant in Page, Arizona (Little, 1977). Unemployment in the community is expected to rise at the close of the construction phase, but Sweet Home, Oregon, had a healthy labor market when nearby dam construction ceased. Therefore, many problems of boom towns are fairly predictable, but assessors should also be prepared for surprises.

*Chapter 7*

# COMMUNITY DECLINE IN RURAL AREAS

## Introduction

Many public projects or actions are related to the growth or decline of rural communities. The previous chapter reviewed the consequences of very rapid growth. In this chapter we describe both gradual and precipitous decline (bust towns). We leave unexamined the fourth type of change: gradual growth. It is generally the desired type of change, and, therefore, is not generally problematic for impact assessors. When gradual growth does have significant negative consequences it is usually in the less extreme forms of the negative consequences of boom towns. As such, it does not warrant a separate discussion.

Community decline is a major negative impact of some public projects and policies. This fact is often overlooked because public projects are known to stimulate economic activity and community growth and are often justified, in part, on this basis. But booms often become busts, military bases close, and project-induced economic growth in some communities may mean decline in other communities. An example of the latter is the proposed enlargement of Locks and Dam # 26 on the Mississippi River by the Corps of Engineers. By facilitating barge transportation on the Mississippi, the enlarged lock would divert freight from competing railroad lines and thus accelerate railroad line abandonment. The communities along the affected railroad lines expect to lose some of their industries and population. Accordingly, they oppose the project.

In the majority of SIAs involving community decline, the decline is accounted as a negative impact of the no-action or no-build option. Therefore, social impact assessors need to understand the changes associated with community decline in order to evaluate the consequences of not carrying out a project which would cause community development. Many rural communities are declining and are trying to attract industry and other types of economic activity in order to provide badly needed employment for community residents. The advocates of development are anxious to protect their investments and make more money, but they also want to counter the social consequences of community decline, including the outmigration of young adults. The impact assessor must determine the probable negative impacts of the proposed project and the likelihood, extent, and negative impacts of community decline without the project. In sum, social impact assessors need to be experts on community change, whether it is growth or decline.

Gradually and rapidly declining communities are discussed separately in this chapter, although the distinction is often hard to make. Rapidly declining towns are further divided into boom/bust and stable/bust towns. Construction projects typically produce the former and military base closings are more typical of the latter. In the boom/bust pattern, many newcomers arrive to work on the project but leave again in a few years. The town normally returns more or less to its old ways, but not always. Sometimes the town learns to plan and to undertake challenging projects as a by-product of adjusting to the boom problems. If it does adapt, then even after the bust the town may have a new dynamism and pursue growth objectives rather than settle back into comfortable old ways.

The second type of rapidly declining rural community is the stable/bust town. When a stable town experiences a bust, a sudden economic decline due to a mine, plant, or military base closing, the negative impacts can be severe. It is not the temporary construction worker who must seek employment elsewhere, but the long-term resident. The Migration of townspeople is not evidenced by trailers being towed out of town, but by abandoned houses and boarded up stores. The bust does not return the town to its prior *gemeinschaft*, but forces the distancing of friends and relatives as many residents must leave. Depression and discouragement generally pervade the shrunken town.

Most declining rural communities are slowly dying towns rather than bust towns. Nevertheless, there are probably more case studies of bust towns than declining towns, although there are not many of either. On the other hand, considerable research on aggregate growth, change, and decline in rural areas is available for describing the general conditions of rural America and explaining why some rural communities decline while others prosper economically. The next section examines gradually declining rural communities, but it also describes how rural America is changing. Thus, a baseline picture is provided for impact assessors who must evaluate the consequences of project- or policy-induced growth, change, or decline on rural communities. The next section begins with the facts and figures on demographic and economic changes in rural America, and then reviews the theories which try to explain declining towns. It also considers the consequences of gradual decline, which are largely negative. This is why many rural communities launch development programs to halt their decline.

## Declining Rural Towns

### FACTS AND FIGURES ON DEMOGRAPHIC CHANGES IN RURAL AREAS

The national population has grown moderately and unevenly. It increased 18.5 percent from 1950 to 1960 and 13.3 percent from 1960 to 1970, but almost all of the growth has been in urban areas. The rural population remained relatively stable from 1930 to 1970 at around 54 million, while the urban population increased from 69 million to 149 million. Urban growth results from the natural increase of urban population and the substantial rural to urban migration. The reclassification of some of the rural areas as urban areas also accounts for some of the urban growth. The definition of urban includes all persons in urbanized areas and in places of 2500 or more outside of urbanized areas. Between censuses the borders of some urban areas expand, and some places become urban by growing past 2500. The area in the 290 largest cities increased from 7610 to 15,588 square miles from 1950 to 1970. Thus, the rural area has declined while the rural population has remained constant, indicating that the density of rural areas has increased (Campbell, 1975).

The focus of this chapter is on the population changes in nonmetropolitan United States. Overall nonmetropolitan population increased only 6.7 percent from 1960 to 1970, while metropolitan population increased 16.6 percent. The low overall nonmetropolitan growth rate combines a healthy growth of the nonfarm population (19.3 percent) with a significant decline in the farm population (-36.0 percent). The farm population was fairly constant from 1920 to 1940 but declined from 30,547,000 in 1940 to 7,806,000 in 1977, only 3.6 percent of the U.S. population. The farm population was 62 percent of the rural population in 1920 and dropped to 15 percent in 1970. It should be noted that further declines in the farm population will have little effect on the nonmetropolitan population growth rate, since the farm population is now such a small percentage of this population.

Rural no longer means agricultural. Rural life is occupationally heterogeneous and urbanized in a number of ways. Campbell (1975) argued that ever since the rural nonfarm surpassed the rural farm population between 1940 and 1950, "the rural population was for the most part urbanized. . . . The residents were now employed in a diversity of occupations, and the homogeneity of interests and other characteristics was disappearing" (1975: 99). According to Haren (1974), employment in manufacturing increased in nonmetropolitan counties twice as rapidly as in metropolitan counties from 1959 to 1969. As a result, the percentage of the labor force which was employed in manufacturing in 1970 was about the same for nonmetropolitan and metropolitan counties, although some nonmetropolitan workers commuted to their jobs in metropolitan counties (Hines et. al., 1975).

Rural areas are further urbanized by the inmigration of urbanites. About one-fourth of the rural white adult population had been reared in cities. Finally, rural areas are urbanized by institutional connections and by the mass media. The isolation and relative self-sufficiency of rural villages has disappeared. Schools have been consolidated into regional school systems, more businesses are extralocally owned, more government functions are provided by higher levels of government, and many goods and services are obtained at the nearest urban center. The mass media provide rural areas with largely the same programs, advertisements, and information that the New Yorker receives. In sum, urban and rural are categories which still refer to differences in size and density but decreasingly distinguish distinct patterns of life.

Since 1970, rural population has grown faster than urban population. From 1970 to 1974 metropolitan counties grew 3.4 percent, while nonmetropolitan counties grew 5.6 percent. Of the latter, counties adjacent to metropolitan areas increased 6.3 percent and nonadjacent counties 4.9 percent, but the entirely rural counties of the nonadjacent group grew 6.1 percent (Beale, 1978). Some of the rural growth involves commuting to urban areas, but much of it is unrelated to urban sprawl. The decline of rural areas has finally been reversed. The entirely rural counties had an inmigration from 1970 to 1974 of 4.4 percent.

Of course, the rural renaissance is strong in some areas while other areas continue to decline. Out of 2469 nonmetropolitan counties, 516 declined in population from 1970 to 1974, although generally their rate of decline was less than before 1970. According to Beale (1978: 50):

Most of them were in the Great Plains, scattered from North Dakota to Texas. The Western Corn Belt and the Mississippi Delta also had noticeable clusters of declining counties. Many of the declining counties are associated with high dependence on agriculture or with high proportions of black population. There is still some force for outmigration in such settings.

The most comprehensive study of population changes in nonmetropolitan areas is by Fugitt (1971). He examined all incorporated centers which were not in the 1960, SMASs, but excluded the communities which had metropolitan characteristics and were in townships and counties adjacent to SMASs. The nonmetropolitan incorporated centers contained 34 million people in 1970, which was 53 percent of the total nonmetropolitan population of 64 million. On the whole, these incorporated places grew 29 percent in population from 1950 to 1970, indicating that rural towns were not dying but were doing fairly well.

The detailed picture for decade population changes from 1950 to 1970 is presented in Table 7.1. In all size groupings but the smallest, more places grew than declined in both decades. In the 1950s 57 percent of all nonmetropolitan incorporated places grew, and in the 1960s 56 percent grew. If the table is reorganized such that places having population changes of less than 10 percent are classified as stable, then a high percentage of places were stable in both decades, with stability increasing from 42 percent in the 1950s to 47 percent in the 1960s. In both decades the number of places with significant growth (10+ percent) were one and a half times the number with significant decline.

The larger the place, the more likely it was to grow and to grow substantially (10 percent or more). In the 1950s 55 percent of places over 10,000 population grew 10 percent or more, and the percentage of places growing substantially declined with each size category to 24 percent for places under 500 population. In the 1960s all size categories had about the same percentage (around 34 percent) of places with 10 percent or more growth. Substantial declines (10 percent or more), on the other hand, occur most frequently in smaller places in both decades. Table 7.1 can be summarized by three points: nonmetropolitan incorporated places tended to grow from 1950 to 1970; growth was positively associated with size of place; and this association was much weaker in the 1960s than in the 1950s.

Beale (1974) replicated Fuguitt's study with finer size categories for rural towns under 1000 population. Using only incorporated places in the north central region, which has an exceptionally high rate of incorporation, Beale calculated the percentage of rural towns with population loss from 1960 to 1970. Only 36.0 percent of places of 1000-2499 lost population, while 67.5 percent of places of under 100 lost population. Places of less than 400 were more likely to decline than to increase, but the opposite was true of communities of 400 or more (Beale, 1974: 6).

From the above it can be concluded that the bulk of the growth that did occur in rural areas in the 1950s and 1960s occurred in the larger places and the cities. Rural residency was becoming more concentrated.

Rural residency in these decades was also becoming more oriented toward metropolitan centers. The interstate highway system and improved state

TABLE 7.1   Distribution of Places by Percentage Change Over a
            Decade, Nonmetropolitan United States, 1950-1960 and
            1960-1970

| Size of Place at Beginning of Decade | Distribution of Places by Percentage Change | | | | | | |
|---|---|---|---|---|---|---|---|
| | Loss | | Gain | | | | |
| | 10+ | 0-9 | 0-9 | 10-19 | 20+ | Total | Number |
| 1950-1960 | | | | percentage | | | |
| All places | 23 | 20 | 22 | 15 | 20 | 100 | 12,809 |
| 10,000 and over | 5 | 14 | 26 | 23 | 32 | 100 | 555 |
| 2500-9999 | 7 | 17 | 26 | 20 | 30 | 100 | 1,718 |
| 1000-2499 | 13 | 20 | 26 | 18 | 23 | 100 | 2,483 |
| 500-999 | 19 | 22 | 25 | 14 | 20 | 100 | 2,728 |
| Less than 500 | 38 | 21 | 17 | 11 | 13 | 100 | 5,325 |
| *1960-1970 (Grouped by size in 1950)* | | | | | | | |
| Places existing 1950 | 21 | 23 | 24 | 14 | 18 | 100 | 12,809 |
| 10,000 and over | 11 | 27 | 28 | 15 | 19 | 100 | 555 |
| 2500-9999 | 11 | 26 | 29 | 16 | 18 | 100 | 1,718 |
| 1000-2499 | 12 | 25 | 28 | 16 | 19 | 100 | 2,483 |
| 500-999 | 17 | 23 | 26 | 16 | 18 | 100 | 2,728 |
| Less than 500 | 32 | 21 | 18 | 11 | 18 | 100 | 5,325 |
| New places, 1960 | 22 | 13 | 14 | 14 | 37 | 100 | 522 |

SOURCE:  Fuguitt (1971: 454).

highway systems facilitated increasing numbers of metropolitan workers
living in nonmetropolitan areas. Morrison and Wheeler (1976) pointed out
that the nonmetropolitan counties from which 20 percent or more of the
labor force commuted to SMSAs had annual population growth rates of .9
percent from 1960 to 1970 and 2.0 percent from 1970 to 1974, while all
nonmetropolitan counties had annual growth rates of only .4 percent and 1.3
percent. A number of studies have compared the growth rates of places which
are near to or far from urban centers, and the near ones grow faster. Campbell
(1975) reported that areas with population 10,000 and over that were within
50 miles of the nearest SMSA grew 22.7 percent from 1950 to 1960, and the
others grew only 10.8 percent. Furthermore, the growth rate was greater
when interstate highways facilitated access. Fuguitt (1971) reported similar
findings for rural places of various sizes.

   Migration is the process which accounts for the above findings. For an
understanding of the situation of rural American, it is important to examine

the migrants. Nonmetropolitan to metropolitan migration selects the young adults, the better educated, the more capable, and the higher occupational classes (Zuiches and Brown, 1978). Migration in the opposite direction selects retired elderly people. As a result, the dependency ratio is high in nonmetropolitan areas. The selective migration, therefore, is unfavorable to nonmetropolitan areas in that those who could contribute the most economically tend to leave.

## EXPLANATIONS OF DECLINING COMMUNITIES

What is the explanation for some communities growing while others decline? Population growth or decline results from economic growth or decline, modified by changing levels of productivity and the percentage of the population in the labor force. The simple answer, therefore, is that communities differ in their ability to attract or retain economic activity. Many factors contribute to this ability, including natural resources, skilled labor, transportation, markets, low wage rates, low taxes, and community inducements to businesses.

At the national level, the decline of rural areas is due to the severe decline in the number of farm workers from 1940 to 1970 due to mechanization. Farm productivity increased, but the farm population decreased from 31 million in 1940 to 10 million in 1970. Contributing to the declining farm population was the decline in the number of farms. From 1960 to 1969 the number of farms declined from four million to three million. The acreage in farms, however, declined very little in the same period, so the average size of farms increased. "The preliminary 1972 average size of farms is 394 acres—an increase of almost 80 acres in ten years. In 1925, the average was 143 acres" (Campbell, 1975: 112). The farm which is disappearing is the small farm. The number of farms with less than $10,000 in sales declined 39 percent from 3,125,000 in 1960 to 1,898,000 in 1969. The number of medium-size farms ($10,000 to $19,999 in sales) remained almost constant, while farms with over $20,000 in sales increased 67 percent from 340,000 in 1960 to 588,000 in 1969 (Campbell, 1975: 115).

A second factor inducing general population loss in rural areas is the reduction of workers in mining, lumbering, and other extraction industries due to mechanization. Compared with the displacement of farm workers, however, their numbers are small.

The explanation for population loss or gain in specific communities or regions focuses more on the increase in nonfarm population than on the decline in farm population. The mechanization of farming is more advanced in some regions and on some types of land than others, leading to different rates of decline of farm workers for regions and for communities. These differences, however, are minor when compared with the changes in the nonfarm population in rural areas. In this regard it is interesting to note that rural counties increased their nonagricultural jobs faster than did urban counties between 1959 and 1969 (Beale, 1974). This enabled many rural communities to expand nonfarm jobs faster than they lost farm jobs.

The question of differential growth or decline, therefore, becomes the question of why some communities are able to generate nonfarm jobs while others are not. There are several approaches to answering this question. The major approach is location theory, which assumes that economic activity will gravitate to locations that have a comparative advantage—that is, those which are most profitable. Comparative advantage takes into account absolute advantage in producing goods and absolute advantage in marketing goods. A community or area has an absolute advantage in production when the factors of production (land, labor, capital, resources, institutions, and so on) are least expensive and most advantageous. A community or area has an absolute advantage in marketing when the profits of marketing are the greatest in that location—that is, when marketing costs are low and the sale price is high. Market and production advantages often diverge, since one requires a location near markets and the other may require a location near resources. Overall absolute advantage for a good or service applies to the location which most profitably balances the production and marketing advantages. Comparative advantage occurs when the profit on a certain commodity is greater than the profit on any other commodity using the same fixed resources. A community might have an absolute advantage relative to other areas in producing and marketing one commodity, and yet use its resources for producing another commodity which returns a better profit.

### Location Theory

Schultz (1953) used location theory to explain differential per capita incomes for regions and communities. As a rule, the production and market advantages occur in or near urban centers. Thus, the spatial pattern of economic activity is shaped by the spatial pattern of cities. As a result, even agricultural activities located near industrial-urban centers have overall advantages compared with those on the periphery. Furthermore, rural communities near urban centers are better able to adjust to the displacement of labor in agriculture. They have sufficient locational advantages to obtain nonagricultural economic activities and to absorb the surplus farm labor. They are also better able to obtain additional capital for agriculture. In constrast, rural communities on the periphery experienced poverty, declining economic activity, and the outmigration of labor.

### Central Place Theory

Another approach to explaining differential economic development is central place theory It is based on the observation that various types of firms or business functions require trading areas of various population sizes. Central places are arranged in a hierarchy on the basis of the types of business functions which they contain. Business functions with similar market thresholds are brought together in central places of the appropriate level and are present also in all higher-level places. Furthermore, central places are spread across the countryside in a pattern which minimizes the distance between buyers and sellers. Unless terrain interferes, the territory would be subdivided into many small, equal-sized hexagons with a first-order place in the center of each. One out of nine of these first-order places will also be a second-order place, and the second-order places will form a similar pattern of hexagons, but on a larger scale. The pattern is repeated up to the single largest city which is at the center of the territory.

Central place theory is a reasonably accurate description of the organization of commercial trade centers where farms are fairly evenly spread throughout the region. Centers based on other extraction industries or manufacturing are less well predicted. It is basically a static theory, but it provides a framework for understanding some differential economic changes of centers. As the means of transportation and the economics of various types of business functions change, the central place pattern is affected. Most areas were settled in horse-and-buggy days and are not efficiently spaced for current means of transportation. Furthermore, new technologies and factors favorable to concentrating economic activity are making some lower levels of central places less viable as currently spaced. For example, Hodge (1965) found that 46 percent of the 358 hamlets in Saskatchewan in 1941 "expired" by 1961 and only two percent moved up to "minimum convenience shopping centers" (see Table 7.2). In the same period, 65 percent of minimum convenience shopping centers lost business functions and regressed to hamlet status or expired altogether. Each subsequent level in the central place hierarchy showed increasing viability.

### Export Base Theory

While central place theory focuses on the spacing, organization, and viability of commercial centers, the third approach to explaining differential economic change, export base theory, focuses on the noncommercial economic activities of a community or region. It divides total employment into employment in basic export industries and nonbasic employment. Export

TABLE 7.2    Changes in the Proportion of Trade Centers Among Classes, Saskatchewan, 1941-1967 (Class of Center in 1961)

| Class of Center of 1941 | Expired by 1961 | Hamlet | Min. Conv. | Full Conv. | Part. Shop. | Comp. Shop. | Sec. W-R[a] | Prim. W-R[a] |
|---|---|---|---|---|---|---|---|---|
| | | | | (percentages) | | | | |
| New Center (1942-1951) | 48 | 52 | | | | | | |
| Hamlet | 46 | 52 | 02 | | | | | |
| Min. Conv. | 02 | 63 | 27 | 07 | 01 | | | |
| Full Conv. | | -6 | 28 | 39 | 26 | 01 | | |
| Part. Shop. | | | 02 | 19 | 63 | 16 | | |
| Compl. Shop. | | | | | 12 | 73 | 15 | |
| Secondary W-R | | | | | | | 100 | |
| Primary W-R | | | | | | | | 100 |

a.  Wholesale-Retail
SOURCE:  Hodge (1965: 96).

industries obtain money from outside the area from customers, taxes, or funding agencies. Nonbasic industries are local service industries. The ratio of nonbasic to basic employment is taken to represent the number of additional jobs which each export industry job generates. Thus, communities or regions must increase their export industries in order to grow. Export industries are increased through the development of natural resources, the expansion of present export industries, and the enticement of businesses and public agencies to locate in the community. Local entrepreneurship and leadership; concessions to businesses; political influence; and effective schools, roads, utilities, and institutions help obtain export industries, but luck also plays a major role.

### Historical Explanation

Another approach to understanding growth and decline of communities and regions is the historical analysis of labor surpluses. The historical analysis considers the early settlement of areas and the subsequent technological, economic, and social developments which form new economic patterns and create shortages or surpluses of labor. Surpluses are indicated by unemployment and low capital inputs per worker. In rural areas some people scratch out a meager living farming poor land with minimal equipment. Their productivity is low and they are inefficiently employed. They and the unemployed should move to areas of greater opportunity. In the long run both labor and capital move to places providing higher returns, but the story of poverty in America indicates how slow and imperfect this adjustment is. Furthermore, it is nearly impossible for certain types of people to get jobs anywhere under present labor market conditions.

The historical approach would consider many unique events and factors for each community in explaining its growth and decline. Nevertheless, several factors apply to a large number of places. For example, Caudill (1965) discussed four historical factors which account for much of the poverty in America today. Three of these factors also account for some of the stagnation, decline, and labor surpluses in many rural communities: settlement patterns, changes in soil quality, and slavery.

The settlement pattern of the frontier involved three "human waves." The first wave consisted of frontiersmen, backwoodsmen, hunters, and wanderers. Behind them came the temporary or scratch farmers. "Behind these waves flowed a third, the farmers and town-builders who secured the continent and began the process of transforming its raw resources into useable wealth" (Caudill, 1965: 4). The third wave, however, did not inundate all areas. Some areas with poor resources remained the preserves of the first two waves. These backwoods areas had a culture that was antithetical to the dominant culture and hindered the assimilation of generations of their populations into the mainstream. "This backwoods subculture is predominant today in Appalachia and the Ozarks, but it also holds sway over destitute millions scattered in other regions" (1965: 5).

Changes in soil quality have also produced destitute people. The frontier situation encouraged improper agricultural practices and profligate uses of resources. Land was cleared by burning and slashing. The tough grasses which hold the soil in place were plowed under and the soil was washed or blown away. The productivity of the soil declined. Poor land supports poor people.

The third factor which produced poverty and hindered the flow of labor to areas of superior opportunity was slavery. Not only did slavery create population densities in rural areas far too great for the resource and capital bases, but it also kept the blacks uneducated before emancipation and poorly educated after emancipation. Discrimination then hindered the absorption of blacks into the industrial labor force. In the past half-century a massive migration of southern blacks to northern cities has occurred, but millions of poor and underemployed blacks remain in southern rural communities.

The major contribution of the historical approach to the explanation of differential economic performance of communities and regions is its emphasis on social factors. Backwoods culture, the social systems of slavery and the postemancipation South, job discrimination in northern cities, attitudes toward nature and land use, and the psychological resistance to pulling up stakes are factors used to explain poverty. In contrast, the earlier approaches deal with abstract economic considerations; they assume that people simply follow economic rules and their "irrational" behavior is simply included in the error term and are soon lost from view.

### Poverty Ghettoization Theory

The final approach considered here for explaining rural economic decline is the rural poverty ghettoization thesis set out by Bender et al. (1971) and reported by Doeksen et al. (1974):

> The thesis proposes three interrelated subprocesses that reinforce each other in such a way that low incomes, inadequate institutions, and poverty prone people tend to accumulate to form a rural ghetto. These subprocesses are termed as: intergenerational familial poverty, class-selective migration, and changes in the productivity of social and economic institutions. The subprocess of intergenerational poverty concerns families with histories of economic and social deprivation. Succeeding generations of these families tend to remain in poverty. Class-selective migration involves the type of migrant who moves into or out of a region. The style of life in a declining region screens out certain classes of potential in-migrants and encourages out-migration of these same classes within the region. The out-migrants are the highly educated and the in-migrants are the unskilled workers with similar values, attitudes, and characteristics to those of the people left in the region. The third subprocess in the poverty ghettoization thesis is the change in the productivity of social and economic institutions. Community leaders and local officials allow private firms to "externalize" their costs, and public goods are supplied inadequately and inefficiently due to sparse population, causing the region to attract low-wage industries. Normally, these industries do not require many complementary community services and are not required to pay taxes to support the complex community infrastructure because of tax exemptions granted by the community.

Tweeten (developed in Tweeten, 1970, and summarized in Tweeten and Brinkman, 1976) provides a theory of economic stagnation which elaborates on the poverty ghettoization thesis. His theory describes three sets of factors which cause cumulative economic depression. The first includes economic and social changes that require adjustment, starting with oversettlement and "including (1) a decline in demand for products produced, (2) a depletion of natural resources through mining or erosion, (3) technical obsolescence, and (4) a social upheaval" (Tweeten and Brinkman, 1976: 159). He cites slavery, the Civil War, and racial discrimination as examples of the last factor.

The second set of factors causing cumulative depression is the capacity of individuals, groups, and areas to adjust to changing economic conditions.

> This capacity to adjust is highest in areas where (1) birthrates are low, (2) educational levels are high, (3) transportation and communication are adequate, (4) people have a "mobility ethic" fostered by past

migration, (5) the culture of the area is compatible with that in areas offering migrants greater economic opportunity, (6) there are no institutional barriers such as racial discrimination to reduce mobility to regions receiving migrants, and (7) the area is in reasonable proximity to an urban-industrial complex.

The above list demonstrates that Tweeten's theory emphasizes migration as the major mode of adjustment.

The third set of factors causing cumulative depression is the negative institutional and attitudinal responses to adverse economic conditions which retard economic adjustment. Schools and the family should prepare people for adjustment responses such as moving. Local leaders and local government should try to maintain quality services even in the face of declining resources in order that the area might attract new economic activities. A climate of optimism and energy is a major inducement to industry, but "general pessimism is apt to pervade the area" (Tweeten and Brinkman 1976: 161). Tweeten describes how alienation, demoralization, fatalism, and hopelessness become widespread and choke off efforts to improve things. Furthermore, as people fail to achieve economically, they elevate family and religion over work as the source of greatest satisfaction in life. Turning inward to the family and withdrawing from organizations outside the family further reduces their ability to adapt and achieve. Finally, Tweeten applies the subculture of poverty thesis to explain the cumulation of depression and the failure of people in depressed rural areas to adapt more successfully. The subculture of poverty includes many attitudes from "pervading mistrust" to a "short-term time perspective" which hinder individual advancement in American society. As Tweeten acknowledges, the validity of the subculture of poverty thesis is still hotly debated. One side contends that this culture causes and perpetuates poverty; the other side contends that the culture results from the circumstances of the poor. According to the second view, when their circumstances improve they will act more like the rest of society. Tweeten holds the first view, and therefore is pessimistic about the effects of programs to help the poor.

The general theories reviewed in the previous discussion fail to mention a number of specific factors which favor community growth. We note that some of the fastest growing rural areas are growing because of an increased demand for a resource of the area. Demand is increasing rapidly for good climate, recreational resources, and energy resources. Retirement communities in attractive climates, recreational areas, and energy boom towns are rapidly growing communities that do not need to be explained by complex theories. Retirement, recreation, and energy are currently rural growth industries.

## THE CONSEQUENCES OF COMMUNITY DECLINE

The consequences of community decline are generally negative for the people who stay in the community and mixed for the migrants. In this section we first follow the plight of those who leave the community to seek their fortune elsewhere and then survey the conditions of those who stay and have to adjust to the ramifications of community decline.

The manner of the exodus is critical to its effects. If it is precipitated by the cut-back, relocation, or demise of industries, the movers are likely to have dim prospects. When skilled and older workers lose their jobs, they are likely to lose all seniority benefits and may find their skills unmarketable. They and their families are also likely to have deep roots in the community and may suffer considerable social costs when moving. If, on the other hand, the decline is gradual and based mainly on the exodus of young people, they are likely to fare well in their new locations which have greater opportunities. In general, migrants fare better than those who stay behind according to several studies reviewed below.

Tweeten and Brinkman (1976) report on numerous studies which show that rural-to-urban migrants are better off than the rural nonmigrant. They present findings from a U.S. Department of Agriculture study (1971: 9, 10), indicating:

> In 1966 median family income of whites was $7,855 for rural-urban migrants, $8,557 for urban nonmigrants, and $6,198 for rural non-migrants. For blacks the median family income was $5,116 for rural-urban migrants, $5,015 for urban nonmigrants, and $2,778 for rural nonmigrants [Tweeten and Brinkman, 1976: 89-90].

Some of these differences are explained by the outmigration of the better educated and more capable young residents, but much of it is due to the greater opportunities in the cities. Numerous other studies indicate that rural-to-urban migrants improve their standard of living (for example, Anschel and Bordeaux, 1972; Deaton and Anschel, 1974; Lansing and Morgan, 1967).

The people who stay in declining communities generally experience negative economic, social, and psychological impacts. Some lose jobs; others have less work or fewer customers, and all suffer a reduction in services or opportunities. Many of these changes are small and even trivial—for example, having to go to the next town for a haircut—but they add up to nontrivial changes in the quality of life.

The major economic change in declining communities is loss of employment, which often means a period of unemployment followed by employment in a less rewarding job. Some are forced to migrate to find work, as discussed above. Most people who retain their jobs maintain their way of life at a somewhat reduced standard. Their income may decline due to less work or fewer customers. The cost of goods and services increases as the market shrinks. Goods and services are more difficult to obtain and require greater transportation costs because some stores and services go out of business. When services like health care are farther away, they are used less frequently and the standard of living declines. The standard of living is also affected by increased per capita costs for services which result from population declines. Cost increases reduce demand further, and so services are cut back even more or else businesses raise their prices to stay in business. Each step produces further losses in standard of living.

The loss of population and economic activity by a community is associated with numerous social changes as religious, recreational, educational, cultural, governmental, welfare, and associational activities likewise decline. For example, Beal (1965) reported on studies which demonstrate declining religious opportunities with declining population. The cost of maintaining churches in open country in Missouri was found to be twice as much per member as churches in towns of over 2500. Churches are not only less expensive per member in larger centers, but they provide more services and activities; their ministers are better trained, more capable, and full-time; and their services are of higher quality (Beal 1965: 155, 156). Other institutions, such as education, also decline in quality as the community declines.

One mode of adjusting to declining population is consolidation or centralization. However, there are unanticipated consequences of these processes. Beal (1965) points out that in many cases when churches consolidate, members of one or both churches are lost in the consolidation process. School consolidation also results in declining participation.

> School reorganization usually means larger units. This often results in greater distances traveled on buses. A study in the South found a significant relationship between the number of high school "drop outs" and the number of miles pupils traveled on the bus. A related generalization was that parents participated less in school affairs the further they lived from the school. . . . Formal group social participation studies indicate a positive relationship between closeness to meeting place and degree of participation [1965: 157].

Another type of unanticipated consequence of community decline is the conflict generated by the adjustment process. Increasing scarcity creates troublesome issues and commonly intensifies conflicts over allocation decisions. Beal (1965) observed these patterns in declining communities.

> Among the greatest problems arising from choosing to reorganize in order to adjust to a declining population are the conflicts among

individuals and groups in deciding, planning and carrying out the action. Many of us have observed widespread and deep-seated conflicts arising from attempts made to reorganize school, church, government or group economic activities [1965: 158].

Community decline also has psychological costs, ad described by Wilkinson (1974: 50): "Case study literature provides us with a picture of community decline characterized by frustration, anxiety, ambivalence, cognitive distortion, negativism, and conservatism." The frustration and resentment attendant upon community decline are illustrated in the death by dieselization study reported at length later. In this case the resentment was directed against the railroad company which had closed down its steam locomotive servicing operation in "Caliente" without making any provision for the community that literally existed for the railroad. The frustration found in Caliente and many other rural communities is largely due to being out of step with the times and the larger society. Such towns are the losers in the competitive political economy. They are antiquated by technological advances. What they produce for the larger society loses its value as in Caliente, or they fail to keep up technologically in their methods of production and become economically unviable, as is the case for many small farms. In addition to the frustration of economic problems is the frustration of being on a losing team.

## CASE STUDIES OF GRADUALLY DECLINING TOWNS

### East Parrish, Clyde, and Spiresburg—Three Towns Trying to Survive

Simon and Gagnon (1967) described the plight of three rural towns in southern Illinois which were struggling to survive. The area had poor soils which could only support meager subsistence farming, so farming was a declining industry. The major economic activity of the area was coal mining, which peaked in the mid 1920s and steadily declined thereafter except during World War II. After 25 years of extensive population decline, the three communities took steps to prevent further declines. Simon and Gagnon tell the story of these efforts to recover in the 1950s and 1960s. Coal mining was still declining rapidly. During the 1950s employment in mining decreased by 71 percent in East Parrish, 72 percent in Clyde, and 61 percent in Spiresburg while population declined 21 percent, 11 percent, and six percent, respectively.

East Parrish was the first to take community action to reverse its decline by raising $100,000 from over 2000 public contributors for the East Parrish Industrial Fund in the early 1950s. Little was done with the money, however. The interest it gained was used to subsidize the local Chamber of

Commerce, which did little to promote new economic activity because the chamber was controlled by conservatives who worried more about the problems that new companies could create than about the problems that would result from further declines. After remaining in the bank for eight years, the fund was finally used to rebuild a burned-down dress factory and was used little thereafter. No other measures were taken to prevent the community from declining further. "To date no federal funds have been requested— except for some public housing and clearance--and on at least two occasions they were rejected by community leaders when offered" (Simon and Gagnon, 1967: 44). Politically, East Parrish is the only town with an organized and politically active working class. The middle class, however, is badly split and opposed to the miners. The result is that the formal political system is ineffectual and is not relied upon to get things done.

Clyde is a county seat of about 7000 people, and therefore provides some middle-class jobs in the county government. It is more attractive than typical coal towns and affects a middle-class air. It has been run by a series of strong mayors without significant participation by an apathetic citizenry. Most members of the upper middle class are interested in keeping things as they are, and the few who would like to see significant development acquiesce to the present power holders.

The major developmental effort was a local water development on a nearby lake financed through taxes and intended to make Clyde a recreational center and to attract new industry.

> It is thus not unexpected that Clyde's major bid for renewal came not from some broad, popular campaign, but from an administrative unit of government; that it did not seek funds through public appeal, but through taxation [1967: 48].

Spiresburg is also a county seat, but smaller, with a population of 3000. Its two major mines gave out in the early 1930s, so mining is no longer the major source of employment. It has no natural advantages over the other two towns and countless others in the area, but was the most successful of the three towns in obtaining new industry. Its success is to be credited to the political and community leadership, "a fairly well integrated group of small merchants and independent professionals and semi-professionals. . . . Social contacts among Spiresburg's upper group is the highest for all three communities— while social participation for its workers and reliefers is the lowest for all three" (p. 49). The small size of Spiresburg greatly facilitated the leadership integration.

Spiresburg renewal success consisted of arranging for four plants to locate there. In three cases outside governmental aid was utilized and in the fourth the resources came from the community. These plants were not the most attractive types economically, so Spiresburg's renewal achievements were limited. They paid very low wages and had few white-collar or managerial positions. On the other hand, they did provide employment and helped to stabilize population, even though they will not help retain the more capable young people.

The conclusion drawn by Simon and Gagnon from their ethnographic study of the three towns is that "the quality of community leadership—particularly political leadership—is a crucial determinant of the course of development" (1967: 49). In East Parrish the widespread contributions to the Industrial Fund indicated community support for the idea of development, but the extremely conservative administration of that fund nullified its use in obtaining new economic activities. Furthermore, community conflict hindered all other public efforts at development. In Clyde the political leadership launched the water development project without the participation of the citizenry. The "stand pat" conservatism of the upper middle class made nongovernment development efforts unlikely. In contrast, Spiresburg was not shackled by conflicts or "stand pat" conservatism; it had sufficient leadership to take modest steps for development. The authors, therefore, emphasized the importance of leadership in determining the fate of small towns. They also made it clear that leadership involves more than abilities—it also involves goals and determination. All towns had the goal of development, but only Spiresburg possessed a leadership determined to achieve the goals and the capacity to execute them. Capacity was found to be partly a function of the degree of community conflict and opposition to the endeavor and partly a function of leadership integration.

The authors stressed that the leading groups of all three towns did not really want "genuine community renewal" because that would "rock the boat" and some of them might lose as a result. Real development "might bring competition to established businesses and established allocations of power" (p. 50). In each town, "despite a prevailing rhetoric of community renewal—is a deep-seated resistance to social change of any real significance. And in this respect they resemble hundreds of other declining communities" (p. 50).

The authors collected considerable evidence on the conservatism of the leading groups in the three towns, but they may have overestimated its permanence. These groups are pessimistic about inducing positive social change and with reasonably good cause. After all, how many examples could they find of successfully developing towns under similar circumstances? Optimism needs a realistic basis or it becomes fantasizing. We suggest that a taste of some success whets the appetite for more. If benefits from new plants or development projects rather than costs flow to established business and political interests, then community leaders will become less conservative and more supportive of further changes. The authors themselves point out that in Spiresburg "economic improvement has had an effect on . . . the attitudes of its citizens" (1967: 50). The citizens of Spiresburg were optimistic when asked if they thought things would get better or worse in the next few months. "Worse" was the answer of 50 percent in East Parrish, 27 percent in Clyde, and only 12 percent in Spiresburg. Spiresburg residents were also more likely to feel that their community was ideal and "that most people . . . really care about what happens to the community" than were East Parrish and Clyde residents. They were also more likely to disagree that their town "is no place for a young man just starting out." If these attitudes were changed by economic development, as the authors assume, then the conservatism of the leading group could also change.

### Springdale–An Antigrowth Town

Perhaps the best-known study of a waning American town in the sociological literature is Vidich and Bensman's *Small Town in Mass Society* (1960). It focuses on the economic, political, and social structure of "Springdale" (fictitious name), its values, and its relationship to the larger society. Their discussion of Springdale's values generally agrees with descriptions of other small rural towns and helps to explain why rural towns are not progressing more rapidly and why they are not more successful in adapting to the economic forces shaping their destinies. After presenting a capsule summary of the economic history of Springdale, we will examine its value system.

Springdale, a small rural town in upper New York state, has had several periods of growth and decline. Settlement began in 1793 based on lumbering and subsistence agriculture, and the township of Springdale gradually grew to its peak of 4323 in 1880 and the village of Springdale to 1050. The township declined to 2564 by 1930 and then grew at a slow rate in the next two decades. The decline was due to soil exhaustion and the unsuitability of rolling farmlands to the new machines and methods which were necessary for profitable farming. Lumbering had disappeared by 1880, and small-scale industry did not prosper until World War II. The small growth of population in the 1930s was due to the fact that the depression made the urban areas less attractive than the rural areas. The growth in the 1940s was due to both agricultural prosperity and employment in industry. During the War, farm prices rose and agriculture (which was largely dairy farming by this time) became prosperous for those who modernized. Even most of the traditional farmers managed to survive. In addition to agriculture, industry provided an important source of employment. Local industry remained relatively small, but regional industries expanded during the war. By 1952, one-third of the labor force of Springdale township commuted to industrial and other manual jobs.

The value system of Springdale both contributed to and hindred its economic progress. On the one hand, hard work was highly esteemed. Some marginal farms and businesses survived rough times because of the extra effort which their owners devoted to them. Many workers supplemented their income with second jobs or substantial gardens. In farm families, all members were workers. Associated with the ethic of hard work was a set of goals which justified hard work until retirement, such as "buying a house, setting up a business, raising a family, sending children to college, planning and preparing for self-support in old age" (Vidich and Bensman, 1960: 49). The dominant pattern of life, therefore, was hard work to accumulate money for "useful" rather than "foolish" spending.

The businessman's ethic, on the other hand, was not conducive to economic progress. The businessman in Springdale was a hard worker, but he was not a risk taker, nor was he oriented toward expansion.

> He is geared to the maximum utilization of his existing facilities, eschews measures which would modernize his plant at capital expense and, instead, tries to develop a clientele whose loyalty is based on personal considerations. . . .
>
> Only six out of approximately fifty businessmen are in process of investing capital. However, these are all new businessmen whose investment represents necessary expenditures toward establishing the business rather than a policy of continuous reinvestment and expansion. In the absence of efforts directed toward increasing his profits by increased capital investments and increased inventories (a more favorable merchandizing climate), he directs his efforts at a niggardly cutting of cost [1960: 53-54].

The rational farmer, in contrast, is an investor. He starts with modest capital, works hard, and over time "builds up" his farm by investing in more cows, machinery, building materials, and feed. Luxury consumption is foregone in order to make farm and home more efficient, and the farmer's heavy work schedule leaves little time for social activities. Unlike rational farmers, traditional farmers keep investments to a minimum and survive by cutting costs. They do not engage in outside social activities, but make the family a social enclave. Their social independence is matched by their economic independence. They consume little and are relatively independent of economic conditions in the larger society. They survive hard times by cutting their purchases to almost nothing, supplying their own food, and repairing possessions.

The authors identified five class groups in Springdale:

(1) The middle class, made up of independent entrepreneurs (13 percent), prosperous farmers (25 percent), and professionals and skilled industrial workers (9 percent).

(2) The marginal middle class, made up of aspiring investors (10 percent), economically and socially immobile ritualists (10 percent), and psychological idiosyncratics (2 percent).

(3) Traditional farmers (10 percent);

(4) "Old aristocrats" (1 percent); and

(5) Shack people (10 percent) [1960: 52].

Each of the ten subgroups is described by the authors. We have described the values of the three groups which have the major influence on Springdale's destiny and probably have similar effects in other small towns. The farmers and businessmen are largely responsible for creating or thwarting local economic development by their economic and political activities. The economic activities of the rational farmer generate development, while the businessmen and the traditional farmers seek only to survive, and their political activities are largely against development.

Village politics was dominated by businessmen who ran the village government in the same cost-cutting, unenterprising manner they used in running their own businesses. "It is an outstanding characteristic of village government that it does not initiate new undertakings and new projects" (1960: 114). It operated on the ideology of low taxes and low expenditures. "In the village board no expenditure is approved without a careful prior consideration of its consequences for the tax rate" (p. 119). This policy, not surprisingly, agreed not only with the businessmen's mode of thinking, but was also in accord with their tangible interests. Much of the savings they accumulated was invested in local real estate. Successful businessmen owned five to 15 houses; of course, they did not want to pay high taxes. Economic development should have increased the value of these properties, but this possibility seems to have been ignored.

The major activity of town government was the construction and maintenance of roads, and almost all of its decisions focused on road issues. Town government was dominated by prosperous farmers and was as tight-fisted as the village government on all expenditures except roads. "Prosperous farmers are interested in good roads as an adjunct to their business operations and because a good road fronting their property enhances the value of that property" (1960: 154). Prosperous farmers had little interest in the other functions of town government, except to keep expenditures on them low so that more taxes could go into roads.

Coal Town—A Dying Town

Lantz (1971) wrote an impressionistic but intriguing account of the decline of a coal mining town in Southern Illinois. It depended on two mines, the first opened in 1904 and the second in 1918. Employment in mining peaked in 1919 and declined until World War II caused a temporary mini-boom. The first mine closed in 1948 and the second in 1956. A very small mine opened in 1952 and was operating at one-third of its peak level at the time the study ended in 1958. A few residents of Coal Town felt that the mines would reopen and prosperity would again visit the town. Most residents were pessimistic about both the future of the town and their own futures.

Lantz believed that Coal Town's experience is applicable to many one-industry communities which undergo extensive but gradual decline in that industry. He first discussed the decline in local business, which forced many businesses to shut down. The lumber business is likely to be one of the first to go under: No one builds new houses when the old houses sell for a song.

Migration is a major component of the scenario of community decline. Laid-off company employees leave to look for work elsewhere, and the young people leave for schools and jobs with little likelihood of returning. The extensive mobility ends many friendships. One stayer complained: "most of my friends have gone from this community . . . yes, I am lonely because most of the people here I don't associate with" (1971: 193). The mobility also depresses property values. Furthermore, the lower incomes and the unoccupied housing lead to the deterioration of housing.

Communities in decline, according to Lantz, experience many negative social and psychological changes. Prominent among these is gossip.

> Destructive gossip directed toward others emerges and becomes an important ingredient in the interaction between people. . . . [G]ossip often takes the form of injuring one's personal reputation. . . . During such periods of fear and uncertainty "character assassination becomes a common occurrence." No one is immune and persons presumably friendly are capable of turning on one another [Lantz, 1971: 193-194].

Another negative characteristic is the growing pessimism and hopelessness. As a result, "people are afraid to take a chance or venture into a new situation. Out of such fears much inertia comes" (p. 195). Discouragement is most "acute for middle aged males who encounter difficulty finding employment in new industries" (p. 196). Such men also have investments and roots in the community which make the decision to stay or leave especially painful.

On the other side, Lantz reported that people are more helpful and friendly during the period of decline. They share common stress and fears and identify with one another. The increased integration is reflected at the public level by the increase in civic improvement projects since the decline.

What about the future of Coal Town? Lantz' assessment was pessimistic because Coal Town lacked adequate leadership, was dominated by antiindustrial cultural values, and was left with a population composed of people who resisted change. Part of the failure of leadership was its lack of commitment to the community as a community. Another part was its lack of commitment to economic development. "Coal Town has never had leadership sufficiently interested in or capable of attracting new, stable economic endeavors" (p. 206).

The predominant values were described by Lantz in extremely negative terms, and he pointed out how they hinder adjustment to an industrial order.

> They possess an imitative type of conformity and an explosive individualism, without direction. They resent responsibilities, especially those concerned with meeting working schedules and routines. Absenteeism is high and provoked by the slightest dissatisfaction. Hunting and fishing are important values and have always been more attractive than work. . . . For the few industries present there is always the potential danger that an increase in wages may result in an increase in absenteeism. There is a marked tendency for these people to be satisfied with little and to avoid planning for the future; a way of life not easily changed. If one may earn enough for a week in only three days instead of five, three days' work becomes sufficient [1971: 208].

The experiences of most community residents had been demoralizing and fostered an attitude of resistance to new things.

> [T]here have been relatively few positive human relationships for the vast majority of these people. They have exploited others and have themselves been victims of exploitation. They have grown up amidst patterns of violence, fear, cynicism, and hopelessness.

> Life in the community has fostered skepticism to the point where their confidence in any new enterprise or scheme can readily be undermined and destroyed. . . . The capacity for these people to change, to visualize new alternatives, is limited [1971: 209].

The economic decline of Coal Town and its failure to bring in new industry can be attributed to its leadership, culture and personalities, but structural factors also play a role. Stable industries have little incentive to settle in Coal Town which had "a history of high labor costs and a strong tradition of union organization" (p. 200). The industries which Coal Town was able to obtain provided little benefit to the community.

Economically destitute with little to offer, they have had to contend
with small, unstable industries which expect almost everything but
promise nothing. Such industries demand free rent, low taxes, and
guarantees of cheap labor. At the slightest indication of community
unrest they threaten to leave and to withdraw what little economic
support they may have afforded the community [Lantz, 1971: 204,
205].

## Bust Towns

The literature on declining communities and areas is vast compared with
the literature on bust towns. Rural sociologists and rural economists have
been studying the problems of economic and population decline in rural areas
for many years, but few studies of bust towns exist. The following discussion
of bust towns summarizes this sparse literature.

Bust town conditions differ markedly when preceded by stability or a
boom. Boom/bust towns are less adversely affected by the bust, because the
new people and activities are the ones which disappear. Probably the town
was relatively well adjusted to its economic circumstances before the boom,
because labor surpluses or shortages tend to shrink through migration. (As
pointed out earlier, some "backwoods" areas are exceptions in that they
retain significant labor surpluses). The bust should return the town to a
population/employment equilibrium at the old population level or somewhat
higher. The latter occurs when a facility has been constructed which requires
a small workforce.

Most boom/bust towns anticipate the bust and thereby minimize its
adverse effects. The town expands facilities, goods, and services on a
temporary basis. Some homes are built, but many of the newcomers are
housed in trailers. Temporary classrooms are used to handle expanded school
enrollments. Stores increase their volume of merchandise and extend their
hours of business. The dentist works longer and faster. If all expansion were
on a temporary basis, then contraction would be relatively painless. It is
likely, however, that some new facilities are built and some new businesses
started. As a result, some surplus capacity is left after the bust.

The story of Seneca, Illinois, illustrates a boom/bust town which adjusted
to the bust rather painlessly. According to Havighurst and Morgan (1951), the
World War II shipbuilding boom left hardly a mark on the town when the
shipyard was completely closed down after the war. Most boom/bust towns
are not so lucky, but they have less adjustment problems than bust towns
that were previously stable. The population of boom/bust towns that leaves
during the bust are newcomers with shallow roots. The old-timers stay and
experience the bust as a return to normal rather than as a depression.

In stable/bust towns almost all changes are experienced as losses rather than as the end of the hectic, problem-ridden boom days. The bust shatters the way of life of the town which was premised on stability and possibly on growth. Economic losses are severe and affect those old-timers with the greatest stake in the community the most severely. Unemployment, reduced income, bankrupt businesses, houses for sale without buyers, empty class-rooms, reduced church attendance, and cut-backs in public services for lack of funds are the conditions of stable/bust towns. Psychological depression accompanies the dramatic change in circumstances. Outmigration of the type which is so common for declining towns further alters the social landscape. Young adults are the quickest to seek their fortunes elsewhere. The educated and most enterprising also are not likely to try to make a living in the depressed circumstances.

## CASE STUDIES OF BOOM/BUST TOWNS

### Seneca—A War Boom/Bust Town

A well-documented case study is the boom/bust town of Seneca, Illinois, as told by Havighurst and Morgan (1951; see Chapter 6 for a description of the boom). The bust took place between March and July of 1945 when employment in the shipyard went from 9000 to zero. The Navy asked Congress to declare its Seneca plant to be surplus property in October, and the town's hope for a recovery based on converting the shipyard to other uses was crushed. Most of the government housing was hauled off to other places or torn down. Most of the new businesses closed, and the "schools opened in September, 1945, with only about thirty more students than had been there in June of 1942" (1951: 325). The new policemen were laid off. Things returned to preboom normalcy. Or did they? According to townspeople, Seneca had been changed--it had a new spirit and new ideas.

> The first sign of the new life was the founding of the community club . . . [which] was open to everyone at a fee of a dollar a family.
>
> Two big projects of the Community Club were the organization of a bank and the securing of the War Homes Recreation Building for community use. Success in these projects led to others, such as road improvements to make it easier for farmers to get to Seneca, and the clearing and lighting of the Crothy Park ball field [Havighurst and Morgan, 1951: 327].

Havighurst and Morgan also described numerous small changes which took place up to 1950, concluding: "The sleepy, down-at-the-heel village of 1940 gave way to an enterprising, spic-and-span town in 1950" (p. 330). These changes included the continuance of the movie theater with daily showings, a new bowling alley, an upholsterer moving to Seneca, continued use of the government-built elementary school, tearing down the old elementary school and building in its place an addition to the high school, continuation of the nursery school, incorporation of more rural territory in the high school district, gradual growth of the library, establishment of a Lions' Club, and 30 new houses. These were small changes but they were positive.

### Sweet Home—The Town That Did Not Bust

We have accounts of quite a few boom towns, but most of these studies are produced before the bust occurs. The case of Seneca is the only fully reported boom/bust town we have been able to locate. We therefore include in this section a case that does not literally qualify as a boom/bust town but which illustrates many of the problems of the boom/bust town. It is the story of the aftermath of the mini-boom in Sweet Home (See Chapter 6 for an account of the boom). Sweet Home was the nearest community to two dams built on the Santiam River from 1961 to 1967 (Hogg and Smith, 1970; Smith et al., 1971). At the peak of construction in 1965-1966, the dams employed about 1100 workers. A minor population boom (a 21 percent increase occurred from 1961 to 1966 as Sweet Homes' population climbed from about 3350 to 4060). After construction no bust occurred in Sweet Home itself (only a one percent population decline), but one occurred in the surrounding area.

For example, residential electric customers in the district decreased by one-quarter, and the students in the Sweet Home school district decreased by two-fifths. Hogg and Smith explain the minimal impacts of the downturn of construction on Sweet Home as follows:

> When dam construction began, Sweet Home was experiencing a lumber recession. When the dam construction was completed, the timber industry was healthy again, and this factor greatly mitigated the effects of the rapid decline in the availability of construction work [p. 71].

Another reason for the stable population of Sweet Home was the modest inmigration of people from urban/suburban areas for recreational or retirement purposes.

Although the population of Sweet Home remained stable as construction on the dams declined, the ambience of Sweet Home was one of decline.

> Since the inception of the more quiet operational phase of the reservoir systems in the Sweet Home setting, the town has once more settled down to a degree of depression. The many jobs are gone; some local

mills have closed  Again, the dream of development is yet unrealized. Many gambles taken during construction have proven costly. The make-shift housing and education facilities remain, but are largely vacant. A degree of disillusionment pervades public and private minds, and yet there is fundamental and empirical evidence of a potentially better setting which can result from the dam [Hogg and Smith, 1970: 18].

The postconstruction phase can be considered one of mild decline for Sweet Home, the main apparent result being sharply higher school and municipal taxes. The higher taxes, however, also resulted from other factors, some of which may apply in other postconstruction settings.

Figure 7.1 presents school revenues by sources overlaid on a graph of construction manhours worked. County and local revenues increased to meet peak construction and therefore peak school expenses. These revenues dropped to prepeak levels the following year, but then increased to a new combined high the next year and substantially higher the year when construction was about finished. Most of the increase in school revenue was supplied by local people through increased property taxes. Since the construction workers lived in trailer parks and rentals, they did not contribute significantly to the local tax base.

The consequences for local property owners is explained by Smith et al. (1971) in terms of the effective tax rate as follows:

> The effective tax rate is an index of the tax burden borne by local residents. It is a measure of the ratio of the change in property tax liability to the change in value of property subject to taxation. Positive ratios greater than 1.0 indicate increasing tax severity (Bates, 1969: 14). For the residents of Sweet Home, the average effective school tax rate was 1.29 during the construction period, which is indicative of slightly increasing property tax severity. In the postconstruction period, calculated to include fiscal year 1969-70, the average ratio was 5.75, indicating a marked increase in property tax severity.

Municipal expenses for Sweet Home increased substantially during construction and remained high after peak construction. The sources of revenues for municipal services were such that the construction workers tended to pay their share. Property taxes contributed only an average of 16 percent of these revenues. "Thus, the influx of construction workers cannot be argued to have added substantially to the municipal tax burden of Sweet Home residents during the construction period" (Smith et al., 1971: 111).

The problem of high per capita costs of municipal services occurred after construction. Faulty expectations were largely to blame. "The water system was expanded to accommodate a service capacity of 12,000 people, three

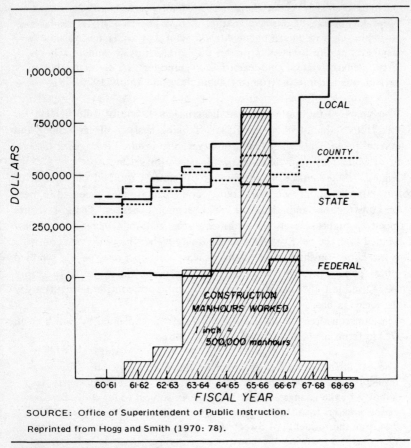

SOURCE: Office of Superintendent of Public Instruction.

Reprinted from Hogg and Smith (1970: 78).

FIGURE 7.1   School Revenue Sources

times the 1970 population which it served" (pp. 181, 182). The planners expected many more people to migrate to Sweet Home after the dams were complete. Other factors cited by the researchers to explain the high postconstruction per capita municipal service expenses are (1) inflation, (2) low public involvement in city government, (3) the increased national concern for law and order, and (4) new community leaders and new community goals. The researchers claim the last factor was

> a sociocultural effect of dam construction on the community. The dams have brought about a change in community self-image. . . . Many sought a new image: a town which was neat, clean, and orderly, a town attractive to suburbanites. . . . Many public officials, the Chamber of Commerce, and other service groups, largely in an effort to attract

recreation enthusiasts and retired people to the community, began appearance-oriented projects. The median down Main Street was beautified; a concerted effort was made to demolish decaying buildings; a new zoning ordinance was passed. . . . The superintendent of schools, city manager, newspaper editor, and president of the Chamber of Commerce are new migrants with urban and suburban backgrounds. (The previous holders of these positions have left the community, mostly because they rejected the pressures, conflicts, and status deprivations associated with change.) All have substantial influence in community decision-making with respect to the allocation of community resources. The urban and suburban migrants bring to Sweet Home their experience with neat, clean, orderly goals for environmental quality which emphasize good schools and adequate municipal services. Their impact on the community had been to intensify programs designed to reach these goals [Smith et al., 1971: 184].

Sweet Home suffered some of the fiscal problems of declining or bust towns, but was exceptional in that its postconstruction depression was mild and short-lived. Leadership in the community was taken by those who believed in its future and sought improvements in public services. Development, not decline, lay ahead.

## CASE STUDIES OF STABLE/BUST TOWNS

### Caliente—A Casualty of New Technology

Probably the best-known case of a stable/bust town is Caliente, a one-industry town in the Southwest United States. Its story is told by Cottrell (1951) in his article, "Death by Dieselization." It grew up on a railroad division point as a town equipped to service steam locomotives. Due to technological developments that lengthened the traveling distance of locomotives, Caliente found itself situated at the appropriate spot to act as a service depot and enjoy the economic growth and outlook this industry engendered. In contrast, many railroad towns located at shorter division points went under. Caliente grew: The community built a new water system, homes, school buildings, a theater, a hospital, and a park. Businesses and various civic organizations were established.

In the mid-1940s the railroad was dieselized, making the steam locomotive service shops obsolete. The company closed them down. Caliente, by this one action, suffered crisis. The community unsuccessfully tried to reverse the company's decision and then appealed to the company to establish some other facility at Caliente. It made several attempts to obtain favorable government action, including an unsuccessful request to the Interstate Commerce Commission that it require inspection of rolling stock at Caliente. It also tried to attract new industry, but all efforts failed.

The impact of the railroad's action devastated the economy and other parts of the community as well. The railroad paid 61 percent of Caliente's taxes, but would pay little after selling or tearing down its buildings and moving its usable capital stock elsewhere. Almost all nonoperating employees lost their jobs. Since their seniority extended only to the local shop, they could make no claims on jobs elsewhere. Some workers, such as boilermakers, took jobs as unskilled laborers, since their old skills were now outmoded. Three out of every four operating employees had to look for new jobs, since the use of diesel engines had reduced the overall need of labor. Some workers were transferred; most left town to look for work but with no immediate prospects. Their departure and the declining incomes in Caliente forced many local businesses to close, further reducing opportunities for employment and further increasing the number of persons experiencing lowered income. Many homeowners lost their homes when they could not keep up their payments. Beyond the economic subsystem, the consequences extended to churches, schools, civic clubs, and recreation programs, all of which experienced devastating decline in financial and personal support (Cottrell, 1951: 19).

Caliente is a case of a bust following stability, a bust that no one expected. The members of the community believed in its future and never suspected that technological developments would make it obsolete. Who in the town could foresee that the steam locomotive would itself become outmoded?

> Based upon the "certainty" of the railroad's need for Caliente, men built their homes there, frequently of concrete and brick, at the cost, in many cases, of their life savings. The water system was laid in cast iron which will last for centuries. Businessmen erected substantial buildings which could be paid for only by profits gained through many years of business. Four churches evidence the faith of Caliente people in the future of their community.... Their school buildings represent the investment of savings guaranteed by bonds and future taxes [pp. 358, 359].

When busts are expected, actions such as building less permanent facilities reduce its negative impacts.

### Presque Isle–Rebounding from a Base Closing

The stable/bust situation which has the greatest likelihood of being reported in the literature is the military base closing or cut-back. Although base closings usually do not cause busts as devastating as in Caliente, they can cause significant declines in the nearby communities. The economic impacts of dozens of base closings have been reported (for example, Lynch, 1970; Daicoff et al., 1970: I, II). Many of the major closed bases were located in the labor markets of metropolitan areas so that their economic impacts could be readily absorbed. A few of the closings occurred in rural areas with principal nearby cities of under 20,000 population. These closings could economically undermine the proximate community. We report on one closing which did and one which did not.

As reported by Lynch (1970), Presque Isle Air Force Base was closed in 1961, at which time it employed 1259 military personnel and 268 civilians. The city of Presque Isle, Maine, is the northern-most city on the eastern seaboard and had a population of about 13,000 in 1961. Next to potato farming, the air base was the principal economic enterprise of the area, and its closing left a large gap in the local economy. The base had an annual payroll of $2.5 million, and local procurement reached $1.8 million annually.

Fortunately, Presque Isle was not a typical small rural city. It had twice received honorable mention in the All-American City competition, and its Chamber of Commerce had an industrial development program even prior to the closing announcement. The development program was successful in arranging the location of a potato processing plant in the community. With the base closure, the Chamber of Commerce and the city combined their development efforts in the Presque Isle Industrial Council with a full-time, tax-supported executive director. Through the efforts of the council, individual citizens, and several organizations, Presque Isle soon generated enough economic development to more than compensate for the closed base.

An important early step toward redevelopment was the request that all installed and semi-installed equipment at the base be left when the base was turned over to the city at a nominal price. As a result, the base was converted into a municipal airport and an industrial park which promised over 800 new jobs. These new economic activities generated 500 new jobs in local industries which supplied these businesses.

By 1968 an estimated 1302 workers were employed at the industrial park as follows:

| | |
|---|---|
| Indian Head Plywood | 200 |
| Aroostock Shoe Company | 320 |
| International Paper | 55 |
| Converse Rubber Company | 350 |
| Northeast Publishing | 58 |
| N. Maine Vocational-Technical Institute (staff) | 55 |
| All other employees | 264 |

Meanwhile, the potato processing plant was successful and its employees increased to 900. "The expansion made the Presque Isle facility the largest producer of frozen potatoes in the world" (1970: 60). It used potato cartons which were cut and printed at International Paper at the industrial park.

Presque Isle also introduced sugar beet production to Aroostock County by securing a 33,000-acre allotment from U.S. Department of Agriculture and financing for a $17.5 million sugar processing plant. The allotment was awarded in 1964, and the plant was in full operation for the 1966 crop.

The air base was also converted to several nonindustrial activities:

One of the former warehouses has been converted to a skating and hockey rink. An eighty-acre camping area has been reserved on the far side of the base. The United States Soil Conservation Service and the city of Presque Isle developed a small artificial lake for recreation, a seaplane base, and trout fishing [1970: 60].

Presque Isle is an exceptional case. Its major economic activity other than farming closed down and it quickly generated much more economic activity than it had lost. Even the 268 base civilian employees fared well, since 178 of them were reemployed to perform other governmental activities, largely at Toring Air Force Base 20 miles away. Presque Isle did suffer a short-term housing surplus of 250 units (previously it had a shortage of 200 units), but it recovered in 18 months. It also suffered a short-term 15 percent decline in retail sales; however, soon the city was better off than before. In fact, the economic development of Presque Isle was so impressive that it won the all-American City award in 1967. And growth is continuing: In 1968 the potato processing plant announced plans for another expansion which would generate 300-400 new jobs. In summary Lynch states, "Presque Isle might well be described as the first community to have successfully adjusted to any of the post-1960 military base closures" (p. 63).

The key to Presque Isle's success, according to Lynch, "was the development of previously untapped local resources (potatoes and lumber) and the creation of still a new resource (sugar beets)" (p. 64). The city also had a pro-expansion attitude and able leadership. Also in its favor was that the Maine congressional delegation, led by Senator Muskie, was concerned about the effects of the base closing and brought about favorable actions in several agencies.

### Edgemont—Suffers a Base Closing

A contrasting case of the economic effects of a military base closing in a small community was the closing of the Black Hills Army Department (BHAD) near Edgemont, South Dakota, with a population of 1680 when closure was announced (Lynch, 1970). Edgemont's economy was based largely on BHAD, which employed 520 civilian and 12 military personnel.

The other sources of basic employment were small uranium and vanadium processing mills, the railroad, and ranching. The closing of BHAD caused the following losses in Edgemont:

(1) Population in Edgemont declined from 1,680 to 1,440.
(2) Net income of Edgemont Businessmen had declined 50 percent in 1967.
(3) Assessed valuation of real estate had dropped from $4.5 million in 1962 to $3.1 million in January 1968.
(4) Homes valued at $16,000 to $18,000 were selling for $3,000 to $4,000.
(5) There were forty-three vacant or abandoned homes in the community [Lynch, 1970: 133].

At least partial economic recovery was underway by the time of Lynch's report in 1968. The recovery was due to a group of outside entrepreneurs "representing an association of businessmen willing and interested in investing in communities similar to their own local areas" (p. 128). The group offered to lease the depot with a five-year option to buy for $450,000. By report time the group had arranged for the facilities to be used by a munitions manufacturer and a nursing home for retarded persons.

### Moses Lake—An Illustration of the Modest Effects of Military Base Closings

In reviewing a number of other cases of base closings it appears that the negative economic impacts generally are small compared with the closings of other types of economic enterprises. Two factors account for the relatively easy recovery. First are the opportunities provided by the facility, which are usually transferred to the local community at a modest price. Second is the relatively low impact of military installations on local economies, because they are more self-sufficient than other types of enterprises. Gordon (1968) studied the economic impact of the closure of Larson Air Force Base on Moses Lake, Washington (population of about 12,750 before closure), and concluded:

In terms of the usual aggregative indicators of the economic health of a community, Moses Lake provides evidence that a relatively small increase in industrial employment can make up for a large loss in military personnel. In the case of Moses Lake, it seems that one industrial worker replaces about ten or eleven military personnel in terms of community impact [1970: 221].

The Larson Air Force Base closure is a good example of minimal long-term negative impacts from base closing. Moses Lake recovered almost immediately even though the base had not begun to be utilized. The base had the second longest runway in the United States and many excellent facilities including 1335 housing units, two elementary schools, a 50-bed hospital, and airport buildings. The reuse of facilities would help Moses Lake expand economically in the future. The present economic good health of Moses Lake, however, was largely due to developments in agriculture and related industries, particularly increased production of potatoes and sugar beets and the addition of two food processing plants.

It is important to note that economic recovery from base closings may involve economic and social changes. In the case of Moses Lake, the labor force changed in character. The operation of the base involved mostly professional and skilled workers, while the replacement activities involved mainly semi-skilled and unskilled workers. The social patterns of the two sets of workers would be different and they would affect the institutions of the community differently.

## Summary

Rural areas as a whole are experiencing more growth than are urban areas, but many individual rural communites are experiencing gradual economic decline. The factors which affect the rate of economic or population decline include size, regional location, natural resources, leadership, businessmen's values, selective migration, and community goals. The larger rural communities are the most likely to grow, and the smaller rural communities are the most likely to decline. Location in the South or West and location near exploitable energy resources are associated with growth.

Quality community leadership and developmental goals are also important catalysts of growth, as the case studies so clearly indicate. Causes of community decline include declining natural resources, conservative and pessimistic viewpoints of businessmen, and outmigration of the most promising young people.

*Chapter 8*

# NOISE IMPACTS

In the inscrutable logic of EIS procedures, noise impacts are normally classified as a social impact and handed over to a social impact assessor for analysis. If the social impact assessor is a sociologist, anthropologist, or social psychologist, there is little substantive knowledge in his training which prepared him for the assignment. This chapter will provide an introduction to the effects of noise on humans and direct the reader to additional sources. Specifically, this chapter will provide an introduction to the physiology of noise and hearing and review the psychological and social effects of noise on people.

Noise is unwanted sound and has become an important social problem affecting the quality of life of many Americans. One report estimates that around 1970 nine million people lived where aircraft and highway noise levels were judged to be incompatible with residential living (Wyle Laboratory, 1971). Many other Americans experience unpleasant noise levels at their working place. Noise is a by-product of all large construction projects and probably also a by-product of the use of the facility constructed. Noise is a negative social impact because it affects sleep, the performance of some kinds of tasks, and communication. Noise levels were found to be an important factor in the evaluation of the area around one's house in Chapter 3 (see Lansing et al., 1970), and noise is a major complaint made about the environment.

After a brief historical note, this chapter describes the hearing process, noise sources, noise standards, the effects of noise, and noise control practices. Extensive research has been conducted on the effects of noise, and the main lesson for assessors is that the noise associated with construction projects can cause considerable annoyance but will generally have mild physiological and performance affects. Community reactions may be strong, and assessments which are responsive to community needs will carefully examine noise impacts.

## Historical Note

Noise sources are increasing rapidly, and noise levels in cities are rising. Street noise rose eight decibels between 1938 and 1952 in portions of Berlin and Dusseldorf, according to one study (Goromosov, 1968). The concern about noise has also increased, but ancient societies also were concerned about noise. Some examples provided by the U.S. Environmental Protection Agency (1973) reveal this concern. Around 2500 years ago the Greek community of Sybaris reportedly issued an ordinance banning metal works and rooster-keeping within the city to protect against noise that interfered with speech and disturbed sleep. In ancient Rome Juvenal complained that noise from wagons and their drivers interfered with sleep. One of Chaucer's poems written around 1350 complained that "no man can get a night's rest" because of the blacksmith's noise. Around 1750 Ben Franklin reportedly moved from one area of Philadelphia to another because "the din of the market increases upon me; and that has I find made me say some things twice over."

The problems but not the associated technologies in the above historical anecdotes have a modern ring to them. Nevertheless, the differences between today and earlier historical periods are greater than their similarities in the area of sound. It is important to note what Bragdon (1971: 1) calls the "auditory regression of modern society." Modern society is based heavily upon visual perceptions, and the auditory senses have atrophied. But it was not always so.

> In the Middle Ages, for example, man's auditory sense was keenly developed. In a world of little artificial light and nearly universal illiteracy, medieval man relied heavily upon his ears for information. He saw with his ears. Throughout that period, the church bell was not rung for esthetic purposes—it ordered men's lives and gave them meaning. The tolling of the bell evoked an encompassing range of emotional responses, from happiness and joy during holy days and festive occasions, to fear when the town was being attacked, and to sadness after battle when the death toll could be heard. The message conveyed was

so precise that the bell's final strokes "indicated the age, sex, and social rank of the dead." Another auditory vehicle important to the medieval townspeople was the crier or bellman. The town crier acted as a verbal newspaper, assisting those responsible for law and order in conveying their messages.

Because auditory communication was essential for community survival, steps were often taken to reduce noises that interfered with this vital function. By the thirteenth century, many towns had enacted laws prohibiting blacksmiths from working in the early morning hours because of bothersome noise. In contrast with today, the population could enjoy relatively noise-free sleep from sunset to sunrise. Among those towns which had a thriving marketplace, paved streets were a major noise source. They became a particular nuisance when iron-rimmed carts entered the market towns from nearby farming areas. Laws were introduced to prohibit the use of these carts in the market-place. In Beverly, England, a fine was imposed on persons driving iron-wheeled carts wherever stone pavement existed. The less noisy and destructive wooden-wheeled carts could operate more freely in most towns [Bragdon, 1971: 3].

The Renaissance started the shift from relying on the sense of hearing to relying on the sense of sight. As a result of living in a sight-based culture, our hearing is underdeveloped and we tolerate abusive noise conditions with surprisingly few objections. In addition, even when the public complains about a noise source, their complaining declines substantially when visual barriers with minimal noise control capabilities are placed around the noise source (Bragdon, 1971: 4). To a surprising extent, what we do not see we do not hear.

## Sound, Hearing, and Noise Measurement

There is no physical or physiological difference between noise and any other sound. Both are processed by the human hearing system in the same way. The only difference is the psychological response of the listener: Noise is unwanted sound.

Sound is simply fluctuation in air pressure or air vibrations. Sound waves move the ear drum and the small ossicle bones of the middle ear. The ossicles translate these vibrations to the fluid in the cochlea where sensory hair cells translate these vibrations into nerve impulses for transmission to the brain where they are interpreted.

The sound source moves back and forth and causes air or some other transmitting substance to vibrate which creates the variations in the normal atmospheric pressure that are sound waves. The basic facts on sound waves are described by the EPA as follows:

> These waves radiate in all directions from the source and may be reflected and scattered or, like other wave actions, may turn corners, or be refracted. They can be combined with or even cancelled by other sound waves. Likewise, the energy contained in the sound can be absorbed. As the waves travel over increasing distances, the amount of energy per unit area contained in them is reduced proportionally to distance. Once the source ceases to be in motion, the movement of the air particles ceases and the sound waves disappear almost instantaneously. Under normal conditions of temperature, pressure, and humidity at sea level, these sound waves travel at approximately 1100 feet per second [U.S. EPA, 1973: I-4, 5].

The three dimensions of sound which are the most important for noise impacts are magnitude, frequency, and duration. Magnitude is the amplitude in the pressure fluctuation and is the main determinant of loudness. Frequency is the cycles of pressure variations per second in the sound wave and is experienced by humans as "pitch." Frequency also is a component in loudness, in that humans are more sensitive to high frequencies than to low frequencies of the same magnitude. Duration is the length of time the sound waves are emitted.

The human ear has tremendous range in the frequencies and magnitudes of sound that it can safely hear. The human ear hears sounds between 20 and 20,000 Hz, or cycles per second. The human voice ranges from 500 to 5000 Hz. The range in magnitudes that the human ear can hear effectively is from 0.0002 to 2000 microbars. A microbar is one-millionth of one "bar," which is the unit of measure for atmospheric pressure (14.7 pounds per square inch). The loudest sound exerts a pressure which is ten million times the pressure of the weakest audible sound and involves one hundred billion times the sound energy. For convenience, the microbar scale is converted into the decibel scale (dB) which compares the existing sound level with 0.0002 microbars in terms of logarithmic ratios. Zero decibels is the softest audible sound and 140 decibels is about the loudest sound that can be accommodated by the human ear. Ordinary conversation is about 60 dB, an automobile at 50 feet is 60 dB, a motorcycle at 50 feet is 85 dB, a jet take-off at 1000 feet is 110 dB, and a rock and roll band is around 108-114 dB. Permanent hearing damage can result from a single brief exposure exceeding 115 dB.

Since loudness and sound impact is a combination of magnitude and frequency, its measurement requires more than decibel measurement. A 2000 Hz tone of 5 dB sounds just as loud as a 20 Hz tone of 70 dB (Goldsmith and Jonsson, 1973: 784). "Loudness" must therefore be measured by a scale which weights magnitude (dB) by frequencies (Hz). Sound level meters are based on this type of scale, and the A-weighted scale is commonly used when noise effects on people are being considered. The A-weighted scale, like the human ear, emphasizes the frequencies in the 800 to 3000 Hz range and discriminates against very high and very low frequencies in determining an overall loudness score in dBA units (A-weighted decibels). On this scale, which is logarithmic, a 10 dBA increase more than triples the sound pressure and sounds twice as loud, a 5 dBA increase is noticeable, and a 3 dBA increase is barely discernible.

The measurement of noise as an environmental variable is further complicated by the duration dimension, or the time factor. A variety of methods have been proposed for measuring noise levels over time; the most commonly used measure in the United States is the Day-Night Average Level ($L_{dn}$). It divides the day into a day period from 7 a.m. to 10 p.m. and a night period from 10 p.m. to 7 a.m., and gives a 10 dBA greater weight to nighttime sound. Thus, a 60 dBA sound after 10 p.m. is counted as a 70 dBA sound. Figure 8.1 provides $L_{dn}$ levels for selected situations.

## Noise Sources

The main sources of noise outside of the workplace are automobiles (buses, trucks, etc.), construction equipment, plants and workshops, playgrounds, motorized recreational equipment, power tools, and home appliances. The noise levels at a distance of 50 feet for a number of noise sources are presented in Table 8.1. All sources in the table are "very noisy" for residential areas (68 dBA and louder) and most exceed 75 dBA, which is the average noise level at which hearing loss begins and when communities are likely to organize opposition to the noise sources.

Noise is a major complaint of urban dwellers, according to a survey of central London (McKennell, 1963). The major source of noise complaints is road traffic except near airports (see Table 8.2). Highway vehicles create noise mainly through their tires, propulsion systems, and aerodynamics. At speeds greater than 50 miles per hour, tires are the dominant noise source for both trucks and cars; and tire noise increases with speed. At speeds below 45 mph for trucks and 35 mph for cars, engine-generated noise (intake, exhaust, and casing vibration) is dominant. Automobile-generated noise increases with speed; truck noise, however, is fairly constant across speeds. The noisiest highway vehicle is the diesel truck; it is generally 8 to 10 dB noisier than gasoline trucks and 12 to 18 dB noisier than cars. One large diesel can produce more noise than 30 cars. Fortunately, only two to three percent of trucks are diesel powered (U.S. EPA, 1972: II-57, 59).

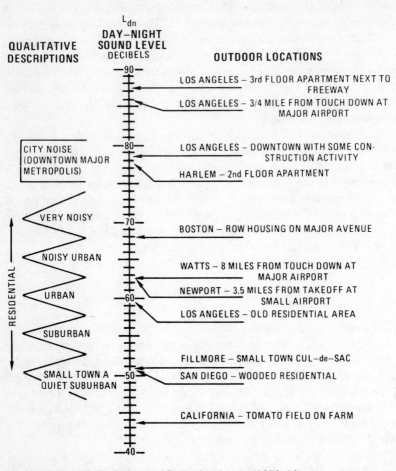

SOURCE: U.S. Environmental Protection Agency (1974: 14).

FIGURE 8.1   Outdoor Day-Night Sound Level in dB (re 20 micropascals) at Various
             Locations

## Noise Level Standards

In 1974 the EPA published noise level standards for various types of sites
which would protect the health and welfare of the exposed population. A
margin of safety is built into the standards which are "to provide a basis for
judgment by states and local governments on a basis for setting standards . . .
along with other relevant factors" (U.S. EPA, 1974: 31). The $L_{dn}$ selected
for residential areas, hospitals, and schools was 45 indoors and 55 outdoors.

TABLE 8.1    Noise Levels in A-Weighted Decibels for Various Noise Sources
at a Distance of 50 Feet (Normal Operating Level)

| Noise Source | dBAs at 50 ft. | Noise Source | dBAs at 50 ft. |
|---|---|---|---|
| Medium & heavy trucks | 84 | Scraper | 88[a] |
| Motorcycle | 82 | Jackhammer | 88[a] |
| Garbage truck | 82 | Tractor | 87 |
| Highway bus | 82 | Concrete | |
| Automobile (sport) | 75 | mixer | 85[a] |
| City bus | 73 | Chain saw | 82 |
| Light truck | 72 | Bulldozer | 80[a] |
| Automobile (standard) | 69 | Lawnmower | 74 |
| Train | 94 | | |
| Rapid transit | 86 | | |
| Off-road motorcycle | 85 | | |
| Snowmobile | 85 | | |
| Motorboat | 80 | | |

SOURCE:  U.S. Environmental Protection Agency (1972: II-77, 87).
a.  Source:  Bolt, Bernack and Newman, Inc. (1971).

Hearing loss is a consideration when noise levels exceed 70 $L_{dn}$ for long
periods of time.

## The Physiological Effects of
## Noise on People

Noise can permanently damage the inner ear, causing slight to total loss of
hearing. It also causes nonauditory physiological effects varying from mus-
cular tension to headaches. Finally, it affects sleep (for general references on
the physiological effects of noise, see U.S. EPA, 1973; Kryter, 1970).

### NOISE-INDUCED HEARING LOSS

Noise causes hearing loss in millions of Americans. According to Carmen
(1977), 15 percent of Americans already have significant hearing loss and the
numbers are increasing rapidly. (Using more severe criteria, Bugliarello et al.
[1976] estimate that 2.5 percent have noise-induced hearing loss.) Carmen's
list is headed by 19 million industrial workers out of a work force of 75
million; below that group are five million young people under the age of 18.
He warned that almost no one over age 10 will escape noise-induced hearing
loss by 2000 if noise continues to increase at its present rate.

The part of the ear which is most sensitive to noise damage is the Organ of
Corti. It is the receptor organ located in the cochlea, a chamber in the inner
ear. It contains many rows of microscopic receptor hair cells which are moved

TABLE 8.2   Noises Which Disturb People at Home, Outdoors, and at Work

|                          | Number of People Disturbed, per 100 Questioned | | |
| Description of Noise | When at Home | When Outdoors | When at Work |
|---|---|---|---|
| Road traffic | 36 | 20 | 7 |
| Air craft | 9 | 4 | 1 |
| Trains | 5 | 1 | – |
| Industry/Construction works | 7 | 3 | 10 |
| Domestic/Light appliances | 4 | – | 4 |
| Neighbors' impact noise (knocking, walking, etc.) | 6 | – | – |
| Children | 9 | 3 | – |
| Adult voices | 10 | 2 | 2 |
| Wireless/T.V. | 7 | 1 | 1 |
| Bells/Alarms | 3 | 1 | 1 |
| Pets | 3 | – | – |
| Other noise | – | – | – |

SOURCE: McKennell (1963).

by the sound vibrations moving through the liquid of the inner ear. They translate the sound messages to the brain through the nerve endings to which they are connected. Loud noises cause vibrations which destroy the delicate hair cells and their auditory nerve connections. "Every exposure to loud noise destroys some cells, and prolonged or repeated exposure causes the destruction of large numbers of cells, and ultimately the collapse of the Organ of Corti" (Bugliarello et al., 1976: 23).

Irreversible hearing loss usually results from prolonged exposure to intense noise, but a single very loud noise can also cause permanent loss. An explosion or gunshot can even vibrate the Organ of Corti so violently that it tears apart.

Even if it does not destroy cells, severe noise can cause structural damage which interferes with the processes which maintain the cells, causing their deterioration. Long exposure to lower-level noise causes another type of deterioration which is not completely understood. One theory is that the cells are made to work at too high a metabolic rate for too long, and they suffer cumulative exhaustion—they die of overwork. Their loss is permanent, as they cannot regenerate.

Temporary hearing loss can result from short-term exposure to severe noise. People appear to have a great capacity to adapt, however, and regain hearing acuity unless the ear is damaged. It is not known how much damage is caused by prolonged exposure to noise of even lower intensity and how much recuperation occurs. In the past it was assumed that progressive hearing loss (presbycusis) is a natural consequence of aging, but now it is suspected that much of the hearing loss with age in modern societies is due to the cumulative effects of noisy environments. Hearing loss with age is trivial among the Mabaan tribe in the Sudan, which suggests that modern life is more at fault than the aging process.

Noise-induced hearing loss usually starts at the 4000 Hz range and later extends to lower frequencies. Thus, higher-noise occupations are likely to expose workers to greater risk of hearing loss; for example, industrial occupations. Traditional noise standards were directed at the more average frequencies from 500 Hz to 2000 Hz because of their importance for hearing speech sounds. The EPA standard presented in the previous section, however, emphasizes protection up to 4000 Hz.

## EXTRAAUDITORY PHYSIOLOGICAL EFFECTS
## OF NOISE ON PEOPLE

Extensive research focuses on the physiological effects of noise on people, varying the noise parameters and the experimental conditions. The effect of exposure to noise includes headaches, muscle tension, higher heart and respiratory rates, and increased blood pressure. It also has effects on brain chemistry, gastrointestinal activity, metabolic activity, pupil size, and sweat gland activity. It can cause nausea, migrane headaches, tinnitus, gastric ulcers, drowsiness, and emotional disturbances. In addition, noise exposure can cause inadequate blood circulation, which may prevent a proper supply of blood to vital organs such as the brain, the inner ear, or infant fetuses.

There is no consensus about the seriousness of the above list of extra-auditory physiological effects of noise. "There is the opinion that hazardous side effects are very probable above the 95 decibel level" (Bragdon, 1971: 72), but some studies show that people are able to adapt to long exposure to higher noise levels without significant physiological effects (see Kryter, 1970). The evidence is not clear-cut and supports differing views. Bragdon's recommendation is, "until someone proves that these changes are negligible, we must assume that the physiological effects of noise on health are hazardous" (1971: 70).

Some, such as Glass and Singer (1972), study the nonauditory physiological effects of noise within a more general theory of stress. Since this viewpoint bridges the physiological and psychological effects of noise, it is of particular interest to social impact assessors. The general relationship between noise and stress has been summarized by Miller (1974: 760-761):

The neuro-endocrine responses to intense sound are similar to the responses to stress. The response to stress is called the general adaptation syndrome. . . . It consists of three stages: an alarm reaction, a stage of resistance, and a stage of exhaustion. If a stressor is very severe and is maintained for prolonged periods of time, an organism passes in succession through the stages of the alarm reaction, resistance, and exhaustion. In the extreme case, the end result is a breakdown of bodily function and death. In a less severe case, there may be a price to be paid in the stage of resistance. This price may include lowered resistance to infection and, perhaps, specific diseases known as the diseases of adaptation. These *may* include, among others, some types of gastrointestinal ulcers, some types of high blood pressure, and some types of arthritis. Many medical authorities do not accept the theory that there are diseases of adaptation. Rather, they theorize that each disease has its own special set of causes.

It is also impossible to make firm statements about the noise levels at which stress occurs, but existing data seem to indicate that the threshold of the stress response is about 65 dBA and becomes pronounced at 80 to 85 dBA.

## SLEEP INTERFERENCE

"Noises which interrupt rest, relaxation, and sleep are the major underlying causes of officially registered complaints of noise pollution" (Goldsmith, 1973: 788). The EPA (1973) cites several researchers who argue that "sleep interruption or sleep modification due to noise exposure is one of the most harmful conditions noise poses for an individual's health" (1973: chap. 7, 19). Noise interferes with sleep by rousing people from sleep, preventing them from going to sleep, shifting them from a deep stage of sleep to a shallower stage, or interfering with dreaming which is important for mental health. Figure 8.2 presents the results of three studies showing the percentage of sleeping subjects who awaken at various noise levels and one showing the percentage of subjects prevented from going to sleep. At the noise level of 45 dBA, at least 20 percent of the subjects were awakened or kept awake; this is the sound level recommended by the EPA (1974) as requisite for public health and welfare for residential areas. Some researchers have recommended much lower allowable noise limits; for example, Karagodina et al. (1972) recommended the 30 dBA level for nighttime noise inside apartments, and Beland et al. (1972) recommended 35 dBA as the maximum allowable steady-state noise level for sleeping. It should be remembered, however, that any impulse noise that exceeds the background noise by more than 10 dB is potentially sleep-disturbing (U.S. EPA, 1974).

Obviously, some people are more prone to sleep distrubance by noise than others, and impact assessors need to know which groups are most sensitive. Bugliarello et al. (1976: 64) summarized the research on group differences as follows:

Aged people, women beyond the menopause, sick people, people afflicted with psychic disturbances, as well as children between 4 and 6

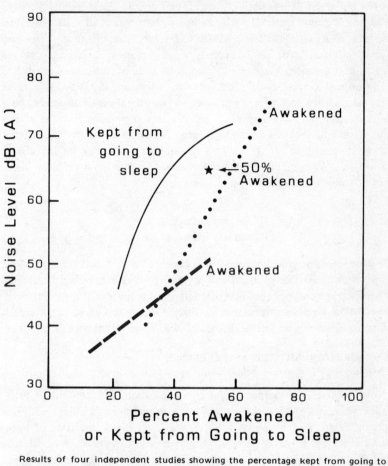

Results of four independent studies showing the percentage kept from going to sleep or the percentage awakened from sleep.

SOURCE: California State Department of Public Health (1971).

**FIGURE 8.2   Sleep Disturbance by Noise**

years old, constitute a portion of the population who are very sensitive to noise or who could be easily disturbed during their sleep by excessive noises. This particularly sensitive group represents more than one-third of the total population. Thus antinoise measures should take into consideration the reactions of this important portion of the population, and not only those of "adult males in good health."

Some research has examined the effects of noise-induced sleep loss on later performance. Chernik (1972) and Johnson et al. (1972) found no significant effects on performance; however, Levere et al. (1972), Roth et al. (1971), and Herbert and Wilkinson (1973) found some effects. Herbert and Wilkinson (1973: 527) found that "the effects upon performance of noise-disturbed sleep were relatively small and confined to the early part of the day" (see also Collins and Iampietro, 1973). The type of performance effects observed suggests that the sleep loss caused "both decreased motivation and disruption of the normal diurnal cycle" (Herbert and Wilkinson, 1973: 537). In other words, the ability to perform the tasks was not significantly impaired, only the motivation to do them well. These authors also found that the effects were not due to absolute amounts of sleep deprivation, but to disruption of normal physiological rhythms. This is similar to the way jet lag affects performance. We conclude from these studies that noise-induced sleep loss is *mainly* an annoyance.

## Social, Psychological, and
## Community Effects of Noise

There is no sharp line between physiological effects of noise and the social and psychological effects. Social and psychological effects have a physiological basis, and physiological effects often have consequences at the psychological and social level. In this section we discuss the effects of noise on speech and communication, performance, mental health, and annoyance.

### SPEECH OR COMMUNICATION INTERFERENCE
### BY NOISE

Noise interferes with speech and communication. The amount of interference associated with various noise levels is presented in Figure 8.3. This figure is based on the Speech Interference Level (SIL), the level of background noise which barely permits ordinary speech to be understood (that is, when 95 percent or more of the key words are not heard). Communication indoors requires lower noise levels because of the build-up of sound by reflection from walls and objects.

Bragdon (1971: 79-80) observed:

An SIL reading of over 75 decibels prohibits telephone conversations; 65-75 decibels would barely permit reliable communication over a two-foot distance with a raised voice; at 55-65 decibels, however, telephone conversations are nearly unimpaired, and normal communication can occur up to three feet; but an SIL of less than 55 decibels is desirable for any office operation. . . . In order to communicate in a normal voice when less than a foot away, noise should not exceed 82

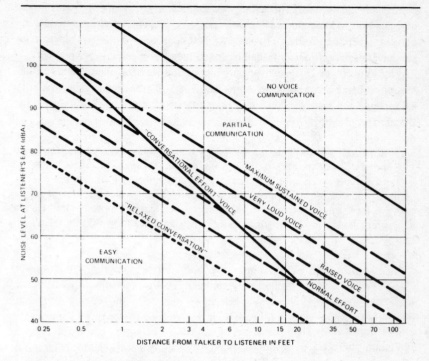

SOURCE: U.S. Environmental Protection Agency (1973: 6.5).

*As a function of A-weighted sound levels of masking noise in the outdoor environment.

**FIGURE 8.3   Distance at which Ordinary Speech can be Understood***
*As a function of A-weighted sound levels of masking noise in the outdoor environment.

dBA. In a recently completed social survey, 64 dBC or 71 dBA was found to be a maximum acceptable level for background noise for voice communication. Above this level, people complained or felt they were less able to perform their jobs properly.

The EPA (1973) suggests that noise in homes should not exceed 40-45 dBA if communication is to be unimpeded. Relaxed conversation is possible up to 10 feet at a SIL of 45 dBA.

Communication interference is prominent among the home activities which are disturbed by aircraft and traffic noise. In a social survey by Tracor (1971) of people living near airports in Chicago, Dallas, Denver, and Los Angeles, 21 percent indicated that television and radio reception were "extremely disturbed." This rating was applied to other activities as follows: conversation, 15 percent; telephone use, 14 percent; relaxing outside, 13 percent; relaxing inside, 11 percent; listening to records or tapes, nine percent; sleep, eight percent; reading, six percent; and eating, four percent.

The importance of speech or communication interference depends on the messages being communicated and activities of the listener. A dramatic example of the adverse effects of communication interference is reported by Bragdon (1971: 65):

> Two people were killed and several injured the day Senator Robert F. Kennedy's southbound funeral train passed through Elizabeth, New Jersey. They were unable to hear the warning horn of a train approaching from the opposite direction, and therefore did not get out of its way. It was later determined that secret service and news media helicopters had completely obliterated the signal warning of this train's approach.

Many motor vehicle accidents have occurred because the vehicle noises mask warning signals of emergency vehicles. This is especially true of trucks: when driving in high gear, the truck driver may hear the warning siren of a passing emergency vehicle for less than one and a half seconds (Vaneklasen, 1969).

Obviously, noise-induced communication interference seldom has fatal consequences and is generally a nuisance rather than a danger. Frequent interference with communication can be annoying, however, even though the effects are not serious. How can assessors evaluate the importance of noise interference with communication? Probably all assessors can do is estimate the number of people who are subjected to various noise levels and convey some understanding of what these noise levels mean for conversation and social life. An example of an effective description of noise impacts is the Jamaica Bay/Kennedy Airport study by the Jamaica Bay Environmental Study Group (1971). It pointed out that 700,000 people lived in areas around Kennedy Airport which were subjected to noise levels that interrupted conversation for a cumulative duration of about a half-hour per day and interrupted the sleep of about half of them. In addition, the report stated:

> The airport noise has a very adverse effect on area schools. Within the present impacted area (NEF 30 or greater) there are 220 schools attended by 280,000 pupils. With normal schoolroom usage, this implies about an hour's interruption of classroom teaching technique to

accommodate the impossibility of communicating with pupils as an aircraft passes overhead. The noise interference with the teaching process goes beyond the periods of enforced noncommunication, for it destroys the spontaneity of the educational process and subjects it to the rhythm of the aeronautical control system [1971: 20].

## NOISE AND PERFORMANCE

Noise interferes with performance by masking necessary messages. But does noise interfere with performance if auditory signals are not involved? The extensive research on this topic has been summarized by Miller (1974: 757) under six general conclusions:

When mental or motor tasks do *not* involve auditory signals, the effects of noise on their performance have been difficult to assess. Human behavior is complicated and it has been difficult to discover exactly how different kinds of noises might influence different kinds of people doing different kinds of tasks. Nonetheless, certain general conclusions have emerged. (1) Steady noises without special meaning do not seem to interfere with human performance that does not include auditory components, unless the A-weighted noise level exceeds about 90 dB. (2) Irregular bursts of noise are more disruptive than steady noises. Even when the A-weighted sound levels of irregular bursts are below 90 dB, they may sometimes interfere with performance of a task. (3) High-frequency components of noise, above about 1000-2000 Hz, may produce more interference with performance than low-frequency components of noise. (4) Noise does not seem to influence the overall rate of work, but high levels of noise may increase the variability of the rate of work. There may be "noise pauses" followed by compensating increases in work rate. (5) Noise is more likely to reduce the accuracy of work than to reduce the total quantity of work. (6) Complex tasks are more likely to be adversely influenced by noise than are simple tasks.

Broadbent (1979) described how and when noise can have both positive and negative impacts on performance:

The common thread in all the findings described in this chapter is that noise increases the general state of arousal or excitement of the nervous system. Like other situations increasing arousal, noise produces a concentration upon some sources of information to the detriment of others. At low noise levels, this process seems positively to increase efficiency, because it means that a worker attends to the task rather than irrelevant surroundings, and to that part of the task which is most likely to need attention. Relatively low levels of noise, therefore, may be positively desirable as compared with quiet. Logically, however, there can be tasks in which such a concentration of attention can be too great and leave parts of the total job neglected more than they should be. This is particularly true when attention needs to be distributed over many sources of information. Even with a single source, as a work period goes on it becomes increasingly unlikely that attention can be held in the same place and it may wander. When it does so, a person working in noise with a narrow span of awareness will cease completely to take in information from the task, while one in quiet, with a wider span of awareness, may still keep some degree of monitoring on the task itself. Thus moments of inefficiency will appear in continuous work. This inefficiency will take the form primarily of failure to consider unexpected information from the outside world; automatic and routine internal operation can continue quite adequately while attention is diverted [1979: chap. 17, 1-2].

One setting where noise levels should not be excessive is the school. Fourteen separate recommended acceptable noise level standards cited by the EPA (1974: D-3) set school classroom levels relatively low: from 30 to 47 dBA and averaging 37 dBA. A number of studies have shown that highway, aircraft, or other environmental noises lower school performance (Cohen et al., 1973; Crook and Langdon, 1974; Bronzaft and McCarthy, 1975; Glass et al., 1973; Highline Public Schools, 1973). Bronzaft and McCarthy (1975) found significantly higher reading achievement for children on the quiet side of a school compared with those on the side facing elevated railroad tracks. They observed that the trains interrupted 11 percent of the teaching time. Not all studies, however, find a significant correlation between environmental noise and school performance. Experiments with school children often fail to find detrimental effects of noise on speed or accuracy of performance on experimental tasks (see for example Slater, 1968). Furthermore, Cohen et al. (1980) failed to find "evidence that aircraft noise affects reading and math skills" (1980: 240). However, the children in the noisy schools were more easily distracted, gave up more often on tasks, and generally performed experimental tasks less well than the children in the quiet schools.

## NOISE AND MENTAL HEALTH

The effects of noise on mental health are not clear. Abey-Wickrama et al. (1969) found higher admission rates to a psychiatric hospital from areas subjected to high noise levels around Heathrow Airport than from less noisy control areas. Furthermore, they reported that the control areas had higher percentages of the groups normally having high rates of mental illness, which suggests that the aircraft noise was responsible for the higher hospital admissions from housing in the airport noise corridor. Chowns (1970) challenged these results, claiming that they were largely due to population differences between the noisy and the control areas. However, the results of Herridge (1974) support (although at lower correlations) the findings of Abey-Wick-rams et al. Napp also (1977) reports on a study by Meechan and Smith of admission rates to mental hospitals from Inglewood, where the Los Angeles airport is located, and El Segundo, a comparable area several miles away. "Allowing for population differences, mental hospital admissions were 29 percent higher in Inglewood, although the two areas were racially, economically and socially similar" (1977: 33).

There is no *definitive* evidence that noise causes mental illness, but informed opinion is that it aggravates already existing mental health problems. This opinion is supported by anecdotal accounts of extreme reactions to noise. Connell (1972, cited by Bugliarello et al., 1976: 71) reports three separate cases of suicide which supposedly were caused by a discotheque, children, and highway noises, respectively. In the latter case, a major new highway had been built near the victim's house. He left a suicide note which read: "The Noise; the Noise; I just couldn't stand the Noise." Another poignant anecdote is presented by Mecklin (1969: 130):

> In the Bronx borough of New York City one evening last spring, four boys were at play, shouting and racing in and out of an apartment building. Suddenly, from a second-floor window, came the crack of a pistol. One of the boys sprawled dead on the pavement. The victim happened to be Roy Innis Jr., thirteen, son of a prominent Negro leader, but there was no political implication in the tragedy. The killer, also a Negro, confessed to police that he was a nightworker who had lost control of himself because the noise from the boys prevented him from sleeping.

## ANNOYANCE AND COMMUNITY RESPONSE

The trouble with noise is that it is annoying. Even when noise is not causing any physiological damage, it is irritating. People prefer living in relatively quiet settings unless they want to subject themselves to loud sounds of their own choosing, such as disco or rock music. Study after study, at home and abroad, shows that the percentage of people who are annoyed correlates highly (around $r = .9$) with noise levels (see, for example, U.S. EPA, 1973; Llewellyn et al., 1975; Alexander, 1973). The National Academy of Science CHABA Committee (1977) developed Table 8.3, which summarizes this relationship and the literature on community reactions. At 55 $L_{dn}$ a community is not likely to react to noise exposure, but at 75 $L_{dn}$ and higher a community would react strongly.

TABLE 8.3  Summary of Human Effects for Outdoor Day-Night Average
Sound Levels of 55, 65, and 75 Decibels

| Type of Effects | Magnitude of Effect | | |
|---|---|---|---|
| | $55L_{dn}$ | $65L_{dn}$ | $75 L_{dn}$ |
| Speech–Indoors | | | |
| a) Speech disturbance | None | Slight | Some |
| b) Sentence intelligibility (average) | 100% | 99% | Less than 99% |
| Speech–Outdoors | | | |
| a) Speech disturbance | Slight | Significant | Very significant |
| b) Distance of 99% sentence intelligibility (average) | 1.0 meter | 0.35 meter | 0.1 meter |
| Average community reaction | None; 7dBA below level of significant "complaints and threats of legal action: | Significant; 3dB above level of significant "complaints and threats of legal action" | Very severe; at least 3 dB above level of "vigorous action" |
| Percent highly annoyed | 5% | 15% | 37% |
| Attitudes toward area | Noise essentially the least important of various factors | Noise is one of the most important adverse aspects of the community | Noise is likely be the most important of all adverse aspects of the community |
| (Percent who complain) | (1%) | (5%) | (15%) |

SOURCE: National Academy of Sciences CHABA Committee (1977).
Figures in parenthesis are from Tracor (1971).

A distinction should be made between annoyance and complaints. Few of
the very annoyed complain by telephone, letter, in person, or in the courts
(see Table 8.3).

Although community annoyance levels are highly correlated with noise
levels, individual annoyance scores and noise ratings are rather poorly correlated (correlations under .5). A number of psychological and social factors
contribute to the variations in individual responses, and these are of special
interest to social impact assessors. According to the EPA (1973: chap. 3, 4),
some of these factors are:

(1) Fear associated with activities of noise sources, such as fear of crashes
    in the case of aircraft noise.

(2) Socioeconomic status and educational level.
(3) The extent to which residents of a community believe that they are being treated fairly.
(4) Attitude of the community residents regarding the contribution of the activities associated with the noise source to the general well-being of the community.
(5) The extent to which residents of the community believe the noise source could be controlled.

To this list should be added fear of harmful physiological and health effects of noise, according to Leonard and Borsky (1973).

## Economic Effects of Noise

Since high noise levels make residential areas less attractive, a major economic impact of noise is reduced property values. Few researchers have tried to estimate the amount of the value reduction because of the difficulties in estimating property values if the noise source were not present. Furthermore, it is difficult to separate the effects of noise from other influences on property values, but several studies have attempted to do just that (except they fail to separate air pollution from noise pollution impacts). Highways and aircraft are the two noise sources with the greatest economic effects on residential areas.

The major reports on the economic impacts of aircraft noise are by Dygert (1973), Feller and Nelson (1973), and Nelson (1975). Feller and Nelson summarize three studies (including Dygert's work) and present their numerical summary in Table 8.4. The studies are based on multiple regressions predicting mean or median property values (Dygert and Sanders, 1970; Paik, 1970) or sales prices (Emerson, 1969). The second row in the table presents Feller and Nelson's best estimate and assumes that "marginal damages are constant throughout the range of noise levels" (1973: 129). The authors point out that the studies are highly consistent when differences in the cost of housing are taken into account, as in the fourth row.

Nelson (1975) found a $174 decrease in median property values for each unit increase in composit noise rating (CNR) due to aircraft noise. Nelson used $188 marginal damages per CNR as the best estimate in Emerson's study, and claimed the two studies have similar results.

However, the results differ substantially from the findings of Paik for New York City and Dygert-Sanders for San Francisco. The differences appear to be due to model specification, since this study and Emerson's use log functional forms while the latter studies rely on linear functional forms.

TABLE 8.4  Summary of Noise Pollution—Property Value Estimates

| Variable | Dygert and Sanders San Francisco (1970) | | Emerson Minneapolis (1969) | | Paik New York (1970) | |
|---|---|---|---|---|---|---|
| Dollar damages per unit CNR per property (observed range due to regression form) | −$440 to $456 | | −$32 to $206 | | −$270 to $440 | |
| Best estimate of dollar damages per unit CNR per property | −$440 | | −$206 | | −$440 | |
| Percent reduction in mean property value—actual mean | 1.6% (mean = $28,000) | | 1.0% (mean = $19,863) | | 1.6% (mean = $28,000) | |
| Percent reduction in adjusted mean property value | 1.6% | | 1.4% | | 1.6% | |
| Level of confidence | Fair | | Good | | Poor | |

a. CNR=composite noise rating.
SOURCE:  Feller and Nelson (1973). Original sources: Dygert and Sanders (1970); Emerson (1969); Paik (1970).

Our results imply that a property located near an airport (CNR 30) would be worth 10 percent less than a property located in an area not affected by aircraft noise (CNR 15), other things being equal. Thus for an average $28,000 dwelling, the decrement due to aircraft noise nuisance is $2,800 [1975: 8.15].

The three major studies of the economic impacts of highway noise are by Gamble and Sauerlender (1976; based on Gamble et al., 1973), Nelson (1975), and Anderson and Wise (1977). Gamble and Sauerlender studied real estate transactions for 324 properties in four suburban communities: Bogota, New Jersey; North Springfield, Virginia; Rosedale, Maryland; and Towson, Maryland. They used many stepwise multiple regressions with 93 independent variables and ended up with one having six significant variables: noise pollution level (dBA scale), number of rooms in house, number of bathrooms, and three dummy variables (central air conditioning, finished basement, and Rosedale). The authors found the following:

> The regression coefficient for NPL shows that for each increase of 1 dBA of noise the value of property decreased $82. This is the marginal capitalized damage estimate due primarily to noise, but reflects also damages from vehicular air pollutants. The difference between the lowest ambient noise level (55 dBA) and the highest (80 dBA) in the sample of properties tested was 25 dBA. This difference times the coefficient of -82, or $2,050, is the estimated amount by which the average price of properties *abutting* the highways in the study areas was affected primarily by vehicular noise. This value represents a decrease of approximately 6.6 percent below the average price of properties in the four study areas. The decrease in NPL is not linearly related to distance from the highway; rather, the rate of decrease in noise lessens as one moves farther from the highway. Consequently the relationship between property damages and distance from the highway is curvilinear in nature; i.e., the rate of increase in damages is higher as one gets closer to the highway [Gamble and Sauerlender, 1976: 37].

Nelson (1975) simulated noise levels in census tracts in the Washington, D.C. SMSA from traffic data and used multiple regression techniques to control for other influences on property values. He found a $58 decrease in median property values in suburban areas for each dBA increase of peak noise over background noise due to traffic. His methodology failed in urban census tracts, probably because noise levels are relatively even there.

Anderson and Wise (1977) obtained results similar to Gamble's from different contexts. Using data from four small communities traversed by a major highway, they found that

[f]or each 10 percent increase in the noise pollution level above
background levels, property values were found to decrease by 1.5
percent. This corresponds to about $75 decrease in value for each dBA
above the background noise level.

None of these studies claim to reliably determine all noise-induced economic costs to property owners. For example, they do not include expenditures made by property owners to reduce noise (such as storm windows,
fencing, or insulation). Nor do they claim that the economic loss in property
values adequately expresses social or psychological negative impacts. A study
by Colony (1967) found no loss in property values due to the Detroit-Toledo
Expressway, but found 32 percent of the nearby residents annoyed to the
point of saying they would not buy, build, or rent so close to an expressway
again. Colony also questioned realtors, who generally believed the expressway
caused a substantial loss in property value.

Finally, the studies point out that new highways also have positive economic effects on nearby properties. In fact, the Gamble team found that the
positive economic effects outweighted the negative economic effects in their
study of North Springfield (see Table 8.5).

Another point to consider in order to have a balanced perspective is the
effect of noise on moving. As seen in Chapter 2, noise is not an important
cause of moving in the general population. The reason is twofold. First, only
a small percentage of the population lives in environments with noise levels
high enough to induce moving. Second, even residents of noisy neighborhoods usually will not move only because of the noise. In keeping with this
pattern, Arvidsson et al. (1965) surveyed residents in a Swedish city and
found that traffic noise was frequently cited as an annoyance in the noisy
district studied (twice as often as in the quiet district). Traffic density and
noise, however, did not seem important enough to justify moving. This is
contrary to a study by Hitchcock and Waterhouse (1979), which found that
residents in apartment houses near an expressway who were disturbed by the
highway noises planned to move substantially more often than did residents
who were not disturbed by the noise. In like manner, Brinton and Bloom
(1969) found high turnover and rent concessions made to tenants living in
units next to the highway.

Finally, according to a survey in Allentown, Pennsylvania, the public is
disinterested in noise control programs (Hawkins, 1979). Two-fifths of the
sample of residents were unwilling to pay even 10 cents extra in taxes for

TABLE 8.5   Estimated Net Effect of the Washington, D.C. Beltway on Abutting Property Values in North Springfield, Virginia

|  | Abutters | % Change | Nonabutters |
|---|---|---|---|
| Basic value | $30,690 |  | $30,690 |
| Effect of regional assessibility | +2950 | +9.6 | +2950 |
| Effect of highway pollutants | -1518 | -4.6 | 0 |
| Net value (selling price) | 32,122 |  | 33,640 |
| Net effect of highway | +1432 | +4.7 | +2950 |

SOURCE: Gamble, et al. (1973: 9.17).

such a program, and only six percent were willing to pay as much as $2.50 per person in taxes. People like the idea of such programs as long as they seem to be free.

## Noise Control

Despite the public's unwillingness to personally sacrifice even small amounts of money for noise control, the public is considerably annoyed by constant noise above 75 dBA (see Table 8.3) and demands public actions to control it. A wide variety of controls can be instituted (see Figure 8.4), but only two will be discussed here: sound barriers and sound insulation.

Barriers are a common means for obtaining a modest reduction in noise from traffic, construction, or other outdoor noise sources. Part of the noise is diffracted over the top of the barrier, but little goes through solid barriers designed for noise control. This feature makes barriers more effective in reducing peak noise than background noise. Even so, their effectiveness is limited: "The maximum noise reductions that can be expected in practice from an acoustic barrier are limited to between 10 and 15 dBA" (Bugliarello et al., 1976: 150). Figure 8.5 presents the amount of reduction in noise effected by a three-meter barrier to receivers at various heights and distances behind the barrier. A person standing on level ground 20 meters behind the barrier would benefit from a 13 dBA decrease in noise.

It is important for assessors and planners to view noise problems in psychological rather than in physical terms. Often the most effective barriers are not as well accepted by the public as are less effective but more natural barriers. For example, as mentioned earlier, a row of trees are popular barriers, but only marginally reduce noise levels.

| Abatement Alternatives | Example* |
|---|---|
| **Operational Restrictions** | |
| Noise Standard | Motor vehicles shall not exceed 86 dB at 15m in speed zones above 64km/h (40 mph). |
| Operational Controls | 1. Speed limit in residential areas changes from 72 to 56km/h (45 to 35 mph). 2. Vehicles shall not operate with excessive acceleration (except where safety requires). |
| Area Restrictions | No thru-trucks allowed in hillside area. |
| Time Restrictions | No loud music exceeding 70 dB at property lines allowed after 10 P.M. |
| Permits | On all construction projects exceeding $10,000 value, equipment must meet municipal noise standard X. |
| **Land Use Restrictions** | |
| Barriers | Construct barrier between highway and school. |
| Building Insulation | Insulate all buildings near airport where $L_{dn} > 75$ dB. |
| Compensation | Reimburse residents under flight path for lowered property values. |
| Population Relocation | Relocate residents living in airport areas where $L_{dn} > 75$ dB. |
| Planning/Zoning | 1. Build new highway through industrial area instead of residential area. 2. Restrict future housing developments near airport. |
| Building Codes | Extra insulation required in zones where $L_{dn}$ 65 dB. |
| **Tax Measures** | |
| Tax Incentives | Commercial establishments installing quiet outdoor furnaces receive tax break. |
| Tax Penalty | Plants are charged $500 per dB in excess of 70 dB ($L_{dn}$) measured at property line per year. |
| **New Product Regulations** | |
| Noise Standard | New lawn mowers sold in the city may not exceed 75 dB at 7.5m. |
| Labeling | New vacuum cleaners sold in the city must not be acoustically labeled. |
| **Equipment Standard** | |
| Maintenance | Registered automobiles must be inspected for proper maintenance once every two years. |
| Retrofit | All motorcycles must have a muffler that produces an insertion loss of at least 20 dB. |
| **Other Alternatives** | |
| Education | 1. Broadcast once-a-month radio programs to help consumer choose quiet products. 2. Inform local airport and pilots of noise-sensitive areas. |
| Complaint Mechanism | Establish noise hotline in cooperation with police. |

*These examples are illustrative and may not completely describe details which must be specified if the abatement alternative is to be properly established. Products mentioned as targets of abatement action may not be the most important noise sources to control.

SOURCE: Wyle Research (1979: 19).

**FIGURE 8.4   List of Abatement Alternatives which Local Governments May Apply to Community Noise Sources**

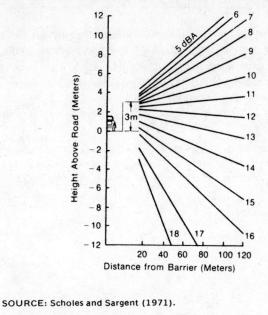

SOURCE: Scholes and Sargent (1971).

*Distance between source and barrier: 25m.

**FIGURE 8.5    Reduction of $L_{10}$ by a Three-Meter Barrier***
*Distance between source and barrier: 25m.

Sound insulation is another noise abatement procedure that should be considered. It is both expensive and effective, but when homes are far apart it is less expensive than constructing barriers. According to Wyle Laboratory (1970), a "Stage One" level of soundproofing cost in 1970 around $3210 for houses valued between $20,000 and $30,000. Although the noise level would be reduced 25 dB, "stage one" modifications were judged to be insufficient by tested homeowners. "Stage Two" modifications costing about $5620 per house and "Stage Three" modifications costing about $12,550 were judged to be adequate: They reduced the noise 35 dB and 50 dB, respectively.

With sound insulation, as with taxes for noise control, what residents want and what they will pay for are quite different. In 1966 London Airport Authority offered to pay two-thirds of the costs for sound insulation and set aside £ 2,000,000 for the program. Only £ 8,500 was spent because homeowners would not pay the £ 100 required on their part (Bragdon, 1971: 189).

## Epilogue

Noise is a byproduct of modern urbanized life, and many people who enjoy the benefits of that life dream of a relaxed, quiet, rustic life which is its antithesis. The public is now speaking out against further noise bombardment. A story told by Baron (1970: 17) expresses an attitude which may have implications for future public actions.

George Bernard Shaw entered a posh London restaurant, took a seat, and was confronted by the waiter. "While you are eating, sir, the orchestra will play anything you like. What would you like them to play?"

Shaw's reply? "Dominoes."

*Chapter 9*

# LEISURE AND RECREATION IMPACTS

A large number of social impact assessments involve leisure/recreational resources. A major social impact of dams and waterworks projects are the recreational resources which they create. In addition, there are vast wilderness recreational areas under the jurisdiction of the Forestry Service or the Bureau of Land Management, both of which produce EISs which assess the land use plans for these areas. Moreover, many government actions have indirect impacts on leisure/recreational activities. However, seldom are leisure/recreational impacts adequately assessed. Generally, they are poorly understood and underevaluated. Policy makers seem to be guided by a work ethic which justifies projects in terms of employment, income, conservation, and savings but give too little weight to leisure/recreational benefits. The general public gives far more weight to the leisure/recreational aspects of their lives than do policy makers.

Impact assessors need to understand the role of leisure/recreation in American life. This chapter describes this role by examining how people use time, what leisure activities they engage in, and what their attitudes are toward work and leisure. The recreational movement and the federal agencies involved in recreation are described. For perspective, we review the role of leisure/recreation in some earlier and contemporary societies. Finally, we discuss leisure/recreational impacts and their measurement.

## Definitions and Concepts

Leisure is generally defined as surplus time or the time not used for working, sleeping, eating, and other necessities. Since many activities such as sociable dining or lawn care are not easily classified as leisure, this definition is not completely satisfactory. Other definitions, however, have even greater difficulties. For example, leisure has been viewed as activities which have certain qualities. In most cases the major defining quality is freedom from external compulsion or proscription. Again, activities are difficult to classify by this or similar criteria.

Recreation is a closely allied concept and is defined with similar difficulties. A simple definition of recreation is pleasurable activity engaged in during leisure time. More complex definitions might include the elements of free choice and intrinsic rewards as opposed to obligations and instrumental purposes. Fuller definitions would also decide whether recreation includes or excludes planned inactivity, contemplation, and rest.

The above statements raise more questions than they answer. However, the pursuit of the ideal definitions of leisure and recreation is vain. For our purposes, leisure means unobligated time and recreation means leisure-time activity undertaken voluntarily. The reader is directed to Kraus (1971) and Neulinger (1974) for more complete discussions of definitional issues.

## Leisure/Recreation
## in Historical Perspective

Historical records of the leisure/recreational activities of ancient peoples is spotty but intriguing. Many current forms of recreation have ancient roots, as the following passage from Carlson et al. (1972: 27) indicates:

> Egyptian reliefs give evidence of an interest in hunting, spearing, wrestling, and fencing. Kite flying provided a dual pleasure for the artistic talent and the physical energy of the Chinese and other Asiatic peoples, 4000 years before the Christian era. Expression in movement of sorrow or delight, or the interpretation of an occupation formed dance patterns which were highly developed in early societies. . . . Contests of speed and endurance gave evidence of the early Persians' use of recreation to train their warriors, and the Japanese board game of "Go" existed 2200 years before the birth of Christ.

Little is known of the role of leisure/recreation in the lives of ancient peoples, but it is generally supposed that work and leisure were not sharply separated for prehistoric man. In contrast, ancient higher civilizations developed leisure classes, and the distinction between leisure and work came into being. In Ancient Greece, members of the leisure class developed sophisticated notions about the role of leisure/recreation in society and in the lives of its citizens. Work was subordinated to leisure in the hierarchy of ancient Greek values, and this was reflected in the way Greek cities were stratified. Salves did much of the work, which enabled the well-born citizens to live lives of leisure. Other citizens were farmers, craftsmen, and tradesmen, but they had less prestige than the leisure class. In Greek society the purpose of work was to provide leisure. However, leisure did not mean idleness. In Athens, leisure was devoted to athletics, the arts, learning, and political participation and was directed toward the development of skills, character, self-discipline, the mind, and the body. The ideal citizen was an accomplished athlete, artist, philosopher, soldier, and statesman. The leisure class also enjoyed amusements, but these were considered secondary to the self-development activities. Leisure may provide pleasure and entertainment, but historically it was intended for the improvement of self and society.

Over time, the Athenian ideal of an athletic, artistic, and learned citizenry declined as sports and the arts became specialized and professionalized. Theater, dance, and sporting contests were performed by specialists before large audiences.

> At its height, though, the Athenian ideal had developed a new concept of recreation and play as a means of preparing children for adulthood and for providing mankind with great creative impulses and enrichment. Play was seen as having the utilitarian purposes of maintaining physical fitness, courage, and readiness to defend the state and also in restoring the energies and health of citizens. It was in the period of the Periclean age that a philosophy of creative play emerged that gave birth to great forms of art, theater, poetry, and dance and that exalted a spiritual concept of democratic man that was not matched during the many centuries that followed [Kraus, 1971: 139].

In Sparta and later in the Roman Empire recreation was also seen as a means for education and development, but the primary purpose of the development was preparation for the requirements of war. In the Middle Ages religious values downgraded leisure and recreation and lauded asceticism. Idleness and sloth were considered evil; only hard work was good. Many forms of play and recreation were allowed but they were not viewed as means for developing the ideal man. During the Renaissance the relative value of the arts increased greatly: They were highly professionalized and their expression attained high levels. The Reformation, however, reinstituted religious values which were antithetical to many forms of leisure activity. Work was viewed as a calling of God, diligence was viewed as an essential characteristic of a virtuous person, churches were devoid of ornate art, and most amusements were viewed as antithetical to a godly life. This ethic extolling hard work and impugning amusements and leisure remains in diluted and secular form today. Working Americans spend less than a quarter of their time working, but work is considered the focus of life. According to time budgets, however, adults spend more time on leisure activities than at working. Perhaps the work ethic is becoming outdated, but a new ethic has not yet crystalized. Many adults are avid joggers, bikers, sportsmen, dancers, hobbyists, or fans, but our society is not yet dominated by an ethic of leisure.

## The Functions of
## Leisure/Recreation

The four major functions of leisure/recreation are generally considered to be entertainment, self-development, renewal, and self-expression. In the ancient Roman Empire entertainment was the main purpose of leisure/recreation, and this emphasis contributed to Rome's reputation as a hedonistic society. Roman emperors provided spectacular contests for the masses in the Circus Maximus (capacity nearly 400,000) and the Colosseum (90,000). "Here the public passively witnessed gladiatorial games, sea battles waged in artificial lakes, chariot races, vicariously enjoying bloodshed and brutality" (Kando, 1980: 26). Among the wealthy there were extravagant feasts where drunkenness and debauchery were expected of the guests. The pursuit of pleasure was the accepted way of life.

Modern America has been compared with hedonistic Rome, often by moralists who predict the fall of America unless it repents. The mushrooming of spectator sports, the mania for wild rock concerts, the widespread use of alcohol and other drugs, and the billions of hours of TV-viewing provide evidence that Americans are heavy entertainment and pleasure consumers. Nevertheless, Americans also use leisure/recreation for considerable self-development, self-expression, and renewal.

The view of leisure/recreation as a means of self-development may not be dominant in American culture, but it has many devotees. Much energy is devoted to body development for appearance and health. Crafts, hobbies, gardening, and participation in thousands of organizations provide creative outlets for millions. Reading, evening courses, and viewing the performing arts combine entertainment with cultural and intellectual self-development. Religion, meditation, and other spiritual endeavors are additional popular leisure activities whose purpose is to improve the self.

The renewal role of leisure/recreation in America also should be recognized. Recreation in the form of strenuous physical activity can serve to refresh mentally fatigued workers. Sedentary white-collar and blue-collar workers with monotonous jobs often are rejuvenated by exercise. Other workers feeling the need to relax and unwind after work may have a drink with the boys" or cocktails at home. Relaxing in front of the TV set provides renewal for many. Television also provides a different type of renewal: Watching an exciting sports event on the weekend can compensate for unexciting work and enable workers to endure their work with more equanimity. Vacations also function to refresh workers.

In *The Theory of the Leisure Class* (1899), Veblen portrayed how the wealthy classes in many periods of history used leisure/recreation as means to exhibit their high status and to set themselves above other classes. A life of leisure was evidence of high standing and natural superiority when masterfully expressed with style and cultivated tastes. The Industrial Revolution diffused both wealth and leisure. Mass production enabled the middle class, and later the working class, to consume the goods which had been available only to the rich. Distinctions of dress practically disappeared. Meanwhile, the work week shortened for manual workers to less than that for managers and professionals, and few of the rich live idle lives today. Most are involved in business or public life. There is no leisure class, unless the nonworking wives of the rich are considered as such. Nevertheless, leisure/recreation are still ways to display one's social standing, taste, and breeding. Equestrian sports, exclusive clubs, formal affairs, and attending high-brow artistic performances supposedly indicate the elite style of life.

Leisure/recreation can serve a host of additional functions for people, from exercising personal power to teaching cooperation. An infinite number of activities are engaged in during leisure for an infinite number of purposes and serve the full range of psychological needs. From the point of view of society, leisure/recreation has been seen to reduce crime and delinquency (Glueck and Glueck, 1950; Bernstein, 1964), providing harmless outlets for aggression. Leisure/recreation also contributes to social solidarity, renews the labor force, contributes to health, advances the arts, and provides a large consumer market.

## Contemporary American Leisure Patterns

### WORK/LEISURE RATIOS

It is a fallacy to think that the Industrial Revolution greatly increased leisure time. This fallacy derives from statistics on working time which go back only a century. The length of the average workweek has been cut almost in half since 1850 (see Table 9.1), dropping from 69.7 hours in 1850 to 37.2 in 1978, for a savings in free time of 32.5 hours per week (Kando, 1980). De Grazia (1962) estimated that paid vacations, holidays, and sick leave add an additional 2.5 hours of free time per week, for a total of 34.6 hours reduction in the modern workweek. If the focus shifts to lifetime labor-force participation versus life-time leisure, several additional factors decrease the ratio: longer schooling, higher absenteeism, and earlier retirement. Increasing life expectancy extends both the work life and life after retirement.

The decline in the workweek pictured in Table 9.1 is exaggerated, however, because part-time workers are included in the later figures but not in the earlier ones, and the number with second jobs has increased. When these factors are taken into account, they reduce the hours saved from work from 34.6 to 26.4, according to De Grazia (1962). When further subtractions are made for the increases in commuting time, the difference is only 18 hours. When increases in home maintenance and house work for men are taken into account, the gain in leisure time for men is only 10.7 hours a week. Thus, the workweek has declined considerably in the past 130 years, but the amount of leisure time gained is modest.

Using statistics which differ considerably from the statistics of de Grazia and Kando, Moore and Hedges (1975: 472) also demonstrated that leisure time has increased only modestly over the past century. "In the 1870's the average workweek was about 53 hours. Today, the average is close to 40 hours—about 13 hours less than a century ago."

No gain in leisure time is evident from a longer historical perspective. Comparisons of current and nineteenth-century work schedules indicate a downward trend, but the nineteenth century was exceptional in world history. Wilensky (1961) noted that around 350 A.D. the average Roman citizen worked only about half a year due to countless holidays. Assuming a twelve-hour work day, he calculated a 2160-hour work year, which is similar to current average work levels for many workers and less than the work years of professional and administrative workers. Wilensky (1961: 34-35) also calculated that:

> From the late middle ages to 1800, the drift in manual occupations was unmistakably toward longer hours. Dolleans and Dehove report work days in the city crafts of 14 to 18 hours. And the number of days off declined from the fifteenth century on. By 1750, day laborers were working perhaps 3,770 hours.
>
> The burden of labor in our century, of course, has lessened; today annual hours are down in the range 1,900-2,500—a return to the work schedules of medieval guildsmen.

As can be seen in Table 9.1, agricultural workers generally have longer workweeks or workyears than do nonagricultural workers. "Estimates for traditional European agriculture put annual hours at 3,500-4,000 throughout

TABLE 9.1   Length of the Average Workweek in
Agriculture and Nonagricultural
Industries, 1850 to 1978

| Years | All Industries | Agriculture | Nonagricultural Industries |
|---|---|---|---|
| 1850 | 69.7 | 72.0 | 65.7 |
| 1860 | 67.8 | 71.0 | 63.3 |
| 1870 | 65.3 | 70.0 | 60.0 |
| 1880 | 63.8 | 69.0 | 58.8 |
| 1890 | 61.7 | 68.0 | 57.1 |
| 1900 | 60.1 | 67.0 | 55.9 |
| 1910 | 54.9 | 65.0 | 50.3 |
| 1920 | 49.4 | 60.0 | 45.5 |
| 1930 | 45.7 | 55.0 | 43.2 |
| 1940 | 43.8 | 54.6 | 41.1 |
| 1950 | 39.9 | 47.2 | 38.8 |
| 1955 | 39.7 | 46.5 | 38.9 |
| 1960 | 38.5 | 44.0 | 38.0 |
| 1965 | 38.0 | 42.1 | 37.7 |
| 1970 | 37.7 | 42.1 | 37.4 |
| 1975 | 36.9 | 39.2 | 36.7 |
| 1978 | 37.2 | 40.1 | 37.0 |

SOURCE:   Kando (1980: 109). Original sources: de Grazia
(1962) for 1850 to 1960 data; Bureau of Labor Statistics
for 1965 to 1978 data, which were adjusted by Kando to
conform to de Grazia's methodology.

the early period; this did not change until the 20th century" (Wilensky,
1961: 34). Currently, workyears in agriculture in the United States are under
2300 hours, less than two-thirds of the work year in traditional European
agricultural societies. However, current workyears in agriculture may be
about the same length or longer than primitive agriculture. Primitive societies
had many holidays or non-workdays, and in many societies people worked
little more than was required to provide for their necessities.

De Grazia (1962), independently of Wilensky, analyzed historical trends in
workweeks, commuting times, and other factors related to work and leisure.

Since 1850 free time has not appreciably increased. It is greater when
compared with the days of Manchesterism or of the sweatshops of New
York. Put alongside modern rural Greece or ancient Greece, though, or
medieval Europe and ancient Rome, free time today suffers by comparison, and leisure even more [1962: 90].

More recently, Kando (1980: 82) concluded his review of comparative studies of work time with the assertion:

> Thus comparing ourselves with most of the worlds' past societies, we seem to be working as hard as ever, and . . . the situation seems to be stabilizing into a permanent one, with little prospect of substantial gain in leisure time in the imminent future.

It is possible to examine post-World War II trends in workweeks with a fairly consistent statistical series and fairly high accuracy. A slight decline in average workweeks occurred in this period, but this decline is due to compositional effects, as explained by Owen (1979: 9-10).

> There was a rather modest decline in measured average weekly hours. Thus average hours of nonagricultural employees went from 40.9 in 1948 to 38.5 in 1977. However, this drop appears to reflect changes in the composition of the labor force rather than a reduction in the hours of work of the individuals or groups that compose the work force. As a result of postwar trends, a larger proportion of the work force are women and students: female nonagricultural employees made up less than 29 percent of the work force in 1940 and are over 41 percent of it today; students made up 1 percent or less in 1940 and 2.5 percent after World War II, but now are over 6 percent. In the same period, the proportion of nonstudent males in the nonagricultural work force dropped to under 57 percent. Because of group differences in hours worked—women average 34 hours, male students 23 hours, and nonstudent males about 43 hours per week—the declining proportion of nonstudent males in the labor force has produced a statistical decline in average weekly hours. However, these compositional shifts do not necessarily reflect a real reduction in working times.

Owen separately examined the workweeks and leisure of employed nonstudent men, nonstudent women, and students, and concluded: "Employed American adults have had no net gain in their leisure time in 30 years" (1976: 3). Table 9.2 presents the workweek for nonstudent men in nonagricultural industries for the post-World War II period. No decline occurred, even when the series is adjusted for the growth in paid vacation and holidays. When we add commuting and housework time (both increasing for men) to worktime, we observe that the time remaining for family and leisure activities has actually declined.

Compositional effects rather than across-the-board gains or losses explain most observed changes in work/leisure time of the remaining two categories of adults: students and nonstudent working women. The average workweek of male students increased about four hours from 1948 to 1975 because the

TABLE 9.2    Weekly Hours of Nonstudent Males
Employed in Nonagricultural Industries

| Year | Unadjusted | Adjusted for Growth in Vacations and Holidays |
|------|------------|-----------------------------------------------|
| 1948 | 42.7 | 41.6 |
| 1950 | 42.2 | 41.0 |
| 1953 | 42.5 | 41.4 |
| 1950 | 43.0 | 41.8 |
| 1959 | 42.0 | 40.7 |
| 1962 | 43.1 | 41.7 |
| 1966 | 43.5 | 42.1 |
| 1969 | 43.5 | 42.0 |
| 1972 | 42.9 | 41.4 |
| 1975 | 42.4 | 40.8 |
| 1976 | 42.4 | 40.9 |
| 1977 | 42.8 | 41.3 |

SOURCE: Owen (1979: 10).

average age of working students has increased and older students work longer hours. At comparable age levels no significant change has taken place. The average workweek for nonstudent working women has declined due to changes in the composition of this group. The percentage of working women who are married and/or have children has increased, and marriage and children under 18 are associated with shorter workweeks for working women.

## TIME BUDGET ANALYSIS OF LEISURE PATTERNS

The best way to get a picture of the role of leisure in American life is to examine time budgets. Table 9.3 presents the time budget for a national urban/suburban sample of adults under age 66 in nonagricultural occupations for 1965-1966 and compares it with a 1934 sample drawn from Westchester County, New York. Great pains were taken to make the two studies as comparable as possible, although some difficulties remain. Table 9.3 indicates that the addition of television accounts for most of the "leisure" time savings in other activities. It appears that Americans are spending less time sleeping, eating, reading, frequenting entertainments (including movies), engaging in sports, listening to the radio, pleasure driving, and participating in clubs. The study (Robinson and Converse, 1972) also indicated less time attending church. On the other hand, Americans are spending more time traveling and taking care of home and family. Time used for "leisure" declined about an

TABLE 9.3 Comparison of Average Time Expenditures for Various Groups in Lundberg et al. (1934) with Similar Groups of the 1965-66 Study (in Parentheses)

| | Men | | | | | | Employed Women | | | | Housewives | |
|---|---|---|---|---|---|---|---|---|---|---|---|---|
| | Executives Professional | | White Collar | | Labor | | White Collar | | Labor | | | |
| (N =) | 97 | (126) | 268 | (97) | 10 | (283) | 276 | (182) | 60 | (112) | 107 | (176) |
| Nonleisure:[a] | | | | | | | | | | | | |
| Sleep | 8.2 | (7.7) | 8.3 | (7.6) | 9.0 | (7.5) | 8.2 | (7.6) | 8.3 | (7.6) | 8.6 | (7.5) |
| Work for pay | 6.2 | (6.8) | 6.4 | (7.2) | 5.9 | (6.8) | 5.9 | (5.4) | 6.7 | (4.5) | 0.1 | (0.2) |
| Care of self | 0.7 | (0.7) | 0.7 | (0.8) | 0.8 | (1.0) | 1.0 | (1.1) | 1.0 | (1.1) | 1.0 | (1.0) |
| Transportation | 1.2 | (1.6) | 0.8 | (1.5) | 0.9 | (1.4) | 1.1 | (1.3) | 1.0 | (1.2) | 0.8 | (1.0) |
| Household and children | 0.9 | (0.7) | 0.5 | (0.6) | 0.6 | (0.6) | 1.2 | (2.9) | 1.4 | (3.4) | 4.2 | (6.2) |
| Total nonleisure hours | 17.2 | (17.5) | 16.7 | (17.7) | 17.2 | (17.3) | 17.4 | (18.3) | 18.4 | (17.8) | 14.7 | (15.9) |
| Shopping | | (0.4) | | (0.3) | | (0.4) | | (0.5) | | (0.7) | | (0.7) |
| Undisclosed, private | | (0.2) | | (0.2) | | (0.2) | | (0.3) | | (0.3) | | (0.3) |

TABLE 9.3 Comparison of Average Time Expenditures for Various Groups in Lundberg et al. (1934) with Similar Groups of the 1965-66 Study (in Parentheses) (Cont)

| | Men | | | | | | Employed Women | | | | Housewives | |
| | Executives Professional | | White Collar | | Labor | | White Collar | | Labor | | | |
| (N =) | 97 | (126) | 268 | (97) | 10 | (283) | 276 | (182) | 60 | (112) | 107 | (176) |
|---|---|---|---|---|---|---|---|---|---|---|---|---|
| Leisure:[b] | | | | | | | | | | | | |
| Eating | 106 | (78) | 114 | (73) | 101 | (70) | 116 | (59) | 109 | (59) | 106 | (79) |
| Visiting | 79 | (68) | 81 | (74) | 94 | (80) | 94 | (74) | 74 | (90) | 151 | (138) |
| Reading | 74 | (50) | 61 | (36) | 95 | (37) | 43 | (29) | 38 | (21) | 84 | (40) |
| Entertainment | 15 | (11) | 45 | (13) | 35 | (6) | 48 | (14) | 29 | (14) | 44 | (10) |
| Sports | 40 | (11) | 34 | (13) | 35 | (13) | 19 | (7) | 20 | (4) | 16 | (4) |
| Radio | 22 | (5) | 34 | (4) | 32 | (5) | 18 | (5) | 45 | (3) | 29 | (2) |
| Motoring | 15 | (2) | 20 | (2) | 12 | (1) | 25 | (4) | 13 | (1) | 10 | (3) |
| Clubs | 10 | (17) | 8 | (10) | 0 | (7) | 3 | (8) | 0 | (4) | 61 | (19) |
| Television | | (80) | | (75) | | (120) | | (58) | | (85) | | (75) |
| Miscellaneous | 40 | (38) | 35 | (54) | 5 | (39) | 33 | (48) | 8 | (53) | 50 | (56) |
| Total leisure minutes | 401 | (360) | 438 | (354) | 409 | (378) | 399 | (306) | 336 | (324) | 551 | (426) |
| Total leisure hours | 6.7 | (6.0) | 7.3 | (5.9) | 6.8 | (6.3) | 6.6 | (5.1) | 5.6 | (5.4) | 9.2 | (7.1) |
| Total hours | 23.9 | (24.1) | 24.0 | (24.1) | 24.0 | (24.2) | 24.0 | (24.2) | 24.0 | (24.0) | 23.9 | (24.0) |

a. Hours per day.
b. Minutes per day.
SOURCE: Robinson and Converse (1972: 74).

231

hour and twenty minutes due to an increase in self-care, transportation, homework, and children.

Since 1965 the main change in the time allocated to various leisure activities has been a 41-minute increase in TV-viewing (from 89 minutes in 1965 to 130 in 1975), according to a 1975 replication (Robinson, 1979) of the 1965 study of Table 9.3. The second largest change was an eight-minute decline in newspaper reading (22 minutes in 1965; 14 in 1975). The following small changes also warrant notice: religion, plus two minutes; education, plus two; rest and relaxation, plus five; hobbies and games, plus three; and visiting and conversation, minus six.

The gain in television-viewing time was offset not by declines in other leisure time activities but by a substantial drop (4.9 hours per week) in time spent in family care and a small decline in workweek time (.5 hours). All of the time saved from family care was gained by women, both working and nonworking. The other significant non-leisure-time allocation change was an average increase of 1.4 hours per week for sleep. The conclusion which Robinson draws from his study is that "there is a trend toward 'post-industrious' society in which decreased work and housework are matched by increases in the least demanding of free time activities—television, resting, and pleasure driving" (1979: 18).

## TIME BUDGETS OF VARIOUS CLASSES

There are important variations in the time budgets of different classes. According to Wilensky (1961), the decline in the workweek in the past century has been mainly in the low-status jobs; "the upper strata have probably lost leisure" (p. 37). As a result, professionals, executives, officials, and proprietors have above-average workweeks and blue-collar workers have below-average workweeks unless they have second jobs. These findings are not borne out in Table 9.3, where executives and professionals worked the same hours in 1965-1966 as blue-collar men, but they are supported in other studies.

Wilensky surveyed six professional groups and a cross-section of middle-level occupations earning between $5000 and $13,000 in 1960. Long work-weeks (exceeding 55 hours) were found most often in occupations which provided high income, self-employment, and control over work schedules. For example, 31 percent of his sample with family income exceeding $10,000 worked at least 55 hours per week, compared with only 19 percent of workers with family income of less than $10,000. However, within each occupational grouping, workers who had control over their work schedules were less likely to work 55 hours or more a week than workers who had no choice. This finding seems to indicate a widespread desire for more leisure, such that when workers are given a choice of working more than 55 hours a week they would choose more leisure over more income. It should be pointed out that a completely different trade-off might occur if the choice was between working more or less than 40 hours.

Linder (1970) presented a novel interpretation of the longer workweek of high income earners. He argued that high income earners consume more goods and therefore are saddled with greater burdens of obtaining and maintaining their goods. Since their productivity and wage rates are high, it is efficient for them to pay others to maintain their goods. They therefore work extra hours on the job in order to pay for maintenance work, and thereby keep their total job and maintenance workload to a minimum. According to Linder, the higher income workers have less total work hours and more leisure (consumption) hours than low income workers even though they spend more time on the job. Another viewpoint is expressed by Levitan and Belous (1977) who find that people in the better occupations work longer because they enjoy their work.

## CHANGES IN THE VALUE OF LEISURE TIME

The interplay among work, income, and leisure raises questions about the economic value of leisure. A general rise in incomes makes leisure both more affordable and more costly. With more money people can afford to pay more for leisure and entertainments. At the same time, however, higher wages mean that leisure costs more in foregone income. It is not clear from economic theory that increasing average incomes will increase leisure. The studies cited above indicate that average workweeks have declined from the unusually high levels of the early nineteenth century, but that average leisure time has not increased much. De Grazia (1962: 96) calculated, with much admitted guessing, that the contemporary worker has only about two and a half hours of free time in an average workday. Clearly, leisure has not been extensively substituted for income over the centuries, and claims about a leisure society are misleading.

A more appropriate description of contemporary society is captured in Linder's book, *The Harried Leisure Class* (1970). His main thesis is that time should be analyzed as a commodity, the price of which is set by supply and demand curves and therefore subject to established economic laws. Thus, time will be allocated to activities in such a way that each activity has equal marginal returns. With economic growth, the yield on time spent working increases. As a result, time allotments to various activities will change "so that the yield on time in all other activities is brought into parity with the yield on working time" (p. 4). As income increases, therefore, time becomes more valuable, more scarce. Thus, economic growth has made goods more abundant and time scarcer. It follows that efforts will increase to get the most out of one's free or leisure time. This is done mainly in two ways. First, the amount of consumer goods enjoyed per time unit is increased. In a sense, these goods make the leisure time more productive. Second, one can increase the number of one's activities in a unit of time. Some people jog in front of the television set, some listen to music while reading, and others mix business with pleasure. The quality of leisure is thus affected by the scarcity of time. Life becomes more hectic and dominated by the clock. Activities which take time to enjoy properly are hurried or neglected. Linder explains the time-shortening of love-making, eating, caring for children, caring for the elderly, and love affairs in this manner.

## LIFETIME LEISURE AND
## THE TIME DISTRIBUTION OF LEISURE

Examinations of work and leisure have been in terms of weekly or yearly ratios. Owen (1970) presented a comparison of 1960 with 1900 showing the average proportion of life spent in the labor force and the average proportion of life spent at work. The former declined slightly from 67 percent in 1900, to 62 percent in 1960, because the percentage increase in expected years of life was greater than the percentage increase in years in the labor force. The proportion of life spent at work declined more substantially from 23 percent in 1900 to 15 percent in 1960, because, Owen calculated, the workweek declined from 58.5 to 41.0 in this period. However, the decline in the proportion of life spent at work "might be eliminated altogether if the data were adjusted for the increase in the number of years of school completed of the average member of the labor force in that period: about six years" (1970: 11). Furthermore, these figures do not reflect the increases in commuting and maintenance time. If leisure does not include schooling, commuting, and maintenance, then it appears that lifetime leisure has not increased since 1900.

Although leisure time has not changed much in the past millennium, the time distribution of leisure has changed. Workers have succeeded in getting their leisure time concentrated (see Wilensky, 1961). They have established the two-day weekend and erected premium penalties for Saturday and Sunday work. They have increased the number of holidays and obtained paid vacations. The push is on for flexible working schedules, the four-day work-week, and longer vacations. This trend toward further bunching of leisure has implications for how leisure time can be used. For example, it favors traveling vacations, major house renovation projects, second homes, and hunting or fishing trips.

## TRENDS IN LEISURE ACTIVITIES

The allocation of leisure time to the major leisure activities was presented in Table 9.2. In rank order are visiting, watching television, eating, and reading. Each of the other activities averages out to less than 15 minutes a day. In the 1934 survey, entertainment, sports, and radio occupied a half-hour or more a day; motoring and clubs, 15 minutes or more per day. All of the 1934 categories of leisure received less time in 1965, while an hour and a half of television was added. The big losers were eating, entertainment, and radio, each of which lost a half-hour or more. The activity which received the most time in 1965 was visiting, and time devoted to visiting was about the same for both dates. Evidently, visiting is not significantly reduced as the value of leisure time increases. On the other hand, eating time is reduced, and television substitutes for reading, sports, and radio.

Television has come to play a central role in the leisure activities of the average American. Its appeal holds for all age, sex, income, ethnic, racial, rural/urban, and educational groups. According to a report by *Public Opinion* (1979), TV-watching is very unevenly distributed in the population. About one-third of all adults watch TV 10 or fewer hours a week, one-third watch it 11-20 hours, and one-third watch it more than 21 hours a week. Sixteen percent even watch it over 30 hours a week. Heavy TV users (over 30 hours per week) in 1978 are most prevalent among women who do not work (31 percent); women working full- or part-time, 17 percent; and men, nine percent.

According to another national survey, people use TV both for entertainment and to keep informed. They were asked:

> Turning now to *all* Television, not just public television, people watch television for many different reasons. Here are some of them. [Card shown respondent] Which two or three of them are you most often looking for when you decide to watch television [Public Opinion, 1979: 28]?

The responses were as follows: "to be entertained," 74 percent; "to keep up with what's going on," 59 percent; "to learn something," 46 percent; "to relax my mind," 27 percent; "to be amused," 17 percent; "to improve my mind," 17 percent; "to forget about the cares of the day," 12 percent; "to have a little excitement," five percent; and "don't know," "none," "other," one percent.

## WEEKLY, MONTHLY, AND
## YEARLY LEISURE PATTERNS

Participation in leisure activities is generally measured by asking survey respondents what leisure activities they engaged in "yesterday," "last week," "last month," or "last year." A 1957 study reported by de Grazia (1962) questioned a national probability sample of 5,021 persons aged 15 and over about yesterday's leisure activities. Again, television and visiting head the list. Yardwork and reading are also popular. Organizational activities and hobbies have fair support, but "cultural" activities receive little attention in national averages. Some interesting differences can be observed among the leisure patterns of various categories of people. About 60 percent viewed television in all income groups except the poorest (47 percent), among whom TV ownership is probably low. More suprising are the small differences among income groups in book reading (except for the richest group); attending plays, concerts, or operas; singing or playing a musical instrument; going out to dinner; hobbies; and attending organizational activities. Differences in leisure activities for education, sex, and income groups are presented in Table 9.4.

Table 9.5 presents the percentage participating in various leisure activities in the month prior to the interviews. The monthly participation rates correlate highly with the weekly and yearly participation rates reported in the same study (Cheek and Burch, 1976). TV, visiting, and reading head the list, followed by driving for pleasure and dining out. The more active leisure activities have only moderate participation rates and the high-brow activities are at the bottom of the list.

Another method for evaluating interest in various leisure activities is to ask how people would like to use additional spare time if they had it. Table 9.6 presents the results of a 1978 national sample survey on this question. Television was not often chosen, suggesting that either people already expose themselves to TV to the saturation point or that they do not believe they *should* watch more TV. The list is headed by constructive and self-development activities. The study also indicated that people are not saturated with socializing, but they are saturated with work. Only three percent would work at a second job and only four percent would put more time into their work even though the question asks about the use of 28 extra hours per week.

At the bottom of the lists in Tables 9.5 and 9.6 are the cultural activities concerts, plays, operas, museums, and galleries. Participation in these activities is low but it is increasing rapidly. The number of concerts has more than doubled from 1955 to 1974; attendance has increased sixfold; and population has increased only 39 percent (U.S. Department of Commerce, 1977). Another cultural indicator, number of books produced annually, has increased fourfold.

TABLE 9.4 Percent of Population Engaging in Various Leisure Activities "Yesterday,"a by Personal Characteristics, 1957

| Rank | Activity | Percent of All Respondents | Highest and Lowest Educational Attainment Groups | | | | Annual Family Income | | | |
|---|---|---|---|---|---|---|---|---|---|---|
| | | | 8th Grade | College | Men | Women | Under $3,000 | $3,000-4,999 | $5,000-6,999 | $7,000 and over |
| 1 | Watching television | 57 | 51 | 55 | 56 | 57 | 47 | 60 | 59 | 59 |
| 2 | Visiting with friends or relatives | 38 | 38 | 36 | 32 | 42 | 39 | 38 | 38 | 39 |
| 3 | Working around yard and in garden | 33 | 35 | 37 | 36 | 34 | 35 | 30 | 33 | 34 |
| 4 | Reading magazines | 27 | 12 | 40 | 25 | 27 | 23 | 25 | 27 | 33 |
| 5 | Reading books | 18 | 12 | 30 | 17 | 18 | 20 | 16 | 18 | 20 |
| 6 | Going pleasure driving | 17 | 10 | 18 | 15 | 16 | 13 | 17 | 18 | 17 |
| 7 | Listening to records | 14 | 8 | 13 | 9 | 13 | 13 | 12 | 14 | 15 |
| 8 | Going to meetings or other organization activities | 11 | 11 | 14 | 10 | 11 | 11 | 10 | 10 | 11 |
| 9 | Special hobbies (woodworking, knitting, etc.) | 10 | 9 | 11 | 8 | 12 | 8 | 12 | 11 | 11 |
| 10 | Going out to dinner | 8 | 5 | 12 | 7 | 9 | 6 | 7 | 7 | 12 |
| 11 | Participating in sports | 8 | 3 | 9 | 8 | 4 | 3 | 8 | 10 | 11 |
| 12 | Playing cards, checkers, etc. | 7 | 5 | 7 | 6 | 7 | 5 | 6 | 8 | 8 |

TABLE 9.4 Percent of Population Engaging in Various Leisure Activities "Yesterday,"a by Personal Characteristics, 1957 (Cont)

| Rank | Activity | Percent of All Respondents | Highest and Lowest Educational Attainment Groups | | | | Annual Family Income | | | |
| | | | 8th Grade | College | Men | Women | Under $3,000 | $3,000-4,999 | $5,000-6,999 | $7,000 and over |
|---|---|---|---|---|---|---|---|---|---|---|
| 13 | None of those listed | 7 | 13 | 6 | 8 | 8 | 10 | 8 | 5 | 6 |
| 14 | Spending time at drugstore, etc. | 6 | 3 | 4 | 5 | 3 | 5 | 6 | 7 | 7 |
| 15 | Singing or playing musical instruments | 5 | 3 | 7 | 4 | 4 | 5 | 4 | 5 | 4 |
| 16 | Going to see sports events | 4 | 1 | 4 | 5 | 2 | 3 | 4 | 5 | 5 |
| 17 | Going to movies in regular theater | 3 | 3 | 3 | 2 | 3 | 3 | 3 | 2 | 4 |
| 18 | Going to drive-in movies | 2 | 2 | 2 | 1 | 1 | 2 | 2 | 1 | 1 |
| 19 | Going to dances | 2 | 2 | 2 | 1 | 1 | 2 | 2 | 1 | 1 |
| 20 | Going to a play, concert, or opera | 1 | 1 | 1 | 0 | 1 | 1 | 1 | 1 | 1 |
| 21 | Going to lectures or adult school | 1 | 1 | 1 | 1 | 1 | 0 | 1 | 1 | 1 |

a. Day prior to that on which respondents were visited.
b. Lowest and highest, respectively. Groups in between were omitted due to space limitations.
SOURCE: de Grazia (1962: 460, 462). Original source: Opinion Research Corporation (1957: II).

TABLE 9.5   Adult Participation in Selected Leisure Activities During Month Prior to Interview, 1973

| Activity Category | % | Activity Category | % |
|---|---|---|---|
| Reading a newspaper | 90 | Playing outdoor sport | 32 |
| Watching television | 88 | Going to movies | 31 |
| Visiting friends/relatives | 86 | Swimming/boating/water-skiing | 28 |
| Reading for pleasure | 75 | Going to zoo/fair/amusement park | 25 |
| Driving for pleasure | 66 | | |
| Dining out | 65 | Watching sporting event | 24 |
| Listening to records/tapes | 62 | Hunting/fishing | 20 |
| Walking for pleasure | 54 | Playing indoor sport | 20 |
| Window-shopping | 48 | Camping/hiking/climbing | 17 |
| Playing table games | 45 | Going to theater/concert | 15 |
| Making things (crafts, woodworking) | 40 | Bicycle riding | 14 |
| Gardening | 38 | Going to museum/gallery | 13 |
| Picnicking | 36 | Taking class for enjoyment | 10 |
| Attending club/religious/civic meetings | 35 | Maintaining collection | 10 |
| Going to nightclub/bar/lounge | 34 | Motorcycling/driving jeep/cross-country skiing | 5 |
| | | Horseback riding | 5 |

Sample:  National probability sample of 692 adults.
SOURCE:  Cheek and Burch (1976: 22).

## PARTICIPATION IN OUTDOOR RECREATIONAL ACTIVITIES

Since projects which require EISs are most likely to impact on outdoor recreational activities, the patterns of participation in outdoor recreation deserve special attention and are reported in Table 9.7. Picnicking is a perennial favorite, as are driving for pleasure and sightseeing. More active outdoor pursuits such as swimming, pleasure walking, jogging, and sports also have high participation levels. When these activities are examined by income groups, the less affluent (under $8000 income in 1972) are found to participate more in hunting, fishing, and driving four-wheel, off-the-road vehicles. The more affluent (over $15,000 income) include sailing and golf among their favorite outdoor recreational activities. The middle income group rather evenly distributes its participation in a range of outdoor activities including picnicking, pleasure driving, sightseeing, swimming, pleasure walking, nature walking, fishing, boating, bicycling, wilderness camping, campground camping, golf, tennis, other outdoor games and sports, attending outdoor sports events, outdoor concerts, hiking and climbing, horseback riding, water-skiing, canoeing, and visiting zoos, fairs, and amusement parks. In the summer of 1972, 39 to 49 percent of the middle income group participated in each of these activities (U.S. Department of Commerce, 1977: 513).

TABLE 9.6   How People Would Use Additional Free Time

| Question: | "I'd like you to imagine a situation in which you had four extra hours every day to do whatever you wanted to do. Which *two* or *three* of these things do you think you would do more of with those extra four hours? (Card shown respondent) . . ." |
|---|---|

|  | *Percentage Choosing Activity* |
|---|---|
| Spend time on hobbies and interests | 37 |
| Fix things around the house | 36 |
| Read | 35 |
| Socialize with friends | 25 |
| Spend more time with family | 24 |
| Exercise or play sports | 21 |
| Put all the things I do now in better order | 15 |
| Take a course or study something | 14 |
| Spend time by myself | 12 |
| Watch television | 11 |
| Sleep | 10 |
| Cook | 8 |
| Put more time into present job or business | 4 |
| Daydream and think | 3 |
| Work at a second job | 3 |
| Eat | 2 |
| Other | 4 |
| None | 1 |

SOURCE: *Public Opinion* (1979: 26).

Table 9.8 presents the 10 most popular outdoor recreational activities, the 10 fastest-growing activities, and the 10 with the highest potential growth. All in the latter two sets of activities require relatively expensive equipment. As presented above, Linder's argument (1970) might explain this finding. Increasing incomes make leisure time more valuable, which increases the effort to get the most out of one's leisure time. Increasing the amount of recreational goods per unit of leisure time is one method of doing this.

### RECREATION EXPENDITURES

Leisure activities can be expensive. In 1979, *U.S. News and World Report* estimated that recreational expenditures in 1978 exceeded $180 billion, which was 12.5 percent above 1977 and was about one-eighth of consumers' personal spending. Heritage Recreation and Conservation Service (1978) estimated that in 1977 U.S. consumers spent $84.3 billion (53 percent of total recreation expenditures) on recreational equipment, sporting goods, admissions, and dues; another $60.2 billion (38 percent) on vacations and trips in the United States; and $3.3 billion (two percent) on vacation

TABLE 9.7 Comparison of Percentages of Respondents Participating in Recreational Activities as Reported by Four National Outdoor Recreation Surveys

| Activity | 1960 | 1965 | 1972[a] | 1977 |
|---|---|---|---|---|
| Picnicking | 53 | 57 | 47 | 72 |
| Driving for pleasure | 52 | 55 | 34 | 69 |
| Sightseeing | 42 | 49 | 37 | 62 |
| Swimming (Pool) | | | (18) | (63) |
| (Other) | 45 | 48 | (34) | (46) |
| Walking for pleasure and jogging | 33 | 48 | 34 | 68 |
| Playing outdoor games or sports | 30 | 38 | 22 | 56 |
| (Golf) | | (9) | (5) | (16) |
| (Tennis) | | (16) | (5) | (33) |
| Fishing | 29 | 30 | 24 | 53 |
| Attending outdoor sports events | 24 | 30 | 12 | 61 |
| Other boating | 22 | 24 | 15 | 34 |
| Bicycling | 9 | 16 | 10 | 47 |
| Nature walks | 14[b] | 14 | 17 | 50 |
| (Bird watching) | | (5) | (4) | |
| (Wildlife and bird photography) | | (2) | (2) | |
| Attending outdoor concerts, plays | 9 | 11 | 7 | 41 |
| Camping | 8 | 10 | | |
| Developed | | | 11 | 30 |
| Backcountry | | | 5 | 21 |
| Horsebacking riding | 6 | 8 | 5 | 15 |
| Hiking or backpacking[c] | 6 | 7 | 5 | 28 |
| Water skiing | 6 | 6 | 5 | 16 |
| Canoeing | 2 | 3 | 3 | 16 |
| Sailing | 2 | 3 | 3 | 11 |
| Mountain climbing | 1 | 1 | – | – |
| Visiting zoos, fairs, amusement parks | – | – | 24 | 73 |
| Off-road driving (motorcycles/ other vehicles) | | | 5/2 | 26 |
| Other activities category | 5 | | 24 | |

NOTE: 1960, 1965 and 1972 participation rates are for the summer only.
a. 1972 Survey data are not directly comparable to previous surveys due to sampling differences.
b. Includes bird watching and photography.
c. Includes mountain climbing from 1972 and 1977 surveys.
SOURCE: Heritage Conservation and Recreation Service, U.S. Department of Interior (1978).

TABLE 9.8   The Ten Top Outdoor Recreational Activities Ranked by
Three Indicators of Popularity and Growth*

| Ten Most Popular [1] | Ten Fastest Growth [2] | Ten Highest Potential Growth [3] |
|---|---|---|
| (73) Visit zoos, aquariums, fairs, carnivals amusement parks | (25) Cross-country ski | (6)  Downhill ski |
| (72) Picnic | (17) Downhill ski | (6)  Tennis |
| (69) Drive for pleasure | (13) Tennis | (5)  Water ski |
| (68) Other walk or jog | (11) Sail | (4)  Horseback ride |
| (63) Pool swim or sunbathe | (11) Snowmobile | |
| (62) Sightsee at historical site or natural wonders | (10) Water ski | (3)  Camp in primitive area |
| (61) Attend sports events | (9) Canoe, kayak or river run | (3)  Sail |
| (56) Other sports or games | (9) Golf | (3)  Golf |
| (53) Fish | (5) Drive vehicles or motorcycles off-road | (3)  Snowmobiles |
| (50) Walk to observe nature, bird watch, or wildlife photography | (4) Horseback ride | (2)  Canoe, kayak or river-run |

*Percentages of respondents to 1977 General Population Survey
[1] Percentage of total population participating in an activity at least once during a 12-month period.
[2] Percentage of participants just starting activity for the first time during previous 12 months.
[3] Percentage nonparticipants that would like to begin participating during "next year or two."
SOURCE:   Heritage Conservation and Recreaton Service, U.S. Department of the Interior (1978).

cottages, homes, and land. With foreign visitors spending another $12.0 billion (eight percent) in the United States, total expenditures for recreation were $160 billion.

The majority of recreational opportunities in America are commercially offered, if we ignore the streets and playgrounds where children play. Even the majority of the places which serve recreational purposes are privately owned. Commercial interests provide most of the television, radio, movies, professional sports, travel, resorts, and many other leisure activities. Assessors need to remember that recreation and leisure usually mean income and jobs in leisure industries.

According to Owen (1970: 84), "The demand for commercial recreation, whether measured by expenditures or in constant dollars, has grown more rapidly than the national economy in the 1900 to 1961 period." Kaplan (1975) reported that recreational expenditures increased 1060 percent from 1909 to 1952, which was much faster than the growth of expenditures for welfare (private—100 percent), religion (330 percent), housing and utilities (360 percent), clothing and accessories (535 percent), food and liquor (695 percent), education (private—750 percent), and household equipment (810 percent). The two types of expenditures which increased faster were medical care and insurance (1100 percent) and consumer transportation (1500 percent). Kaplan also pointed out that American per capita expenditures for recreation and entertainment were the highest in the world in 1962; but all of the European countries devoted a larger percentage of their total consumer expenditures to recreation.

## THE RECREATION MOVEMENT

The recreation movement refers to organized efforts to have government or voluntary agencies provide leisure activities and facilities for the public (see Kraus, 1971, for a fuller description of the recreation movement). One aspect of this movement was the development of national and state parks as a response to the despoilment of natural areas. The first federal land set aside as a preserve was in Hot Springs, Arkansas, in 1832. The first extensive wildlife area set aside by Congress for public use was Yosemite Valley and the Mariposa Grove of Big Trees in California in 1864. Eight years later, Yellowstone was made the first national park. Since then the National Park System grew to 70.5 million acres in 320 areas in 1978, including 40 million acres of public domain in Alaska which was added to the system in 1978. These areas are managed by the National Park Service. In 1978, 283 million visits were made to all areas combined. Yellowstone, with its 2.2 million acres, is considered the foremost area in the National Park System, but it receives fewer visitors than many other areas in the system. For example, its 2.6 million visits in 1978 were small compared with the 15.4 million visits to the Blue Ridge Parkway or the 11.3 million visits to Valley Forge. On the other hand, in overnight stays, Yellowstone ranks third, with 1.5 million, behind Yosemite with 1.8 million and Lake Mead with 1.6 million.

In addition to the National Park Service, many other federal agencies administer or serve lands and waterways with recreational use. The most prominent are the National Forest Service, the Bureau of Land Management, and the U.S. Army Corps of Engineers.

The National Forest Service manages over one and a half times the acreage as the National Park Service (109 million acres), and the recreational use of these lands is growing rapidly. In 1978, these lands experienced 218 million visitor days (12 person-hours), including 340 million visitor days at National Forest campgrounds. The Bureau of Land Management has jurisdiction over an even larger amount of land, which comprises about one-fifth of the land area of the United States. These are federally owned public lands which have not been incorporated into specific national forest parks or other recreational areas. The U.S. Army Corps of Engineers manage rivers and waterways and lead the other agencies, in terms of visitor days, to its sites.

In addition to the federally owned and managed recreational areas, the states manage 9.8 million acres, receiving 566 million visits in 1975. The municipal and county park and recreational areas have not yet been accurately estimated, but the acreage would not be much over a million, and the attendance would be several times the attendance at state and federal areas.

Clawson and Knetsch (1966: 24, 25) estimated leisure time in millions of person-hours spent in various outdoor recreation activities in 1960 as follows:

|  | million person- hours |
|---|---|
| Travel for pleasure | 5330 |
| Visits to public outdoor recreation areas (excluding travel time): | |
|     National park system | 660 |
|     National forests | 2285 |
|     Federal wildlife refuges | 150 |
|     Reservoirs of Corps of Engineers | 900 |
|     TVA reservoirs | 432 |
|     All state parks | 1620 |
|     All municipal and county parks | 5000 |
| Fishing in all areas | 1500 |
| Hunting in all areas | 1125 |
| Boating of all kinds | 600 |
| Bowling | 660 |
| Organized sports, such as baseball, football, basketball, etc., but excluding golf and tennis—spectator as well as participant time included | 600 |
| Horse racing | 150 |
|      Total of enumerated activities, 1960 | 21,012 |

These figures have increased substantially in the past two decades, but the ratios between activities would not change greatly. To give an idea of the high growth rates in the recreational activities which we have been discussing, we include Figure 9.1 from Clawson and Knetsch.

The recreation movement also brought about the development of city parks. American cities lacked the parks which graced European cities, and the public complained. The first major city park in America was Central Park in New York City. This 843-acre park is completely manmade, with lakes, fields, woods, and paths designed for scenic views and a rural appearance. Construction began in 1957, and since that time groups have battled over its use. Should it remain a quiet, secluded natural area, or should it be developed more fully for recreational activities?

The next large city park was the 2816-acre Fairmont Park in Philadelphia in 1867 and the 527-acre Franklin Park in Boston in 1883. By the end of the century it was widely accepted that major cities should have a major park, although suitable land was not always available. Between 1892 and 1902 the number of cities with parks increased from 100 to 800, and all cities have a park system today.

The recreation movement's third impact was the playground movement. As America urbanized in the latter part of the nineteenth century, immigrants and other poor people were crowded into tenements under unhealthy conditions. Social reformers were concerned that the children in the tenement districts have safe places to play. The first facility for this purpose was the Boston Sand Garden in 1885. A pile of sand was placed in the yard of a chapel in a working-class district, and volunteers supervised the children who came to play. Later, the city financed the supervision. As quaint as this episode appears, it is generally regarded as a landmark in the recreation movement. Sand gardens were successful and spread rapidly throughout Boston and to other cities. They were the precursors to planned playgrounds.

The playground movement was launched in New York City when the newly formed New York Society for Parks and Playgrounds, backed by private subscription, established two model playgrounds in the tenement areas in 1889 and 1891. Playgrounds were needed because parks had been designed mainly for adults and did not serve the needs of children. First, they were fairly long distances from most residences. Playgrounds were for children; they were placed in the poor neighborhoods. It was thought, with some justification, that supervised and safe play areas for children would reduce their vandalism and delinquency. Before long New York City developed a network of playgrounds and required all new schools to build playgrounds and programs for their use. The playground movement had caught on. In 1906, the National Playground Association was organized, which became the National Recreation Association in 1930.

The fourth impact of the recreation movement was the development of certain voluntary organizations which advocated recreation as part of their

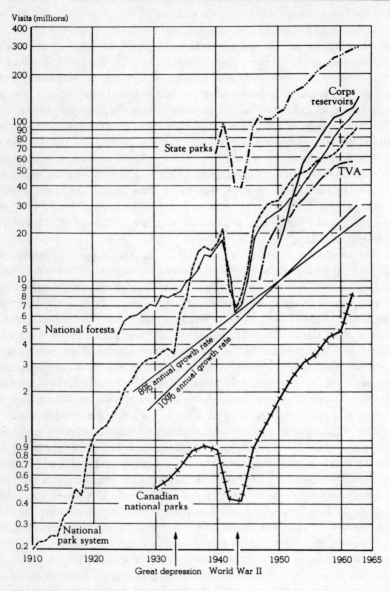

Visits (millions)

FIGURE 9.1    Attendance at Major Types of Outdoor Recreation Areas, Years of
Record

programs. The YMCA was founded in 1851 with a focus on religious activities, but gradually it enlarged its program to include sports and group recreation. Another important organization for the growth of publicly provided recreational activities was the settlement house, starting with University Settlement in 1886 and the Neighborhood Guild in 1887 in New York City and Chicago's Hull House in 1889. These included recreation in their programs and were precursors of neighborhood recreation centers.

Recreational activities have increased rapidly in the twentieth century in conjunction with increasing affluence and the reduction of the workweek. The family automobile made the parks more accessible, and the recreation industries aggressively tried to capture some of the extra money people were earning. Even the two world wars and the Depression stimulated the recreation movement. In World War I, communities near military bases were mobilized to provide wholesome recreational activities. The value of community recreation programs was demonstrated, and Community Service, Inc. sought to spread the lesson after the war. By the end of the 1920s organized park and recreation services were active in most urban communities. During the Depression the Works Progress Administration provided personnel for operating 23,000 community centers and supervisors for playgrounds, beaches, and pools. "In 1939, over 5 million people, not counting spectators, were estimated to be taking part in the programs of the WPA's Recreational Division each week" (Kraus, 1971: 204). The National Youth Administration and the Civilian Conservation Corps constructed or upgraded countless recreational facilities, and the CCC helped establish many state park systems. During World War II massive recreation programs were provided for servicemen at home and throughout the world. Many participants in these programs became recreation professionals after the war.

Since World War II, recreation programs and participation have grown at phenomenal rates. In the 1950s a national concern with physical fitness developed after comparative studies found American youths less fit than the youths of other nations. In the 1970s a health and fitness craze seized this country, and there are as yet no signs of its waning. Meanwhile, both commercial and noncommercial provision of recreational activities, goods, and facilities have mushroomed. Now Americans are well provided with recreational opportunities by both the private and public sectors.

Government concern with recreation is gargantuan. Town, city, county, state, and federal levels of government are all very active. At the federal level alone over 100 agencies are responsible for recreation functions. In terms of visitor days per year, the Army Corps of Engineers, the National Park Service, and the National Forest Service have the largest role in recreation. Other agencies with important recreation functions include the Bureau of Land Management, the Bureau of Indian Affairs, the Fish and Wildlife Service, the

Bureau of Outdoor Recreation, the Bureau of Reclamation, the Tennessee Valley Authority, and the Land and Water Conservation Fund Program. The federal government not only manages important recreation lands, but also provides recreation services (including recreation in the armed forces), trains recreational personnel, and supports recreation research.

## Assessing Leisure/Recreation Impacts

### IMPACT AREAS

The main direct impacts of construction projects are the construction or destruction of recreation resources. Water works construction creates bodies of water with recreational and scenic value. At the same time, they usually destroy or diminish the natural setting that existed before construction, such as streams and natural canyons, which have their own recreational and scenic value. Other projects, such as highways, displace natural areas, parks, and other recreational facilities. However, highways may also make parks and natural areas accessible to more users, and pleasure driving on scenic roadways is a favorite American pasttime. In sum, major direct recreational impacts of large construction projects are

(1) creating entirely new resources,
(2) destroying or diminishing existing resources,
(3) enhancing existing resources,
(4) opening or closing access to existing resources,
(5) crowding existing resources, and
(6) changing the resource mix.

In the evaluation process, it should be noted, different groups will disagree about which of the above impacts the project will have.

Large construction projects have indirect or secondary recreational impacts, most of which result from direct population or economic impacts. Both population and economic changes are likely to impact on amounts of recreational activities and rates of recreational resource use. Projects might also contribute to the transformation of rural communities into tourist, recreational, or retirement communities.

### BASIC APPROACHES TO
### EVALUATING RECREATIONAL IMPACTS

Assessments of project impacts would describe the recreational resources created, destroyed, enhanced, diminished, accessed, or cut off. However, there are several alternative ways to describe recreational resources, and these will be reviewed in this section. These approaches have been drawn in part from the literature on planning for outdoor recreation. Assessors probably will want to use more than one approach when assessing recreational impacts.

### Resource-Based Approach

The simplest method for describing recreational resources which may be impacted by construction projects is the resource-based approach. It quantitatively and qualitatively describes the recreational resource. Parklands or other natural areas would be described in terms of acres; landscape features such as streams, hills, beaches, lakes, canyons, forests, swamps, and fields and manmade facilities such as buildings, trails, roads, campsites, picnic areas, marinas, and swimming areas. Other recreational resources such as playgrounds, museums, concert halls, amusement parks, and resorts would be described quantitatively and qualitatively in terms which are suited to each specific type of resource.

The resource-based approach can be elaborated into a complex evaluation methodology with a scoring system for component features of the resource being evaluated. One example is the environmental corridor approach developed by Phillip H. Lewis for Wisconsin's Department of Resource Development. As described by Donald Wolbrink and Associates (1967: 9), it was used to evaluate 61 areas of distinctive landscape character for selection for outdoor recreational use.

> In applying this concept to the Wisconsin Outdoor Recreation Plan, three overlay maps were prepared showing primary resources: (1) roads, trails, and railroads; (2) lakes, rivers, and wetlands; and (3) significant topography which included all slopes exceeding 12% in grade and over 40 feet in elevated change. Next, a fourth overlay was prepared showing over 200 secondary resources (natural and man-made), ranging from balanced rocks and caves to marinas and museums. When the four overlays were combined, the "environmental corridors" were found to contain about 90% of all secondary resources.

> After numerous trials and errors, a numerical point system was developed for both primary and secondary resources occurring in these concentration areas. Based upon these numerical evaluations and on-site field inspections, the "best" sites for outdoor recreation in Wisconsin were then selected.

### Demand-Based Approach

The value of a recreational resource involves more than acres or other counts of recreational facilities. Nor is the value of a resource coterminous with scorings for intrinsic beauty or attractiveness for recreational purposes. An additional aspect of the value of a recreational resource is its rate of use.

An unsightly playfield where many children are always playing is a valuable resource in spite of its few acres and low score on the environmental corridor rating. Its high use gives it value, and this type of value is captured in the demand-based approach to describing and evaluating recreational resources.

Quantitative measures of demand are usually counts of visitors or estimates of visitor days. Qualitative measures of demand usually involve sample surveys of users on their satisfaction with the recreational resource. Often it is informative to supplement these basic measures of demand with a user/non-user ratio and a measure of crowding, both of which might indicate disadvantages of recreational resources which have large numbers of visitors. The value of the resource is adjusted downward for either of two situations: (1) when only a small proportion of the community or population for which it was created uses it, and (2) when it is overcrowded. It should be noted that there are wide variations in the evaluations by citizens of area or facility crowding. Only when waiting lines are long or many visitors are denied the use of facilities is crowding obvious to all. Presumably, recreation experts can determine when overcrowding occurs much before this point.

The demand-base approach is often used to project either the future demand for a recreational resource or the future recreational needs for a specified population (see, for example, the needs projection prepared by the Department of Resource Development [1966] for the citizens of Wisconsin). A variety of techniques are used, including surveys, models, visitor counts, expert opinions, and statistical analyses. Usually, visitors or citizens are surveyed on their recreational activities and desires, and the results are combined with demographic and socioeconomic projections to estimate future recreation demands.

The demand-base approach to projecting demand came into prominent use in the early 1960s when the Outdoor Recreation Resources Review Commission employed it in their comprehensive study of outdoor recreation in America. With modification and differences in emphasis, this demand-based approach has been adopted and used in many agencies. It essentially tries to discover

the relationship between various social and economic characteristics of the population or a particular user-group, and the extent of participation in recreation activities. Through statistical analysis, the most important socio-economic factors are projected to a given future year from which an estimation of the probable participation in outdoor recreation activities is then derived.

In the ORRRC (Outdoor Recreation Resources Review Commission) study, for example, detailed interviews in 16,000 households located in 333 primary sampling areas throughout the nation were conducted. Information was obtained regarding the participation rate of each family in 22 activities, as well as other information regarding such socioeconomic factors as family income, education, occupation, place of residence, age, and sex. Other factors such as the season, the region of the nation, the size of the city in which the respondents lived, and the availability of facilities were also considered in determining the type and frequency of outdoor recreation participation.

The collected data were then analyzed and compounded to secure composite participation rates (as measured by "user-days" per person, stratification by socioeconomic status factors, region, and season of use) for 17 of the activities. The different participation rates were then applied to total population estimates to arrive at the total number of recreation occasions during 1960 and projected for the years 1976 and 2000. Although the ORRRC study did not take the next step, which would have involved making estimates of the amounts of land and water area required to meet this demand, this step was later taken in studies which drew upon the ORRRC design [Donald Wolbrink and Associates, 1967: 11].

A comprehensive list of factors that affect demand for a particular recreation area is presented by Clawson and Knetsch (1966: 60):

(1) Factors relating to the potential recreation users, as individuals:
 (a) their total number in the surrounding tributary area;
 (b) their geographic distribution within this tributary area—how many are relatively near, how many relatively far, etc.;
 (c) their socioeconomic characteristics, such as age, sex, occupation, family size and composition, educational status, and race;
 (d) their average incomes, and the distribution of income among individuals;
 (e) their average leisure, and the time distribution of that leisure;
 (f) their specific education, their past experiences, and present knowledge relating to outdoor recreation;
 (g) their tastes for outdoor recreation.
(2) Factors relating to the recreation area itself:
 (a) its innate attractiveness, as judged by the average user;
 (b) the intensity and character of its management as a recreation area;
 (c) the availability of alternative recreation sites, and the degree to which they are substitutes for the area under study;
 (d) the capacity of the area to accommodate recreationists;
 (e) climatic and weather characteristics of the area, the latter during the period under study.
(3) Relationships between potential users and the recreation area:
 (a) the time required to travel from home to the area, and return;
 (b) the comfort or discomfort of the travel;

(c)  the monetary costs involved in a recreation visit to the area;

(d)  the extent to which demand has been stimulated by advertising.

Clawson and Knetsch recognized that actual estimations of park demand would select only a few of these variables for use in a prediction model. Furthermore, in estimating future total national demand for outdoor recreation they use only four factors: population; leisure time; travel mileage, time, and costs; and per capita real incomes. (For detailed discussions of the demand-based approach, see Clawson and Knetsch, 1966; Bannon, 1976; U.S. Army Engineer District, Sacramento, 1976; Outdoor Recreation Resources Review Commission, 1962.)

### Standards Approach

The third approach to describing recreational resources which may be impacted by construction projects is the standards approach. The National Park and Recreation Association and the National Recreation Association have developed over the years standards for the amount of recreational resources which should be provided for various sizes of population. This approach is not very helpful for rural areas where population is too sparse for meaningful standards and natural recreational resources are abundant anyway. In urban areas, however, standards of "adequate" or "desirable" levels of provision of parklands and open spaces are useful both for recreational resource planning and impact assessment. The rule of thumb of the standards approach is that projects should try not to remove recreational resources, but if they must, they should avoid decreasing recreational resources in an area to below the standard of adequacy.

The major source for standards was *Standards for Municipal Recreation Areas* by Butler (1962), published by the National Recreation and Park Association. It was slightly revised in 1967 (see U.S. Department of Interior, 1967) and updated in 1971 (Buechner, 1971). The NRPA has always emphasized that these standards are only guides for minimum requirements but they tend to be followed rather rigidly and treated as ideal levels of recreational services. The traditional NRPA rule of thumb was 10 acres of parks and open space per 1000 population for cities between 8000 and 500,000 and five acres for cities between 500,000 and 1,000,000. According to the 1971 standards, the 10 acres per 1000 people is divided into 2.5 acres for neighborhood parks, 2.5 acres for district parks, and five acres for large urban parks (see Table 9.9).

We present in Tables 9.10-9.12 the 1971 standards for special facilities, neighborhood parks, and district parks.

Standards serve two objectives: (1) to encourage the provision of adequate or desirable levels of recreational resources, and (2) to preserve the quality of

TABLE 9.9    Recreational Area Standards

| Classification | Acres/ 1000 People | Size Range | Population Served | Service Area |
|---|---|---|---|---|
| Playlets | * | 2,500 sq. ft. to 1 acre | 500-2,500 | Sub-neighborhood |
| Vest pocket parks | * | 2,500 sq. ft. to 1 acre | 500-2,500 | Sub-neighborhood |
| Neighborhood parks | 2.5 | Min. 5 acres up to 20 acres | 2,000-10,000 | 1/4-1/2 mile |
| District parks | 2.5 | 20-100 acres | 10,000-50,000 | 1/2-3 miles |
| Large urban parks | 5.0 | 100+ acres | One for each 50,000 | Within 1/2 hour driving time |
| Regional parks | 20.0 | 250+ acres | Serves entire population in smaller communities; should be distributed throughout larger metro areas | Within 1 hour driving time |
| Special areas and facilities | | Includes parkways, beaches, plazas, historical sites, flood plains, downtown malls, and small parks, tree lawns, etc. *No standard applicable.* | | |

*Not applicable

By Percentage of Area

The National Recreation and Park Association recommends that a minimum of 25% of new towns, planned unit developments, and large subdivisions be devoted to park and recreation lands and open space.

SOURCE: Buechner (1971).

the resources by indicating when actions are required to prevent their over-use. For the latter purpose "use ceilings" are required, because use beyond certain levels causes a decline in quality and the resource may deteriorate rapidly. The basic work on quality controls for recreation areas is by Chubb and Ashton (1969) for NRPA.

### Resource-Value Approach

The final approach for describing recreational resources for impact assessments or planning purposes is the resource-value approach. This approach

TABLE 9.10    Standards for Special Facilities

*The following standards are recommended for individual recreation facilities:*

| Facility (Outdoor) | Standard/ 1000 People | Comment |
|---|---|---|
| Baseball diamonds | 1 per 6,000 | Regulation 90 ft. |
| Softball diamonds (and/or youth diamonds) | 1 per 3,000 | |
| Tennis courts | 1 per 2,000 | (Best in battery of 4) |
| Basektball courts | 1 per 500 | |
| Swimming pools—25 meter | 1 per 10,000 | Based on 15 sq. ft. of |
| Swimming pools—50 meter | 1 per 20,000 | water for each 3% of population |
| Skating rinks (artificial) | 1 per 30,000 | |
| Neighborhood centers | 1 per 10,000 | |
| Community centers | 1 per 25,000 | |
| Outdoor theaters (noncommerical) | 1 per 20,000 | |
| Shooting ranges | 1 per 50,000 | Complete complex including high power, small-bore, trap and skeet, field archery, etc. |
| Golf courses (18 hole) | 1 per 25,000 | |

NOTE: All of the above mentioned facilities are desirable in small communities, even though their population may actually be less than the standard. Every effort should be made to light all facilities for night use, thus extending their utility.
SOURCE: Buechner (1971).

applies cost-benefit thinking to the evaluation of recreational resources and their uses. It has been developed to a sophisticated level in the evaluation of the relative desirability of alternative water resource projects and alternative uses of water resources, and now is widely accepted for all public resource development programs. In these contexts this approach would place a value on recreation for comparison with other uses. The method, however, is hampered by lack of agreement on the appropriate value for recreation. Theoretically, the problem is solvable. Economic value is usually measured by how much people are willing to give up—that is, what they are willing to pay. In practice the evaluation task is made difficult by the fact that the recreation resources being evaluated are public goods which are provided free or at only nominal costs. Therefore, the users bear only part of the costs.

Perhaps the best method for estimating recreational value of a resource is the travel cost approach. It uses the number of visitors and the costs of visitation by distance zones to construct the demand curve of users for the

TABLE 9.11   Space Standards for Neighborhood Parks

*Suggested space standards for various units within the park. The minimum size is 5 acres.*

| | Area in Acres | |
| Facility of Unit | Park Adjoining School | Separate Park |
|---|---|---|
| Play apparatus area—preschool | .25 | .25 |
| Play apparatus area—older children | .25 | .25 |
| Paved multi-purpose courts | .50 | .50 |
| Recreation center building | * | .25 |
| Sports fields | * | 5.00 |
| Senior citizens' area | .50 | .50 |
| Quiet areas & outdoor classroom | 1.00 | 1.00 |
| Open or "free play" area | .50 | .50 |
| Family picnic area | 1.00 | 1.00 |
| Off-street parking | * | 2.30** |
| Subtotal | 4.00 | 11.55 |
| Landscaping (buffer & special areas) | 2.50 | 3.00 |
| Undesignated space (10%) | .65 | 1.45 |
| Total | 7.15 acres | 16.00 acres |

*Provided by elementary school
**Based on 25 cars @ 400 sq. ft. per car
SOURCE: Buechner (1971).

recreational experience. The total area under the demand curve measures the total economic worth to society of the recreational services provided by the resource (see Clawson and Knetsch, 1966; Water Resources Council, 1973; U.S. Army Corps of Engineers, 1974).

An alternative method for estimating recreation benefits is the unit day value approach (Water Resources Council, 1973; U.S. Senate, 1962). It establishes a value for a unit day and multiplies it by the total number of visit days. According to 1973 standards of the Water Resources Council, the unit day value varied from $.75 to $2.25 depending on the quality of the recreational experience obtainable at the resource.

## Concluding Comment

This chapter has reviewed the evolution of public provisions for recreation in the United States and trends in leisure/recreational activity patterns. We note that leisure/recreational activities and expenses have increased more

TABLE 9.12   Space Standards for District Parks

*Suggested space requirements for various units within the park. the minimum size is 20 acres.*

| Facility of Unit | Area in Acres | |
|---|---|---|
| | Park Adjoining School | Separate Park |
| Play apparatus area—preschool | .35 | .35 |
| Play apparatus—older children | .35 | .35 |
| Paved multi-purpose courts | 1.25 | 1.75 |
| Tennis complex | 1.00 | 1.00 |
| Recreation center building | * | 1.00 |
| Sports fields | 1.00 | 10.00 |
| Senior citizens' complex | 1.90 | 1.90 |
| Open or "free play" area | 2.00 | 2.00 |
| Archery range | .75 | .75 |
| Swimming pool | 1.00 | 1.00 |
| Outdoor theater | .50 | .50 |
| Ice rink (artificial) | 1.00 | 1.00 |
| Family picnic area | 2.00 | 2.00 |
| Outdoor classroom area | 1.00 | 1.00 |
| Golf practice hole | * | .75 |
| Off-street parking | 1.50 | 3.00** |
| Subtotal | 15.60 | 28.35 |
| Landscaping (buffer & special areas) | 3.00 | 6.00 |
| Undesignated space (10%) | 1.86 | 3.43 |
| Total | 20.46 acres | 37.78 acres |

*Provided by Junior or Senior High School
**Based on 330 cars @ 400 sq. ft. per car
SOURCE:  Buechner (1971).

rapidly than incomes, and conclude that leisure/recreation is increasing in importance in American society. Leisure/recreation has always been valued as a means to renew us for our more functional tasks. As Cervantes states in *Don Quixote*, "The bow cannot always stand bent, nor can human fraility subsist without some lawful recreation." Now, in postindustrial society, leisure/recreation is also valued in its own right. Thus, the assessment of leisure/recreation impacts is increasing in importance.

*Chapter 10*

# UNEMPLOYMENT

Unemployment is a major problem. The unemployed suffer economic hardships, and if the unemployment is fairly long-term, they suffer social deprivations and psychological problems. The society loses in terms of production, taxes, and the discontent of its members. The federal government is therefore committed to policies for stimulating employment when unemployment rises. Furthermore, almost all programs and projects are evaluated in terms of the additional jobs which they create and/or the jobs they will eliminate. In general, employment considerations are probably second only to the benefit-cost ratio as a major criterion for assessing government actions. The unemployment which would result from the economic failure of a large corporation is one reason why the federal government props up large corporations in financial crisis (for example, Lockheed and Chrysler) by guaranteeing loans or taking other actions. The employment impacts of foreign competition justify import quotas and taxes. Construction projects are usually promoted to people in the host community on the basis of the employment they will directly or indirectly bring to a community. In this work-oriented society it is widely believed that everyone who wants to work should be able to get a job, and the federal government, starting with the Employment Act of 1946, has assumed responsibility for actualizing this principle to the degree that is possible within a market-oriented economy. Low unemployment as a goal, however, often conflicts with other major national goals, such as minimum inflation, price stability, favorable balance of trade, and long-term growth.

Impact assessors invariably estimate unemployment impacts of projects and policies whenever they are likely to involve more than a few dozen workers. Frequently, unemployment assessments are inadequate because they estimate only the number of workers who lose their jobs. They should also describe the conditions of life of the unemployed and their prospects for getting other jobs. This chapter will provide the general picture on job prospects and the social conditions of the unemployed. It reviews the general unemployment picture in the United States and the explanations for the high rates of unemployment which currently exist. The general unemployment picture provides the macro context which the newly unemployed must face. It determines to some extent their chances of finding another job, and assessments are inadequate which fail to describe these chances. Assessments are also inadequate which speak only in terms of numbers; they should also convey a sense for the social and psychological costs of unemployment. To assist assessors in this task, this chapter reviews the research on personal and family adjustment to unemployment and the case studies of worker sufferings in plant closings.

## Statistics on Employment and Unemployment

### THE COMBINED PICTURE

To aid in fulfilling the goal of full employment, the federal government collects and analyzes periodic data on employment and unemployment. The Bureau of the Census conducts monthly the Current Population Survey of approximately 50,000 households for the Bureau of Labor Statistics. Persons who worked at least one hour for pay or profit in the survey week plus those who were absent from their jobs for sickness, vacation, or strikes are counted among the employed. To be counted among the unemployed, a jobless person had to make some effort to get a job in the past four weeks unless they had a job which was to start soon. People who are under 16 or unable to work or not desiring work (such as housewives and the retired) are excluded from the labor force. The unemployment rate is the percentage of persons in the labor force who are unemployed. It fails to take note of part-time or seasonal workers who desire full-time or year-round work and people who want jobs but have lost hope and stopped looking (discouraged workers). The latter category is estimated at around 900,000 (Finegan, 1978: 15).

Table 10.1 presents the employed and unemployed components of the civilian labor force and the population not in the labor force for selected years from 1948 to 1978. This table indicates that the unemployment rate was high in the 1970s relative to the previous two decades. It also indicates,

TABLE 10.1   Civilian Employment Status of the Noninstitutional
Population, 16 Years and Over, for Selected Years 1948–1978
(numbers in thousands)

| | | Unemployed | | |
| Year | Number Employed | Number | Percent of Labor Force | Not in Labor Force |
| --- | --- | --- | --- | --- |
| 1948 | 58,344 | 2,276 | 3.8 | 42,447 |
| 1950 | 58,920 | 3,288 | 5.3 | 42.787 |
| 1955 | 62,171 | 2,852 | 4.4 | 44,660 |
| 1958 | 63,036 | 4,602 | 6.8 | 46,088 |
| 1960 | 65,778 | 3,852 | 5.5 | 47,617 |
| 1965 | 71,088 | 3,366 | 4.5 | 52,058 |
| 1968 | 75,920 | 2,817 | 3.6 | 53,291 |
| 1970 | 78,627 | 4,088 | 4.9 | 54,280 |
| 1971 | 79,120 | 4,993 | 5.9 | 55,666 |
| 1972 | 81,702 | 4,840 | 5.6 | 56,785 |
| 1973 | 84,409 | 4,304 | 4.9 | 57,222 |
| 1974 | 85,936 | 5,076 | 5.6 | 57,587 |
| 1975 | 84,783 | 7,830 | 8.5 | 58,655 |
| 1976 | 87,485 | 7,288 | 7.7 | 59,130 |
| 1977 | 90,546 | 6,855 | 7.0 | 59,025 |
| 1978 | 94,373 | 6,047 | 6.0 | 58,521 |

SOURCE: Bureau of Labor Statistics (1979).

however, that the employed have increased much more rapidly than the nonworkers (unemployed and persons not in the labor force). Employment has expanded 62 percent from 58 million to 94 million, while the nonworking population 16 years and over expanded only 44 percent from 45 million to 65 million. The high unemployment rate, therefore, is not the result of declining jobs or even that job expansion is slower than population expansion; rather, it is because the job market is not expanding as fast as people are entering the labor force. In 1948, the total noninstitutional population 16 years and over exclusive of military personnel was 103 million, of which 56.6 percent were employed, 2.2 percent were unemployed, and 41.2 percent were not in the labor force. In 1978, the total noninstitutional, nonmilitary adult population was 159 million, of which 59.4 percent were employed, 3.8 percent were unemployed, and 36.8 percent were not in the labor force. Both employment and unemployment expanded relative to those not in the labor force.

The growth in employment relative to the nonwork force was due to the increasing percentage of women in the labor force, as demonstrated in Table 10.2. The most striking increase in female employment is for the 25- to 34-year-old group. This suggests that the normally low labor force participation of these age groups due to family responsibilities no longer applies. On the other hand, the proportion of the adult male population which was employed declined from 1967 to 1977, especially black males and young black males. Reflected in this picture is the increased proportion of males who retire at 65 and the rapid increase in early retirement (before 65).

Included in the proportion working in Table 10.2 are many persons who were unemployed part of the year. Table 10.3 presents the work experience of the proportion working in Table 10.2. About two-thirds of the working men work full-time for at least 50 weeks of the year. Only one-eighth of the men work part-time, and 42 percent of these work less than half a year. One-third of the women worked part-time, and 41 percent of these worked less than half a year. Only 42 percent of the working women worked full-time for at least 50 weeks of the year.

## THE UNEMPLOYMENT PICTURE

Table 10.4 looks more closely at the unemployed component of the labor force. In 1977, 17.8 percent of the labor force was unemployed for a time during the year, while the average unemployment rate at any one time in 1977 was 7.0 percent (see Table 10.1). Of the 19.5 million who experienced unemployment in 1977, only 13 percent did not work at all, another 14 percent were unemployed for more than half a year, 30 percent were unemployed 11 to 16 weeks, and 43.6 percent were unemployed less than 11 weeks. Although about the same proportion of men and women experienced unemployment in 1977, only 1.6 percent of the male labor force did not work at all during the year, and 3.4 percent of the female labor force never worked in 1977. In other words, 8.9 percent of the male unemployed never worked in 1977 compared with 18.3 percent of women. On length of unemployment, blacks did worse than whites: A higher proportion of blacks in the labor force never found work in 1977 than whites—20.7 percent for black males compared with 7.0 percent for white males. In addition, 50 percent of the unemployed black males with work experience were out of work 15 or more weeks compared with 39 percent of white males (Young, 1979: 55).

In 1977, the average duration of unemployment was 14.3 weeks, which declined to 11.9 weeks in 1978 (*Monthly Labor Review* 1979: 75). The average duration of unemployment has varied in the past three decades from a high of 15.8 weeks in 1976 to a low of 8.0 weeks in both 1953 and 1969 (Bureau of Labor Statistics, 1979: 199).

The reasons for unemployment are shown in Table 10.5. The most common reason is loss of job (41.0 percent). Only 15.1 percent of the unemployed chose to leave their jobs. New entrants comprise only 13.7 percent of the unemployed, but reentrants comprise 30.2.

TABLE 10.2    Proportion of the Population Who Worked During the Year,
by Sex, Age, and Race, 1967 and 1977

| Sex and Age | Total | | White[1] | | Black | |
| --- | --- | --- | --- | --- | --- | --- |
| | 1967 | 1977 | 1967 | 1977 | 1967 | 1977 |
| Men total | 85.1 | 81.2 | 85.3 | 82.2 | 83.3 | 71.3 |
| 16 to 19 years | 75.1 | 69.9 | 76.0 | 73.8 | 69.3 | 45.3 |
| 20 to 24 years | 90.2 | 91.1 | 90.5 | 93.2 | 88.2 | 75.8 |
| 25 to 34 years | 98.1 | 95.8 | 98.2 | 96.5 | 96.9 | 89.8 |
| 35 to 44 years | 97.9 | 95.9 | 98.2 | 96.6 | 95.6 | 89.6 |
| 45 to 64 years | 92.8 | 85.8 | 93.2 | 86.6 | 88.8 | 78.1 |
| 65 years and over | 34.9 | 26.7 | 34.9 | 26.9 | 34.2 | 26.3 |
| Women total | 51.3 | 55.6 | 50.4 | 55.7 | 59.1 | 54.5 |
| 16 to 19 years | 59.8 | 60.5 | 61.3 | 64.8 | 49.8 | 36.3 |
| 20 to 24 years | 71.0 | 76.7 | 71.2 | 79.0 | 69.2 | 62.4 |
| 25 to 34 years | 53.7 | 68.1 | 51.6 | 67.8 | 68.1 | 71.1 |
| 35 to 44 years | 56.8 | 68.1 | 55.5 | 65.9 | 67.0 | 67.1 |
| 45 to 64 years | 55.3 | 55.2 | 54.5 | 55.1 | 63.2 | 55.4 |
| 65 years and over | 13.9 | 12.0 | 13.6 | 11.6 | 17.8 | 16.6 |

[1] Data for 1967 also include black and other races and are not strictly comparable with data for 1977
SOURCE:  Young (1979: 54).

In order to obtain an accurate picture of unemployment, the national unemployment rate must be disaggregated geographically. The Northeast and the West have the most acute unemployment problems, while the South and the North Central have less trouble with unemployment. Unemployment would have been much worse in the South if southern, young workers, especially blacks, did not migrate north and west. The cutbacks in the defense and aerospace industries are responsible for the jump in unemployment in the West. The slow rate of recovery in the West is largely attributable to net migration into the region. The 11 states with the highest unemployment rates in 1977 in rank order are Washington, D.C., 9.7 percent; Alaska and New Jersey, 9.4 percent; New York, 9.1 percent; Washington, 8.8 percent; Rhode Island, 8.6 percent; Maine, 8.4 percent; and Arizona, California, Florida, and Michigan, 8.2 percent.

An important characteristic of the geographic distribution of unemployment is its concentration. High unemployment rates for decades have plagued economically declining rural regions such as Appalachia and the Ozarks and are also concentrated in the poverty neighborhoods of central cities. Not only are unemployment rates high in the urban ghettos, but subemployment rates are also high. Harrison (1972) computed both rates for 10 urban ghettos (see Table 10.6). In eight out of 10 ghettos, the unemployment rate is more than

TABLE 10.3   Work Experience During the Year of Persons 16 and
Older, by Extent of Employment and Sex, 1977

| Extent of Employment | Both Sexes | Men | Women |
|---|---|---|---|
| | Percent Distribution | | |
| Persons who worked during the year[1] | 100.0 | 100.0 | 100.0 |
| Full time[2] | 78.8 | 87.5 | 67.0 |
| 50 to 52 weeks | 54.9 | 64.7 | 42.1 |
| 48 or 49 weeks | 2.4 | 2.6 | 2.0 |
| 40 to 47 weeks | 5.0 | 5.2 | 4.7 |
| 27 to 39 weeks | 5.6 | 5.5 | 5.7 |
| 14 to 26 weeks | 5.6 | 5.0 | 6.4 |
| 1 to 13 weeks | 5.1 | 4.4 | 6.0 |
| Part time[3] | 21.4 | 12.5 | 33.0 |
| 50 to 52 weeks | 7.2 | 4.1 | 11.2 |
| 48 or 49 weeks | .7 | .4 | 1.1 |
| 40 to 47 weeks | 1.9 | 1.1 | 2.9 |
| 27 to 39 weeks | 2.8 | 1.5 | 4.4 |
| 14 to 26 weeks | 4.0 | 2.4 | 6.0 |
| 1 to 13 weeks | 4.9 | 2.9 | 7.5 |

[1] Time worked includes paid vacation and sick leave
[2] Usually worked 35 hours or more per week
[3] Usually worked 1 to 34 hours per week
NOTE:   Because of rounding sums of individual items may not equal totals
SOURCE:   Young (1979: 54).

twice the SMSA unemployment rate. The ghetto subemployment rate varies
from one-quarter of the persons in the labor force to almost one-half in the
10 ghettos. The subemployment rate includes not only the unemployed but
also part-time workers who want full-time work, full-time workers earning
under $60 a week (under $56 for non-heads of households), half the males
not in the labor force, and half the "unfound" males. It should be pointed
out that ghetto unemployment has increased greatly since Harrison's compu-
tations for 1966, a year of very low unemployment rates. The national
average unemployment rate in 1966 was 3.8 percent compared with 8.5
percent in 1975 and 6.0 percent in 1978.

Harrison calculated the subemployment rate because he judged that the
unemployment rate failed to adequately portray the failure of the labor
market in the ghetto. There is widespread agreement that the unemployment
rate understates job market inadequacies, but there is no consensus on
alternative measures. Accordingly, we will continue to use it in this report
even though we recognize that it is only the tip of the iceberg. For example,
Eli Ginzberg said in 1977, "My own calculations . . . show a minimum of 20
million who would show up sooner or later in the labor market, under certain

TABLE 10.4  Persons 16 Years and Over Who Experienced Some
Unemployment During Year, by Sex, 1977

| Extent of Unemployment | Both Sexes 1977 | Men 1977 | Women 1977 |
|---|---|---|---|
| Persons who worked or looked for work during the year | 109,663 | 61,675 | 47,989 |
| Percentage with unemployment | 17.8 | 17.4 | 18.3 |
| Persons with unemployment | 19,512 | 10,727 | 8785 |
| Did not work but looked for work | 2568 | 958 | 1610 |
| With work experience | 16,944 | 9770 | 7175 |
| | Percent distribution | | |
| Did not work but looked for work | 100.0 | 100.0 | 100.0 |
| 1 to 14 weeks | 57.7 | 42.7 | 66.7 |
| 15 weeks or more | 42.3 | 57.3 | 33.3 |
| Unemployed persons with work experience | 100.0 | 100.0 | 100.0 |
| Year round workers' unemployed | | | |
| 1 or 2 weeks | 3.8 | 4.3 | 3.2 |
| Part-time workers unemployed | 96.2 | 95.7 | 96.8 |
| 1 to 4 weeks | 24.7 | 20.5 | 30.4 |
| 5 to 10 weeks | 21.2 | 21.5 | 20.8 |
| 11 to 14 weeks | 12.4 | 13.6 | 11.1 |
| 15 to 26 weeks | 21.6 | 24.4 | 18.5 |
| 27 weeks or more | 15.8 | 15.7 | 15.9 |
| With 2 spells or more of unemployment | 32.6 | 36.2 | 27.8 |
| 2 spells | 17.2 | 18.7 | 15.1 |
| 3 spells | 15.4 | 17.5 | 12.7 |

NOTE:  Because of rounding sums of individual items may not equal totals
SOURCE:  Young (1979: 55).

conditions—that is, if the government guaranteed a job at prevailing wages to everyone who might need one" (in Lecht, 1977: 26). In other words, if attractive opportunities were available, many more people would enter the labor force than are currently unemployed.

**THE EMPLOYMENT PICTURE**

Part of the unemployment picture is the shifting of employment among industries and among occupational groupings (see Tables 10.7 and 10.8). These figures indicate where job opportunities are shrinking or expanding and identify some unemployment problems. Even when the total demand for labor equals the total supply of labor, considerable unemployment could result from an imperfect fit between the types of jobs and types of workers that are available. The industry and occupational shifts in employment

TABLE 10.5  Unemployed Persons, by
            Reason for Unemployment

| Reason for Unemployment | June 1979 |
|---|---|
| Percentage Distribution | |
| Total unemployed (2,358,000) | 100.00 |
| Job losers | 41.0 |
|    On layoff | 13.8 |
|    Other job losers | 27.2 |
| Job leavers | 15.1 |
| Reentrants | 30.2 |
| New entrants | 13.7 |
| Unemployed as a Percentage of the Civilian Labor Force | |
| Job losers | 2.3 |
| Job leavers | .8 |
| Reentrants | 1.7 |
| New entrants | .8 |

SOURCE: *Monthly Labor Review* (1979: 75).

TABLE 10.6  Unemployment and Subemployment in Ten Urban Ghettos,
            1966

| Ghetto and City | Unemployment Rate | | Ghetto Subemployment Rate[a] |
|---|---|---|---|
| | Ghetto | SMSA | |
| Roxbury (Boston) | 6.5 | 2.9 | 24.2 |
| Central Harlem (New York City) | 8.3 | 3.7 | 28.6 |
| East Harlem (New York City) | 9.1 | 3.7 | 33.1 |
| Bedford-Stuyvesant (New York City) | 6.3 | 3.7 | 27.6 |
| North Philadelphia | 9.1 | 3.7 | 34.2 |
| North Side (St. Louis) | 12.5 | 4.4 | 38.9 |
| Slums of San Antonio | 7.8 | 4.2 | 47.4 |
| Mission Fillmore (San Francisco) | 11.4 | 5.4 | 24.6 |
| Salt River Bed (Phoenix) | 12.5 | 3.3 | 41.7 |
| Slums of New Orleans | 9.5 | 3.3 | 45.3 |

a.  Subemployment includes the unemployed, part-time workers wanting full-time work, full-time workers earning under $60 a week, half the males not in the labor force, and half of the "unfound" males.
SOURCE: Harrison (1972; 74).

TABLE 10.7   Distribution of Nonagricultural Employment by Industry

|                                    | 1950  | 1960  | 1970  | 1978  |
|------------------------------------|-------|-------|-------|-------|
| Mining                             | 2.0   | 1.3   | .9    | 1.0   |
| Construction                       | 5.2   | 5.4   | 5.1   | 4.9   |
| Manufacturing                      | 33.7  | 31.0  | 27.3  | 23.7  |
| Transportation/Utilities           | 8.9   | 7.4   | 6.4   | 5.7   |
| Wholesale Trade                    | 5.8   | 5.8   | 5.6   | 5.7   |
| Retail Trade                       | 14.9  | 15.2  | 15.6  | 16.9  |
| Finance, Insurance, Real Estate    | 4.2   | 4.9   | 5.1   | 5.5   |
| Services                           | 11.9  | 13.6  | 16.3  | 18.6  |
| Federal Government                 | 4.3   | 4.2   | 3.9   | 3.2   |
| State and Local Government         | 9.1   | 11.2  | 13.9  | 14.8  |
| Total                              | 100.0 | 100.0 | 100.1 | 100.0 |

SOURCE:  Bureau of Labor Statistics (1979).

indicate that workers who lose their jobs tend not to have the skills for the jobs which are expanding.

Of the ninefold classification of industries used by the Bureau of Labor Statistics, only mining and agriculture had an absolute decline in workers from 1950 to 1978. Actually, employment in mining is reviving from a low point of 606,000 workers in 1968 to 837,000 workers in 1978, which is 93 percent of the 1950 employment level. Transportation and public utilities employment has increased only 20 percent since 1950, manufacturing employment only 33 percent, and federal government employment only 44 percent. All other major categories increased more than 50 percent, led by state and local government and services with threefold increases.

Table 10.7 presents the distribution of employment by nonagricultural industries from 1950 to 1978; Table 10.8 presents the distribution of employment by major occupational cateogries from 1940 to 1977. Sectors with significant relative declines are mining, manufacturing, transportation and utilities, and federal government. The rapidly expanding sectors are services and state and local government, closely followed by finance, insurance, and real estate. The service sector includes health services and education, which mushroomed in this period. These changes indicate a significant decrease in the proportion of jobs in the goods-producing sector and an increase in the proportion in the service-producing sector. The former dropped from 40.9 percent in 1950 to 29.6 percent in 1978; the latter increased from 59.1 percent to 70.4 percent. Within the goods-producing industries, similar shifts have occurred. These are described by Sorkin (1974: 20, 22).

In most of these industries, the proportion of jobs directly related to production has decreased since the end of World War II, while the percentage of non-production workers has increased. In manufacturing, for example, non-production employees constituted 16.4 percent of all employees in 1947, as compared with 26.9 percent in 1972. Moreover, in mining, the number of production workers declined by over 400,000 in the postwar period, while the number of non-production workers *rose* by over 60,000.

Table 10.8 documents the shift from blue-collar to white-collar work from 1940 to 1977 and the shrinking of unskilled work within the blue-collar occupations. Farm laborers and other laborers declined from 25.0 percent of the jobs in 1940 to 6.4 percent in 1977, while the more skilled blue-collar workers held their own. In the white-collar category both clerical workers and professional/technical workers tripled their proportion of the employed. Unfortunately, unemployed workers in declining occupational sectors generally cannot be retrained for opportunities in the expanding occupational sectors. The growing participation of women in the labor force is being absorbed largely by the growth in clerical employment, and the rapid growth the college-educated young workers is being absorbed by the growth in professional/technical employment.

**DISTRIBUTION OF UNEMPLOYMENT**

Tables 10.7 and 10.8 focus on employment. Tables 10.9 and 10.10 present unemployment rates for industries and occupational sectors. Table 10.9 indicates that unemployment rates are fairly uniform across industries, except for high unemployment rates in construction and low rates in finance, insurance, real estate, and government. Table 10.10 indicates that white-collar occupations have less than half the unemployment rate of blue-collar occupations (except for 1977). Nonfarm laborers have the highest unemployment rate, followed by operatives.

Unemployment is very unequally distributed among social groups. It is highest among minority groups, young men, the old, the unskilled, and the uneducated (Wolfbein, 1965; Sorkin, 1974). The high rates of unemployment for these groups indicate two problems in the American economy. First, discrimination contributes to unemployment. Minorities and the older workers are turned away from jobs for which they qualify. Second, not all persons in the labor force are employable under present labor market arrangements. Specifically, the unskilled and the uneducated are more numerous than the jobs for which they qualify.

TABLE 10.8  Occupational Composition of the United States Labor Force, 1940, 1960, 1970, and 1977 (percentage distribution)

| Occupational Group | 1940 | 1960 | 1970 | 1977 |
|---|---|---|---|---|
| Professional, Technical, and Kindred Workers | 4.6 | 11.4 | 14.2 | 15.1 |
| Farmers and Farm Managers | 17.3 | 4.2 | 2.2 | 1.6 |
| Managers, Officials, and Proprietors, Except Farm | 7.2 | 10.7 | 10.5 | 10.7 |
| Clerical and Kindred Workers | 5.5 | 14.8 | 17.4 | 17.8 |
| Sales Workers | 5.0 | 6.4 | 6.2 | 6.3 |
| Craftsmen, Foremen, and Kindred Workers | 11.7 | 13.0 | 12.9 | 13.1 |
| Operatives and Kindred Workers | 14.1 | 18.2 | 17.7 | 15.3 |
| Service Workers | 9.6 | 12.2 | 12.4 | 13.7 |
| Farm Laborers and Foreman | 13.4 | 3.6 | 1.7 | 1.4 |
| Laborers, except Farm and Mine | 11.6 | 5.4 | 4.7 | 5.0 |
| | 100.0% | 99.9% | 99.9% | 100.0% |

SOURCE: For 1940—U.S. Bureau of the Census (1943); for 1960 and 1970—U.S. Department of Labor (1972); for 1977—U.S. Department of Labor (1979: Table 19, 82-84).

## Theories of Unemployment

The national unemployment rate is largely the combination of four types of unemployment: frictional, seasonal, cyclical, and structural. Frictional unemployment is the time lag between when people start looking for work and when they find it, or the time between jobs for people who quit to take new jobs. Even when there is a match between jobs and workers, some unemployment must occur in the process of getting the worker into the job. Seasonal unemployment is unavoidable in many industries, particularly in agriculture and construction, which have wide variations in seasonal demands for labor. Levitan et al. observe: "While precise measures are difficult . . . the BLS estimated that seasonal unemployment accounted for about one-fourth of total forced idleness in the late 1950's; reexamination of comparable data for the late 1960's suggests a similar conclusion" (1976: 39, 40).

Cyclical unemployment is generated by the recession side of the business cycle. Until the Depression the federal government let the market adjust itself throughout the business cycle, and Hoover took this tack in 1929 and 1930. Never again will the government stand by during depressions. Roosevelt experimented with government programs to generate private economic activ-

TABLE 10.9 Unemployment Rates by Industry, 1948-1977 (persons 16 years of age and over)

| Year | Total Unemployment Rate | Experienced Wage and Salary Workers | | | | | | | | | |
| | | | | Wage and Salary Workers in Private Nonagricultural Industries | | | | | | | |
| | | Total | Agriculture | Mining | Construction | Manufacturing | Transportation and Public Utilities | Wholesale and Retail Trade | Finance Insurance and Real Estate | Service Industries | Government |
| | | | | | | Unemployment Rate | | | | | |
| 1948 | 3.8 | 4.3 | 5.5 | 3.0 | 8.7 | 4.2 | 3.5 | 4.7 | 1.8 | 4.8 | 2.2 |
| 1950 | 5.3 | 6.0 | 9.0 | 6.7 | 12.2 | 6.2 | 4.7 | 6.0 | 2.2 | 6.4 | 3.0 |
| 1955 | 4.4 | 4.8 | 7.2 | 9.0 | 10.9 | 4.7 | 4.0 | 4.7 | 2.3 | 5.2 | 2.0 |
| 1960 | 5.5 | 5.7 | 8.3 | 9.5 | 13.5 | 6.2 | 4.6 | 5.9 | 2.4 | 5.1 | 2.4 |
| 1965 | 4.5 | 4.3 | 7.5 | 5.3 | 10.1 | 4.0 | 2.9 | 5.0 | 2.3 | 4.6 | 1.9 |
| 1970 | 4.9 | 4.8 | 7.5 | 3.1 | 9.7 | 5.6 | 3.2 | 5.3 | 2.8 | 4.7 | 2.2 |
| 1975 | 8.5 | 8.2 | 10.3 | 4.0 | 18.1 | 10.9 | 5.6 | 8.7 | 4.9 | 7.1 | 4.0 |
| 1976 | 7.7 | 7.3 | 11.7 | 4.7 | 15.6 | 7.9 | 5.0 | 8.6 | 4.4 | 7.2 | 4.4 |
| 1977 | 7.0 | 6.6 | 11.1 | 3.8 | 12.7 | 6.7 | 4.7 | 8.0 | 3.9 | 6.6 | 4.2 |

SOURCE: Bureau of Labor Statistics (1979: 213).

TABLE 10.10   Unemployment Rates, by Occupation, 1958-1977 (persons 16 years of age and older)

| Year and Month | White-collar Workers | | | | | Blue-collar Workers | | | | Service Workers | Farm Workers |
|---|---|---|---|---|---|---|---|---|---|---|---|
| | Total | Professional and Technical | Managers and Administrators Except Farm | Sales Workers | Clerical Workers | Total | Craft and Kindred | Operatives | Nonfarm Laborers | | |
| 1958 | 3.1 | 2.0 | 1.7 | 4.1 | 4.4 | 10.2 | 6.8 | 11.0 | 15.1 | 6.9 | 3.2 |
| 1960 | 2.7 | 1.7 | 1.4 | 3.8 | 3.8 | 7.8 | 5.3 | 8.0 | 12.6 | 5.8 | 2.7 |
| 1965 | 2.3 | 1.5 | 1.1 | 3.4 | 3.3 | 5.3 | 3.6 | 5.5 | 8.6 | 5.3 | 2.6 |
| 1971 | 2.8 | 2.0 | 1.3 | 3.9 | 4.1 | 6.2 | 3.8 | 7.1 | 9.5 | 5.3 | 2.6 |
| 1975 | 4.7 | 3.2 | 3.0 | 5.8 | 6.6 | 11.7 | 8.3 | 13.2 | 15.6 | 8.6 | 3.5 |
| 1976 | 4.6 | 3.2 | 3.1 | 5.4 | 6.4 | 9.4 | 6.9 | 10.1 | 13.7 | 8.7 | 4.5 |
| 1977 | 4.3 | 3.0 | 2.8 | 5.3 | 5.9 | 8.1 | 5.6 | 8.8 | 12.0 | 8.2 | 4.6 |

SOURCE: Bureau of Labor Statistics (1979: 191).

ity and to provide employment in the public sector. Gradually, Keynesian economic theory came to be accepted, which justified and prescribed federal actions for stimulating the economy, reducing unemployment, and controlling inflation. Since World War II, recessions have been relatively mild and short. Nevertheless, they have not been eliminated, and unemployment has varied from a low of 2.9 percent in 1953 to a high of 8.5 percent in 1975. An unemployment rate of 4.0 percent is considered very low in this country, but other industrialized western countries generally have much lower unemployment rates (see Table 10.11).

Structural unemployment involves structural changes in the economy which eliminate jobs in some industries while expanding jobs in others. Unfortunately, the workers who lose their jobs in the process generally are not qualified for the new jobs which are opening up. For example, the decline in railroad employment with the switch to diesel locomotives and the shifts to other modes of travel put men out of work whose craft could not be used readily elsewhere. The two principal causes of structural unemployment are technological progress and industrial relocation. Technology tends to displace manual workers and to create jobs for technical and professional workers. Industrial relocation to areas of lower costs (mainly wages) may not reduce net total employment, but it does put workers out of work. When, for example, the textile industry of New York and New England moved to Appalachia and the South, unemployment increased in the former areas and decreased in the latter.

Low levels of unemployment are readily explained by the unavoidable occurrence of minimal amounts of the four types of unemployment. High levels of unemployment, however, require additional explanations; two theories are considered here. The first argues that high levels of unemployment are due to insufficient demand for goods and service. Because of inadequate demand, production does not expand rapidly enough to absorb all of the new entrants and workers displaced by technological changes. The second explanation of high levels of unemployment is that they are due to the growth of structural unemployment. "In other words, the job requirements of modern industry were not consonant with the skills and abilities of the unemployed" (Sorkin, 1974: 75). The first explanation calls for fiscal and monetary policies to stimulate the economy; the second explanation denies the effectiveness of these policies for dealing with unemployment. The solutions proposed by the second explanation are manpower programs and improvements in employment exchanges, but the structural explanation is not really optimistic that even these programs will help a great deal.

Which explanation is right? Probably the high unemployment in the late 1950s and early 1960s was due to insufficient demand. "Most of the research undertaken in the early and middle 1960's concluded that the primary explan-

TABLE 10.11   Unemployment Rates
in the United States and
Eight Industrialized
Nations, 1962 and 1972

|                | 1962 | 1972 |
|----------------|------|------|
| United States  | 5.5% | 5.6% |
| Australia      | n.a. | 2.2  |
| Canada         | 5.9  | 6.3  |
| France         | 1.8  | 2.9  |
| Germany        | 0.4  | 0.9  |
| Great Britain  | 2.8  | 6.2  |
| Italy          | 3.2  | 4.0  |
| Japan          | 1.3  | 1.4  |
| Sweden         | 1.5  | 2.7  |

NOTE:   Rates are adjusted to U.S. concepts.
SOURCE:   Sorrentino (1970: 14); Sorrentino
and Moy (1974: 48).

ation of the prevailing high rates of joblessness was a lack of demand"
(Sorkin, 1974: 76). As a result, the efforts to stimulate the economy were
highly successful in reducing unemployment. High unemployment in the
1970s was also primarily the result of insufficient demand, but much of the
demand shortfall was due to the greatly inflated costs of raw materials. Even
though the insufficient demand theory of unemployment seems to best
explain the times of high unemployment in the past two decades, nevertheless, structural unemployment is an important part of the current picture of
unemployment, as Tables 10.7 and 10.8 suggest.

## Social and Psychological Impacts
## of Unemployment

While the statistics on unemployment are voluminous, the qualitative
descriptions of the economic, social, and psychological conditions of the
unemployed are few. The two best general studies are by Bakke and his
associates conducted during the Depression, one in America and the other in
England. Another valuable study of the social and psychological impacts of
unemployment for Americans is by Komarovsky and also dates from the
Depression. It focuses on the impacts on family relations. A few studies of
plant shutdowns in the 1960s and recent work on unemployment and mental
health round out the surprisingly sparse literature on social and psychological
impacts. These will be reviewed and then summarized in this section.

## DEPRESSION UNEMPLOYMENT IN
## NEW HAVEN: BAKKE

An important finding of Bakke's study (1940a) is the degree of isolation of the unemployed men. In the high-unemployment neighborhoods of New Haven where the study was conducted, there was little intimacy among neighbors generally. Unemployment failed to reduce this isolation even though many men in the same neighborhoods were at home during weekdays. "Men tend to hold more to themselves in unemployment than otherwise" (Bakke, 1940a: 7). Furthermore, if unemployment lasts more than one or two months, the family is forced to move to a less desirable neighborhood. The move weakens their ties to old friends because of their shame in their poor living conditions and because of the greater distance for visiting. However, more important than moving for isolation is the fact "that the lack of money is a serious handicap in the maintenance of friendships or cliques" (1940a: 10). Again and again the families experiencing unemployment commented on the need to be able to reciprocate in order to sustain compatible social relationships, but their relative poverty prevented this. The wife of a former contractor said:

> Suppose you go to a friend's house and she gives you a cup of tea and something. You feel ashamed. You think—now I got to do the same when she comes to my house. You know you can't, so you stay home. If you walk a long way to see a friend you get thirsty and your friend will feel that she must at least give you a cup of coffee, and often she can ill afford to do this, so you don't go [p. 10].

Bakke concludes that a requirement for friendships and cliques "is that participants shall have enough money to provide for the events on which such friendships thrive" (p. 9).

Another requirement of friendship is that "the economic fortunes of those who participate in the clique must not be too diverse" (p. 9). Inequality obstructs reciprocity, as discussed above, and results in negative comparisons or the fear of negative comparisons. Entertaining in the home cannot be completely relaxed if the hosts worry about negative evaluations of the conditions and furnishings of the home. Bakke observed:

> Since "keeping up a front" is very difficult when one is unemployed, the general tendency is to withdraw from those contacts in which it is necessary. Even the reputation for hospitality can survive only by objective evidence, and objective evidence costs money [1940a: 13].

Table 10.12 documents the decline in socializing which results from unemployment. It describes the participation in recreational activities before

TABLE 10.12    Proportion of the 200 Unemployed Families Participating
in Various Forms of Recration Before and During
Unemployment

| Type of Recreation | Proportion Participating While Employed | | Proportion Participating During Unemployment | |
|---|---|---|---|---|
| | Number | Per Cent | Number | Per Cent |
| Visits with Family and Friends | 132 | 66.0 | 58 | 29.0 |
| Clubs | 119 | 59.5 | 61 | 30.5 |
| Movies | 111 | 55.5 | 32 | 16.0 |
| Trade Unions | 64 | 32.0 | 29 | 14.5 |
| Excursions | 47 | 23.5 | 4 | 2.0 |
| Parties | 40 | 20.0 | 6 | 3.0 |
| Auto Trips | 38 | 19.0 | 6 | 3.0 |
| Walking | 30 | 15.0 | 33 | 16.5 |
| Sitting around Home | 26 | 13.0 | 49 | 24.5 |
| Cards | 25 | 12.5 | 10 | 5.0 |
| Watching Athletics | 25 | 12.5 | 12 | 6.0 |
| Bathing | 24 | 12.0 | 4 | 2.0 |
| Reading | 18 | 9.0 | 17 | 8.5 |
| Dances | 17 | 8.5 | 4 | 2.0 |
| Participation in Athletics | 12 | 6.0 | 8 | 4.0 |
| Church | 10 | 5.0 | 6 | 3.0 |
| Gardening, Home Repair | 8 | 4.0 | 19 | 9.5 |
| Italian Shows | 8 | 4.0 | 0 | 0 |
| Picnics | 4 | 2.0 | 2 | 1.0 |
| Lecture and Discussion Groups | 4 | 2.0 | 4 | 2.0 |
| Singing | 3 | 1.5 | 0 | 0 |
| Saloons | 3 | 1.5 | 0 | 0 |
| Chatting and Gossiping at Corner Store, Gas Staions and on Street | 0 | 0 | 24 | 12.0 |
| Sleep (during the Daytime) | 0 | 0 | 8 | 4.0 |

SOURCE: Bakke (1940a: 14).

and during unemployment (as reported after). The major recreational activity
was visiting with friends and relatives. "Over half had discontinued these
friendly contacts and the other half continued them on a much-reduced
scale. . . . Visiting with relatives did not decline as much as visiting with
friends" (p. 15).

Most other recreational activities which required money were severely
curtailed. When they were not stopped altogether, they were greatly reduced
and their costs were slashed. The number participating in clubs was cut only
in half, but "the average amount spent on them fell from $20.50 to $3.82 a
year" (p. 15). The activities which increased were staying at home, puttering

around the house, and gossiping at daytime hang-out spots. These do not cost money and suggest a greater supply of time than of worthwhile activities for using the time.

Bakke studied the effects of unemployment on religious and political relations and practices and found surprisingly little change. There was no significant incidence of turning to religion or political action in the crisis of unemployment. As Table 10.12 indicates, few were active churchgoers before unemployment, and unemployment further reduced the number. Many unemployed church members expressed discomfort over being too poor to put money in the church offering even though no one is required to give. Many non-churchgoers, however, did maintain nominal contact with the church, but few saw it as a resource for coping with unemployment. A few used the church to make contacts for securing jobs, and some churches set up a clearinghouse for odd jobs which its members required. The clearinghouse did not greatly help the unemployed: The wages offered were generally low and the unemployed worker who got the job was expected to show gratitude. The unemployed sometimes also sought out ministers for secular advice which would normally be given by lawyers, doctors, realtors, brokers, and others who charge fees for their services.

Bakke explained the political inactivity of the unemployed man as a continuation of his political inactivity while employed. Except for voting, almost all manual workers did not participate in politics. It had little relevance for them. Politicians were accepted as self-interested party servers and were not expected to achieve important gains for the working class or the unemployed.

> He has enough contact with the game of politics to know that the game is not a free-for-all. He has enough contacts with those who do play the leading roles to know that they are primarily job holders or hangers-on working in self-interest, that their first concern is to keep the machine they serve in power. He does not resent that; "they have their living to make too, you know." But the knowledge does not stimulate confidence that government is "of the people, by the people, and for the people" [Bakke, 1940a: 48].

Radicals tried to organize marches and demonstrations but failed to mobilize the unemployed in significant numbers, for several reasons. First, their description of the evils of the present system were not sufficiently confirmed in the experiences of the unemployed. Second, radical solutions were seen as foreign and therefore suspect as un-American and pro-Russian. Third, they feared the economic consequences of being identified as radical.

The unemployed also failed to support organizations which claimed to speak and work in their behalf. In New Haven, the principal organizations for the unemployed were:

(1) Unemployed Protective Association,
(2) Unemployed League,
(3) F.E.R.A. Union,
(4) Project Workers Union, and
(5) Workers Alliance.

Although unemployment in New Haven fluctuated between 13,000 and 18,000, these organizations claimed less than 1000 members and probably had less than 500. Most of the unemployed viewed their condition as temporary, and few had prior experience with special influence organizations. Bakke observed: "There was little evidence of a spontaneous grouping of the unemployed for their own protection in spite of the common lot of distress which was theirs" (p. 72).

The main focus of Bakke's study was on the impacts of unemployment on family life. Two-fifths of his book is devoted to this topic, even though he studied only 24 families. Bakke reported the experience of five families in detail with considerable benefit to an understanding of the impact of unemployment on family life. Both generalities and exceptions surfaced in these case histories. The 24 families were studied intensively over an eight-year period, and the study transcended superficial understandings of unemployment impacts. The following description of the family history of the Cohens includes a description of typical impacts but also shows the superficialily of the typical pattern.

Man and wife and two children are living happily together. The man loses his job. Savings are soon gone. Job hunting is fruitless. Discipline problems with the children become difficult. Health is impaired for all by reduced expenditures for food. Debts pile up. Tempers become worn. Arguments increase. Discouragement gets the upper hand. The man, realizing his failure, wishes he could die and contemplates suicide. In a wave of despair the wife, losing patience with her husband, takes the children and goes back to her mother. All of this and much more happened to the Cohens. But such a record does not present an accurate picture of what unemployment did to their family. It gives only superficial and sometimes misleading indications of the changes taking place in the institution of the family and of its struggle to survive [Bakke, 1940a: 111].

Mrs. Cohen could not adjust at first to the family's loss of status as Mr. Cohen went from being a well-paid professional musician to unemployment and then to manual labor. After a very difficult period of adjustment, however, they became a closer and more cooperative family and adjusted to their new working-class style of life.

In each of the five cases reported, the husband lost status and authority relative to the wife. In several cases, the change improved the functioning and integration of the family to better than that prior to unemployment. In no case, however, was the transition easy and without pain. Bakke emphasized that the manner of adjustment is dynamic and variable. Weak marriages can fall apart or come together in new patterns of cooperation. Strong marriages can slowly disintegrate, rapidly disintegrate, or adjust. Readjustment, however, always took place sooner or later. "None of the families stayed for long in the disorganization stage" (p. 175). Expenditures were adjusted to income, attitudes were adjusted to the new standard of living, and the family authority structure adjusted to the new status and resources of its members. The later changes conflicted with traditional values about appropriate roles of husbands and wives. "The husband's status in the eyes of both wife and children tends to decline" (p. 184). The husband is reluctant to do housework, but generally is pressed into it if the wife works while he is unemployed. The wife has a greater authority in family decisions, and some come to dominate their husbands. Almost invariably, wives gain greater control over the family budget.

Bakke came to the surprising conclusion that only five of his 24 families became less stable than before unemployment. One became highly unstable, two considerably unstable, and two reestablished a degree of stability but less than that before unemployment.

> The remaining nineteen of the twenty-four came out of the period of unemployment with, or soon progresses to, a degree of stability equal to or greater than that which characterized them prior to the onset of unemployment [1940a: 228].

Bakke emphasized that readjustment does take place, but he also described the pain of the poverty, status loss, and disorganization which unemployment generally brings. Some families did not get medical attention which was badly needed. Another family had to sell the musical instruments which provided the main family entertainment. In all families countless money problems became occasions for bitter debates. Sometimes all social contacts outside the family were severed, and social contact within the family became tense and disappointing. The children were harder to discipline, and tempers were short. An extended period of unemployment for the male head of the family caused considerable suffering.

In a companion volume, *The Unemployed Worker* (1940b), Bakke described the effects of unemployment on male worker's self-reliance which was critical to his pride. Most socially respected roles require a job which gives both income and a degree of financial autonomy.The working-class male is to be a "Provider," a hard worker, a good father, holder of a good job, and a good comrade. Unemployment undermines each of these roles. Relief makes the failure public. Most of the studied families delayed going for relief for several months out of pride. Furthermore, in most cases where relief was sought, the goal of self-reliance was only temporarily given up.

## UNEMPLOYMENT AND
## HUSBAND'S STATUS: KOMAROVSKY

Bakke's analysis of the effects of unemployment on family structure and functioning is supported, albeit weakly, by Komarovsky's study (1940) of 59 families in 1935-1936 in New York City. "Unemployment does tend to lower the status of the husband. It has had this effect in 13 out of 58 families included in the study" (1940: 23). It is surprising that the authority of the husband did not decline in the other 45 cases (78 percent). One reason offered by Komarovsky is that she confined her study to families with teenage children. Therefore, most of her respondents were married for 15 to 20 years. Patterns that have developed over such long periods of time can survive even the husband's unemployment.

Komarovsky tried to identify the kinds of families which experienced no loss of status for the husband and the kinds which did. In 35 families the husband's authority was derived from love, admiration, or the traditional role of husband. In only two of these cases did the husband lose status. In contrast, in eight of the 12 cases where the husband's authority was based on utilitarian considerations or fear, the husband lost status. In three of the 11 families in which the husband's authority was based on a mixture of the two sets of considerations, the husband experienced a loss of status. Komarovsky explained the association of husband's status loss with utilitarian rather than love/tradition authority by the ability of the latter wives to excuse or forgive their husbands' economic failure. Some put the blame on the economic system or bad luck. Others emphasized the areas where the husband did not fail the family. On the other hand, utilitarian authority does not encourage wives to interpret the husband's unemployment in a charitable light.

Komarovsky also studied personality changes of the unemployed husbands; she classified 22 of them as experiencing "deterioration of personality: loss of emotional stability, breakdown of morale, irritability, new faults such as drinking, unfaithfulness to the wife, and so on" (1940: 66). Only 11 experienced personality improvement: for example, "the man became more thoughtful toward members of the family, more helpful, less irritable" (p. 66). Two of the 59 husbands could not be classified on this dimension, and 24 experienced no personality change.

Personality deterioration is strongly associated with husband's loss of authority. Of the 13 husbands experiencing loss of authority, seven (54 percent) experienced personality deterioration; while of the 44 husbands not experiencing loss of authority, only 15 (34 percent) experienced personality deterioration.

Personality deterioration is modestly related to the wife's attitude toward the husband being based on instrumental considerations rather than on love/tradition. Only 34 percent of husbands whose wives had attitudes based on love/tradition experienced personality deterioration, while 45 percent of husbands whose wives had attitudes based on instrumental considerations experienced personality deterioration.

Personality deterioration and wife's attitude account almost completely for husband's loss of status. These two factors in combination explain 12 of the 13 cases of husbands' loss of status and 38 out of 44 cases of no loss of status. In other words, the unemployed husband's status is secure if (1) it is based on his wife's love or on tradition or (2) his status is based on a mixture of love/tradition and instrumental considerations and his personality does not change for the worse.

Komarovsky further probed the effect of unemployment on the personalities of the husbands by inquiring about self-esteem and means of self-expression. The general pattern was that husbands' self-esteem suffered greatly from their failure to filfill the provider role, and that they suffered somewhat less from being economic failures. Komarovsky described the importance of the role of provider.

The general impression that the interviews make is that in addition to sheer economic anxiety the man suffers from deep humiliation. He experiences a sense of deep frustration because in his own estimation he fails to fulfill what is the central duty of his life, the very touchstone of his manhood—the role of family provider. The man appears bewildered and humiliated. It is as if the ground has gone out from under his feet [1940: 74].

In some cases considerable emotional investment and identification is made in the provider role, as indicated in the following two respondent's statements: "I would rather starve than let my wife work." "I would rather turn on the gas and put an end to the whole family than let my wife support me" (p. 76).

With regard to the loss of self-esteem associated with the failure to succeed economically, Komarovsky observed that all of the unemployed men sampled recognized that economic success leads to prestige in American society and worried over the loss of social status. The intensity of the reaction to this loss of status, however, varied greatly. Some took it in stride and remained proud; others were bitterly disappointed and embarrassed by their poverty. The different responses were primarily due to different goals. The former placed greater importance on family life or other noneconomic values, while the latter were ambitious for economic and social gain.

Work not only provides income; it also provides a major means of expression for male adults.

> Furthermore, for most of the men in our culture, work is apparently the sole organizing principle and the only means of self-expression. The other interests that existed in the lives of these men—active sports, hobbies, political and civic interests, personal and social relations—turned out to be too weak and insignificant for their personalities to furnish any meaning to their lives. Work, the chief, and in many cases only, outlet was closed to the men, and they faced complete emptiness.

> There are several factors which make it difficult for unemployed men to pursue even such hobbies as they may have had, or to develop new interests. Many men testify that their acute anxiety concerning the welfare of their families is so demoralizing that they cannot concentrate even on their usual hobbies and activities. Several remarked that the busier they were the more they got done, and complained about having too much time. Apparently, the very formlessness of the day and the week, the absence of any required tasks, caused a letdown and weakened the drive for any activity. This reaction is typical of the unemployed and is part of the generally paralyzing effect of unemployment which has been noted in several studies [Komarovsky, 1940: 81].

Unemployment did not have much impact on the father's authority over children seven years old and over. No change in the father's authority was detected for 75 percent of the 153 children studied. The father's authority increased for 7 percent of the children and decreased for 18 percent of the children. The increases were largely because he was home more often. None of these children, however, were 15 and over. In contrast, among the cases of declining father's authority, 63 percent of the children were 15 and over. One reason for the worsening relationship of father with children was the lack of money to use in ways which control children, such as bribes, withholding money as punishment, or sponsoring substitutes for undesirable activities. Some fathers lost authority because they became more irritable or unpleasant. Other fathers lost authority because their children were forced to work and so became more independent and less honorific.

Komarovsky also commented on a number of effects of unemployment outside the family. In the political sphere little change occurred. "In only one-sixth of the cases was there an inkling of attitudes changing toward the left" (1940: 118). They still aspired to improve their standard of living in the traditional manner of hard work within the given economic system. In the social sphere major changes occurred. Four out of five said unemployment had reduced social life. Komarovsky summarized the situation as follows:

> The unemployed man and his wife have no social life outside the family. The extent of the social isolation of the family is truly striking. This refers not only to formal club affiliations but also to informal social life. The typical family in our group does not attend church, does not belong to clubs, and for months at a time does not have social contacts with anyone outside the family. Furthermore, the families do not give the impression of maintaining any ties with the community as a whole.
>
> Some attributed the change to the disloyalty of friends. Others stressed the economic aspect of social life. Social life costs money and they simply could not afford it. Another group of families gave a still different explanation. They had, themselves, withdrawn from social life because they felt humiliated by their present status and inferior to most of their friends. Partly to protect themselves from being snubbed, partly to spare themselves the humiliation of comparisons, they had preferred to withdraw from all social life [1940: 123-124].

Finally, Komarovsky's study found that unemployment negatively affected the sexual relations between husbands and wives in 58 percent of the 38 families providing adequate information on this topic. This was especially true for older couples.

## UNEMPLOYED MEN IN LONDON
## IN 1931: BAKKE

Another study from the Depression of the 1930s will be briefly cited. Bakke studied unemployed men in the Greenwich Borough of London in 1931. He journeyed to England to see "whether or not Unemployment Insurance has had a detrimental effect on the willingness and the ability of workers to support themselves" (1934: 268). He concluded that it is not a disincentive to working for the majority of unemployed recipients. Almost all unemployed workers want to be self-supporting and earn the respect of the community.

In analyzing the physical, psychological, social, and political effects of unemployment, Bakke concluded that unemployment causes little or no physical decline, criminal behavior, revolutionary activities, or political activities other than voting. Unemployment did not cause physical decline, as earlier studies had indicated, because unemployment insurance or relief provided for a reduced but sufficient diet for health. Nor did unemployment stimulate a tendency toward crime, except perhaps among the unusually low-paid workers. Nor did the unemployed turn to political and revolutionary activity.

> When the invitation was issued by the agitators in Greenwich for men to take part in what was termed the largest demonstration of the year, there were only ten men from that community at the appointed meeting-place. Ten men are not conspicuous among the more than 3,000 unemployed in Greenwich [1934: 62].

Unemployment reduced social contacts and social life. The family and the home are central to the life of the English working man, and the unemployed worker retreated further into the family. Because of unemployment insurance, however, unemployed workers were able to keep up most of their important social contacts and to continue to participate in their church or their clubs, although usually at reduced levels.

Probably the greatest effect of unemployment was psychological. The workers found unemployment disorienting. Many respondents expressed a "sense of being lost without the work to which they were accustomed" (1934: 62). Obviously, the young and/or unsteady workers were less troubled in this regard.

The main psychological problem of unemployment is the loss of self-respect and pride. At first, workers work hard at finding a job. As the weeks pass into months, however, they become increasingly discouraged and their pride suffers. Eventually, many take jobs which they consider beneath them. After seven months of unemployment, an electrical engineer was at the point of accepting any job just to be working. The pain of his defeat is expressed in his comment: "No one who hasn't gone through it, knows how that tears you up in here" (1934: 70).

## PACKARD PLANT SHUTDOWN: AIKEN

The above works provide a poignant portrait of unemployment almost two generations ago. Today's unemployed would experience some of the same problems but not all. The best work on the social and psychological impacts of unemployment since World War II have been studies of plant shutdowns. Three major plant shutdown studies will be reviewed in this section. The first is a study by Aiken et al. (1968) of the effects of the shutdown of Packard's Detroit plant in 1956. The focus of the study is on the consequences of unemployment for personal alienation and political extremism. It is based on a survey of 305 ex-Packard workers, 27 months after the announcement of the shutdown. At the time of the announcement of the shutdown in June 1956, there were 4016 workers at the company. At the time almost "95 percent were forty years old or more and nearly 90 percent had at least twenty-three years seniority with the company" (1968: 29). Layoffs of younger workers with little seniority had been proceeding for months, and rumors of the impending shutdown had caused some workers to seek other jobs on their own. A sample of 400 was drawn from the June workforce, and 314 were interviewed. The following results are based on the 260 white manual workers among the 314.

"The Packard workers found themselves jobless in an area marked by the loss of defense jobs, a trend toward geographical decentralization of the auto industry, a labor market in the throes of recession, and an increasing unemployment rate" (p. 29). For the 260 white respondents the average length of unemployment prior to the interview was 10.3 months (longer for blacks) and 21.35 months for the 23 percent who were not reemployed before the interview. The older workers had the most difficulty finding work: Workers over 60 averaged 14.7 months unemployment and workers under 60 averaged 7.7 months. Second to age, the best predictor of months of unemployment was skill level. The unskilled averaged 13.9 months and the skilled averaged 7.3 months unemployment. Education also was associated (negatively) with months of unemployment. The association of age, low skill, and low education with long-term unemployment is corroborated by other studies (for example, Foltman, 1968; Haber et al., 1963; Wilcock and Franke, 1963).

Aiken et al. created an Index of Anomie based on agreement/disagreement with seven statements, such as "most people don't really care what happens to the next fellow" (1968: 67). High anomie was evidenced by "workers who had reduced savings, increased debts, and who had gone without essentials, such as food, clothing, shelter and transportation" (p. 69). Age, education, skill level, months unemployed, and current employment status were correlated with anomie but not as strongly as the above economic deprivations, and these were not significantly related to anomie when other factors were taken into account. Exactly the same pattern of association was found between the above variables and an Index of Satisfaction which was based on four questions, such as: "On the whole, how satisfied would you say you are with your life today?" (p. 73). Again, economic deprivation is the most strongly associated with dissatisfaction; it is also the best predictor of reduced contact with relatives and friends. Aiken et al. summarized their findings as follows:

In this chapter, we have seen that economic deprivation was the variable most strongly associated with anomie and satisfaction with life as well as with social participation with friends and relatives. In each case, the loss of economic integrity resulted in reduced social interaction. Thus, we have shown that the effects of economic deprivation may lead not only to psychic withdrawal—tendencies to define the world as unintelligible, hostile, unpredictable, and unsatisfying—but also to social withdrawal, as manifested in reduced social contact with relatives and friends [1968: 86].

The displaced workers were not politically apathetic. Only five percent failed to vote in the 1956 elections shortly after the shutdown. Ninety percent agreed "that people should be just as concerned about things that happen in politics as they are about things that happen in their personal lives," and 95 percent agreed "that even when your party doesn't have a chance to win, it is important to vote" (p. 100).

In political attitudes these workers were not extreme but did tend to favor government intervention. Over 75 percent felt that the government should intervene to keep shutdowns similar to Packard's from occurring and should help laid-off employees find jobs. Less than three out of 10, however, thought "that the government should take over a plant and run it in a situation similar to the Packard shutdown" (p. 110). Senator McCarthy's anticommunist activities were supported by 38 percent of these workers, but this attitude was not significantly related to months of unemployment or extent of economic deprivation. Anticommunism was strong among these workers, 89 percent of whom agreed that "steps should be taken right away to outlaw the Communist Party in the United States" (p. 119).

## BAKER PLANT SHUTDOWN: SLOTE

The second study of a shutdown to be reviewed is Slote's study (1969) of the closing of the Baker paint plant in 1965. The book tries to portray the drama of what the workers were going through in novelistic style. It is difficult to summarize, except to point out that Slote succeeded in portraying the suffering involved in a shutdown. His story does not go beyond the actual closing, but it tells of the plight in the following year of some of the laid-off workers. His research is impressionistic rather than systematic, but it is based on many interviews. It portrays the economic and psychological deprivations resulting from the shutdown. It also reports the findings of a study of health data on the Baker closing, which found a much higher rate of sickness among the terminated men than among the control groups.

## FIVE PLANT CLOSINGS: WILCOCK AND FRANKE

The third shutdown study is by Wilcock and Franke (1963). They interviewed workers three times in five plants in five separate communities:

(1) before closing,
(2) four months to a little over a year after closing, and
(3) about one and a half years later.

Response rates were high; over 2600 workers responded to the first two interviews and over 2200 responded to the last interview. A major conclusion of the study was that,

> Even though none of the five areas was depressed . . . and all have been expanding in population and economic activity in recent years, none was able to absorb effectively into its economy the workers displaced from a single plant. Data from other studies . . . indicate that our results are typical. . . . Case studies thus far suggest, therefore, that long-term unemployment can normally be expected when plant shutdowns occur, in or out of depressed areas. . . . Among the long term unemployed there were above average proportions of women, Negroes, older workers, the lowest educated, the least skilled, and those whose skills were not transferable to other industries [1963: 162-163].

The authors did not directly study the noneconomic personal effects of displacement and joblessness, but they found ample evidence in the comments of respondents that the unemployed felt stigmatized and suffered other social and psychological deprivations.

> The economic and financial hardships were accompanied by the social and psychological problems associated with prolonged unemployment. Permanent layoffs after years of company tenure meant a traumatic shock, particularly for the long-tenure Armour workers. Facing a labor market in which jobs were scarce was a difficult experience for many, particularly for those who suddenly discovered they had become "old" in the eyes of potential employers.
>
> Anger, resentment, bitterness, frustration, and bewilderment are a few of the words used by the interviewers to describe the emotions of many of the unemployed. One interviewer described some of the respondents as "blighted men." The long-term unemployed had been uprooted from a productive institutional tie and a seemingly secure place in society and, as a result, had become isolated from the work environment and a large part of their usual human associations [1963: 92].

Wilcock and Franke studied how laid-off workers went about finding other jobs. Few understood the difficulties they would face. They were overly optimistic about their job prospects and the amount of help they would receive. Most expected help from the employment service, the company, and the union, and most were disappointed. "Among the former Armour workers in the four cities only 6 percent reported specific help from the union, 9 percent from the company, and 13 percent from the state employment service" (1963: 168). Most found jobs in the traditional manner of using their informal networks for leads and help and "plant-gate" application. The geographic range of their job search was narrow: "In each city from 80 to 90 percent of the job seekers confined their search to the local labor market area" (pp. 168-169). However, only 31 percent in the first three Armour cities indicated at the time of layoff that they were unwilling to move to another city to accept an Armour job.

## Summary

In this chapter unemployment has been described statistically, impressionistically, and theoretically. The statistical description notes that the recent unemployment rate is unusually high for the period since the Depression, but so is the employment rate. Both are high simultaneously because the percentage of the population which is not in the labor force has declined from 1948 to 1978, with increased labor force penetration by women.

Most unemployment is relatively short term. Less than three in 10 were unemployed more than half a year in 1978, and the average duration of unemployment was 12 weeks.

Unemployment is unequally distributed among regions, groups, and industries. It is the most acute in the Northeast and the West and concentrated in economically declining rural areas and in urban ghettos. It is higher for blacks than for whites and is especially high for young men. Unemployment is highest in construction and agriculture and almost twice as high for blue-collar workers as for white-collar workers.

Some unemployment is inevitable. It occurs in the process of changing jobs or looking for work. Workers with seasonal or weather-dependent jobs are unemployed part of the year. Short of a completely planned economy, business cycles and cyclical unemployment are inevitable. Finally, structural changes in the economy occur constantly which both eliminate and create jobs. Those who lose employment, however, often are not suited for the new jobs.

One theoretical explanation for recent high levels of unemployment attributes them to the growth of structural unemployment. On the other hand, a more likely explanation attributes them to insufficient demand for goods and services. Accordingly, policies which stimulated demand in the 1950s and 1960s were successful in reducing unemployment. The same policies were not as effective in the 1970s because they were inflationary, and the insufficient demand was largely due to inflated costs of raw materials.

The impressionistic description of unemployment in this chapter focused on its social and psychological impacts. Some of the studies reviewed date from the Depression and would not hold today in all of their details. Even fairly recent studies, however, confirm that unemployment causes considerable suffering. One reason is that the work ethic is a core value in American society. Although it may have waned in the past few decades while Americans were increasing their emotional investments in leisure activities, nevertheless, work is still essential to male self-esteem and increasingly important for women, and economic success is still the basic goal for males in the United States. Unemployment therefore causes psychological as well as economic deprivations which in turn produce social deprivations. These deprivations have been effectively summarized by Aiken et al.:

> The loss of work is viewed as weakening and impairing the individual's ability to remain socially and emotionally attached to the main currents of the society. Job displacement may result in (1) depletion of financial resources and reduced contact with kin or friends because the worker cannot reciprocate his social obligations; (2) temporary or permanent loss of social relationships in the work situation that have provided affective support and functional aid; (3) loss of contact with one of the primary social institutions, the union, through which the worker gains a sense of competence or influence in the control of his environment; (4) erosion of a socially useful role that has given the individual a sense of social identity; and (5) redistribution of wage-earning responsibilities with the family which may result in drastic readjustment of role expectations and behavior of the family members [1968: 2].

# EPILOGUE

Forewarned is forearmed. We desire to know the future so that we can take present actions to prevent the tragedies which are foreseen. The Club of Rome Project on the Predicament of Mankind predicts world ecological catastrophe in about 70 years on the basis of a complex computerized model using the present trends in population, production, capital investment, and the evolution of technology (Meadows et al. 1972). The purpose of its prediction was to jar the world into actions which would prevent the catastrophe: stabilize population and production, use resources more efficiently, and control pollution. Social impact assessment also predicts the future in order to change it. The social impacts of policy alternatives are estimated so that the "least adverse" or "best" alternative can be selected and its negative impacts ameliorated. At least, this is what SIA and the assessment of other impacts are supposed to do.

The principle which underlies SIA is that we should learn from the mistakes of the past. It is cumulated knowledge on the social impacts of past projects and policies which helps us design better projects and policies in the present. In this book we present cumulated knowledge on social impact areas as an aid to social impact assessors. To the social impact assessor is left the often difficult task of translating this knowledge base into SIAs which increase the benefits and reduce the adverse effects of public actions.

# REFERENCES

Abey-Wickrama, I. et al. (1969) "Mental hospital admissions and aircraft noise." Lancet 2: 1275-1277.

Abrahamson, J. (1971) A Neighborhood Finds Itself. New York: Biblo and Tannen.

Abu-Lughod, J. and M. M. Foley (1960) "Consumer strategies," in N. N. Foote et al. (eds.) Housing Choices and Housing Constraints. New York: McGraw-Hill.

Adkins, W. G. (1957) Effects of the Dallas Central Expressway on Land Values and Land Use. Bulletin No. 6. College Station, Texas Transportation Institute, Texas A & M University.

Adler, S. P. and E. F. Jansen, Jr. (1978) Hill Reestablishment: Retrospective Community Study of a Relocated New England Town. Report for U.S. Army Engineer Institute for Water Resources. Ft. Belvoir, VA.

Aiken, M. et al. (1968) Economic Failure, Alienation and Extremism. Ann Arbor: University of Michigan Press.

Alexander, C. (1967) "The city as a mechanism for sustaining human contact," in W. R. Ewald, Jr. (ed.) Environment for Man: The Next Fifty Years. Bloomington: Indiana University Press.

Alexandre, A. (1973) "Decision criteria based on spatio-temporal comparisons of surveys on aircraft noise," in W. D. Ward (ed.) Proceedings of the International Congress on Noise as a Public Health Problem, Dubrovnik, Yugoslavia, 1973. Washington, DC: U.S. EPA.

Alonso, W. (1978) Testimony before the Joint Economic Committee, U.S. Congress (May 31).

Anderson, R. J., Jr. and D. E. Wise (1977) The Effects of Highway Noise and Accessibility on Residential Property Values. Final Report for Federal Highway Administration. Princeton, NJ: Mathtech, Inc.

Andrews, F. M. and S. B. Withey (1976) Social Indicators of Well-Being. New York: Plenum Press.

Anschel, K. and A. F. Bordeaux, Jr. (1972) "The realities of migration," in The Labor Force: Migration, Earnings and Growth. Muscle Shoals, AL: Tennessee Valley Authority.

Arvidsson, O. et al. (1965) "Community noise—a social psychological study." Nordisk Hygienisk Tidskrift 46: 153-188.

Bach, R. L. and J. Smith (1977) "Community satisfaction, expectations of moving, and migration." Demography 14: 147-167.

Back, K. W. (1962) Slums, Projects and People: Social Psychological Problems in Relocation in Puerto Rico. Durham, NC: Duke University Press.

Bakke, E. Wight (1940a) Citizens Without Work. New Haven, CT: Yale University Press.
——— (1940b) The Unemployed Worker. New Haven, CT: Yale University Press.
——— (1934) The Unemployed Man. New York: E. P. Dutton.
Bannon, J. J. (1976) Leisure Resources: Its Comprehensive Planning. Englewood Cliffs, NJ: Prentice-Hall.
Bardach, E. and L. Pugliaresi (1977) "The environmental-impact statement vs. the real world." The Public Interest 49: 22-38.
Baron, R. A. (1970) The Tyranny of Noise. New York: St. Martin's Press.
Barrett, C. L. and H. Noble (1973) "Mother's anxieties versus the effects of long distance move on children." Journal of Marriage and the Family 35: 181-188.
Barrett, F. A. (1973) Residential Search Behavior. Geographical Monographs No. 1. Toronto, Ontario, Canada: York University.
Bates, V. E. (1978) "The impact of energy boom-town growth on rural areas." Social Casework 59: 73-82.
Beal, G. (1965) "Communities with declining populations," in Iowa State University Center for Agricultural and Economic Development (eds.) Family Mobility in our Dynamic Society. Ames: Iowa State University Press.
Beale, C. L. (1978) "People on the land," in T. R. Ford (ed.) Rural U.S.A.: Persistence and Change. Ames: Iowa State University Press.
——— (1974) "Quantitative dimensions of decline and stability among rural communities," in L. R. Whiting (ed.) Communities Left Behind. Ames: Iowa State University Press.
Beland, R. D. et al. (1972) Aircraft Noise Impact-Planning Guidelines for Local Agencies. South Pasadena: Wiley and Horn.
Bell, W. (1959) "Social areas: typology of urban neighborhoods," in M. B. Sussman (ed.) Community Structure and Analysis. New York: Crowell and Company.
Bender, L. D. et al. (1971) "The process of rural poverty ghettoization." Presented at the Annual Meeting of the American Association for the Advancement of Science, December 28, Philadelphia.
Bennis, W. G. (1968) "The temporary society," in W. G. Bennis and P. E. Slater, The Temporary Society. New York: Harper & Row.
Berger, B. N. (1960) Working-Class Suburb. Berkeley: University of California Press.
Bernard, J. (1937) "An instrument for the measurement of neighborhood relationships with experimental applications." Southwestern Social Science Quarterly 16: 145-158.
Bernstein, S. (1964) Youth on the Streets: Work with Alienated Youth Groups. New York: Association Press.
Bettelheim, B. (1971) Ladies Home Journal, October: 38-41.
Blumberg, L. and R. R. Bell (1959) "Urban migration and kinship ties." Social Problems 6: 328-333.
Bollenbacher, J. (1962) "Study of the effects of mobility in reading achievement." Reading Teacher 15: 356-360.
Bolt, Beranek and Newman, Inc. (1971) Noise From Construction Equipment and Operations, Building Equipment, and Home Appliances. Report for the U.S. Environmental Protection Agency, Washington, D.C.
Bott, E. (1957) Family and Social Network, Roles, Norms, and External Relationships in Ordinary Urban Families. London: Tavistock Publications.
Bragdon, C. R. (1971) Noise Pollution: The Unquiet Crisis. Philadelphia: University of Pennsylvania Press.

Brayfield, A. H. and H. F. Rothe (1951) "An index of job satisfaction." Journal of Applied Psychology 35: 307-11.

Breese, G. (1965) "Fairless works of U.S. Steel in Lower Bucks County, Pennsylvania," in G. Breese et al., The Impact of Large Installations on Nearby Areas: Accelerated Urban Growth. (Beverly Hills, CA: Sage.

Brinton, J. H. and J. N. Bloom (1969) Effect of Highway Landscape Development on Nearby Property. National Cooperative Highway Research Program Report 75. Washington, DC: National Academy of Sciences, Highway Research Program.

Broadbent, D. E. (1979) "Human performance and noise," in C. M. Harris (ed.) Handbook of Noise Control. New York: McGraw-Hill.

Bronzaft, A. L. and D. P. McCarthy (1975) "The effects of elevated train noise on reading ability." Environment and Behavior 7: 517-527.

Bruyn, S. (1966) The Human Perspective in Sociology. Englewood Cliffs, NJ: Prentice-Hall.

Buckley, W. (1967) Sociology and Modern Systems Theory. Englewood Cliffs, NJ: Prentice-Hall.

Buechner, R. D. [ed.] (1971) National Park Recreation and Open Space Standards. Washington, DC: National Recreation and Park Association.

Buffington, J. L. (1974) "Economic consequences of freeway displacement to residents relocated under the 1968 and 1970 Relocation Programs." Transportation Research Record Vol. 481: 29-42.

—— (1973) Consequences of Freeway Displacement to Urban Residents in Low Valued Housing. Texas Transportation Institute, Texas A & M University (February).

—— (1964) Restudy of Changes in Land Values, Land Use and Business Activity along a Section of Interstate Highway 35, Austin, Texas. Bulletin No. 26. College Station: Texas Transportation Institute Texas A & M University.

—— et al. (1974) Attitudes, Opinions, and Experiences of Residents Displaced by Highways Under the 1970 Relocation Assistance Program. College Park: Texas A & M University.

Bugliarello, G. et al. (1976) The Impact of Noise Pollution. New York: Pergamon Press.

Burdge, R. J. and K. S. Johnson (1973) Social Costs and Benefits of Water Resource Construction. Research Report No. 64, Lexington's Water Resources Research Institute. University of Kentucky.

Burdge, R. J. and R. L. Ludtke (1973) "Social separation among displaced rural families: the case of flood control reservoirs," in W. R. Busch et al. (eds.) Social Behavior, Natural Resources and the Environment. New York: Harper & Row.

Bureau of the Census (1978a) Marital Status and Living Arrangements: March 1977. Current Population Reports, Population Characteristics, Series P-20, No. 323 (April). Washington, DC: U.S. Government Printing Office.

—— (1978b) "Estimates of the Population of States: July 1, 1977 and 1978 (Advance Report)." Current Population Reports, Population Estimates and Projection, Series P-25, No. 790 (December).

—— (1978c) Statistical Abstract of the United States, 99th Edition.

—— (1977) Geographical Mobility: March 1975 to March 1976. Current Population Reports, Population Characteristics, Series P-20, No. 305 (January).

—— (1976) "Estimates of the Population of States with Components of Change, 1970 to 1975." Current Population Reports, Series P-25, No. 640.

—— (1975) Mobility of the Population of the United States March 1970 to March 1975. Current Population Reports, Population Characteristics, Series P-20., No. 285.

—— (1943) 1940 Census of Population, The Labor Force.

Bureau of Labor Statistics (1980) Employment and Earnings, February 1980, 27, 2. Washington, DC: U.S. Government Printing Office.

—— (1979) Handbook of Labor Statistics, 1978.

—— (1977) News release, March 8.

Burgess, E. W. and D. J. Bogue [eds.] (1964) Contributions to Urban Sociology. Chicago: University of Chicago Press.

Burkhardt, J. E. and N. L. Chinlund (1971) Anticipation of the Effects of an Urban Highway Improvement on the Highway Corridor. Bethesda, MD: Resource Management Corporation.

Burkhardt, J. E. and M. T. Shaffer (1972) "Social and psychological impacts of transportation improvements." Transportation 1: 207-226.

Burkhardt, J. E. et al. (1976) Residential Dislocation: Consequences and Compensation. Final Report. NCHR Program.

—— (1971) Changes in Neighborhood Social Interaction. Bethesda, MD: Resource Management Corporation.

Butler, E. W. and E. J. Kaiser (1971) "Prediction of residential movement and spatial allocation." Urban Affairs Quarterly 6: 477-494.

Butler, E. W. et al. (1973) "The effects of voluntary and involuntary residential mobility on females and males." Journal of Marriage and the Family 35: 219-227.

—— (1969) Moving Behavior and Residential Choice—A National Survey. National Cooperative Highway Research Program, Report No. 81. Washington, D.C.

Butler, G. O. (1962) Standards for Municipal Recreation Areas. New York: National Recreation and Park Association.

Cagle, L. T. and I. Deutscher (1970) "Housing aspirations and housing achievement: the relocation of poor families." Social Problems 18: 243-256.

California State Department of Public Health (1971) A Report to the 1971 Legislation on the Subject Noise Pursuant to Assembly Concurrent Resolution 165, 1970.

Campbell, A. et al. (1976) The Quality of American Life. New York: Russell Sage.

Campbell, R. R. (1975) "Beyond the suburbs: the changing rural scene," in A. H. Hawley and V. P. Rock (eds.) Metropolitan American in Contemporary Perspective. New York: Russell Sage.

Caplow, T. and R. Forman (1950) "Neighborhood interaction in a homogeneous community." American Sociological Review 15: 357-366.

Carasso, M. et al. (1975) The Energy Supply Planning Model, San Francisco: Bechtel Corp.

Carlson, R. E. et al. (1972) Recreation in American Life. Belmont, CA: Wadsworth.

Carmen, R. (1977) Our Endangered Hearing. Emmau, PA: Rodele Press.

Carp, F. M. et al. (1976) "Dimensions of urban environmental quality." Environment and Behavior 8: 239-264.

Caudill, H. (1965) "Reflections on poverty in America," in A. B. Shostak and W. Gornberg (eds.) New Perspectives on Poverty. Englewood Cliffs, NJ: Prentice-Hall.

Chapin, F. S., Jr. (1974) Human Activity Patterns in the City. New York: John Wiley.

Cheek, N. H., Jr. and W. R. Burch, Jr. (1976) The Social Organization of Leisure in Human Society. New York: Harper & Row.

Chernik, D. A. (1972) "Effects of REM sleep deprivation on learning and recall by humans." Perceptual Motor Skills 34: 283-294.

Chevan, A. (1971) "Family growth, household density, and moving." Demography 8: 451-458.

Chowns, R. H. (1970) "Mental-hospital admissions and aircraft noise." Lancet 3: 467.

Chubb, M. and P. Ashton (1969) Park and Recreation Standards Research: The Creation of Environmental Quality Controls for Recreation. Report to the National Recreation and Park Association. East Lansing, MI: Department of Park and Recreation Resources.

Claire, W. H. [ed.] (1973) Handbook on Urban Planning. New York: Van Nostrand Reinhold.

Clawson, M. and J. L. Knetsch (1966) Economics of Outdoor Recreation. Baltimore: Johns Hopkins University Press.

Cline, M. G. (1963) "Urban freeways and social structures: some problems and proposals." Highway Research Record 2: 12-20.

Cohen, S. et al. (1980) "Physiological, motivational, and cognitive effects of aircraft noise on children." American Psychologist 35: 231-243.

—— (1973) "Apartment noise, auditory discrimination, and reading ability in children." Journal of Experimental Social Psychology 9: 407-422.

Colborn, F. M. (1963) The Neighborhood and Urban Renewal. New York: National Federation of Settlement and Neighborhood Centers.

Coleman, R. P. (1978) Attitudes Toward Neighborhoods: How Americans Choose to Live. Working Paper No. 49. Cambridge, MA: Joint Center for Urban Studies of MIT and Harvard University.

Collins, W. E. and P. F. Iampietro (1973) "Effects on sleep of hourly presentations of simulated sonic booms (50 N/M$^2$)," in W. D. Ward (ed.) Proceedings of the International Congress on Noise as a Public Health Problem, Dubrovnik, Yugoslavia, 1973. Washington, DC: U.S. EPA.

Colony, D. C. (1973) Residential Relocation: The Impact of Allowances and Procedure in Effect Since July 1, 1970. University of Toledo for the Ohio Department of Transportation.

—— (1972) "Study of the impact on households of relocation from a highway right-of-way." Highway Research Record 399: 12-26.

—— (1971) Socio-Economic and Environmental Effects of Right-of-Way Acquisition. Ohio Department of Highways (April).

—— (1967) Expressway Traffic Noise and Residential Properties. Report for the Bureau of Public Roads, U.S. Department of Transportation (July 1).

Cooper, C. (1972) "The house as symbol." Design and Environment 3: 30-37.

Cooper, F. (1964) Property Replacement Study: Effects on Property Owners Displaced by Freeway Construction. Oregon State Highway Department.

Corrigan, R. (1976) "The western boom towns—'going crazy,' going it alone." National Journal (August 14): 1150-1152.

Cortese, C. F. (1979) "The social impacts of energy development in the west: an introduction." The Social Science Journal 16: 1-7.

—— and B. Jones (1977) "The sociological analysis of boom towns." Western Sociological Review 8: 76-90.

Cottrell, W. F. (1951) "Death by dieselization: a case study in the reaction to technological change." American Sociological Review 16: 358-365.

CEQ [Council on Environmental Quality] (1978) "National environmental policy act—regulations." Federal Register 43: 230 (Wednesday, November 29). Washington, DC: U.S. Government Printing Office.

—— (1976) Analysis of Six Years Experience by Seventy Federal Agencies.

Crook, M. A. and F. J. Langdon (1974) "The effects of aircraft noise in schools around London Airport." Journal of Sound and Vibration 34: 221-232.

Daicoff, D. W. et al. (1970) Economic Impact of Military Base Closings, Vols. 1, 2. Prepared for the U.S. Arms Control and Disarmament Agency. Lawrence: University of Kansas.

Davis, J. C. III (1966) Neighborhood Groups and Urban Renewal. New York: Columbia University Press.

Dear, M. J. (1976) "Abandoned housing," in J. S. Adams (ed.) Urban Policymaking and Metropolitan Dynamics. Cambridge, MA: Ballinger.

Deaton, B. and K. Anschel (1974) "Migration and return migration." Southern Journal of Agricultural Economics 6: 185-191.

De Grazia, S. (1962) Of Time, Work, and Leisure. New York: The Twentieth Century Fund.

Denver Research Institute (1975) The Social, Economic and Land Use Impacts of a Fort Union Coal Processing Complex. Denver: University of Denver Research Institute.

Department of Resource Development (1966) The Outdoor Recreation Plan. Madison: State of Wisconsin.

Dillman, D. A. et al. (1979) "Influence of housing norms and personal characteristics on stated housing preferences." Housing and Society 6: 2-19.

Dixon, M. (1978) What Happened to Fairbanks? Boulder, CO: Westview Press.

Doeksen, G. A. et al. (1974) "Consequences of decline and community economic adjustment to it," in L. R. Whiting (ed.) Communities Left Behind. Ames: Iowa State University Press.

Donald Wolbrink and Associates, Inc. (1967) Planning for Recreation: A Methodology for Functional Planning. State of Hawaii General Plan Revision Program, Part 6. Prepared for State of Hawaii Department of Planning and Economic Development, Honolulu, Hawaii.

Droettboom, T., Jr. et al. (1971) "Urban violence and residential mobility." Journal of the American Institute of Planners 37: 319-325.

Durand, R. and D. R. Eckart (1973) "Social rank, residential effects and community satisfaction." Social Forces 52: 74-85.

Durkheim, E. (1933) The Division of Labor in Society (G. Simpson, trans.). New York: Free Press.

Dygert, P. K. (1973) Estimation of the Cost of Aircraft Noise to Residential Activities. Ph.D. dissertation. Ann Arbor: University of Michigan.

――― and D. L. Sanders (1970) On Measuring the Costs of Noise from Subsonic Aircraft. Berkeley: University of California, Institute of Transportation and Traffic Engineering.

Emerson, F. C. (1969) The Determinants of Residential Value with Special Reference to the Effects of Aircraft Nuisance and Other Environmental Features. Ph.D. dissertation. University of Minnesota.

Erikson, K. T. (1976) Everything in Its Path: Destruction of Community in the Buffalo Creek Flood. New York: Simon and Schuster.

Ermuth, F. (1974) Residential Satisfaction and Urban Environmental Preferences. Geographical Monographs No. 3. Toronto, Ontario, Canada: York University.

Evans, J. W. (1966) "The effect of pupil mobility upon academic achievement." National Elementary Principal 45: 18-22.

Federal Highway Administration (1974) Social and Economic Effects of Highways. Washington, DC: U.S. Government Printing Office.

Federal Highway Administration, U.S. Department of Transportation (1976) Social and Economic Effects of Highways. Washington, DC: U.S. Government Printing Office.

Feller, I. and J. P. Nelson (1973) Economic Aspects of Noise Pollution. Report for U.S. Department of Transportation by Pennsylvania State University, Institute for Research on Human Resources (April).

Fellman, G. and B. Brandt (1973) The Deceived Majority: Politics and Protest in Middle America. New Brunswick, NJ: Transaction Books.

——— (1970) "A neighborhood a highway would destroy." Environment and Behavior 2: 281-301.

Fernandez, R. R. and D. A. Dillman (1979) "The influence of community attachment on geographic mobility." Rural Sociology 44: 345-360.

Fessler, D. R. (1952) "The development of a scale for measuring community solidarity." Rural Sociology 17: 144-152.

Festinger, L. et al. (1950) Social Pressures in Informal Groups. Stanford, CA: Stanford University Press.

Finegan, T. A. (1978) "Improving our information on discouraged workers." Monthly Labor Review 101: 15-25.

Finsterbusch, K. (1977) "Suggestions for estimating policy consequences for individuals, organizations, and communities," in K. Finsterbusch and C. P. Wolf (eds.) The Methodology of Social Impact Assessment. Stroudsburg, PA: Dowden, Hutchinson, and Ross.

——— (1976a) A Methodology for Social Impact Assessments of Highway Locations. Interim Report for Maryland State Highway Administration and the Federal Highway Administration. University of Maryland.

——— (1976b) "Demonstrating the value of mini surveys in social research." Sociological Methods and Research 5: 117-135.

——— (1975) A Methodology for the Analyses of Social Impacts of Public Policies. Vienna, VA: BDM Corporation.

Fischer, C. S. (1976) The Urban Experience. New York: Harcourt Brace Jovanovich.

——— (1975) "The study of urban community and personality," in A. Inkeles et al. (eds.) Annual Review of Sociology, Volume 1. Palo Alto, CA: Annual Reviews, Inc.

——— and R. M. Jackson (1976) "Suburbs, networks, and attitudes," in B. Schwartz (ed.) Changing Face of the Suburbs. Chicago: University of Chicago Press.

Fischer, C. S. et al. (1977) Networks and Places. New York: Free Press.

Fitch, C. and J. Hoffer (1964) "Geographical mobility and academic achievement of a group of junior high students." Home Economics 5: 334-335.

Foley, D. L. (1952) Neighbors or Urbanites? Rochester, NY: University of Rochester.

Foltman, F. F. (1968) White-and Blue-Collars in a Mill Shutdown: A Case Study in Relative Redundancy. Ithaca, NY: Cornell University.

Foote, N. N. et al. (1960) Housing Choices and Housing Constraints. New York: McGraw-Hill.

Fredland, D. R. (1974) Residential Mobility and Home Purchase. Lexington, MA: D. C. Heath.

Freudenburg, W. R. (1978a) "Toward ending the inattention: a report on the social consequences of energy boomtown developments." Presented at the annual meetings of the American Association for the Advancement of Science, February.

——— (1978b) "A *social* social impact analysis of a Rocky Mountain energy boomtown." Presented at the annual meetings of the American Sociological Association, San Francisco, August.

——— L. M. Bacigalupi, A. Clay, C. Landoll, and K. N. Deeds (1977) "Subjective responses to an energy boomtown situation: a preliminary report on research in progress in four Western Colorado towns." Presented at the annual meetings of the American Sociological Association, Chicago, September.

Fried, M. (1967) "Functions of the working-class community in modern urban society: implications for forced relocation." Journal of the American Institute of Planners 33: 90-103.

––––– (1963) "Grieving for a lost home," in L. J. Duhl (ed.) The Urban Condition. New York: Simon and Schuster.

––––– and P. Gleicher (1961) "Some sources of residential satisfaction in an urban slum." Journal of the American Institute of Planners 27: 305-315.

Friesema, H. P. and P. J. Culhane (1976) "Social impacts, politics, and the environmental impact statement process." Natural Resources Journal 16: 339-356.

Fuguitt, G. V. (1971) "The places left behind: population trends and policy for rural America." Rural Sociology 36: 449-470.

Galpin, C. J. (1915) The Social Anatomy of an Agricultural Community. Madison: Wisconsin Agricultural Experiment Station, Research Bulletin 34.

Galster, G. C. and G. W. Hesser (1979) "Compositional and contextual determinants of residential satisfaction." Presented at the annual meetings of the American Sociological Association, Boston, August.

Gamble, H. B. et al. (1973) Community Effects of Highways Reflected by Property Values. Report for Federal Highway Administration. Institute for Research on Land and Water Resources, Pennsylvania State University, August.

Gamble, H. B. and O. H. Sauerlender (1976) "Effects of highway noise in residential communities," in P. Laconte et al. (eds.) The Environment of Human Settlements. Proceedings of the conference held in Brussels, Belgium, April. Oxford: Pergamon Press.

Gans, H. J. (1967) The Levittowners. New York: Random House.

––––– (1963) "Effects of the move from city to suburb," in L. J. Duhl (ed.) The Urban Condition. New York: Basic Books.

––––– (1962a) The Urban Villages. New York: Free Press.

––––– (1962b) "Urbanism and suburbanism as ways of life: a revolution of definitions," in A. M. Rose (ed.) Human Behavior and Social Processes. Boston: Houghton Mifflin.

––––– (1961) "Planning and social life: friendship and neighborhood relations in suburban communities." Journal of the American Institute of Planners 27: 134-140.

Garn, H. A. (1978) "Urban economic development strategies: improving economic and fiscal performance." Final report for Economic Development Administration, U.S. Department of Commerce. Washington, DC: The Urban Institute.

Garrison, C. B. (1972) "The impact of new industry: an application of the economic base multiplier to small rural areas." Land Economics 48: 329-337.

Gates, A. S. et al. (1973) "What makes a good neighbor?" Presented at the annual meeting of the American Sociological Association, New York, August.

Gilmore, J. S. (1976) "Boom towns may hinder energy resource development." Science 191: 535-540.

––––– and M. K. Duff (1975) Boom Town Growth Management: A Case Study of Rock Springs-Green River, Wyoming. Boulder, CO: Westview Press.

Ginzberg, E. (1977) Panel discussion in L. A. Lecht (ed.) Employment and Unemployment: Priorities for the Next Five Years. New York: The Conference Board.

Glass, D. C. and J. E. Singer (1972) Urban Stress: Experiments on Noise and Social Stressors. New York: Academic Press.

Glass, D. C. et al. (1973) "Urban din fogs the brain." Psychology Today 6: 306-326.

Glueck, S. and E. Glueck (1950) Unraveling Juvenile Delinquency. New York: The Commonwealth Fund.

Goffman, E. (1959) The Presentation of Self in Everyday Life. New York: Doubleday.

Golden, J. S. (1968) Land Values in Chicago: Before and After Expressway Construction. Chicago: Chicago Area Transportation Study.

Goldsmith, J. R. and E. Jonsson (1973) "Health effects of community noise." American Journal of Public Health 63: 782-793.

Goldstein, G. S. (1973) "Household behavior in the housing market: the decision to move and the decision to buy or rent housing," in E. G. More (ed.) Models of Residential Location and Relocation in the City. Studies in Geography No. 20. Evanston, IL: Northwestern University.

Goodman, J. (1974) "Local residential mobility and family housing adjustments," in J. N. Morgan (ed.) Five Thousand American Families—Patterns of Economic Progress, Vol. II. Ann Arbor, MI: Survey Research Center.

Gordon, G. G. (1968) "A case study of the phase-out of Larson AFB, Moses Lake, Washington," in Economic Impact of Military Base Closings, Vol. II. Prepared by University of Kansas for the U.S. Arms Control and Government Agency.

Gordon, H. E. and K. K. Gordon (1958) "Emotional disorders of children in a rapidly growing suburb." International Journal of Social Psychiatry 4: 85-97.

Gordon, S. (1975) Lonely in America. New York: Simon and Schuster.

Goromosov, M. S. (1968) The Physiological Basis of Health Standard for Dwellings. Public Health Paper #33. Geneva: World Health Organization.

Greene, J. E. and S. L. Daughtry (1961) "Factors associated with school mobility." Journal of Educational Sociology 35: 36-40.

Greer, S. (1956) "Urbanism reconsidered: a comparative study of local areas in a metropolis." American Sociological Review 21: 19-25.

——— and A. L. Greer [eds.] (1974) Neighborhood and Ghetto: The Local Area in Large Scale Society. New York: Basic Books.

Gulick, J. et al. (1962) "Newcomer enculturation in the city: attitudes and participation," in F. S. Chapin, Jr. and S. F. Weiss (eds.) Urban Growth Dynamics. New York: John Wiley.

Haber, W. et al. (1963) The Impact of Technological Change. Kalamazoo, MI: W. E. Upjohn Institute for Employment Research.

Haga, W. J. and C. L. Folse (1971) "Trade patterns and community identity." Rural Sociology 36: 42-51.

Hamilton, J. R. et al. (1976) Small Towns in a Rural Area: A Study of the Problems of Small Towns in Idaho. Research Bulletin No. 91. Agricultural Experiment Station, University of Idaho.

Hamilton, M. R. et al. (1980) Addendum to Volume II: The Social Impact of Urban Highways: A Review of Empirical Studies. Washington, DC: Federal Highway Administration.

Haney, W. G. and E. S. Knowles (1978) "Perception of neighborhood by city and suburban residents." Human Ecology 6: 201-214.

Haren, C. C. (1974a) "Current spatial organization of industrial production and distribution activity," in U.S. Senate, Committee on Agriculture and Forestry, Subcommittee on Rural Development, Rural Industrialization: Prospects, Problems, Impacts, and Methods. 93rd Congress, 2nd Session, Committee Prints, April 19.

——— (1974b) "Location of industrial production and distribution," in Rural Industrialization: Problems and Potentials, produced by North Central Regional Center for Rural Development. Ames: Iowa State University Press.

Harrison, B. (1972) Education, Training and the Urban Ghetto. Baltimore, MD: Johns Hopkins University Press.

Hartman, C. (1964) "The housing of relocated families." Journal of the American Institute of Planners 30: 266-286.

Hartnagel, T. F. (1979) "The perception and fear of crime: implications for neighborhood cohesion, social activity, and community affect." Social Forces 58: 176-193.

Havighurst, R. and K. Feigenbaum (1959) "Leisure and life style." American Journal of Sociology 64: 396-404.

Havighurst, R. J. and H. G. Morgan (1951) The Social History of a War Boom Community. New York: Greenwood Press.

Hawkins, D. G. (1979) Statement by the Assistant Administrator for Air Noise, and Radiation, U.S. EPA before the Subcommittee on Transportation and Commerce, Committee on Interstate and Foreign Commerce, House of Representatives, March 21.

Heberle, R. (1960) "The normative element in neighborhood relations." Pacific Sociological Review 3: 3-11.

Herbert, M. and R. T. Wilkinson (1973) "The effects of noise-disturbed sleep on subsequent performance," in W. D. Ward (ed.) Proceedings of the International Congress on Noise as a Public Health Problem, Dubrovnik, Yugoslavia, 1973. Washington, DC: U.S. Government Printing Office.

Heritage Conservation and Recreation Service, U.S. Department of Interior (1978) "National outdoor recreation survey 1977. (unpublished)

Herman, M. W. (1964) Comparative Studies of Identification Areas in Philadelphia. City of Philadelphia Community Renewal Program, Technical Report No. 9. (mimeo)

Herridge, C. F. (1974) "Aircraft noise and mental health." Journal of Psychosomatic Research 18: 239-243.

Highline Public Schools (1973) Aircraft Noise Study. Seattle, WA. (August)

Hill, S. L. (1967) "The effect of freeways on neighborhoods." Transportation Agency of the State of California (June).

Hillery, G. A., Jr. (1955) "Definitions of community: areas of agreement." Rural Sociology 20: 111-123.

Hines, F. et al. (1975) Social and Economic Characteristics of the Population in Metro and Nonmetro Counties. Agricultural Economic Report 272. Washington, DC: U.S. Department of Agriculture.

Hitchcock, J. and A. Waterhouse (1979) "Expressway noise and apartment tenant response." Environment and Behavior 11: 251-267.

Hodge, G. (1965) "The prediction of trade center viability in the Great Plains." The Regional Science Association: Papers 15: 87-115.

Hogg, T. C. and C. L. Smith (1970) Socio-Cultural Impacts of Water Resource Development in the Santiam River Basin. Corvalles: Oregon State University.

Holmes, T. H. and R. H. Rahe (1967) "The social readjustment scale." Journal of Psychosematic Research 11: 213-218.

Hormachea, M. N. and C. R. Hormachea (1972) Recreation in Modern Society. Boston: Holbrook Press.

House, P. A. (1970) "Relocation of families displaced by expressway development: Milwaukee case study." Land Economics 46: 75-78.

Howard, Needles, Tammen and Bergendoff (1975) Review of Socio-Economic Impacts of the Calvert Cliffs Nuclear Power Plant in Calvert County Maryland and Comparison with Kent County, Maryland. Report for Maryland Power Plant Siting Program, Department of Natural Resources (January).

Hudson Guild Neighborhood House and New York University Center for Human Relations and Community Studies (1960) Human Relations in Chelsea. Report of the Chelsea Housing and Human Relations Cooperative Project.

Hunter, A. (1978) "Persistence of local sentiments in mass society," in D. Street (ed.) Handbook of Contemporary Urban Life. San Francisco: Jossey-Bass.

––– (1975) "The loss of community: an empirical test through replication." American Sociological Review 40: 537-552.

––– (1974) Symbolic Communities: The Persistence and Change of Chicago's Local Communities. Chicago: University of Chicago Press.

Hutchison, R. (1977) "Sentiment and attachment in the urban community." Presented at the annual meeting of the American Sociological Association, Chicago, September.

Institute of Public Administration (1973) Assessment of Flood Management Alternatives Against Social Performance Criteria. Phase II Report (Preliminary). (April 15).

Irving, H. W. (1977) "Social networks in the modern city." Social Forces 55: 867-880.

Jacobs, J. (1961) The Death and Life of Great American Cities. New York: Random House.

Jacobson, D. (1971) "Mobility, continuity, and urban social organization." Man 6: 630-644.

Jamaica Bay Environmental Study Group (1971) Jamaica Bay and Kennedy Airport: A Multidisciplinary Environmental Study, Vols. I, II. Washington, DC: National Academy of Sciences.

Janowitz, M. (1967) The Community Press in an Urban Setting. Chicago: University of Chicago Press.

––– and J. D. Kasarda (1974) "The social construction of local communities," in T. Leggett (ed.) Sociological Theory and Survey Research. Beverly Hills, CA: Sage.

Janowitz, M. and D. Street (1978) "Changing social order of the metropolitan area," in D. Street (ed.) Handbook of Contemporary Urban Life. San Francisco: Jossey-Bass.

Johnson, L. et al. (1972) "Sleep stages and performance," in W. P. Colquhoun (ed.) Aspects of Human Efficiency: Diurnal Rhythm and Loss of Sleep. London: English University Press.

Johnson, S. and R. J. Burdge (1974) "An analysis of community and individual reactions to forced migration due to reservoir construction," in D. R. Field et al. (eds.) Water and Community Development. Ann Arbor, MI: Ann Arbor Science Publishers.

Jones, S. B. (1973) "Geographic mobility as seen by the wife and mother." Journal of Marriage and the Family 35: 210-218.

Kando, T. M. (1980) Leisure and Popular Culture in Transition. St. Louis: C. V. Mosby.

Kantor, M. B. [ed.] (1965) Mobility and Mental Health. Springfield, IL: Charles C Thomas.

Kaplan, M. (1975) Leisure: Theory and Policy. New York: John Wiley.

Karagodina, I. L. et al. (1972) "Effects of apartment noise on sleep," in I. L. Karagodina (ed.) The Fight Against Noise in Cities. Moscow.

Kasarda, J. D. (1978) "Urbanization, community, and the metropolitan problem," in D. Street (ed.) Handbook of Contemporary Urban Life. San Francisco: Jossey-Bass.

––– and M. Janowitz (1974) "Community attachment in mass society." American Sociological Review 39: 328-339.

Kasl, S. V. (1974) "Effects of housing on mental and physical health." Man-Environment System 4: 207-226.

––– and E. Harburg (1972) "Perceptions of the neighborhood and the desire to move out." Journal of the American Institute of Planners 38: 318-324.

Keller, S. (1968) The Urban Neighborhood. New York: Random House.

Kemp, B. H. (1965) "Social impact of a highway on an urban community." Highway Research Record 75: 92-102.

Key, W. H. (1967) When People Are Forced to Move. (mimeograph)

––– (1965) "Urbanism and neighboring." The Sociological Quarterly 6: 379-385.

Kolb, J. H. and L. J. Day (1950) Interdependence in Town and Country Relations in Rural Society. Research Bulletin 172. Madison: Wisconsin Agricultural Experiment Stations.

Komarovsky, M. (1940) [1971] The Unemployed Man and His Family: The Effect of Unemployment Upon the Status of the Man in Fifty-Nine Families. New York: Octagon Books.

Kraus, R. (1971) Recreation and Leisure in Modern Society. New York: Appleton-Century-Crofts.

Kryter, K. D. (1970) The Effects of Noise on Man. New York: Academic Press.

Landis, J. R. and T. Stoetzer (1966) "An exploratory study of middle-class migrant families." Journal of Marriage and the Family 28: 51-53.

Lane, J. S. et al. (1975) The No-Build Alternative, Parts 1 and 2. National Cooperative Highway Research Program, Transportation Research Board, National Research Council (December).

Langner, T. S. and S. T. Michael (1963) Life Stress and Mental Health: The Midtown Manhattan Study. New York: Free Press.

Lansing, J. B. and R. W. Marans (1969) "Evaluation of neighborhood quality." Journal of the American Institute of Planners 35: 195-199.

Lansing, J. B. and M. Morgan (1967) "The effects of geographic mobility on income." Journal of Human Resources 2: 449-460.

Lansing, J. B. et al. (1970) Planned Residential Environments. Ann Arbor, MI: Institute for Social Research.

Lansing, J. B. et al. (1963) The Geographic Mobility of Labor. First report for Area Redevelopment Administration, U.S. Department of Commerce. Ann Arbor, MI: Survey Research Center.

Lantz, H. R. (1971) People of Coal Town. Carbondale: Southern Illinois University Press.

Laumann, E. O. (1973) Bonds of Pluralism: The Form and Substance of Urban Social Networks. New York: John Wiley.

Lazarus, J. et al. (1963) "Migration differentials in mental disease." Milbank Memorial Fund Quarterly 41: 25-42.

Lecht, L. A. (1977) Employment and Unemployment: Priorities for the Next Five Years. Boulder, CO: Westview Press.

Lee, B. A. and A. M. Guest (1979) "Subjective evaluations of metropolitan neighborhood quality." Presented at the annual meeting of the American Sociological Asociation, Boston, August.

Leighton, D. C. et al. (1963) The Stirling County Study of Psychiatric Disorder and Sociocultural Environment. New York: Basic Books.

Leonard, S. and P. M. Borsky (1973) "A causal model for relating noise exposure, psycho-social variables and aircraft noise annoyance," in W. D. Ward (ed.) Proceedings of the International Congress on Noise as a Public Health Problem, Dubrovnik, Yugoslavia. Washington, DC: U.S. Government Printing Office.

Levere, T. E. et al. (1972) "Electroencephalographic and behavioral effects of nocturnally occurring jet aircraft sounds." Aeorospace Medicine 43: 384-389.

Levine, M. (1966) "Residential change and school adjustment." Community Mental Health Journal 2: 61-69.

––– et al. (1966) "Pupil turnover and academic performance in an inner city, elementary school." Psychology in the Schools 3: 153-158.

Levitan, S. A. and R. S. Belous (1977) Shorter Hours, Shorter Weeks: Spreading the Work to Reduce Unemployment. Baltimore, MD: Johns Hopkins University Press.

Levitan, S. A. et al. (1976) Human Resources and Labor Markets. New York: Harper & Row.

Lewis, W. C. (1976) "Export base theory and multiplier estimations: a critique." The Annals of Regional Science 10: 58-70.

Ley, D. (1974) The Black Inner City as Frontier Outpost. Washington, DC: Association of American Geographers.

Linder, S. B. (1970) The Harried Leisure Class. New York: Columbia University Press.

Little, R. L. (1977) "Some social consequences of boom towns." North Dakota Law Review 53: 401-425.

––– and S. B. Lovejoy (1977) Employment Benefits from Rural Industrialization. Los Angeles: Lake Powell Research Project.

Litwak, E. (1960) "Geographic mobility and extended family cohesion." American Sociological Review 25: 385-394.

––– and I. Szelenyi (1969) "Primary group structures and their functions: kin, neighbors and friends." American Sociological Review 34: 465-481.

Llewellyn, L. et al. (1979) "An analysis of public comment on coyote management alternatives." U.S. Fish and Wildlife Service (mimeo)

––– (1975) Social Impact Assessment: A Sourcebook for Highway Planners, Vol. II, The Social Impact of Urban Highways: A Review of Emperical Studies. Report for Federal Highway Administration (June).

Lofting, E. M. and P. H. McGauhy (1968) Economic Evaluation of Water, Part IV: An Input-Output and Linear Programming Analysis of California Water Requirements. Contribution No. 116. Berkeley: Water Resources Center, University of California.

Long, H. H. (1975) "Does migration interfere with children's progress in school?" Sociology of Education 48: 369-381.

––– and C. G. Boertlein (1976) The Geographic Mobility of Americans: An International Comparison. Current Population Report, Special Studies Series P. 23, No. 64. Bureau of the Census. Washington, DC: U.S. Government Printing Office.

Long, H. H. and K. A. Hansen (1979) Reasons for Interstate Migration. Current Population Reports, Special Studies Series P. 23, No. 81 (March), Bureau of the Census. Washington, DC: U.S. Government Printing Office.

Lundberg, F. M. et al. (1934) Leisure: A Suburban Study. New York: Columbia University Press.

Lundberg, G. A. and E. Steele (1937) "Social attraction patterns in a village." Sociometry 1: 18-26.

Lynch, J. E. (1970) Local Economic Development After Military Base Closures. New York: Praeger.

McAllister, R. J. et al. (1973) "The Adaptation of women to residential mobility." Journal of Marriage and the Family 35: 197-204.

Maccoby, E. E. et al. (1958) "Community integration and the social control of juvenile delinquency." Journal of Social Issues 14: 38-51.

McKennell, A. C. (1963) Aircraft Noise Annoyance Around London Heathrow Airport. London: Central Ofice of Information, SS 337.

McKenzie, R. D. (1921) "The neighborhood: a study of local life in the city of Columbus, Ohio." American Journal of Sociology 27 (2, 3, 4, 5, and 6): 145-168, 344-363, 486-509, 588-610, 780-799.

McKeown, R. L. and A. Lantz (1977) "Rapid growth and the impact on quality of life in rural communities: a case study." Craig, CO: Colorado West Regional Mental Health Center, Inc.

Maine, H. (1964) Ancient Law. New York: Scribner.

Malzberg, B. (1967) "Internal migration and mental disease among the white population of New York State 1960-1961." International Journal of Social Psychiatry 13: 184-191.

——— and Lee, E. S. (1956) Migration and Mental Disease: A Study of First Admissions to Hospitals for Mental Disease, New York, 1939-1941. New York: Social Science Research Council.

Mann, P. (1968) "Neighborhood," in G. D. Mitchell (ed.) A Dictionary of Sociology. Chicago: AVC.

Marans, R. W. and W. Rodgers (1975) "Toward an understanding of community satisfaction," in A. H. Hawley and V. P. Rock (eds.) Metropolitan America in Contemporary Perspective. New York: Russell Sage.

Marsh, R. M. (1970) Family Disruption During the Moving Process. Ph.D. dissertation. Brandeis University, Florence Heller Graduate School for Advanced Studies in Social Welfare.

Mead, M. (1966) "Neighborhoods and human needs." Ekistics 21: 124-126.

Meadows, D. H. et al. (1972) The Limits to Growth. New York: Universe Books.

Mecklin, J. M. (1969) "It's time to turn down all that noise." Fortune (October): 130-133.

Meidinger, E. E. (1977) "Projecting secondary jobs: an empirical examination and epistemological critique." Presented at the annual meetings of the American Sociological Association, Chicago, September.

Menchik, M. D. (1973) "Income and residential location in Alonso's model of urban form," in E. G. Moore (ed.) Models of Residential Location and Relocation in the City. Studies in Geography Number 20. Evanston, IL: Northwestern University Press.

Meyers, G. C. et al. (1967) "The duration of residence approach to dynamic stochastic process model of internal migration: a test of the axiom of cumulative inertia." Engenics Quarterly 14: 121-126.

Michelson, W. (1977) Environmental Choice, Human Behavior, and Residential Satisfaction. New York: Oxford University Press.

Milgram, S. (1970) "The experience of living in cities." Science 167: 1461-1468.

Miller, J. D. (1974) "Effects of noise on people." Journal of the Accoustical Society of America 56: 729-764.

Miller, S. F., Jr. (1971) Effects of Proposed Highway Improvements on Property Values. Report No. 114 for National Cooperative Highway Research Program.

Mintz, N. L. (1959) "Concerning some effects of aesthetic surroundings." Presented at third housing conference, Oklahoma State University.

Mogey, J. M. (1956) Family and Neighborhood. London: Oxford University Press.

——— et al. (1971) Social Effect of Eminent Domain Changes in Households After Involuntary Relocation for Southwest Expressway, (I-95) Boston, 1968-1970. Boston University.

Montgomery, J. E. (1967) "Human needs in housing." Economy Housing Seminar, Conference Proceedings sponsored by the American Society of Agricultural Engineers, pp. 5-9.

Monthly Labor Review (1979) 102 (August).

Moody, H. T. and F. W. Puffer (1970) "The empirical verification of the urban base multiplier: traditional and adjustment process models." Land Economics 46: 91-98.

Moore, G. H. and J. N. Hedges (1975) "Trends in labor and leisure." Monthly Labor Review Reader. Washington, DC: U.S. Government Printing Office.

Morris, E. W. and M. Winter (1978) Housing Family, and Society. New York: John Wiley.

Morrison, P. A. (1978) "Overview of demographic trends shaping the nation's future." Testimony before the Joint Economic Committee, U.S. Congress, May 31.

——— (1967) "Duration of residence and prospective migration: the evaluation of a stochastic model." Demography 4: 53-561.

——— (1970a) "Implications of migration histories for model design." Rand Report P-4342.

——— (1970b) "Chronic movers and the future redistribution of population: a longitudinal analysis." Rand Report P-4440.

——— and J. P. Wheeler (1976) "Rural renaissance in America." Population Bulletin 31: 1-26.

Mountain West Research (1975) Construction Worker Profile. Final report for the Old West Regional Commission, Washington, D.C. (December)

Mueller, B. (1965) A Statistical Handbook of the North Atlantic Area. New York: Twentieth Century Fund.

Muller, T. (1976) Economic Effects of Land Development: Employment Housing and Land Values. Washington, DC: The Urban Institute.

——— et al. (1978) The Fiscal Impact of Trident on Local and State Government. Draft report for Office of Economic Adjustment. (January)

Myers, P. and G. Binder (1977) Neighborhood Conservation. Washington, DC: Conservation Foundation.

Myhra, D. (1977) "Socioeconomic impacts at energy construction sites." Power Engineering (August): 54-57.

——— (1975) "Projection and mitigation: examples of successful applications at nuclear power plant and western coal mining sites." Presented at the annual meetings of the Environmental Design Research Association University of Kansas, Lawrence, Kansas, (April 21).

Napier, T. L. (1973) "Social-psychological responses to forced relocation due to watershed-development." Water Resources Bulletin 8: 784-795.

Napp, N. (1977) "Newsline: environment. Noise to drive you cracy—jets and mental hospitals." Psychology Today (June): 3.

Nathanson, C. A. (1974) "Moving preferences and plans among urban Black families." Journal of the American Institute of Planners 40: 353-359.

National Academy of Sciences CHABA Committee (1977) Guidelines for Preparing Environmental Impact Statements on Noise. Report of the Committee on Housing, Biocoustics and Biomechanics Working Group 69. Washington, D.C.

National Bureau of Standards (1971) The Economic Impact of Noise. Report for U.S. EPA. Washington, DC: U.S. Government Printing Ofice.

National Research Council [Social Research Panel] (1974) Toward An Understanding of Metropolitan America. San Francisco: Canfield Press.

Nelson, J. P. (1975) The Effects of Mobile-Source Air and Noise Pollution on Residential Property Values. Report for U.S. Department of Transportation. (April)

Neulinger, J. (1974) The Psychology of Leisure. Springfield, IL: Charles C Thomas.

Newman, S. (1975) "Objective and subjective determinants of prospective residential mobility." Social Indicators Research 2: 53-63.

――― (1974) The Residential Environment and the Desire to Move. Ann Arbor, MI: Institute for Social Research.

New York State Department of Transportation (1974) Draft Environmental Impact Statement and Section 4 (f) Statement for West Side Highway. Submitted for approval to the Federal Highway Administration.

Niebanck, P. L. (1965) The Elderly in Older Urban Areas. Institute for Environmental Studies, University of Pennsylvania.

――― and M. R. Yessian (1968) Relocation in Urban Planning: From Obstacle to Opportunity. Philadelphia: University of Pennsylvania Press.

Northwood, L. R. (1967) "The impact of forced relocation on children," in W. H. Key (ed.) When People are Forced to Move. (mimeo)

Olson, S. (1976) "Baltimore," in J. S. Adams (ed.) Contemporary Metropolitan America Vol. 2 Nineteenth Century Port. Cambridge, MA: Ballinger.

Opinion Research Corporation (1957) "The public appraises movies," in A Survey for Motion Picture Association of America, Inc., Vol. 11. Princeton, NJ.

Outdoor Recreation Resources Review Commission (1962) Prospective Demand for Outdoor Recreation. Study Report No. 26. Washington, DC: U.S. Government Printing Office.

Owen, J. D. (1979) Working Hours: An Economic Analysis. Lexington, MA: D. C. Heath.

――― (1976) "Workweeks and leisure: an analysis of trends 1948-75." Monthly Labor Review 99: 3-8.

――― (1970) The Price of Leisure. Montreal: McGill-Queen's University Press.

Packard, V. (1972) A Nation of Strangers. New York: David McKay.

Paik, I. K. (1970) Impact of Transportation Noise on Urban Residential Property Values With Special Reference to Aircraft Noise. Springfield, VA: National Technical Information Service. (August)

Parker, S. (1976) The Sociology of Leisure. New York: International Publications Service.

Pastalan, L. A. (1973) "Involuntary environmental relocation: death and survival," in E. H. Steinfield (ed.) Environmental Design Research Volume II, Symposia and Workshops. Strausberg, PA: Dowden, Hutchinson and Ross.

Pederson, F. A. and E. J. Sullivan (1964) "Effects of geographic mobility and parent personality factors on emotional disorders in children." American Journal of Orthopsychiatry 34: 575-580.

Peele, E. et al. (1978) "Social impact analysis," in Energy Division Annual Progress Report: Period Ending September 30, 1977 (ORNL-5364, April 1978). by Oak Ridge National Laboratory.

Pepenoe, D. (1973) "Urban residential differentiation: an overview of patterns, trends, and problems." Sociological Inquiry 43: 35-56.

Perfater, M. A. (1972) The Social and Economic Effects of Relocation Due to Highway Takings. Charlottesville: Virginia Highway Research Council, October.

Perfater, M. A. and G. R. Allen (1976) Relocation Due to Highway Takings: A Diachronic Analysis of Social and Economic Effects. Virginia Highway and Transportation Research Council.

Philliber, W. W. (1976) "Prior training, opportunity, and vested interest as factors influencing neighborhood integration." Pacific Sociological Review 19: 231-244.

Pikarsky, M. (1967) "Comprehensive planning for the Chicago Crosstown Expressway." Highway Research Record 180: 35-51.

Pilarsky, M. (1967) "Comprehensive planning for the Chicago Crosstown Expressway." Highway Research Record 180: 35-51.

Public Opinion (1979) "The 28-hour day." 26, 28.

Queen, S. A. (1949) "Social participation in relation to social disorganization." American Sociological Review 14: 251-257.

Quigley, J. M. and D. Weinberg (1977) "Intra-urban residential mobility: a review and synthesis." International Regional Science Review 2: 41-66.

Rainwater, L. (1966) "Fear and the house-as-haven in the lower class." Journal of the American Institute of Planners 32: 23-30.

Reagan, J. A. and C. A. Grant (1977) Highway Construction Noise: Measurement, Prediction and Mitigation. Special Report, Federal Highway Administration. (July 18)

Redfield, R. (1947) "The folk society." American Journal of Sociology 52: 293-308.

Redpath, B. (1974) "The hard case for community." New Society 28: 541, 542.

Reiss, A. J., Jr. (1959) "Rural-urban status differences in interpersonal contacts." American Journal of Sociology 65: 182-195.

Richardson, H. W. (1973) Regional Growth Theory. New York: John Wiley.

Riemer, S. (1945) "Maladjustment to family home." American Sociological Review 10: 642-648.

Robinson, I. M. et al. (1975) "Trade-off games," in W. Michelson (ed.) Behavioral Research Methods in Environmental Design. Stroudsburg, PA: Dowden, Hutchinson and Ross.

Robinson, J. P. (1979) "Changes in Americans' use of free time: towards a post-industrious society?" Unpublished paper of which important parts are presented in J. P. Robinson in "Toward a post-industrious society." Public Opinion 2: 41-46.

——— (1967) "Social change as measured by time budgets." Presented at the annual meetings of the American Sociological Association, San Francisco.

——— and P. Converse (1972) "Social change as reflected in the use of time," in A. Campbell and P. Converse (eds.) The Human Meaning of Social Change. New York: Russell Sage.

Roistacher, E. (1975) "Residential mobility: planners, movers and multiple movers," in G. J. Duncan and J. H. Morgan (eds.) Five Thousand American Families-Patterns of Economic Progress, Vol. III. Ann Arbor: Survey Research Center.

——— (1974) "Residential mobility," in J. H. Morgan (ed.) Five Thousand American Families-Patterns of Economic Progress, Vol. II. Ann Arbor: Survey Research Center.

Ross, H. L. (1962) "The local community: a survey approach." American Sociological Review 37: 75-84.

Rossi, P. H. (1972) "Community social indicators," in A. Campbell and P. E. Converse (eds.) The Human Meaning of Social Change. New York: Russell Sage.

——— (1955) Why Families Move. New York: Free Press.

Roth, J. et al. (1971) "Noise, sleep and post sleep behavior." Presented at the 124th Annual Meeting of the American Psychiatric Association, Washington, D.C.

Sackman, H. (1975) "Summary evaluation of Delphi." Policy Analysis 1: 693-718.

Sale, J. and E. Steinberg (1971) "Effects on nonrelated households of building a highway in a dense urban residential area." Highway Research Record 356.

Sanua, V. D. (1969) "Immigration, migration and mental illness: a review of the literature with special emphasis on schizophrenia," in E. B. Brody (ed.) Behavior in New Environments. Beverly Hills, CA: Sage.

Schacter, S. (1968) "Social cohesion," in International Encyclopedia of the Social Sciences, Vol. 2. New York: Macmillan.

Scholes, W. E. and J. W. Sargent (1971) Designing Against Noise from Road Traffic. Building Research Station, Report No. 20/21, United Kingdom.

Schorr, P. (1975) Planned Relocation. Lexington, MA: D. C. Heath.

Schultz, T. W. (1953) The Economic Organization of Agriculture. New York: McGraw-Hill.

Schwab, P. M. (1970) "Unemployment by region and in the ten largest states." Monthly Labor Review 93: 3-12.

Searles, H. F. (1960) The Non-Human Environment in Normal Development and in Schizophrenia. New York: Internal Universities Press.

Seiler, L. H. and G. F. Summers (1974) "Locating community boundaries: an integration of theory and empirical techniques." Sociological Methods and Research 2: 259-280.

Shaw, C. R. and H. D. McKay (1931) Social Factors in Juvenile Delinquency. For National Commission on Law Observance and Enforcement, Publication No. 132, Vol. II, of Report on the Causes of Crime. Washington, DC: U.S. Government Printing Office.

Shevsky, E. and W. Bell (1955) Social Area Analysis. Stanford, CA: Stanford University Press.

Shields, M. A. et al. (1979) Socioeconomic Impacts of Nuclear Power Plants: A Paired Comparison of Operating Facilities. Report for the Nuclear Regulatory Commission by Oak Ridge National Laboratory. (July)

Simmons, J. W. (1974) Patterns of Residential Movement in Metropolitan Toronto. Toronto: University of Toronto Press.

Simon, W. and J. H. Gagnon (1967) "The decline and fall of the small town." Trans-action 4: 42-51.

Slater, B. R. (1968) "Effects of noise on pupil performance." Journal of Educational Psychology 59: 239-243.

Slote, A. (1969) Termination: The Closing at Baker Plant. Indianapolis: Bobbs-Merrill.

Smigel, E. O. [ed.] (1963) Work and Leisure: A Contemporary Social Problem. New Haven College and University Press.

Smith, C. L. et al. (1971) "Economic Development: panacea or perplexity for rural areas?" Rural Sociology 36: 173-186.

Smith, J. et al. (1954) "Local intimacy in a middle-sized city." American Journal of Sociology 60: 276-284.

Smith, R. and V. A. Christopherson (1966) "Migration and family adjustment." Journal of Home Economics 58: 670-671.

Smith, R. A. (1975) "Measuring neighborhood cohesion: a review and some suggestions." Human Ecology 3: 143-160.

Sorkin, A. L. (1974) Education, Unemployment, and Economic Growth. Lexington, MA: D. C. Heath.

Sorrentino, C. (1970) "Unemployment in the United States and seven foreign countries." Monthly Labor Review 93: 12-23.

———— and J. Moy (1974) "Unemployment in the United States and eight foreign countries." Monthly Labor Review 97: 47-52.

Speare, A., Jr. (1970) "Life cycle and residential mobility." Demography 7: 451-458.

Srole, L. et al. (1962) Mental Health in the Metropolis: The Midtown Manhattan Study. New York: McGraw-Hill.

———— et al. (1974) "Residential satisfaction as an intervening variable in residential mobility." Demography 11: 173-188.

Stegman, M. A. (1969) "Accessibility models and residential location." Journal of the American Institute of Planners 35: 22-29.

Steidl, R. E. (1972) "Difficulty factors in homemaking tasks: implications for environmental designs." Human Factors 14: 471-482.

Stein, M. (1964) The Eclipse of Community. New York: Harper & Row.

Stone, C. M. (1976) Economic Growth and Neighborhood Discontent. Chapel Hill: University of North Carolina Press.

Stone, G. P. (1954) "City shoppers and urban identification: observations of the social psychology of city life." American Journal of Sociology 60: 35-45.

Straszheim, M. R. (1973) "Modelling urban housing markets and metropolitan change: an econometric approach," in E. G. Moore (ed.) Models of Residential Location and Relocation in the City. Studies in Geography Number 20. Evanston, IL: Northwestern University Press.

Stubblefield, R. L. (1955) "Children's emotional problems aggravated by family moves." American Journal of Orthopsychiatry 25: 120-126.

Sussman, M. B. (1959) "The isolated nuclear family: fact or fiction." Social Problems 6: 333-340.

Sutcliffe, J. P. and B. D. Crabbe (1963) "Incidence and degrees of friendship in urban and rural areas." Social Forces 42: 60-67.

Suttles, G. D. (1975) "Community design: the search for participation in a metropolitan society," in A. H. Hawley and V. P. Rock (eds.) Metropolitan America in Contemporary Perspective. New York: Russell Sage.

——— (1968) The Social Order of the Slum. Chicago: University of Chicago Press.

Sutton, W. A., Jr. and T. Munson (1976) "Definitions of community: 1954 through 1973." Presented at the annual meetings of the American Sociological Association, August 1976.

Tamney, J. B. (1975) Solidarity in a Slum. New York: John Wiley.

Theodorson, G. A. and A. G. Theodorson (1969) "Cohesion, social," in A Modern Dictionary of Sociology. New York: Thomas Y. Crowell.

Thursz, D. (1966) Where Are They Now? Washington, DC: District of Columbia Redevelopment Land Agency.

Tietze, C. et al. (1942) "Personality disorder and spatial mobility." American Journal of Sociology 48: 29-40.

Tilly, C. and C. H. Brown (1967) "On uprooting, kinship and the auspices of migration." International Journal of Comparative Sociology 8: 139-164.

Toennies, F. (1957) Community and Society. New York: Harper & Row.

Toth, W. J. (1979) Noise Abatement Techniques for Construction Equipment. Warrendale, PA. (August)

Tracor (1971) "Community reaction to airport noise." NASA Report CR-1761.

Tweeten, L. (1970) Foundations of Farm Policy. Lincoln: University of Nebraska Press.

——— and G. L. Brinkman (1976) Micropolitan Development. Ames: Iowa State University Press.

Tyron, R. C. (1955) Identification of Social Areas by Cluster Analysis. Berkeley: University of California Press.

U.S. Army Corps of Engineers (1974) "A preliminary analysis of day use recreation and benefit estimation models for selected reservoirs." Plan Formulation and Evaluation Studies-Recreation. Institute for Water Resources Research Report 74-R1 Volume III of V.

U.S. Army Engineer Division, New England (1977) Draft Environmental Statement Dickey-Lincoln School Lake Project at Dickey, Maine. Waltham, MA.

U.S. Army Engineer District, Sacramento (1976) Analysis of Supply and Demand of Urban Oriented Non Reservoir Recreation. Institute for Water Resources Research Report 76-R2.

U.S. Department of Agriculture (1971) Farm Index. Washington, DC: Economic Research Service.

U.S. Department of Commerce (1977) Social Indicators 1976. Washington, DC: U.S. Government Printing Office.

U.S. Department of the Interior, Bureau of Outdoor Recreation (1967) Outdoor Recreation and Space Standards. Washington, DC: U.S. Government Printing Office.

U.S. Department of Labor (1972) Manpower Report of the President, 1972. Washington, DC: U.S. Government Printing Office.

U.S. Environmental Protection Agency (1974) Information on Levels of Environmental Noise Requisite to Protect Public Health and Welfare With an Adequate Margin of Safety. Washington, DC: U.S. Government Printing Office.

——— (1973) Public Health and Welfare Criteria for Noise, July 27, 1973. Washington, DC: U.S. Government Printing Office.

——— (1972) Report to the President and Congress on Noise. Washington, DC: U.S. Government Printing Office.

U.S. Fish and Wildlife Service (1978) Draft Environmental Impact Analysis for the U.S. Fish and Wildlife Service's Mammalian Predator Damage Management for Livestock Protection in the Western United States. Submitted to Council on Environmental Quality, November 21.

U.S. National Bureau of Standards (1971) The Social Impact of Noise. Report for U.S. Environmental Protection Agency. Washington, DC: U.S. Government Printing Office.

U.S. News and World Report (1979) "Leisure: when no Russian is in sight." January 15: 41-44.

U.S. Senate (1962) Policies, Standards, and Procedures in the Formulation, Evaluation, and Review of Plans for Use and Development of Water and Related Land Resources. Document No. 97 and Supplement No. 1, "Evaluation standards for primary outdoor recreation benefits." Washington, DC: U.S. Government Printing Office.

Vaneklasen, P. S. (1969) "Community noise control," in D. W. Ward and J. Fricke (eds.) Noise as a Public Health Hazard. Washington, DC: American Speech and Hearing Association.

Veblen, T. (1899) [1934] The Theory of the Leisure Class. New York: Modern Library.

Vidich, A. J. and J. Bensman (1960) Small Town in Mass Society. Garden City, NY: Doubleday.

Vlachos, E. (1976) Secondary Impacts and Consequences of Highway Projects on Natural Areas. Report for U.S. Department of Transportation.

Wallin, P. (1953) "A Guttman scale for measuring women's neighborliness." American Journal of Sociology Vol. 59 (November): 241-246.

Warren, D. I. (1977) "The functional diversity of urban neighborhoods." Urban Affairs Quarterly 13: 151-180.

Water Resources Council (1973) "Water and related land resources, establishment of principles and standards for planning." Federal Register 38, 174, Part III (September 10).

Wellman, B. (1979) "The community question: the intimate networks of East Yonkers." American Journal of Sociology 84: 1201-1229.

——— (1972) "Who needs neighborhoods?" in A. Powell (ed.) Attacking Modern Myths. Toronto: McClelland and Stewart.

––– and B. Leighton (1979) "Networks, neighborhoods and communities." Urban Affairs Quarterly 14: 363-390.

White, I. L. et al. (1978) Energy from the West: Draft Policy Analysis Report. Prepared for U.S. Environmental Protection Agency.

––– (1977) Energy from the West: A Progress Report of a Technology Assessment of Western Energy Resource Development. Volume II: Detailed Analyses and Supporting Materials. Washington, DC: U.S. Environmental Protection Agency.

Whyte, W. F., Jr. (1955) Street Corner Society. Chicago: University of Chicago Press.

Wilcock, R. C. and W. H. Franke (1963) Unwanted Workers. New York: Free Press.

Wilensky, H. L. (1961) "The uneven distribution of leisure: the impact of economic growth on 'free time.' " Social Problems 9: 32-56.

Wilkinson, K. P. (1974) "Consequences of decline and social adjustment to it," in L. R. Whiting (ed.) Communities Left Behind. Ames: Iowa State University Press.

Wilson, J. Q. (1968) "The urban unease." The Public Interest 12: 25-39.

Wilson, J. W. (1973) People in the Way. Toronto: University of Toronto Press.

Wireman, P. (1978) "Intimate secondary relationships," Presented at the annual meeting of the American Sociological Association, San Francisco, September.

Wirth, L. (1938) "Urbanism as a way of life." American Journal of Sociology 44: 3-24.

Wolf, E. P. and C. H. Lebeaux (1967) "On the destruction of poor neighborhoods by urban renewal." Social Problems 15: 3-8.

Wolfbein, S. L. (1965) Employment, Unemployment, and Public Policy. New York: Random House.

Wyle Laboratory (1971) Community Noise, Transportation Noise, and Noise from Equipment Powered by Internal Combustion Engines. Report for U.S. Environmental Protection Agency, MTID 300-3.

––– (1970) Final Report on the Sound-proofing Pilot Project for the Los Angeles Department of Airports. Report No. WCR 70-1.

Wyle Research (1979) Community Noise Abatement Manual, Strategy Guidelines. El Segundo, CA. (August)

Young, A. M. (1979) "Work experience of the population in 1977." Monthly Labor Review 102: 53-57.

Young, M. and P. Willmott (1957) Family and Kinship in East London. New York: Penguin.

Zehner, R. B. (1971) "Neighborhood and community satisfaction in new towns and less planned suburbs." Journal of the American Institute of Planners 37: 379-385.

Zeitz, E. (1979) Private Urban Renewal. Lexington, MA: D. C. Heath.

Zimmer, B. G. (1973) "Residential mobility and housing." Land Economics 49: 344-350.

––– (1955) "Participation of migrants in urban structures." American Sociological Review 20: 218-224.

Zuiches, J. J. and D. L. Brown (1978) "The changing character of the nonmetropolitan population, 1950-1975," in T. R. Ford (ed.) Rural U.S.A.: Persistance and Change. Ames: Iowa State University Press.

# ABOUT THE AUTHOR

KURT FINSTERBUSCH (Ph.D. Columbia University) is Associate Professor of Sociology at the University of Maryland. He has been active in the field of social impact assessment since 1974, when he developed a general social impact assessment methodology for technology assessments. Subsequently he has been involved in several SIAs, has developed several special SIA techniques, and has written extensively on SIA. He edited, with C. P. Wolf, *The Methodology of Social Impact Assessment* (1977), which continues to be the major work in the field. He wrote (with Annabelle Motz) *Social Research for Policy Decisions* (1980) and several articles on applied sociology. His more basic research examines patterns of development in neighborhoods, communities, and nations, and he is currently working on codifying sociological theories for predicting structural changes in nations under conditions of increasing scarcity, structural changes in communities under conditions of rapid population growth, and social changes in neighborhoods when new facilities are introduced into the area.

# Date Due

| | | | |
|---|---|---|---|
| JUN 3 '89 | | | |
| 5-23-8↓ RETURNED | | | |
| du/per APR 2 8 1998 | | | |
| | | | |
| | | | |
| | | | |
| | | | |
| | | | |
| | | | |
| | | | |
| | | | |
| | | | |
| | | | |
| | | | |